Plays from

The Circle
Repertory Company

BROADWAY PLAY PUBLISHING INC

357 W 20th St., NY NY 10011
212 627-1055

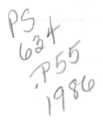

First printing: December 1986

ISBN: 0-88145-037-5

Cover illustration by Winslow Pinney Pels
Cover design by Mary Mietzelfeld
Text design by Marie Donovan
Set in Aster by Ampersand, Rutland, VT
Printed on acid-free paper and bound by BookCrafters, Chelsea, MI

Contents

Introduction

The question I am most frequently asked as Artistic Director of the Circle Repertory Company is, "Why did you do this play?" The immediate answer, "Because it was the best I had available," is both true and evasive. Other factors are often involved, such as the development of a playwright, for whom production at a particular point may be needed in his or her overall growth. Or it may provide an extraordinary opportunity for the Company of actors. It may also be a play with an important or relevant theme for a specific time. It may be because I feel the audience will enjoy their evening in the theater, whether I expect the critics to endorse it or not. But, in short, these rationalizations really add up to the simple case that, for whatever reasons, I felt it was the best play we had for the time period it was needed. Play selection in a situation of presenting five or six new plays per season is a very pragmatically guided activity.

There need be no apology for any of the plays in this volume, although they do not necessarily represent the Best Plays from Circle Rep in any historical context. They do represent the range and variety that Circle Rep has always provided, despite public attempts to categorize our plays as "lyric realism."

Of the six plays here presented, only *The Diviners, Snow Orchid,* and *The Mound Builders* can comfortably be classified as "lyric realism," while *Knock Knock* is a contemporary fairy tale, *Waterlilies* is a gothic absurdist melodrama, and *Jedediah Kohler* is a sassy satire. All, however, share a common interest in the human condition. They dramatize three-dimensional characters, who struggle with the forces of circumstance to make some meaning out of life.

The Mound Builders is a play of tragic dimensions by Circle Rep's foremost playwright and co-founder, Lanford Wilson. He has long considered it his most important play. Rich and complex, *The Mound Builders* illuminates the universal desire to shape our passing experience into a lasting memorial of our existence. It contains some of

Lanford Wilson's most beautiful writing, and in the character of Delia, one of his most indelible portraits.

Down by the River Where the Waterlilies Are Disfigured Every Day was produced in the same season (1974-75) and started a ten-year association between Julie Bovasso (one America's foremost experimentalists) and Circle Rep (most often categorized as a haven for naturalism). *Waterlilies* demonstrates the powerful imagination of its visionary author, which was matched in a surrealistic production designed by John Lee Beatty, directed by Marshall Oglesby, and featuring remarkable performances by a cast that included Linda Hunt, Cathryn Damon, Bobo Lewis, and Neil Flanagan.

Knock Knock by Jules Feiffer, a year later, was one of the high points of Circle Rep's production history. (To this day, it remains my mother's favorite of all the productions I have directed.) It became our first Broadway transfer, where it flourished with great success and awards and Tony nominations, until the producers decided four months into its Broadway run that "stars" would stimulate the box office and replaced me (with the brilliant José Quintero) and the Circle Rep cast (with luminaries like Lynn Redgrave and Charles Durning) only to have the plan backfire. The "improved" production closed within two weeks (a costly validation of the original Circle Rep production). However, before commercial interests killed the golden goose, *Knock Knock* demonstrated that the interaction of playwright and actors and designers and director at Circle Rep could provide potent entertainment and provoke thoughtful laughter.

Jim Leonard's *The Diviners* came to Circle Rep from the American College Theater Festival, where it won national honors. Written in frank admiration of Lanford Wilson's *Rimers of Eldritch*, it fit the Circle Rep aesthetic sensibilities like a glove. In this play, ensemble acting is mandatory, and Circle Rep once again proved equal to the task. Revived the following summer at the Saratoga Performing Arts Center in upstate New York, it initiated Circle Rep's continuing summer residence in Saratoga Springs, along with the Philadelphia Orchestra and the New York City Ballet. Subsequently, this beautifully American play was sent by the State Department for an extensive tour in Southeast Asia, making friends everywhere it played.

Snow Orchid was developed through Circle Rep's developmental process. Joe Pintauro, who had written successful novels, submitted his play to the Projects-in-Progress program at Circle Rep, where it improved with each rewrite until it became a major production. A hauntingly evocative mirror of an Italian family, *Snow Orchid* resonates with the truth of psychological foundation, while ordinary "slice-of-life" dialogue is elevated into realistic poetry. The play depicts a family breaking free from the fears of the past, as a new life of the spirit is nurtured through the first tentative steps toward freedom.

The Great-Great Grandson of Jedediah Kohler is John Bishop's satiric celebration of the perseverance of heroism even in our mundane lives. Jed struggles to shed the weight of historic heroism that is his inheritance from his legendary great-great grandfather, a gun-toting hero of the law of the Old West. Trapped in a life of minutiae where packaging is valued over contents, Jed nevertheless finds his contemporary brand of heroism.

I am very proud of having brought these plays to the attention of our audiences, and it is a special pleasure to know they will now be enjoyed by a larger public through this publication.

When Circle Rep presented in its fifth season *When You Comin' Back, Red Ryder?* and *The Sea Horse* the same season, it was considered miraculous that any theater company should have such luck as to contribute two major plays to the American repertoire. *The New York Times* took the opportunity to declare that Circle Rep was the "major source of new American plays."

Now in our seventeenth season, the expectations have grown so large that when we find only one play in a year, the press wonders what's wrong. For example, last season, our production of *As Is* moved to Broadway, where it won the Drama Desk Award for the Best Play of the season. Yet *The New York Times* greeted the current season with the mournful headline: "Circle Rep seeks to rekindle past glory." In 1974, two great plays in one season was a miracle. In 1986, one great play per season apparently signifies failure. O Tempora, O Mores!

New York City   MARSHALL W. MASON
December 1986   Artistic Director

Growing Playwrights

For every play produced at Circle Rep there are dozens of plays that have been part of our development process, and hundreds more that have been received, read, and returned with varying degrees of encouragement. It's hard to write a play—particularly when the strongest influence on today's young writers is TV and not theater at all. It's harder still to write a *good* play; and, when a solid work by a new writer seems ready for production, it's difficult in the extreme to convince a theater to produce it when the risks in New York today are so high. Thus a paradox: Playwrights need to see their plays produced in order to progress from "promising" to "good", but for theaters to agree to spend money on full productions, they want excellent scripts to begin with.

Here at Circle Rep we can address the problem *in part* because we are a *company* of actors, playwrights, directors, and designers, and provide a home where a limited number of talented artists can work at honing their skills. In our Playwrights Workshop, unproduced writers join our company playwrights to discuss their works in progress and to talk about technique and structure. At least once a week actors join us in our offices to read scripts to the entire company. And, in subsequent discussions, we respond to specific questions posed by the playwright in order to help with the play's revision. Our subscribers become involved in the Extended Reading and Projects in Progress series in our theater; they, too, respond to questions from playwright, directors, and dramaturg in order to discover what, exactly, has been communicated.

I believe that all of these steps are helpful not only for the nurturing of new talent but also for the creation of good plays by established playwrights; yet to be *really* helpful we need a larger theater for our mainstage productions so that our present space can be used as an experimental house to give writers modest productions, and the remarkable learning process that such productions entail.

We are dedicated to American writers at Circle Rep, and I hope we will be able to continue to help for years to come.

New York City
December 1986

B. RODNEY MARRIOTT
Associate Artistic Director

A Note from The Publisher

This book marks the first collection of plays from the Circle Repertory Company, one of America's most important theaters. Circle Rep is, as you may know, the "home" of Pulitzer prize-winning playwright Lanford Wilson, and the combination of Lanford Wilson and Circle Repertory makes this a heaven-made project for a play publisher.

Apart from *The Mound Builders*, which Mr. Wilson calls his favorite play, the question was which other plays from their distinguished production past would best represent this theater's work. We felt that *Knock Knock* and *The Diviners*, two wonderful plays that have had long and fruitful lives after their initial productions, were typical (if such a thing can be said of any developmental theater) Circle Rep plays.

My only proviso for the other three plays was that they have no prior publication history. It makes no sense to print a book of already available plays; as a publisher we have the responsibility to expose the public to works that might be lost forever. There is no question that Joe Pintauro, John Bishop, and Julie Bovasso are all very talented. This is demonstrated not only by their plays in this volume, but by the formidable body of work each has accumulated. Naturally, we hope producers will think they are as interesting as we do, and that these plays will enjoy further life on the stage.

New York City   Christopher Gould
December 1986

Lanford Wilson

The Mound Builders

LANFORD WILSON is a founding member of the Circle Repertory Company. His plays include: *Balm in Gilead, The Rimers of Eldritch, Lemon Sky, The Gingham Dog, THE HOT L BALTIMORE, Angels Fall,* and the Talley Trilogy: *Fifth of July, Talley & Son,* and *Talley's Folly.* His most recent play is *Burn This.* He is the recipient of the Brandeis University Creative Arts Award, the Vernon Rice Award, three Obies, the Outer Critics Circle Award, two Drama Critics Circle Awards, and the 1980 Pulitzer Prize for Drama. He is a member of the Dramatists Guild Council.

The Mound Builders was first performed in New York City by the Circle Repertory Company under Marshall W. Mason's direction, previewing on January 29, 1975 (Press Opening: February 2), with the following cast:

DR. AUGUST HOWE .... Rob Thirkield
D. K. ERIKSEN .... Tanya Berezin
CYNTHIA .... Stephanie Gordon
DR. DAN LOGGINS .... Jonathan Hogan
DR. JEAN LOGGINS .... Trish Hawkins
CHAD JASKER .... John Strasberg
KIRSTEN .... Lauren Jacobs

A subsequent production was performed at The Triplex during the Spring of 1986, with the following cast:

DR. AUGUST HOWE .... Edward Seamon
CYNTHIA HOWE .... Stephanie Gordon
CHAD JASKER .... James McDaniel
DR. DAN LOGGINS .... Jay Patterson
DR. JEAN LOGGINS .... Trish Hawkins
D. K. (DELIA) ERIKSEN .... Tanya Berezin

The Mound Builders is for Roy London

For information regarding stock and amateur production rights, contact: Bridget Aschenberg, International Creative Management, 40 West 57 Street, New York, NY 10019.

Characters

PROFESSOR AUGUST HOWE, an archaeologist, forty
CYNTHIA HOWE, his wife, thirty-five
D.K. (DELIA) ERIKSEN, his sister, thirty-eight
DR. DAN LOGGINS, his assistant, an archaeologist, twenty-nine
DR. JEAN LOGGINS, Dan's wife, a gynecologist, twenty-five
CHAD JASKER, the landowner's son, twenty-five

The Scene

AUGUST's study in Urbana is indicated only by a desk or table that can be easily incorporated into the house at Blue Shoals. When AUGUST is alone, the lights confine us to his immediate desk area. From this light he wanders, while recording, off into the dark, and back again, sitting, standing, messing with things on his desk.

As we move into the previous summer, the house around him is revealed: An old farmhouse with a large living-dining room transformed into a living-dining-working area by the archaeologists. A stairway leads off to the bedrooms, a door opens to AUGUST's office, doors lead to an unseen front porch and a back porch that might be incorporated into the set and used as a playing area for a number of the scenes. An arch allows us to see part of the kitchen, in which there is a refrigerator.

The back wall of the set serves as a screen onto which are back-projected slides from the previous summer that serve AUGUST as the backbone of his recorded notes. He need not literally control the projector.

Scenes in the house are accompanied by a dense orchestration of the outside sounds, opening the house onto its surroundings. The night is filled with noises of the country, and the day with the sounds of bulldozers and workmen preparing the lakebed, which will flood the valley.

The Time

February in Urbana and the previous summer in Blue Shoals, Illinois—located in the extreme south of that state, in the five-state area of Kentucky, Missouri, Indiana, Arkansas, and Illinois—at the confluence of the Wabash, Cumberland, Ohio, and Mississippi Rivers.

Act One

(*As the house lights dim,* DELIA's *voice is heard.*)

DELIA'S VOICE: The Aztec year was divided into eighteen months of twenty days each. Then there were five extra days before the calendar started over. These five days in February were the no-name days. Fires were extinguished, families fasted, household furniture was destroyed. They stayed inside, waiting, having no idea if the sun would rise on the first day of the new year. Then, when the Pleiedes crossed the sky's meridian, signifying that a new year would come, a young warrior was sacrificed. His chest split open, his heart removed, and a new fire was kindled in the cavity of his breast. I see my brother in Champaign-Urbana, in February, during the no-name days, going over again the tragedy, the disaster of the previous summer. Having no idea if the sun will rise the next morning on a new year . . .

AUGUST: (*Sits at a desk, speaking into the microphone of a small tape recorder.*) One, two, three, four, five . . . (*Getting up, walking a few paces away.*) The quick gray fox jumped over . . . whatever it was the quick gray fox jumped over. (*He returns to the desk, clicks off the tape, rewinds it and clicks it on. We hear his voice repeating "... three, four, five ... the quick gray fox jumped—" He clicks the machine off, then back to record.*) Dianne . . . ah . . . good morning. Or, knowing your habits, I should probably say, good afternoon. (*Pause. He walks away a few paces.*) After months of procrastination, with which I'm sure you're sympathetic, I intend to go through what is left of the wreckage of last summer's expedition. (*He returns to the desk.*) You may type this up, or go out to lunch. I'll understand either. (*He touches something on the desk. The back screen is filled with a scenic photograph of a lake at morning.*) This is the lake, against which we were racing time. (*Slide: the house.*) This is the house in which we were staying. After we spent three summers of excavation (*Slide: dam construction.*) on the mounds—within earshot of the construction of the Blue Shoals Dam (*Slide: bulldozer.*)—engineers preparing the lake bed (*Slide: the dig.*)—uncovered evidence of an extensive village site not six hundred yards from the front door (*We hear a car stopping outside, doors slamming, and the lights of the stage begin to reveal the house in Blue Shoals.*) of the house in which we stayed. Excavation of the Jasker Village site was a salvage operation undertaken literally as the lake basin filled behind us.

CYNTHIA: God, I thought they'd never get here. They must have come through Blue Shoals. (*She goes to the door.*)

CHAD: (*Off*) Window's been opened for a week, I was telling the professor we had a hell of a spring. Thought it wasn't gonna be any good for you folks, but it's dried up the last week.

AUGUST: Thank God you're here. (*As* DON, CHAD, *and* JEAN *enter, carrying luggage, etc.*) Everything possible has conspired against us.

DON: Girls getting to you?

AUGUST: The place looks like a resort. You've never seen so many tourists in your life.

CHAD: (*Going out to the car.*) I told him.

AUGUST: It gets worse every year. The girls? No, the girls are fine. They pitched their tents, made a cooking pit. Every goddamned one of them is an Eagle Scout.

DAN: Or whatever.

AUGUST: They're happy as bugs. Ask about you and Jean every ten minutes.

DAN: Don't say anything about Jean being pregnant; she doesn't want them pestering her.

AUGUST: I'm going to be so busy I doubt I'll see them till September. On top of which, I'm going to have to go to the Paducah airport. How far is Paducah?

CYNTHIA: If there is such a place.

CHAD: About an hour.

CYNTHIA: Auggie's sister is being dumped on us.

AUGUST: My sister is dying again; she was scraped up off the street in Cleveland; apparently the hospitals there haven't the facilities or the will. How the hell they found us here—the man came to install the telephone, ten minutes later it was ringing.

DAN: She's dying?

AUGUST: Of course not, and she claims poverty so—Well, it's not worth talking about.

DAN: I've never met the lady.

AUGUST: I'm afraid there's no way I can protect you from it now. Jean, I'm really sorry about this.

JEAN: What's wrong with her?

AUGUST: (*Speaking in* CHAD'S *presence as one might speak before a waiter.*) . . . I wouldn't know.

CYNTHIA: Acute "I wouldn't know," chronic "I suspect."

AUGUST: The hospital is flying her down tomorrow, unconscious and incognito.

CYNTHIA: And collect. (*To* JEAN) Let me help you with this jazz.

JEAN: There's not much, Dan said to travel light.

CHAD: I had the windows opened forever. It's been a sopping spring; thought it wasn't gonna be any good for you guys. But it's cleared up some the last week.

DAN: Thank God.

AUGUST: Conditions are excellent. (JEAN *and* CYNTHIA *re-enter for suitcases and knapsacks.*) We've got the bulldozer lined up for day after tomorrow; you might even be ready for it.

DAN: Oh, hell, let me help.

JEAN: That's it.

CHAD: You visiting again, Doctor, or you planning to stay awhile?

JEAN: No, I'm booked for the duration.

CHAD: We'll have to get her out with us.

JEAN: Don't tell me Blue Shoals swings.

DAN: Out fishing, out to the lake. (*He takes what he can carry of the baggage upstairs.*)

JEAN: No way. Is the lake going to completely cover this house?

AUGUST: Completely.

JEAN: You'll have to move it.

CHAD: Electric company charge you a thousand bucks for every line you cut . . . probably cost six, seven thousand to move it up the hill.

JEAN: You couldn't build it for that.

CHAD: Nobody'd want to either. Beams probably rotten, you couldn't get a block under it.

JEAN: Is it haunted?

CYNTHIA: Not that we've noticed.

CHAD: What do you want? You want it haunted or you want it unhaunted? I'll go either way.

DAN: Come down to the site, you've got time.

AUGUST: I've got to talk money with some St. Louis real-estate men this evening. This isn't going to be much of a vacation for you, Jean.

DAN: (*Leaving.*) Sure it will.

JEAN: Sure it will.

CYNTHIA: (*Opening refrigerator.*) Sure it will. How about a drink? (*She slams the door, effecting a blackout.*)

AUGUST: (*Slide: townspeople.*) Townspeople who awaited with bated breath our discovery of King Tut's tomb. (*Slide: students.*) Alleged students. (*Slide: more students.*) We were assisted last summer by eight girls and (*Slide: male student.*) one presumed male from Dr. Loggins' class in field archaeology. (*Slide: drawing of God King's temple.*) This is one of the students' fanciful renderings of what the God King's temple might have looked like. They were understandably excited, as were we all, by the discovery of the God King's tomb. And of course devastated by its destruction. As you know my regard for fancy, you can disregard this slide. (*Slide: Cynthia.*) Ex-relation by marriage. (*Slide: campsite.*) This is the campsite of the students, pitched well out of earshot of the house. (*Slide: Cynthia.*) Ex-relation. (*Slide: Kirsten.*) Alleged daughter Kirsten, fortunately away at camp last summer. (*Slide: picnic.*) Picnic. (*Slide: people playing.*) Horse play. (*Slide: more horse play, this time on the porch.*) Horse play on the porch. (*Slide: Cynthia.*) Horse.

(*The stage goes black except for a flashlight beam shining from the stair landing.*)

DAN'S VOICE: Is someone there? Hello? (*Flashlight out.*) Hello? (*Sound of a stumble. Mumbled.*) Oh, damnit. (*The flashlight comes on. DAN, in pajamas, gets up, goes to the lamp, turns it on.*)

CYNTHIA: (*Entering from the door, opening a carton of cigarettes.*) Good Lord, I thought you'd be asleep hours ago.

DAN: I was, heard the weirdest . . .

CYNTHIA: Probably the kids on the dig.

DAN: Thought we were being burglarized.

CYNTHIA: Not much to worry about that.

DAN: Are you just getting in? It must be two in the morning.

CYNTHIA: Cigarettes. You working tomorrow?

DAN: Oh, yeah, I'll be up and—

CYNTHIA: (*Cutting him off. Reaching for the lamp switch.*) Better get to bed then.

(*BLACKOUT.*)

(*Sundown the next evening.* CHAD *opens the front door as* CYNTHIA *comes downstairs.*)

CHAD: Got a delivery for you.

(AUGUST *enters,* CHAD *follows carrying* DELIA.)

AUGUST: Please don't squirm. He's not that strong and you're not as dissipated as you'd like to believe.

DELIA: There is no point in dragging me inside. I'm not staying—

AUGUST: If you want to fight, wait till he sets you down!

CYNTHIA: Just here on the—

DELIA: I'll go to the state hospital.

AUGUST: (*Panting*) No state has that kind of money.

(CHAD *carries* DELIA *to a lounge.*)

DELIA: I'm not going to die in this godforsaken Grant Wood mausoleum.

AUGUST: (*Beat.*) Good.

DELIA: How the hell did they find you?

AUGUST: I was wondering.

DELIA: You're making quite a name for yourself. That must be gratifying after all these—

AUGUST: —I've always been satisfied to leave the limelight to those—

DELIA: —That's the God's truth.

AUGUST: —to those who required it.

DELIA: (*Beat.*) Yes, well, just as well.

AUGUST: Why were you in Cleveland?

DELIA: I don't know. It was important to go to—I met someone from Cleveland, or I don't know. I was in Casablanca. Detroit with palm trees! Vile people! Vile air! Vile climate! I went to Annaba, I went to Benghazi, I met someone from Portugal, I started to go back to Lisbon, I changed my mind and went to—(*Interrupted by a violent coughing spell.*)

AUGUST: (*Stands unmoved, watching her. Finally, as she relaxes.*) Where.

DELIA: (*After relaxing. Calmly.*) Cleveland. (*Pause.*) How long did they keep me? They kept me a month, didn't they? Why?

DAN: (*Off, calling.*) Jean?

DELIA: I don't mean that; I'm not that bad.

JEAN: (*From upstairs*) I'm up, I'll be down.

AUGUST: (*Taking medicine and papers from* CHAD.) I've got instructions, yet. You were glad enough to get away.

DELIA: They were trying to kill me in that goddamned hospital. (JEAN comes down.)

AUGUST: They were not trying to kill—

DELIA	DAN
Whether they were killing me through malice and intention or killing me through ignorance of medicine is immaterial. It amounts to the same torture.	(*Entering, dirty and mildly refractory.*) What a day. Hi. Be glad you didn't come down.

JEAN

Cynthia said.

AUGUST

(*Handing the paper to her.*) Jean, can you make any sense of that?

CHAD: You're going to have a lot of fun with her.

CYNTHIA: We can do very well without that.

AUGUST: Thank you very much, Mr. Jasker. We'll see ya tomorrow.

CHAD: Yeah, I'll see you around. (*He exits.*)

AUGUST: Jean, I don't think you and Dan have had the pleasure of meeting my sister. Dan and Jean Loggins, D.K. Eriksen.

DAN: I talked to you on the phone once.

AUGUST: Dan's my assistant. Jean's an intern gynecologist. If you're interested in discussing medicine, I'm sure she'll listen to you.

DELIA: "D.K." Call me Delia, that's the name Dad gave me.

JEAN: I've read your books, of course.

DELIA: That was another life, Doctor.

JEAN: If you're going to call me doctor, I'll have to call you Miss Eriksen.

DELIA: You know me. I don't *meet people*.

AUGUST: You're not to be moved.

DELIA: You know quite well this is just the sort of cozily scientific, zenobitic community that'll drive me bananas.

DAN: Oh, fine. You should see it down there. It's a mob scene.

DELIA: No, thank you.

CYNTHIA: (*Getting a glass of wine.*) Anyone else?

DAN: I'm trying to direct some jerk with a bulldozer ...

JEAN: I saw the cars from upstairs.

DAN: All day long it's been a cavalcade pouring into the field. Every family from the Mississippi to the Walbash. They got their kids, they got their picnic lunches, it looks like a fucking fairground. Where you been, people? I mean, we been here twenty-four hours already. You missed Professor Howe pulling up a patch of ragweed.

CYNTHIA: I enjoy the people showing up.

DAN: Oh, sure. "What's that thing?" Well, ma'am, that *thing* is a surveyor's alidade. It sits on a tripod and you look through here and see a family from Carbondale eating fried chicken.

CYNTHIA: After August explains what we hope to find, the crowd gets so bored they leave him talking to himself.

DAN: A girl says, "Why did they build those mounds?" What mounds? Oh, the one over there. That they're using for a parking lot. Well, honey, we excavated that mound last summer and we found they had built that mound over ninty-three Paducah High School cheerleaders. (*Begins to roll a joint.*)

JEAN: He loves it, of course; he performs for them like a dancing bear. The girls line up for his classes. They eat him up. I don't know if they learn anything.

AUGUST: Any number of things, I'd think.

JEAN: (*Re: the medication.*) This is morning and evening—this is four times a day.

DAN: "Why did they build the mounds?"! They built the mounds for the same reason I'd build the mounds. Because I wanted to make myself conspicuous; to sacrifice to the gods; to protect me from floods, or animals; because my grandfather built mounds; because I was sick of digging holes; because I didn't have the technology to build pyramids and a person isn't happy unless he's building something.

CYNTHIA: There are people who'd be perfectly happy tearing something down.

DAN: A person isn't happy unless he's building something. Scratch a fry cook, you'll find an architect. Listen to Chad Jasker tell you about the restaurant he's going to build. I mean, he knows the kind of light fixtures he's going to have. For an accomplishment, honey; to bring me closer to Elysium; to leave something behind me for my grandchildren to marvel at. To say I'd built something!

AUGUST: *I.e.*, if we find out, we'll let you know.

DELIA: Jesus, dear God, but it's bleak here. Bleak, bleak, bleak, bleak . . . Bleak farmland on a bleak pond by a bleak—I can't stay here, I—

AUGUST: Normally I might try to excuse her egocentric excen—

DELIA: (*Riding over*) But my exploits are so notorious it's useless to closet my presence here and we are forced to admit that I am convalescing from a riding accident . . . I fell from my horse.

(AUGUST *is pouring medicine for her.*)

AUGUST. It's rather more serious than it might sound, as it was a flying horse. (*He gives her a spoonful.*)

DELIA: Jean, what is he giving me? I can't breathe. They gave him something to give me, it's preventing me from—

AUGUST: The only drugs in your system are residual from your binges in Benghazi and—wherever.

DELIA: I can't get air.

JEAN: You're breathing perfectly normally; if you weren't getting air, you'd be turning purple.

DELIA: What the hell does a gynecologist know about cirrhosis of the liver?

JEAN: Absolutely nothing except that it doesn't occur in the respiratory system.

DELIA: All right, I'm a hypochondriac, Jean. Ignore all requests for medical advice.

JEAN: Delia, after one week in the clinic I could spot a hypochondriac at forty feet.

DAN: (*Who has been rolling a joint; passing it to* CYNTHIA, *who takes it, and* JEAN, *who passes it back.*) She's not on call this summer, Delia, she's taking off eighteen months to have a baby.

JEAN: After that I might have a better idea of what I've been talking about.

DELIA: It doesn't take eighteen months to have a baby. It takes eighteen months to have a rhinoceros.

DAN: (*Regarding the joint. To* JEAN:) Take it.

JEAN: No, I said.

DAN: It's not tobacco, it won't kill you.

JEAN: Not now, thank you.

DAN: Only girl I've ever met who's a bigger drughead than I am, she gets pregnant and goes cold turkey on me.

JEAN: Don't mention the offspring to the girls, we don't want it generally—

DELIA: I will not be cross-examined by a mob of swaddling adolescents.

CYNTHIA: Never fear; they aren't allowed near the place.

JEAN: I thought they might.

CYNTHIA: —That's verboten. No students, no dogs.

DAN: I mean, I can understand giving up alcohol and meat. Well, meat, but an innocent joint.

JEAN: (*From "giving up"*) Oh, come on, really—I don't know why it should bother you; I'm the one who's straight.

CYNTHIA: You can't give up meat. You need all the protein you can get.

JEAN: (*Overlapping*) No, I'm eating perfectly normally; I'm just trying to avoid toxins. And you don't require nearly the amount of protein you're led to believe. We just thought we'd give it every opportunity to make its own problems.

CYNTHIA: Don't think it won't.

DAN: I can imagine the little bugger deprived of—

JEAN: O.K., so it will. That's a person's prerogative; we'll try to help, and undoubtedly screw up completely. Good God, it's lousy grass anyway.

DAN: O.K., O.K., go to bed.

JEAN: (*Leaving.*) I am, thank you.

DELIA: (*Overlapping*) Get me out of this thing. I'm going to be sick.

DAN: Where's she staying?

CYNTHIA: Up in Kirsten's room.

DELIA: Oh, dear God—

DAN: I'll take you. (*Picking her up and carrying her off.*) If you bite me or throw up, I'll drop you right on the floor.

(*Beat*)

CYNTHIA: Is she all right?

AUGUST: She's fine.

CYNTHIA: I realize she's down and out; she's undoubtedly broke.

AUGUST: I don't think so.

CYNTHIA: And although she's not bothered to contact us more than three times in ten years, you could feel that we've neglected her—

AUGUST: Not as much as she's neglected herself.

CYNTHIA: Or been neglected by her reading public.

AUGUST: I doubt she ever had a reading public.

CYNTHIA: August, it is a challenge enough to maintain civilisation on these summer-long bivouacs without nursing—

AUGUST: Ignore her; Dad did. Laugh at her.

CYNTHIA: She isn't funny. Could you at least get someone out here to look after her so—

AUGUST: We can't begin to afford it.

CYNTHIA: One of the girls could help—

AUGUST: Their parents are paying a thousand dollars a head for a credit in field archaeology, not for nursing—

CYNTHIA: They're paying to get them out of the house.

AUGUST: Jean is a practicing intern at—

CYNTHIA: —You can't expect Jean to take up residence as the—

AUGUST: Ignore her, damnit, you have enough to do. Ignore her. She doesn't like you anyway.

DAN: (*In from upstairs, out the door.*) I'm going to take a walk. The girls said someone was snooping around the dig last night. We haven't even started, we've got prowlers; I don't know what they think we're going to find. What do they think we're going to find?

CYNTHIA: (*Going upstairs.*) She likes me fine, August. She always has. It's you she can't stand.

AUGUST: (*Alone.*) Well, fine, fine, fine, good, good. (*As the slides change furiously.*) Dianne, this wreckage appears to be in a state of organization you will undoubtedly recognize as typical of my wife. Please throw away those works of her genius that do not pertain to the excavation The ex-Mrs. Howe, with stunning evidence to the contrary, persists in believing she is Diane Arbus. My sister, for instance, is of marginal archaeological interest. (*Slide: site.*) This is the rather unprepossessing site as we found it. The trial pit (*Slide*) stratigraphy (*Slide*) exposed seven separate layers of occupation on the site. (*Site.*) A bulldozer was employed to remove a dense growth of weeds and about four inches of root-bearing topsoil. (*Slide.*) The remaining four to six inches of humus above the plow sole was cleared by hand and screened. (*Slide: projectile points.*) This soil proved to be the repository of Late Woodland (*Slide*) artifacts (*Slide*) of unsurpassing (*Slide*) mediocrity. which were joyfully displayed to me chip by chip. (*Six quick slides of the lake.*) This is the lake. (*As* JEAN *comes down, dawn arrives and* CHAD *enters.*) This is the lake. This is the lake. This is the lake. This is the lake. This is the—

(CHAD *framed against the lake.*)

CHAD: (*Immediately, as* AUGUST *stands in stunned remembrance.*) Last summer I didn't really figure you to marry Dan. You seemed to be pretty sure of what you wanted.

JEAN: Dan and I wanted more or less the same thing, I think.

CHAD: I tell you what, I got the car out front; there's something I want to show you.

JEAN: I don't think so.

CHAD: —You don't even know what it is.

JEAN: —I know, but nevertheless—

CHAD: —You only live once.

JEAN: I'm not sure that can be proved.

CHAD: The courthouse. What can happen? Who's gonna miss you?

JEAN: I've seen it.

CHAD: Inside?

JEAN: No, I haven't been inside.

CHAD: —See, now , you don't know. I want to show you.

JEAN: What?

CHAD: Will you come?

JEAN: No. I can't, Chad; what?

CHAD: You'll promise to see it?

JEAN: When I go to town again.

CHAD: There's a model of damn near the whole county laid out—it's huge—guess what it's called. The whole model—

JEAN: I can't guess, I really don't think—

CHAD: (*Overlapping*)—O.K., O.K., I'm not playing with you—you promised. It's called Jasker's Development. The Jasker Development. They got . . . the hills, they got all the buildings, the mounds are on it—the ones that are left—they even got little trees set up—and this big, beautifull blue lake—like—not round, but maple shaped, hand-shaped. We been talking six years to get Washington to give it to us.

JEAN: The mounds that are left?

CHAD: Four of them will be left, the other five the Interstate will take out. It's all part and parcel with the development. The lake and the new Interstate. See, we got 57 from Chicago already, which they're widening, and the new Interstate cuts across us the other way with all these interchanges and all. It all goes—aw, hell, it'll just take fifteen minutes to see the damn model and understand what's happening—

JEAN: —No, I'm sure. You can feel it. We're an anachronism. Squint your eyes and you can already see girls water-skiing over the tops of the hawthorn trees. Restaurants with dance bands. It's all changing. The lake has become the fact, hasn't it?

CHAD: Pretty much.

JEAN: And you'll own a lot of the shoreline, won't you?

CHAD: Good piece. I could show you if we—

JEAN: —Come on, really—

CHAD: —Well, it's not how much we own, it's where it is. See—Dad was smart enough not to sell. Only thing he ever did—Guys were coming down from Memphis—See, we're sitting on the lake and the interchange.

JEAN: So you're right in the middle of it.

CHAD: We *are* the middle of it—we didn't even know. You wouldn't recognize this town if you'd seen it five years ago. Like, it didn't start being a tourist attraction till a few years ago; but all of a sudden Lily-Tulip is buying up twenty acres to build a new home office, a national headquarters with landscaping, and another one—a box company—cardboard boxes, and everybody's trying to buy our place. These guys from Memphis are talking to brokers and the brokers are driving out to chew it over with us, you know. And their offer goes up and it goes up, Dad just sits tight on it—and finally these guys come down to talk to us themselves, and they say, all right, you're not going to sell—you got the place we want to build on—what would you say about giving us a lease.

JEAN: Oh . . .

CHAD: Yeah.

JEAN: . . . that could mean a lot more.

CHAD: Every month, month on month for as long as they're in operation. They been working over a year. Memphis is the main office of the Holiday Inn people. They've got their market studies, their books full of figures, they've got their artists'-concepts drawings already. They got their 800-unit motel, they got their swimming pools, and the facilities to the lake, they got a layout would amaze . . . (*Floating*) . . . Dream of something. Dream of something you want ... anything. A restaurant with twenty-four-hour service—dream of anything you want. They showed us rug samples that thick—with padding under it. See, we're sitting on the lake and the interchange.

JEAN: All first-class stuff.

CHAD: A barber sh—ah, beauty parlor. A uh—the clubs, the little—with clubs ...

JEAN: Sauna?

CHAD: No, you hit the damn ball, the little setup for a—

JEAN: Tennis court?

CHAD: Tennis court, too, but those—oh, shit. Golf! Little golf—

JEAN: Miniature golf.

CHAD: No, that's kids, that's toys—Chip and putt! Chip and putt. For practicing.

JEAN: Never heard of it.

CHAD: It's like where you learn, you practice—*you* never heard of it! *I* never had a golf club in my *hand!* There's a golf course at Marion, eighty miles off, probably the closest place you could go—I probably couldn't hit—(*Enjoying himself, nearly laughing*)—I'd dig up the green; they'd kick me off the—but I'm going to! Hell! Go out chipping and putting; get me a pair of shorts and the socks and the cap and those gloves they wear—Chip and putt with the pros, man. Lee Trevino's.

JEAN: You'll be terrific.

CHAD: You know what we get? Three percent. On every dollar spent.

JEAN: That's amazing; that's a lot.

CHAD: Of everything except food. One percent on food and drink ... that's the deal they're offering us.

JEAN: You will be rich. That's what I find so profound about politics; the grace notes of that kind of power. The signing of an energy bill in Washington transforms rural areas into resorts—field hands into busboys.

CHAD: Yeah.

JEAN: They shall beat their plowshares into Pontiacs.

CHAD: (*Almost holding his breath.*) ... I ... got six acres all my own. For a house. On an island. I got an island—it will be. Out a little bit on the lake. Looks right across to it. Be able to sit on the lawn and watch people drive up off there to the motel—say that's another ten bucks. That guy over there's havin' himself a beer, that's two cents!—

(A long pause; as she starts to move.)

JEAN: You'll get a kick out of it.

CHAD: Hey . . . *(She stops.)* I'll give it to you . . . Anything you want, it's yours. I'll sign it over. You're the only thing I ever saw I really wanted.

JEAN: *(Long pause.)* No.

CHAD: I want you to—

JEAN: —Chad—get lost.

(CYNTHIA enters.)

CHAD: Thought I'd come over and see if you people got rained on last night.

CYNTHIA: Did we? You didn't say anything.

JEAN: No.

(JEAN leaves.)

CHAD: I'm gonna need some bread.

CYNTHIA: *(Beat.)* So you can have another night out with the locals.

CHAD: Come on, I got some buddies waiting for me in town.

(CYNTHIA reaches for her purse as they exit.)

AUGUST: *(Alone—no slide.)* Note to myself. Separate personal from professional. Discard personal. Separate separate from separate; separate personal from imaginary, illusion from family, ancient from contemporary, etc., if possible. Organize if possible and separate if possible from if impossible. Catalogue what shards remain from the dig; celebrate separation; also, organize (a) brain, (b) photographic material, (c) letter of resignation, (d) health, (e) budget, (f) family, (f-1) family—ties, (g) life. Not necessarily in that order. Dianne, if you're still with me, copy that out and don't worry about it.

(Slide of a pot. DELIA is on the lounge; JEAN is repeatedly doing a sit-up exercise during the following scene.)

AUGUST: This is a shell-tempered pot that we found four years ago in one of the mounds. What the hell it's doing in here only God and the photographer could tell you. *(Slide)* These post molds marked the walls of a round house under which we discovered a burial. This is the beginning of our work to uncover the burial of the God King's retainers.

CYNTHIA: *(Entering from door.)* My eyes are driving me crazy. I don't think the muscles have the strength to focus on anything more this morning.

JEAN: Spots?

CYNTHIA: (*Falling back into a chair.*) Worse: one spot. I've been batting at a nonexistent fly all day. Everyone at the site waved at me.

JEAN: I might wander down and see how they're doing later.

CYNTHIA: They'll be up. Don't go today, it's too slow. They've been working for two weeks and they haven't found anything except post molds. It takes forever and they're not uncovering anything but dark spots. (*To* DELIA) I hope you weren't cold last night; it can get pretty nippy in June, we—

DELIA: I froze.

CYNTHIA: What?

DELIA: I froze.

CYNTHIA: (*Getting up again.*) I'll get the blankets from our room. We all practically sleep outside from March to November.

DELIA: (*Overlapping from* CYNTHIA's "all") I'm fine now. I'm fine now.

CYNTHIA: Do you have clothes or anything that we should send for? Other than what's in the trunk?

DELIA: What trunk?

CYNTHIA: The trunk you shipped from Oran.

DELIA: Did I? Good.

CYNTHIA: The hospital discovered your identity by redeeming the claim check on your trunk.

DELIA: That's—very resourceful of them.

CYNTHIA: Do you have anything that—

DELIA: Don't worry about it.

CYNTHIA: We're so schizophrenic since we've been coming down here. Just as I begin adjusting to a life stripped down to what I can carry on my back we pull up camp and migrate back to eleven rooms of memorabilia.

JEAN: I don't think Delia's a collector.

DELIA: I collect with one hand and mislay with the other. The world's unclaimed-baggage departments are crammed with my paraphernalia.

CYNTHIA: I know it's going to sound fatuously supportive, but for only two weeks you're looking better. How are you feeling?

DELIA: Better. (*Beat.*) Don't stare at the Gorgon, Jean, you'll turn to stone.

JEAN: (*To* CYNTHIA) Don't rub your eyes.

CYNTHIA: Oh, I know...

JEAN: Where's Oran?

DELIA: Tunisia—Algeria.

JEAN: That sounds very glamorous to us landlubbers.

DELIA: It isn't. Oran was Camus's model for the *locus in quo* of *The Plague*. We were host to every fly on the Mediterranean.

JEAN: Were you there with your husband?

CYNTHIA: She isn't married any more.

DELIA: (*Simultaneously*) Good God, I haven't been married since before you were born. I don't even remember being married. I can't believe— (*Trailing into laugh.*)

JEAN: You don't remember being married?

DELIA: —I was very young, darling; I was terrified of rejection; what I remember is an anxiety to please so severe I could hardly fight down the panic long enough to get drunk. I was bonded, I wasn't—(*Coughs*)

JEAN: What'd he look like?

CYNTHIA: He was a looker.

DELIA: He was a strong, hirsute, sweating, horny cocksman. He sold drilling equipment. I was so captivated that that didn't strike me as funny until years after I got out from under him.

JEAN: I thought he was an artist.

DELIA: God, no, God, no—God no! He has not eyes in his head! We traveled through the East. He traveled, I trailed. Egypt, Lebanon, Syria, Cyprus, Metaxa, Ouzo, Grappa, Cinzano...

JEAN: You were working, though.

DELIA: Self-defense.

AUGUST: (*Off*)... as long as it's considered subservient to anthropology. We'll never have sufficient clout till we have a separate autonomous department.

DAN: (*As he and* AUGUST *enter*) Man, it's hotter than a pistol out there.

(AUGUST *goes to his office,* DAN *to the refrigerator.*)

CYNTHIA: Tell me about it.

JEAN: (*After* AUGUST *has exited.*) And you split.

DELIA: And I split. But once set in motion, the moving object tends to remain in motion.

CYNTHIA: Well, maybe the stationary object now will tend to remain stationary.

DELIA: Couldn't do that. Couldn't do that. I have a very real terror of gathering moss.

(DAN *opens a beer.*)

DAN: (*To* DELIA) I think I might welcome a little moss after your experiences.

DELIA: After how many years? Eight, nine—

JEAN: Don't, I'm counting—

DELIA: —After living in the liquid world, wouldn't I welcome being washed up onto some sandy lakeshore-front property in the sun to dry out. Out in the thin air where the hand is quicker than the eye and noises are distinct and occur at their source rather than inside your head. Well, I'm—vaguely conscious of allowing myself to float up toward the surface—at least to look around.

CYNTHIA: Good.

DELIA: Whereupon I'm certain I'll want to drown myself.

DAN: Again.

JEAN: (*Giving up the exercises.*) Oh. Uncle. A hundred ten.

JEAN: Is that O.K.?

DAN: (*Looking through typed pages.*) All that only typed up to four pages?

JEAN: How are the post molds coming?

DAN: "Post molds"? You've been reading books.

JEAN: Talking to Cynthia.

DAN: (*To* CYNTHIA) We're ready on the third section while the girls are taking a lunch break if you want to get at it.

CYNTHIA: They can wait.

JEAN: What were the posts for?

CYNTHIA: Walls. You've never seen so many holes in your life.

DAN: These are for the walls of a roundhouse. They set posts around in a circle about every two feet then filled in the walls with mud and dabble. Walls about yea thick—fire pit in the middle—no chimney, only one door—must have been smokey as hell. Men only—sat around telling hunting stories.

JEAN: This isn't really a typical village, is it?

DAN: Oh, yeah, pretty much.

CYNTHIA: Boringly so.

JEAN: In your notes you say that the typical village configuration is a large plaza with a mound at each end—

DAN: The downtown area. A mound for the high muck-a-muck God-King, and a mound for the temple. Roundhouse we're working on is down here in the corner.

JEAN: Swell. Only where are the mounds in the middle of the plaza?

CYNTHIA: Old Man Jasker plowed them under.

DAN: That's why we didn't know there was a village here.

JEAN: And they weren't burial mounds so who would know—

DAN: No. Burial mounds were built by hunters and gatherers. There weren't any villages to speak of until the Mississippians began to develop agriculture.

CYNTHIA: Then they had to hang around the house and tend the fields—sacrifice to the gods of harvest and whatnot.

DAN: There's been at least three different cultures who built mounds in the area—the Adena, back around 600 B.C.

JEAN: B.C.? 600 B.C.?

CYNTHIA: Don't ask; you don't want to know.

DAN: 600 B.C. Then the Hopewell Culture. Then the Temple Mound People. Or for short, the early Mississippian Culture.

JEAN: And those are our guys.

CYNTHIA: All very filled with pomp and circumstance.

DAN: Cahokia, up in St. Louis, was one of the Mississippian cities. Probably forty, fifty thousand people. Bigger than Paris or London at the time.

JEAN: I know, I was reading your book on it.

DAN: I knew it; don't read books. Let me tell you.

JEAN: Do you get the feeling that they were just the least bit weird?

CYNTHIA: Oh, definitely.

JEAN: There's a grave with six men all laid out ceremonially, with their right hands chopped off.

CYNTHIA: You see that all the time.

JEAN: Well, I mean, really. Do they have an explanation for that ?

CYNTHIA: Maybe they were caught masturbating. (*Beat.*) Where's your book on circulation? I haven't seen you crack a medical book since you've been here.

JEAN: What's more immediate is a stack of articles I've intended to read for three months.

CYNTHIA: Well, don't hire out as a typist. August spends all his time drumming up money to hire secretaries to type up Dan's notes.

JEAN: You don't know how ignorant I am about the—

CYNTHIA: Well, stay that way. I'm not joking. Don't start. (*To* DAN) Have one of the girls do it. (*To* JEAN) It's a full-time job and you already have one.

JEAN: Two.

DAN: (*Unfazed by anything.*) I'd do it myself but I can't type and I can't spell.

JEAN: What will you do after the Interstate levels the mounds you're supposed to dig next summer?

AUGUST: (*Off, calling*)—Dan? Where'd you put it?

DAN: (*Laying down pages.*) Where'd I put what?

CYNTHIA: Really, don't bother with it.

DAN: (*Giving* JEAN *a pat in passing.*) That's terrific. Come down later.

JEAN: Oh, God. I don't mind correcting your spelling, but please don't pat me on the head.

DAN: (*Laughing, going into the office.*) Where'd I put what? (*He shuts the door behind him.*)

CYNTHIA: Have you learned anything about pregnancy that's going to revolutionize childbirth?

JEAN: Oh . . . no. The source of that smug glow pregnant women have. You really do feel the miracle of it all. Every woman is the only woman who's ever been pregnant. That—and one moment of blinding damnation that was probably singular to me. After two immediate miscarriages and all kinds of anxiety about it—

CYNTHIA: I didn't realize you'd—

JEAN: Well, as grandmother would say, "Our women have a history of it"—That's why I'm reluctant to accept premature congratulations. Still, when I finally managed to stay pregnant for two months and thought that maybe we were O.K., I told Dan and I felt for one second that in telling him I had breached a covenant between me and the baby. As though I had—forever fallen from grace. Did you feel that?

CYNTHIA: Fallen from grace, I wouldn't remember; the miracle yes.

AUGUST: (*Re-entering with* DAN.) But that has nothing to do with us.

DAN: Just tell them we've thought of calling the dig the First National Bank of Carbondale Village.

AUGUST: That would do it.

DAN. (*To* JEAN) Come down and dig out a post mold with us. (DELIA *laughs.*)

JEAN: It doesn't sound very romantic. It's more—what—rural, than the spectacular cultures, isn't it?

AUGUST: It was quite spectacular—take her up to the Koster Site.

JEAN: I mean like the Aztec Empire.

AUGUST: The Aztec culture was not really an empire.

JEAN: Well, or the Incan culture.

AUGUST: The Incans had an empire. We'd be working somewhere else if our work here weren't important.

DAN: If Cortes had landed here in 1250, you wouldn't be talking about the Aztecs at all; you'd be talking about the glory that was Jasker's Field. They had longer trade routes—they just didn't leave anyone around to translate their poetry.

JEAN: They had poetry?

AUGUST: I would imagine. Poetry, drama—the Aztecs did.

JEAN: Do we know any of it? The Aztec—

AUGUST: Yes, otherwise we—

JEAN: What did it sound like?

DAN: Free verse, rhyming verse. Think Emily Dickinson.

AUGUST: (*To* CYNTHIA) I'll give you a ring about five. (*He exits.*)

DAN: Here are our precious flowers and songs
May our friends delight in them,
May the sadness fade out of our hearts.
This earth is only lent to us.
We shall have to leave our fine work.
We shall have to leave our beautiful flowers.
That is why I am sad as I sing for the sun.

DELIA: Who was that?

DAN: We don't know his name, Delia. We only know his work. (*He exits.*)

CYNTHIA: (*Picking up her equipment as* JEAN *begins exercising.*) Do you really think you'll go on with a medical career after you have the baby?

JEAN: (*Stops dead. Beat.*) It didn't stop you. You managed. Don't rub your—

CYNTHIA: I have several thousand photographs of Kirsten. Maybe you'll run a day care center. (*Pause.*) If you come down, bring a hat; the sun's murder. (*Starts out.*)

JEAN: Did you want to do something else with your photography?

CYNTHIA: (*Overlapping*) Not at all, not at all. I'm sorry I brought it up.

JEAN: (*After* CYNTHIA *has gone, looking after her.*) Oh, brother.

DELIA: Did they fight? (JEAN *looks around to her.*) The Temple Mound people?

JEAN: (*Not really thinking about it.*) Apparently. The built the first fortifications and all that. Probably kept the first slaves.

DELIA: You feed it all into a computer—all the facts and fancies the scholars have compiled and the computer would print out NOTHING APPLIES. It doesn't scan.

JEAN: You have a way of conveying the impression you know all the answers.

DELIA: The answer to which is, Yes, but I don't know any of the questions.

JEAN: Neat.

DELIA: Isn't that neat? It's a lie, but it's neat. I know the questions by rote. I just don't stand up well under them.

JEAN: No, neither do I. I won the spelling bee when I was a kid. Did beautifully, then had a complete collapse.

DELIA: Spelling bee? God.

JEAN: The spelling bee. When I was what? Twelve. National Champion.

DELIA: Dear God.

JEAN: No one in the neighborhood went to the dictionary, they all came to me. I was tutored by my grandmother so I was the only kid who used the old-fashioned English grammar school method of syllable spelling. Charmed the pants off them. It started out as a kind of phenomenon or trick—then when my teachers realized they had a certifiable freak on their hands, they made me study for it.

DELIA: We're all freaks—all us bright sisters.

JEAN: It wasn't so bad until the competitions started. I mean, it wasn't like the little girl practicing her violin with her nose against the windowpane, watching all the other little girls at play. But I managed to work it into a nervous breakdown. (*Pause.*) I couldn't stop. Every word that was said to me, I spelled in my head. (*In an easy, flowing, but mechanical rhythm.*) Mary, go to bed. Mary go to bed. Mary. M-A-R-Y. Mary. Go. G-O. Go. Mary go. To T-O. To. Mary go to. Bed. B-E-D. Bed. Mary go to bed. Mary go to bed: M-A-R-Y-G-O-T-O-B-E-D. Mary, go to bed.

DELIA: Mary?

JEAN: Mary Jean. (*She wanders to the door to gaze out.*) That, and I lost the meaning. Mary, go to bed was syllables, not sense. (*Beat.*) Then there were days when the world and its objects separated, disintegrated into their atomic structure. And nothing held its form. The air was the same as the trees and a table was no more substantial than the lady sitting at it . . . Those were . . . not good days.

DELIA: I don't imagine. But you got it together.

JEAN: Oh, yes, juvenile resilience.

DELIA: And that led one directly into gynecology.

JEAN: That led one directly into an institution, and contact with some very sick kids. Some of them more physically ill than neurotic—who were not being particularly well cared for; and that led to an interest in medicine. And reading your books and others at an impressionable age led to gynecology. (*Beat.*) Also, living with my grandmother and her cronies, who were preoccupied with illness, kept it pretty much in my curiosity. They were always talking about friends with female troubles, problems with their organs. Of course, the only organ I knew was at church. I developed a theory of musical instruments as families. The cello was the mother, the base was the father, and all the violins were the children. And the reason the big grandfather organ at Grace Methodist Church made such a mournful sound was that female organs were always having something wrong with them.

DELIA: Round John Virgin.

JEAN: Exactly.

DELIA: Have you seen Dad's book on the eye? Vision, actually?

JEAN: I didn't know he had one. He was a doctor?

DELIA: Physiologist. Hated practicing physicians. Eye, ear, nose, throat.

JEAN: Somewhat different field.

DELIA: I'd guess. The downstairs of the house was his, his consultation room, his office, his examination rooms: big square masculine Victorian rooms with oversized charts of the musculature of the neck and diagrams of the eye with the retina and rods and cones and iris and lens and those lines projected out into space indicating sight. And it appeared to me—still does—that rather than the eye being a muscle that collects light, those beams indicated that the eye projects vision onto the outside.

(*Pause.*)

JEAN: The place has changed since last year. I came down a couple of times last summer—weekends—watching their progress. But something odd is happening now—or not happening. There's something . . . I don't think it's the pregnancy. I think it's here. Or maybe my eyes are just projecting vision onto the outside.

DELIA: No, I think something odd is happening.

JEAN: I have an intense desire to turn to the end of the chapter and see how it all comes out. You don't happen to have a deck of tarot on you, do you?

DELIA: No, I just look that way.

JEAN: It's only an anxiety.

DELIA: Generally speaking, Jean, ignore the Ides of March, but beware soothsayers. (JEAN *laughs.*) The old woman in *Dombey and Son* comes upon Edith in a lonely wood and says: "Give me a shilling and I'll tell your fortune." And Edith, of course, cuts her dead and goes on—Edith cuts everyone dead. And the old woman screams: "Give me a shilling or I'll yell your fortune after you."

JEAN: Oh, God. I'd pay. God, would I pay.

DELIA: That's what I thought.

JEAN: Jesus. Would I ever. What was the fortune? (*Pause.*) What was the—

DELIA: Give me a shilling or I'll tell you.

JEAN: Don't! Don't do that. What was the fortune?

DELIA: Uh, someone intervened.

JEAN: The hero.

DELIA: The villain actually.

JEAN: Do you do that? Turn to the end of a book to find out—

DELIA: No, I don't—I don't read any more.

JEAN: You do, of course. What's wrong is this inaction. I'm used to doing things. The university funds a clinic, you can't imagine. Coming off that is like coming off speed.

DELIA: And that's your answer. Why do you want to be a doctor when we get such a kick from diagnosing our own case? What seems to be the problem, Mrs. Blue—"Well, Doctor, I'm afraid I'm going to require twenty-five 300-milligram capsules of Declomycin."

JEAN: Oh, it's true. A gargle and forty Ornade spansules.

DELIA: Jeans's only coming down off work and D.K. is frantically beating the bushes for something to believe in. Something with passion to warm up the blood and make her forget where it hurts. Great blinders is believing in and she's a great believer in blinders.

JEAN: Where does it hurt, D.K.?

DELIA: Doctor, it's a pain in the ass.

JEAN: Where does it hurt, D.K.?

DELIA: I thought we agreed not to ask.

(*Blackout.*)

CHAD's voice: (*Drunk, pounding the door.*) Goddamn! Cynthia?

CYNTHIA's VOICE: (*Harsh whisper*) What are you doing? The house is full of people, none of whom have ever been known to sleep!

CHAD's VOICE: (*Drunk, urgent*) I gotta go. I had to come over. I had to come.

CYNTHIA's VOICE: Shhhhhh! Good God, are you drunk?

CHAD's VOICE: I drunk thirty dollar's worth of rye-and-ginger since six o'clock.

CYNTHIA's VOICE: Oh, God. Come outside.

CHAD's VOICE: When you need it, we go. We gotta go when I need it, damnit.

CYNTHIA's VOICE: Come outside; come on outside.

CHAD's VOICE: (*Louder, insistent*) I'm hot, baby—get down; take it, goddamnit; it'll just be ten seconds; nobody's gonna come in in ten seconds.

CYNTHIA's VOICE: Shhhh. Come on.

CHAD's VOICE: Come on.

CYNTHIA's VOICE: Shh. Come on, come outside.

(*The screen-door spring sounds as they are heard to go outside. Flashlight.*)

DAN: Is someone there? Hello? (*Flashlight out.*) Hello? (*Stumbles.*) Oh, goddamnit. (*Flashlight on, he's on his knees, the light finds the lamp,he turns it on.* DELIA *is on the lounge, a hand averting the light from her eyes.*) Oh. Oh! Shit. Oh, baby. Oh, wow! I'm sorry. Oh, Jesus . . . I thought we were being burglarized . . . Oh, you scared the piss out of me. (*He sits down.*)

DELIA: (*Still with her hand averting the light. Flatly.*) Any time.

DAN: Couldn't you have coughed or something? Were you asleep?

DELIA: No.

DAN: Wooooooooow! You expect to see someone. Then you *do* see someone. Wow! You couldn't sleep?

DELIA: I don't know.

DAN: I'm a light sleeper.

DELIA: (*Only a glance at him.*) Why don't you straighten up like a man? Your posture is a disgrace to the species.

DAN: That's probably from working in—

DELIA: —Oh, for godsake, put your shoulders down, you look like a capon. I'm not talking about your physical health. I'm talking about this Howdy-Dowdy, hale-fellow, nice-guy, innocent-babe-in-the-wood facade you splash over every—I'm a writer, I'm not a chiropractor.

DAN: You still think of yourself as a writer? (*She looks at him directly for the first time.*) I mean, I'm glad; are you working? Are you writing? You know, I knew August for two years before I knew you were his sister? We read you at school . . . Contemporary American Lit. Professor . . . can't remember. Read half your second book aloud. Second one was *Spindrift*? (*Pause.*) He was wild about it. Read everything aloud because he knew (a) we wouldn't read anything he assigned, and he had this thing that any really good book should be read aloud (b). (*He begins rolling a joint.*)

DELIA: Sounds like a lousy disciplinarian.

DAN: Frustrated actor. Read terrifically.

DELIA: Snap course.

DAN: No shit, that's all I took my last year.

DELIA: Where was this?

DAN: Columbia. Said you were the last defender of a woman's right to make a fool of herself.

DELIA: Oh, surely not the last. Tell him I was drunk.

DAN: When you wrote it? Does that make it bad?

DELIA: No. It makes it easier. No, it doesn't. Nothing makes it easier— (*Mumbles, a light cough.*)

DAN: What?

DELIA: (*Forced out.*) I said nothing makes it easier once it starts becoming difficult! Half of it. Half of it should read very nicely. Half of it was dictated into a tape recorder. Because I couldn't find the typewriter—keys.

DAN: I liked it.

DELIA: The half you heard.

DAN: I read it. I liked it a lot. I realize you couldn't care less one way or the other whether I—

DELIA: (*Overlapping almost from "realize".*) Oh, I couldn't. I had a little secretary come in from some agency and type it for me. Temporary help. She looked . . . "temporary." Very neat, sweet, meek. She typed eight hours a day for five days, never misspelling a word, stacked the manuscript on the desk, put on her neat, sweet, meek gloves while I wrote out a check; took her check sweetly, put on her coat meekly, and left by the front door neatly. And I took the manuscript, put it in a box, wrapped it in vinegar and brown paper, addressed it to my publisher, who had been expecting it daily for over five months, threw it on the closet floor, and got drunk for three days. Wouldn't answer the phone.

DAN: Because it was finished?

DELIA: Because I thought she hadn't like it.

DAN: (*Pause.*) And after three days?

DELIA: The police, with my publisher, broke the door in. I told him it was going to be a failure. Later on he told me the book was a success but I was a failure.

DAN: I liked it very much. (*Beat. He gets up, looking out again.*) Was that you? That clamor down here?

DELIA: You've been coming here four summers? You and Auggie and Cynthia? I'd think you'd have noticed that you're in the country out here. The natives get restless at night. The dogs raid the hen house. They get hungry.

DAN: (*Offering the joint.*) Want a toke?

DELIA: How did you ever survive four years in New York?

DAN: Five, I got my M.S. (DELIA *laughs.*) It was really intimidating, but I kinda loved it. I had this great roommate who worried about me. Thought he was Seymour Glass. The guy in all the—

DELIA: I'm familiar—

DAN: Studied medieval history, but he was a great roommate.

DELIA: —Well, though, medieval history isn't something to cross off lightly, he probably taught you how the Flemish used a virgin to distract the horny unicorn.

DAN: We used to put him on.

DELIA: Yes, I'm sure—

DAN: —Well, then, also, I really believed the only way to feel completely safe on the sidewalks of New York is to be completely, knockdown drunk. I mean visibly, stinking, reeling, dangerously drunk.

DELIA: How many times have you been dangerously—

DAN: On the sidewalks of New York? Once. But it's the only time I felt safe. I was badly drunk. In a bad drunk way.

DELIA: I'm familiar. Sick drunk.

DAN: Sick doesn't even begin. I saw signs, sidewalks, people veering out of my way. Taxies *avoiding* me. I fell off the curb—had no idea what it was—got up, staggered across the street wondering where all the *buildings* had gone—realized just as I got to the other side that probably I was crossing a street—looked around to confirm it, and fell over the other curb. (*Pause.*) In the rain. I remember walking up to a street light. I thought it was a street light, it wasn't a street light, I thought it was a street light, and wrapping my arms around it like it was my mother. Cold hard wet beautiful mother. Stood there forever. Long enough to lose all orientation. Finally opened my eyes and right at my nose this sign says: "You must answer to get help." (*Pause.*) White letters on a red field. "You must answer to get help." Blackout. Next thing I know, my roommate's shaking me awake asking me what time I got in. I said, "You must answer to get help." (*Pause.*) You ever see that sign? (*Pause.*) "You must answer . . ."

DELIA: I missed that one.

DAN: One on every block. I saw it about a month later. Old friend. Little letters: "Break glass; life receiver; answer operator." Big print: "You must answer to get help." No more metaphysical than anything else in this world. (*Pause.*) Fire-alarm box. One on every box. (*Pause, look at her.* DELIA *stares blankly off into space.*) Friend of man and dog. (*Long pause. He gets up, reaches for the lamp.*) Light on or off? (*Pause.*) Delia? D.K.? . . . light on or off?

(*A pause. He turns off the light. BLACKOUT.*)

Act Two

AUGUST: (*Slide: Mr. Jasker.*) This is old man Jasker himself. The wise old bird who owns the place. After being made famous with the arrival of the college, he was looking forward to being made rich by the arrival of the lake and Interstate 64. We see him twice each year, on our arrival and departure. This is a June Hello—there was no September Goodbye last summer. (*Slide: the moon.*) This is the moon.

(DELIA *is seated in the swing.* CHAD *and* DAN *are noisily divesting themself of rods, reels, creels, etc. Enjoying the noise; oblivious to the silence of the house.* DAN *goes to the cooler.*)

DAN: Nothing!

CHAD: Nothing?

DAN: Nothing to drink. Do you want to eat?

CHAD: God, no—

DAN: Food?

CHAD: Never again in my life. (*He has found a bottle of Scotch.*)

DAN: Well, then there's nothing.

CHAD: You call that nothing?

DAN: Are you crazy; you want to kill yourself?

CHAD: No—you go. "Beer on whiskey—mightly." Mightly?

DAN: Mightly?

CHAD: What is it? You say it.

DAN: You're saying it. I don't know what—

CHAD: I'm telling you, it's an old wives' tale—there's a *thing*—a saying that tells you how to judge.

DAN: A what? What's the thing?

CHAD: You're the educated member of the family—you're supposed—

DAN: But not in FOLKLORE! Not in—

CHAD: I'm not talking—

DAN: —Absolute blind spot in folklore!

CHAD: I'm talking words—it's a epigram or epitaph or aphorism or anagram.

DAN: Axiom.

CHAD: It's not an axiom.

DAN: Well, what is it? Is it—

CHAD: It's not a godamned axiom. It's an easy word—it's a word! It's a saying—a truth!

DAN: That's the word. It's a truth.

CHAD: It's a truth, but that's not the word—ANYWAY!

DAN: Anyway. How does it go? Tell us! Are we safe? Will we survive?

CHAD: It goes ... (*Pause,trying to frame it.*)

DAN: (*Under*) How does ...

CHAD: (*Under*) Just cool it a minute, will you? It goes: (*Headline*) "BEER ON WHISKEY."

DAN: Sounds bad.

CHAD: "MIGHTY RISKY ... WHISKEY, ON BEER NEVER FEAR."

DAN: (*Pause.*) It's an aphorism.

CHAD: So. (*Pours a glass each.*) Whiskey on beer—(*Toast.*)

DAN: Cheers.

CHAD: WHISKEY ON BEER ...

DAN: That's what I said: "Never fear."

CHAD: Cheers.

(*They drink.*)

DAN: This will probably kill us.

CHAD: Hey! Have you ever seen anything as beautiful as that moon?

DAN: Never.

CHAD: As big?

DAN: Never. When's the harvest moon?

CHAD: October.

DAN: Only the harvest moon.

CHAD: November.

DAN: Only the harvest moon.

CHAD: October.

DAN: Only the harvest moon.

CHAD: September.

DAN: As golden?

CHAD: Never.

DAN: What is it? June 21, 23—that's the summer solstice—moon.

CHAD: (*Simple*) It's a full moon.

DAN: It's a full moon.

CHAD: And you're full of shit.

DAN: I'm fulla beer.

CHAD: I gotta piss.

DAN: (*Alone.*) What'd we do?

CHAD: (*Off*) Twelve.

DAN: Twelve's ass. I caught five and you caught what?

CHAD: (*Off*) You caught five, I caught seven.

DAN: They be all right out in that tub?

CHAD: (*Off*) You want to clean 'em?

DAN: Hell, I couldn't clean me.

CHAD: (*Off*) You better manage it; Jean'll kick your ass out on the floor.

DAN: Hell she will. (*He stands, miming rod: casting, catch.*) Strike! Shitfire! Strike! Get the net!

CHAD: (*Off*) What?

DAN: Get the net, goddamnit, I got another one!

CHAD: (*Off*) Get your own damn net; I got a seven-pounder out there.

DAN: (*Dropping it.*) He who brags about size of meat—I forget what it was, but Confucius said something very appropriate to that. What'll it weight? The big one. Five pounds?

CHAD: Six.

DAN: Was that one motherfuckin' fish? Was that a *fight?* To the *death?*

CHAD: (*Entering.*) That was a fight to the death.

DAN: Was that the biggest bass you ever saw in your life?

CHAD: No.

DAN: Shit.

CHAD: No.

DAN: You've seen a bigger bass?

CHAD: I've seen a bigger bass.

DAN: Drink your beer.

CHAD: I gotta get my ass home.

DAN: Would you drink your damn beer?

CHAD: You better get your duds off; get up to that warm bed, you're gonna be diggin' tomorrow.

DAN: Terrific. You know why? Cause what's happening is, it's all gone wrong. And that's always very terrific.

CHAD: Get up and have your girl give you a rubdown, huh?

DAN: Everything's looking like a typical village, right? And all of a sudden it's not typical any more. They got something under the roundhouse.

CHAD: Isn't that right?

DAN: We don't know what yet. What?

CHAD: You gotta get up to your girl.

DAN: She's beautiful, isn't she?

CHAD: She is that.

DAN: And bright—you wouldn't believe it.

CHAD: No, I'm counting on it. Let's take you up, put you to bed.

DAN: And sweet; you wouldn't believe it.

CHAD: No, I'm a believer.

DAN: You better believe it.

CHAD: Let's get you up to bed, come on.

DAN: I'm all wet.

CHAD: Come on.

DAN: I'm all wet, come on.

CHAD: Well, you said it.

DAN: Drink your—Scotch.

CHAD: Wore your life preserver, didn't you? That's nice out there, just you and me, huh?

DAN: Beautiful.

CHAD: Wouldn't be right with no one else, huh?

DAN: No way.

CHAD: You gettin' warm?

DAN: I'm fine.

CHAD: (*Very close to him.*) You gonna be O.K.?

DAN: I am.

CHAD: (*Pulling him closer.*) You sure? You sure?

DAN: Yeah, well, I didn't drown, I can survive without mouth-to-mouth resuscitation.

CHAD: Huh?

DAN: I'm fine.

CHAD: You know why you didn't drown—because you got a cork head!

JEAN: (*Entering.*) You've got to be kidding; it's one-thirty in the morning.

DAN: (*Whispering.*) Oh, damn! NO! It's the night of nights! People should be up.

JEAN: Do you drink when you go out fishing? No wonder people go fishing. (*To* DELIA) Are you all right? I mean, are they bothering you?

DELIA: Not at all.

DAN: Jesus Christ! I might have sat on you! We're all here. (*To* JEAN, *moving toward her.*) This is the night—

JEAN: Shhh! The night of nights; I hear you. Come on, really. I'm all over calamine lotion . . . I'm itching all—

DAN: (*Softly, singing, waltzing her gently a few steps.*) Gently, gently, gently—"We're gonna fill an ocean of calamine lotion . . ."

JEAN: Come on, you'll wake me up; you'll wake me—(*Breaks off.*) Oh, well, hell, it's too late; I'm awake. Damn. Damn. Damn. Are you sure we won't bother you? Were you sleeping out here?

DELIA: No, you won't bother me. No, I wasn't sleeping.

JEAN: (*Opening refrigerator.*) You hungry? I'm starved.

DAN: Is anybody hungry? No one is hungry.

DELIA: Whattaya say, Jasker? You hungry?

JEAN: What are you drinking? Is that straight Scotch?

DAN: Well, yeah, it's . . . We're sipping.

CHAD: I'm gonna leave you all to your dig.

DAN: Stay. Stay.

CHAD: Later. (*Leaving.*)

DAN: Stay awhile. (*Chad is gone.*) Eat! We'll all eat! What's the matter with him?

(JEAN *is making a sandwich.*)

DELIA: What's he got on you?

DAN: Got on me? Nothing. What are you talking about, he's not got anything on me. I owe him my life—he's not got anything on me.

DELIA: Nobody owes their life to—

DAN: Well—some things you don't know, do you? He pulled me out of the drink last summer. We were rowing out; I was pulling back on the oar, it came out of the socket, hit me right in the face—I passed out and slid over the side in twenty feet of water.

JEAN: You're really too much.

DAN: Pulled me out by the hair of my head.

JEAN: What did you catch?

DAN: Oh! Incredible!

JEAN: Come on.

DAN: (*Whispers.*) Four very friable, skillet-size bass. And one—mammoth . . .

DELIA: Motherfucking.

DAN: Motherfucking President of the Lake. Come and look!

JEAN: No, I haven't got any—

JEAN	DAN
—It's wet! I'm barefoot. I hate fish. I mean, I'll eat it, I'm glad you caught it, but I don't like live fish.	Come out and look. Come— Would you come out here and look.

DAN: What do you do when they got no sense of adventure?

JEAN: How big?

DAN: Very big. Formidable. Six pounds. If she hadn't been here, I'd of said twelve. But a fighter! A very . . . vicious opponent. Only six pounds, but solid muscle. Look at the moon at least—come look at the moon, you can see the moon from here; you don't even have to put your shoes on. Where'd it go? (*He has taken her arm.*)

JEAN: You're soaking wet. Did you fall in?

DAN: I jumped in. I wanted to test my lifejacket.

JEAN: Did it work?

DAN: Uh . . . inconclusive. Anyway! I thought we were getting a late start. I mean, what do I know, right? But it was hot. And bass are hedonists. When it's hot on top they puddle about down at the bottom, doing whatever they do when it's hot on top. You got to know the psychology

of the mothers. To be a fisherman you have to be a kind of amateur—

JEAN: Ichthyologist.

DAN: Ichthyopsychologist. But what do I know. So, no sign. We row
miles. Miles. (*Slowing down, tiring.* JEAN *has sat down.*) You wouldn't
believe the size of—there's one spot that's surrounded—both sides—
with pines. Miles and miles, both sides. Anyway—(*Getting comfortable,
against her, or on her lap.* JEAN *continues to munch her sandwich.*) The
sun goes down. No big deal.

JEAN: No big deal.

DAN: A little rose, a little amber. Nothing to notice. Basic everyday sundown. Then a bunch of disinterested strikes.

JEAN: Uninterested.

DAN: Uninterested strikes, all in a row. One two three four five six. So.
There are fish in there; we just don't interest them much.

JEAN: Is this the fish or is this the moon?

DAN: Shhhh. This is the moon. This is the moon and the fish. This is
both . . . We're busy with the strikes; we don't even notice it's getting
dark. Another couple of strikes, nibbles—bait stealings—nothing serious. And all of a sudden it's night. Pitch. Ink. We're two hours away
easily. Might as well turn around. So we start back—and . . . up . . .
drifts . . . this . . . orange . . . deep orange . . . unstable . . . major moon.
(*Beat.*) The lake is like . . .

JEAN: Glass.

DAN: . . . Very calm. We're rowing back—it's just beautiful. It's important. We stopped rowing and watched it. And then I threw my line in—
(*Simply*)—just because we were stopping. And—"Galoompa." Immediately. (*Lying in her lap. Swaying with it.*) They swam up to that light
like they were mesmerized by the light, dizzy on it . . .

JEAN: And that's when you caught them.

DAN: All—however many of them. Five and seven.

JEAN: Twelve.

DAN: All twelve of them.

JEAN: And by this time you were stoned.

DAN: Uhhh.

JEAN: Importantly stoned.

DAN: Uhhh.

JEAN: You bring back any grass?

DAN: Of course not.

JEAN: And what did you drink? (*Pause. Shakes him lightly.*) And what did you drink?

DAN: We drank . . . sunshine . . . and moonshine . . . and the air . . . and trees . . . and singing . . . singing! And fish . . . and comraderie, and . . . (*Mentally counts.*) Five six-packs.

JEAN: You don't swim that well.

DAN: Chad swims like a duck.

JEAN: Ducks have rarely been know to save anyone from drowning more than once.

DAN: This is true. I'm going to go to bed. (*Gets up.*) Give me a kiss. (*Kisses her lightly.*) I'm going to go to bed. (*Exits.*)

JEAN: (*Pause.*) I don't think I've ever been more awake. (*Pause.*) There's an old Chinese proverb: If you save someone from drowning, you're responsible for them for the rest of their life. I think Dan feels it's the other way around.

DELIA: I wasn't overly enthusiastic about the Orient.

JEAN: I'd like to see India. Japan.

DELIA: No, no . . . I couldn't take the Indian deities with their fucking Mona Lisa smiles saying: "Well, that's for us to know and you to find out." I made the only rationalization possible. I decided they didn't know at all. Come drift with me on a raft in the sea of tranquility. I'd go nuts. All of which would have served me very well if I could have forgotten it was a rationalization.

JEAN: Don't you make yourself tired with all that?

DELIA: (*Profound sigh; pause.*) Yes.

JEAN: I mean, they're only pieces of sculpture. They're art objects. They're not Shiva and Shakti themselves. Shakti didn't come down and sit for her portrait. She didn't pose for the artist.

DELIA: (*Beat.*) I believe she did. I think that she did. You're not easily quailed by the inscrutable.

JEAN: Inscrutable. In. I-N, in. Scrut. S-C-R-U-T, scrut. Inscrut. Ah. A, ah. Inscruta—ble. B-L-E, ble. Inscrutable. Inscrutable: I-N-S-C-R-U-T-A-B-L-E, inscrutable.

(CYNTHIA, *in a robe, comes down, mildly surprised to see them. She hesitates only a second, then, without thinking further about it, crosses the room to the back door and lets herself out. They watch but do not comment.*)

DELIA: (*After a moment.*) Men. God, they're sad—depressing poor bastards, breaking their balls for their families. We're their reflection, I suppose, but I don't know as they love us for it. (AUGUST *enters.*) Who would have the time? I wonder, do we drive them to it?

JEAN: Women?

DELIA: No. Wives. I have an odd vision that women are wonderful. It's the wives. Sad old wives. I wouldn't be man. Not and carry the dumbfounding load they've saddled themselves with. Actually, now that I think of it, being a woman is worse. We're the remains. We're what's left. We're the lees in the bottom of the bottle. You know how the world ends? You know what the "with a whimper" is? A sad old world of widows: wizened old women, lined up on beaches along all the Southern coastlines looking out over the water and trying to keep warm. (*Beat.*) Good lord. That sounds so horribly right I'll bet it's prophetic. The species crawls up out of the warm ocean for a few million years and crawls back to it again to die. Why don't you make me a drink?

JEAN: No.

(*BLACKOUT.*)

AUGUST: (*Slide: God King's Burial.*) Oh, yes . . . take a good look at this, Dianne. If you want to you can have it laminated in plastic and carry it about with you. This is the beginning of our work to uncover the burial of the God King. The shaded are in the center, pointing straight to the rising midsummer sun. This is the sort of sight that makes an experienced archaeologist quake in his boots and remember his dreams.

(*Everyone is onstage,* DAN *presiding.*)

DAN: Well, it's wrong is what it is. It's all wrong. Show her the Polaroid.

CYNTHIA: (*Handing* DAN *a print.*) You won't be able to tell much.

AUGUST: Burials have a way of turning up just as the light goes.

JEAN: I can't tell a thing from this.

DAN: (*Looking over her shoulder.*) See, he's laid out straight, head to the right.

JEAN: He isn't missing a hand, by any chance?

DAN: No, he's got the usual number of hands and three feet. Which is kinda funny when you see it.

CYNTHIA: Very awkward for dancing.

JEAN: Are you going to play with me, or are you going to tell me what you've found?

CYNTHIA: The third foot is incursive from some neighbor.

DAN: We don't know what we've found until we go over and see who his buddy is, and how many of them there are.

AUGUST: Tomorrow.

DAN: You're damn right.

CYNTHIA: Come out tomorrow, you might actually see August with a trowel in his hand.

DAN: Something's up; it's all wrong. Remember the roundhouse I showed you? With the fire in the middle? Well, these guys are buried under the round house.

AUGUST: Looks almost as if the house was built over them.

JEAN: And that's not cricket.

DAN: Uh—no. That's not cricket.

JEAN: Does he have artifacts around him?

DAN: Very low caste. Not so much as a little stone pipe.

JEAN: You think they had a caste system?

CYNTHIA: All the latest advancements.

DAN: As a matter of fact, around 1500 a tribe called the Natchez ended up down in Mississippi, around 1700 some French settlers moved in, studied them for about fifty years, decided they were dangerous, and rubbed them out—

JEAN: —Oh, God—

DAN: —Exactly. And it looks like the Natchez might have been the last of the Mound Builders. Hey, Deek—want to write a book? *Last of the Mound Builders*—I'd be glad to advise for a small consideration.

DELIA: Delia or D.K. Not "Deek."

DAN: So. If our guys were anything like the Natchez, they had a really off-the-wall, really bizarre, caste system.

AUGUST: Four distinct castes: The Suns—S-U-N-S..

DAN: Who were the very big muck-a-mucks, led by the Great Sun, who was a god-king.

AUGUST: Then the Nobles, then the Honored Men, and then the Stink-ards.

DAN: Really. Stinkards. Or that's the French translation. And of course most everybody was a Stinkard.

CYNTHIA: So things haven't changed all that much.

AUGUST: —And the Suns, the Nobles, and the Honored Men could only marry into the Stinkard class, with the second generation assuming the class of the mother. So only someone with a Sun mother and a Stinkard father could become the new God-King.

DAN: And everybody married Stinkards. Including the other Stinkards.

CYNTHIA: I didn't realize that.

AUGUST: I thought probably you did.

DAN: So they were an "upward-mobile," matriarchal society with a god-king muck-a-muck. All dressed in swan feathers. Carried on a litter everywhere he went. Like Delia; huh, D.K.

DELIA: Dan, it has been years since I've dressed in swan feathers.

JEAN: How long did they live? Not the Natchez, our guys.

DAN: Short.

JEAN: How long? How short?

AUGUST: If they reached the age of fifteen, their life expectancy was maybe thirty.

(A light thunder is heard, and gradually a wind rises.)

DAN: Do not ask how old I'll be on my next birthday.

CYNTHIA: You haven't reached the age of fifteen.

JEAN: And won't. The head of the department calls him "Polly-andy" to his face.

AUGUST: The head of the department is an extremely nihilistic individual.

DAN: This is true.

JEAN: What did they eat?

DAN: (Who has gone back to studying drawings of the grave site.) Huh? Oh-corn, squash, beans—

CHAD: That's succotash.

DAN: You kill, right? When you can't flunk 'em? They ate everything. Shellfish, deer . . .

CHAD: For all you know, they were cannibals.

AUGUST: They were not cannibals.

DAN: Of course; you know, I'd love to discover they were cannibals. Only I doubt if we'd ever be funded again. They had fairly elaborate ritualistic human sacrifices, but they weren't barbarians.

CYNTHIA: Actually, there's evidence that they did practice cannibalism.

DAN: None. Here? None. You're talking about Wisconsin. The people of southern Illinois are certainly not responsible for the perverted table manners of the people of Wisconsin. I personally wouldn't be surprised at anything that was discovered in Wisconsin. I think there's something in the water that twists their minds.

CHAD: Beer.

DAN: Very likely. Exactly.

AUGUST: Is that rain?

DAN: Is it raining? Damn. I better go down and see that they got every-thing covered. (*Getting a slicker.*) Let up already. (*Going out.*) My God, it's pouring.

JEAN: Put the hood up.

DAN: (*Off*) What?

JEAN: Your hood, dummy. Put the hood up.

(*Several slides of rain and the lake.*)

AUGUST: (*Isolated by the light to his desk area.*) Up, up, up, up. Every morning Dr. Loggins pushed a stake into the edge of the lake, trying, I think, to kill it. And every evening the lake had covered it. Nine tributaries empty into the basin, draining almost all of two counties. By the time the lake overran the site, it didn't at all matter.

(CHAD *knocks at the door. After a moment,* JEAN *comes down.*)

CHAD: I've been wanting to talk to you.

JEAN: (*After an audible sigh.*) I think maybe if you didn't come here . . . I mean, I know it's your house, and Dan likes you, you're a terrific relief from his gaggle of volunteers, but—you're putting yourself through something that seems so unnecessary.

CHAD: I thought we should talk. Just with nobody—

JEAN: We're talking, I don't mind; I'm perfectly willing to talk, but you can't expect it to be the sort of talk—

CHAD: (*Overlapping from "expect," letting himself in.*) What? Are you try-ing to make a fool of me? We're not talking; I got my boat over here. We'll go over to the place, the six acres I told you about—it's gonna be an island when the lake fills, I want to show you. There's a cave. It's going to be under water in another couple of days . . .

JEAN: (*A long pause.*) No.

CHAD: I thought you said we'd talk.

JEAN: Say whatever it is you want to say. It won't improve with the change in scene.

CHAD: It's just down at the landing—

JEAN: You have some kind of romantic fantasy going on that frankly frightens—

CHAD: I gave it a paint job; you ought to look at it.

JEAN: Chad, for godsake, I don't even swim, I don't like water, I don't like boats, it's pouring rain, and I'm not at all attracted to you.

CHAD: You don't know anything about me, you don't know—

JEAN: That is absolutely true, but I can live with it. You said you wanted to talk; you don't want to talk, you want to bludgeon. I'm married to a guy you claim is your friend—I'm going—I'm very much committed to him—I'm really sorry, but you make me feel foolish.

CHAD: O.K., O.K., O.K., you don't want to be with just me. Maybe what you want is for the three of us to get together. Go out fishing . . .

JEAN: (*Going.*) You're too much of a sport for me, Chad, you're too sporty for me.

CHAD: I thought you said we'd talk.

JEAN: Please put it out of your head, I don't like it. You make me uncomfortable.

CHAD: You said we'd talk. (AUGUST *enters.*) Bitch of a day, huh?

AUGUST: (*Shaking water from his hat.*) None too bright. (CHAD *exits.*) I don't know, Jean—I think it's not a good idea to socialize too much with our surrogate landlord.

JEAN: Socialize—Dan seems to like him.

AUGUST: Well, Dan, for all his ebullience, is quite tactful really.

JEAN: And I'm not—or women aren't.

DAN: (*Entering soaked.*) Brother! Drowned.

JEAN: You really are. (*Hands him a towel.*) You get the girls into the motel?

DAN: Yeah, their tents were almost washing out from under them; they're game, but they're stupid. The lake is insane; it's ten feet higher than it's supposed to be—if it's raining tomorrow, we're going to have to work anyway.

JEAN: You get dried off?

DAN: Yeah, I'm fine.

(DELIA *dressed in a clean robe, walks unsteadily but unaided down the stairs.*)

DAN: Well. It walks, it talks. It takes nourishment from a spoon.

(AUGUST *moves into the office.*)

DELIA: Spiritually it still crawls on its belly like a reptile—And it no longer takes nourishment from a spoon.

JEAN: You didn't.

DAN: You know the Contemporary Lit. professor I told you about? Used to read your stuff out loud?

DELIA: (*Sits.*) Don't push.

DAN: Thought of his name. Dr. Landau. Had a great voice. Said—what do you think about this?—said—

DELIA: I don't want to know what he said.

DAN: No, you'll get a kick out of it.

JEAN: This is about which one, this is *Spindrift?*

DAN: Yeah, said you were checking off the possibilities of the species.

DAN: You know, if it hadn't been for the—

DELIA: That's such a load of crap, what a load of—you know what I wrote? How I teased myself through it? I set a simple problem and tried to solve it. Write a Chinese puzzle box. Write a Russian doll. A box within a box within a box within a box. Every time something was solved, within the solution was another problem, and within the solving of the second riddle another question arose. And when that riddle was unwound there was still a knot. And you know why I failed? For me? Because either a Chinese puzzle box must go on ad infinitum or there must finally be a last box. And when that box is opened, something must finally be in it. Something simple like maybe an answer. Or a question. Or a fact, since we all seem to be compulsive compilers. Look at you, digging your evidence, piecing together shards, fragments, shards. Clues, footnotes, artifacts, pollen grains, bones, chips.

DAN: (*Overlapping from "pollen grains"*) Not of themselves—in association. Where are they, why are they there?

DELIA: Boxes in boxes.

DAN: (*Simultaneously overlapping second "boxes"*) Boxes in boxes. And when you got all the knots unwound in your book, and all the problems untied, and got down to the final little box—

DELIA: The Russian doll.

DAN: —and it was opened, what was inside?

DELIA: (*Pause.*) Another book.

DAN: (*Pause.*) I didn't know there was another . . .

DELIA: Well, that shows what you know. I thought it should be for Dad. A simple . . . simple . . . Then, of course, Dad died, and I—(*Pause.*)

JEAN: What?

DELIA: "In Memoriam" never interested me much.

DAN: (*Softly*) There wasn't another . . .

DELIA: For you to see? For Dr. Landau to read alout? I heard it—I saw it down there somewhere . . . that graceful, trim, and dangerous leviathan that got away—it moved in the cold depths of some uncharted secret currents where the sun has never warmed the shadows. Graceful and taunting. Moving through a spectrum of dark colors alien to the un-aided eye. I could have captured it and displayed to the light some un-discovered color. But it was deaf to my charms and tokens and incan-tations. I called the son of a bitch, but it wouldn't rise. So I went down to find it.

DAN: (*Pause.*) And it got away . . .

DELIA: (*Laughs.*) Well, I didn't get away. It caught me!

DAN: Tell me about—

DELIA: Tell me about the three—footed skeleton you've found.

DAN: We can't work, Delia; how can we work in this? (*Goes to office door.*)

AUGUST: (*Entering*) If it's this bad tomorrow, we'll put up tarps.

JEAN: I've thought about that house you grew up in. Big old masculine rooms with medical charts.

DELIA: Oak floors and old oak furniture. And light. The whole place filled with sunlight. Expecially in the winter.

AUGUST: She left when she was seventeen; I'm surprised she'd tell any-one about it.

DELIA: I'm the one who liked it, so I'm the one who remembers it.

AUGUST: I never said I didn't like it.

DELIA: He liked it so much he sold it the first week he could. Without mentioning to me that it was up for sale—

AUGUST: You were being sick in Mexico, as I recall, and couldn't come to the funeral.

JEAN: Boy, you two make me glad I'm an only child and grew up with grandparents.

AUGUST: It's all quite past. That's all past. Water under the bridge. Water under the bridge.

DAN: Water, water, water, water, water—

(*Slide of bone awl.*)

AUGUST: This bone awl you might as well enter as made by one Mr. Cochise Mississippi, around A.D. 1100.

DAN: (*Overlapping*) Around A.D. 1100, Mississippian; give or take fifty years; it's made from a turkey metacarpal bone.

JEAN: You get into some far-afield studies, don't you?

DAN: Umm.

(CYNTHIA *enters.*)

DELIA: (*Handing the bone to* JEAN) Well, that's a real keen bone awl, Cochise, but what have you done recently?

CYNTHIA: More recently they vanished without a trace. Along with the whole Mississippian Culture.

DELIA: Along with nearly everyone; vanished without a trace.

DAN: (*Still leaning against the screen, watching the rain.*) Vanished without a trace, vanished without a trace, vanished without a trace. God, I wish it would stop raining. Vanished without a trace. Nine mounds and a hothouse do not constitute without a trace. We've seen the outline of the foundations of houses used for gentlemen's clubs, complete with fireplace, never mind the ventilation. Vanished without a trace. It happens that this awl is one of the finest-crafted utilitarian tools discovered in North America—Cochise did not disappear without a trace. I think we have palpable evidence of his craft, of a subtle skill and imagination, of his care and conscientiousness. I think with his example his family stood proud and neat. I think his wife fashioned for him quilled buckskin aprons and kilts of surpassing brilliance that dazzled the tribe. Past? Vanished? Without a trace? Cochise? His passing, women, was mourned by tribes up and down the length of this river. I think his friends told histories around the fire of his craftiness in trapping game. Women cried and brave warriors walked out into the woods to be alone and fathom his loss. I think odes were composed and spoken and learned and repeated down the generations; songs were sung. I think so sure and strong a warrior stood as an example that young braves and children held up to themselves; I think Cochise was extraordinary beyond precedent. He danced with grace, he bathed twice a day, he spoke with simplicity and truth, and nursed the sick back to strength; he tamed wild animals and laughed when the children were frightened at night. I think he spread his arms out in an open field in the sun and yellow-green parakeets that he had tamed to sit on his hands came when he called them. I think wolves nuzzled his thighs and allowed him to walk in the wild as their comrade four hundred years before anyone named Francis walked in Assisi! Goddamn this rain! (*He grabs his slicker, kicks the screen door open, and charges out into the rain.*)

JEAN: Put the hood up! (*Pause.*) I have a feeling he really believes that. If it weren't for August, nothing they write would ever get published.

CYNTHIA: If it weren't for Dan, the work wouldn't get done in the first place.

DELIA: Parakeets?

CYNTHIA: Don't get him started. Parakeets were as common in Illinois as the sparrow is now.

JEAN: They weren't tropical?

DELIA: Some things we don't know, huh?

AUGUST: We have no clear idea what the bone awl was actually used for, but it was undoubtedly used for something. This is a particularly good one. (*He goes into the office.*)

CYNTHIA: Chad Jasker said he'd drive me into town; I think he's changed my plans.

JEAN: He was—

DELIA: I just left him standing on every corner; all the Mediterranean youths are hustlers.

CYNTHIA: Hustlers? I don't know why you call him a hustler. The Mediterraneans are probably poor, and he's poor.

DELIA: Not by their standards he isn't. Poor hustlers, rich hustlers—

CYNTHIA: You talk about how rich they're going to be—

JEAN: They are though—

CYNTHIA: Oh, they are not.

JEAN: No, really, When the lake comes in, God, he and his dad will own about a mile of the shoreline.

CYNTHIA: Poor people don't become rich. It takes capital to develop a lakeshore—they're rich with fantasy. They'll sell for what they think is money and be ripped off. They're not going to be rich.

JEAN: To hear him tell it, it's settled. You've heard about the Holiday Inn and all that . . . the place is going to be a spa . . . they're sitting right in the middle of it.

CYNTHIA: I'm sure they'll borrow from the usurers and have the whole property extorted out from under them.

DELIA: I was only thinking, there are those who hustle and those who don't.

CYNTHIA: There are winners and losers, givers and takers; there's the quick and the dead; Chad tries to be among the quick. Sometimes it shows. What are you? Or do you know?

DELIA: I'm a nomad.

CYNTHIA: And you're happy with that?

DELIA: Happy has nothing to do with it, Cynthia.

CYNTHIA: Well, it sure as hell wouldn't seem to.

DELIA: (*Pause. Friendly.*) If it applied, I could ask you the same thing: Are you happy with that? But it doesn't apply.

CYNTHIA: (*Backing down.*) There are things I need that perhaps you don't.

DELIA: We all need them. It's a question of what you're willing to pay.

CYNTHIA: Well. You're willing to pay a good deal more than I am.

JEAN: No. She isn't.

DELIA: I'm used to shopping in bargain basements, peasant bazaars. You're paying the gold of the realm for bazaar merchandise.

CYNTHIA: All that glitters . . .

JEAN: I don't believe that.

CYNTHIA: (*Letting it pass.*) I thought you had given up on men. Wasn't there some woman sculptor or someone?

DELIA: Good God, no. Never. I know—I should have. A long time ago; I just never got around to it. Isn't it pathetic, it's too late to change.

JEAN: I don't think I could get into it. (*They laugh.*) Is that funny? I guess it is. Wasn't there a story about you and some woman? About tearing up some bar?

DELIA: Which bar?

JEAN: In Spain or somewhere. Oh, no! You were fighting. You were arrested.

DELIA: Not in Spain; I'd still be there.

JEAN: Did you know you made all the newspapers?

DELIA: Of course I knew. Why do you think I did it?

CYNTHIA: They used to call us for comments; we hadn't heard from her in four years.

DELIA: Now no one has. That was Cannes, Nice . . . along that winding, cliff—hanging—in a Mazerati. That was P.R. That wasn't me. A couple of times I allowed myself to cause a brawl or pass out in the middle of the ring because I knew it was good for the biographer. If there's such a thing as sin any more, that must be high on the list. Which of the commandments would that come under? It's not really so bad to lie; sometimes it's kinder. Go ahead and steal, really, most of the bastards deserve to lose it. But I've "sinned." I've humiliated myself because people expected it of me.

(*BLACKOUT.*)

AUGUST: Dianne, would you just note marginally that I have decided I am definitely sick of aesthetics. Aesthetics and all the representatives of the humanities ransacking anthropological collections for pots they find pleasingly shaped and carrying them off to museums, where they lecture without content on form—and without the least ethnological information or understanding. Aesthetics is becoming an enemy of thought. (*Pause. Slide: college graduation.*) What the hell is—Christ, this is my graduation—notice the innocent and hopeful countenance. Prepared to conquer lost worlds with a doctorate in one hand and a trowel in the other. (*Slide:* DAN—*a pause.*) A man's life work is taken up, undertaken, I have no doubt, to blind him to the passing moon. I have no doubt that in an area of his almost unconscious he knows this and therefore is not blinded but only driven. The dig at Jasker's Field was unfinished. A salvage operation from which we salvaged nothing. Slides of picnics, slides of houses, slides of water, slides of ducks, slides of boats, slides of pain, slides of need, slides of spear points. A great amount of work has been done on the early cultures of North America and we have found only the periphery of the culture. Three hundred mounds, numberless graves have been opened, usually seconds before the builders plowed them under. And of the Mississippian Culture— never before had the grave of a god-king been discovered. The most important find in forty years of work. We do not allow ourselves to dream of finding what we might find and dream every sweep of a trowel. And what is salvaged? Nothing. Nothing. (*To the slides.*) Nothing. Nothing. Nothing. Nothing. Nothing. Nothing.

(JEAN *and* DELIA *are reading. There are approaching sounds of girls yelling, everyone yelling,* DAN's *voice heard approaching. They stand as he enters. The slides continue flicking repeatedly across the screen.*)

DAN: Jean, Jean, Jean, Jean—Come out—come down—the muck-a-muck. The high and holy muck-a-muck—

JEAN: —What? Who is it? In the grave?—

DAN: Not one—I'll be very calm, I'm not trembling, shit, I'm fine—We started clearing away toward the third foot—you remember the—grave, the—

JEAN: —Sure, sure . . . The Stinkard—

DAN: —third foot? He isn't a Stinkard, he's a retainer, dozens of them—all over the place—and in the center the ground is dark—a big black square where there has been a long tomb. It's all rotted away, but the ground is dark. August said, Oh, my God. Oh, my God. It's the tomb of a god-king. Nobody's ever found—(*Breathes deeply.*) You have never seen anything like it. Never. We didn't know if they had gold—but a gold thing on his face—and copper—beautiful copper breastplates—everywhere —pearls like—obsidian axes, beads, thousands of tons of—come on. Delia, if you don't come out and see this, I'll never read another word you—I swear to you, two more days and the lake would have flooded it. We're going to have to break our asses.

JEAN: A muck-a-muck? A god-king?

DAN: Oh, God, what a god he must have been! Pottery. *Glazed* pots—fifty, sixty of them. It's going to be dark in no time; hurry up. Oh, my God, how famous we're going to be! You gotta write the book, Delia, you really gotta write it.

DELIA: I'll come down and see. If I can't make it, I expect to be carried on the muck-a-muck's litter.

DAN: I'll carry you on my back.

JEAN: Pearls?

DAN: A room full—and maybe *gold.* This mask thing. We thought they might have gold. They had trade routes into country where there's gold. Copper armbands, bracelets. I am perfectly calm. I am a mature and balanced scientist. I wish you could see August up to his ass in mud. He said "This is a very high muck-a-muck." (DELIA *and* JEAN *hurry off.*) What am I supposed to get? I was supposed to get something.

(AUGUST, CHAD, CYNTHIA, JEAN *all carrying boxes, overrun him, pass back and forth, busy with things, working, tired and high, but preoccupied.* DELIA *is on the chaise.*)

CYNTHIA: Pitch black, it's absolutely maddening. You know you're not going to keep it under your hat.

AUGUST: For a while; for a day.

CYNTHIA: (*To* CHAD) You're pledged, you know that—not a word. Because if it gets out, it's all over; we'll have to set up guards.

CHAD: You could get lights, you could work at night—

AUGUST: That would be subtle.

DAN: We'd draw a larger crowd than the World Series.

AUGUST: You called Croff?

CYNTHIA: Yes, again. You want to know what he said again? (*They go back to working—she tells the women.*) He pissed. He was absolutely wetting his pants. he kept saying. Where's August? I said, he's down at the goddamned dig, where would you be? He started looking up charter-plane companies. I said, Croff, don't sweat it, we won't be doing anything until it gets light; drive down in the morning. He's already calculating the size of the grant the college will be getting from this. He sees his picture on the cover of *Newsweek*. He honest-to-God asked me when *Scientific American* went to press.

DAN: Jasker's the one who's going to be famous, you know that don't you?

(*As the work organizes itself,* DAN *is painting green copper beads with nail polish;* AUGUST *is cleaning something as delicately as an artist;* CYNTHIA *is writing the location and date numbers on projectile points, pottery shards, and small envelopes of pearls;* JEAN *is entering the numbers on a chart.*)

CYNTHIA: It's going to be the most important archaeological dig in America.

DAN: Well, north of the Rio.

CHAD: You know, no bull, I admire you people. You're really trying to make something of yourself. You could have been on vacation like everybody else. I'd just make a bet—you're not doing it for what you get. I've watched you down there and I wouldn't have the patience for it.

CYNTHIA: They wouldn't have the patience to bust down a transmission or any of the tinkerings that—

CHAD: —No, you do that 'cause you got to do it; 'cause you'd be embarrassed not to. But see—you guys are finding a little piece of charcoal last week and stuff if I saw on the ground I wouldn't bother to bend down for, but now that you found something—what's something in that grave that's valuable? I mean, that you could sell?

CYNTHIA: Almost everything.

DAN: —No more hitches for funding, you realize that. We'll be turning people down.

AUGUST: Well, now, no point in being high-handed.

CHAD: If someone came along and offered you—where's the thing? The gold thing? The bead?

DAN: Jean?

JEAN: On the table.

CHAD: See? Sitting on the table. If someone offered to buy this—

AUGUST: Very carefully, Mr. Jasker. That's the first gold ever—

CHAD: I know, I watched you with it. How much would you ask for that, how much is that worth?

AUGUST: (*Carefully.*) The gold in it—is worth maybe two or three dollars. It's beaten very thin and spread around a wooden bead. The wood has long since disintegrated. (*Taking it.*) You can hear it rattle inside. You felt how light it was.

CHAD: See, two dollars. You'd only ask what it was really worth—you wouldn't try to make anything for—Like what you really want to know is—aw, no—well—

AUGUST: I suppose if we knew that—

CHAD: (*Over*)No, forget I said it, I can't say it; I'm not saying it right; I don't know what I'm trying to say. What are these?

AUGUST: (*Taking them from him.*) Why did you come here?

CHAD: (*Beat.*) Beg pardon, Doc? Whatta you mean?

AUGUST: You could be any number of places.

CYNTHIA: We undoubtedly have our attractions, August.

AUGUST: You were down at the dig last week watching the excavation of a fire pit. Charcoal and split rocks. Anyone could see there was no intrinsic material value in that find.

CHAD: Yeah, I know, but it's—

AUGUST: You asked when it had been built, how old it was—which were the precise questions we were asking ourselves.

CHAD: No, I'm not putting it right.

AUGUST: People are drawn to speculate. Even my sister, who has no curiosity about anything—

DAN: I'm going to get her to write us up, though. Fictionalized of course.

DELIA: Of course.

AUGUST: I think archaeology can survive without that.

CHAD: Now you got your boss impressed; he's going to be down—

DAN: Something like this, we need people to verify that we aren't faking it—it's—

AUGUST: (*Minimizing.*) He's the sort that likes to check up on his employees. He's come down a number of times. Generally unannounced.

CHAD: I gotta have another beer. See, that's why I come here; I can always count on Dan to turn me on.

CYNTHIA: Oh, I think you can be turned on by any number of things.

AUGUST: (*He lifts from the table the fragile gold mask he has been cleaning.*) Look at this, coming out beautifully.

CYNTHIA: (*Getting her camera and a flash unit.*) I want to get this.

DAN: It's a death mask—we guess. It might have had feathers around it here. We have to guess. We've never seen anything like it before. (*He holds it up to his face, and almost inadvertently it stays in place.*)

JEAN: Don't put that—

DAN: I didn't do a thing. Is that incredible?

CYNTHIA: Smile. Or can you?

(*Flash.*)

DAN: Let me see. I'm blind. Help me with it. (AUGUST *carefully lifts it from* DAN's *face.*) That's the same design we've seen on gorgets, and assumed it was meant to represent pigmentation.

CHAD: That thing's solid gold, isn't it?

AUGUST: (*A lie.*) That's copper—they valued it above gold.

DAN: It's fragile as hell. He didn't wear it, you know—they made it for him after he died. If you can imagine it completely surrounded with feathers.

JEAN: I really didn't like it on you at all.

DAN: Are you crazy; every dead god-king is wearing one this year. It may take a while to catch on.

CHAD: These are beads; they're copper too?

DAN: Those will fall right apart, Chad, they're corroded right through. They're made the same as the gold—they beat out a solid nugget of copper—they had no metallurgical knowledge, to speak of.

CYNTHIA: What have you got all over your hands?

CHAD: Oh that's uh—paint; got more on me than I did on the car.

CYNTHIA: You painted your car?

DELIA: It's a different car.

CHAD: Got a new one; painted it black. I had 'em put on the papers that it was black, it was some kind of green, all rusted off; I had to paint it before I got stopped.

CYNTHIA: You sold the blue one?

CHAD: Wrapped it up.

CYNTHIA: The Olds?

CHAD: Couple a days ago, over on 14.

DAN: He wraps it around a tree, gets out, leaves it there, and hitches a lift home.

CHAD: Sheriff comes by, says they towed it to the dump, tried to give me a summons for abandoning it. I told him I was dazed; I didn't know what I was doing . . .

DAN: How'd you know it was a different car?

DELIA: I'm familiar with all possible transportation in and out of here.

JEAN: What's that stuff you're putting on that?

DAN: Just nail polish, help hold it together.

JEAN: Smells vile.

DAN: You look tired; don't get sick again.

CHAD: You been sick?

JEAN: No. Woozy; tired, not sick.

DAN: I think she's developing evening sickness. You've heard of morning sickness; she's getting evening sickness.

JEAN: (*To* CYNTHIA) Did you have that?

CYNTHIA: Boring as hell, isn't it?

CHAD: What from?

DAN: Who knows the metabolism of a pregnant woman? She'll feel better tomorrow; she can diagnose what was wrong with her and write a paper on it.

JEAN: Might do it too.

CHAD: Since when was you— (*A long pause. His face registers the implication of the statement. They do not notice and continue working.*)

AUGUST: (*To* DAN) What are you hiding there?

(DAN *gives him a box, which* AUGUST *begins to sort through.*)

CHAD: (*Finally, pinched.*) When's it due?

DAN: December, January.

CHAD: Hell, probably ought to celebrate.

DAN: Thought I told you.

CHAD: Not me.

DAN: As big as the hole is in the gold bead, what would you think—these are all small—if several ropes of copper beads came down like this and then the strings went through the gold one.

AUGUST: Where's the Polaroid of his chest; how was the copper situated?

CYNTHIA: (*Overlapping* DAN *from "gold bead."*) What did you say you were going to show me on your car?

CHAD: Me?

CYNTHIA: I don't know; you said you had something in the trunk.

CHAD: Trunk's locked. I don't have the key for it.

CYNTHIA: Maybe it was the hood, I don't know.

CHAD: I think you're thinking of someone else.

CYNTHIA: (*Going out the door.*) Well, anyway, I want to see this famous paint job.

CHAD: I ain't got time. I gotta get going. (*Steps outside a second.*) Leave me alone.

CYNTHIA: (*Goes to the refrigerator, gets a beer.*) Anyone else? Auggie?

AUGUST: I'm fine.

CHAD: (*Finally. Hardly audible, but hard.*) Whatta you gonna call it? (*As* JEAN, *who has heard, starts to leave.*) HEY! (*Everyone freezes.*) Said, what name you gonna name it?

DAN: What?

CHAD: (*Almost in tears.*) The baby.

DAN: We're taking all suggestions, putting them in a hat.

CHAD: What then, you'll pull it out like a rabbit? It's no more important to you than that?

DAN: Well, we figure when we have a palpable, honest-to-God kid, with a gender, we'll think of something.

CHAD: Boy, you guys are supercool, supercool. Down here in the sticks, you got your little harem of ugly girl students around you watching every little brush stroke and pick and pry like you was painting the world's last masterpiece. You got your pretty wives and your drug-addict sister. You really got everything going for you. Cynthia says you're going to be getting write-ups in *Time* magazine.

CYNTHIA: I said Croff envisions his mug on the cover.

CHAD: You got the place all tied up so anything you find belongs to you. You're really knocking it.

AUGUST: That was the agreement your father signed.

CHAD: (*Not hearing.*) I really got to admire your supercool.

DAN: We got it knocked.

CHAD: You really got it knocked. You're digging up all these old battle weapons—(*Lifting from the box a foot-long spear point.*) Just look at the craftsmanship on that—what'd you say that was? You called that a spear point. Who'd think those old boys would have the tools to make something like that.

AUGUST: That's very dangerous.

CYNTHIA: You said you had to be somewhere by—

CHAD: Hell, you don't even need—you can break someone's neck just by putting the right twist in the right place. (*He has, as quick as a snake, reached around* CYNTHIA'S *neck with his arm.*) You know that?

CYNTHIA: I'm sure you could. You're a lot stronger than I.

(*He releases her.*)

CHAD: It's a damn shame you're going to have to find yourself some other field of operation.

DAN: We'll be a while on this one yet.

CHAD: I'm talking about next year.

DAN: Next year we can get back to those mounds you think are so important.

CHAD: I gues you can if you can find where the road construction crew scatters them. Only I don't think the Holiday Inn people are going to much appreciate a scruffy gang of ugly virgins digging up the front yard of their motel.

CYNTHIA: I don't know why you think they're virgins.

DAN: People eating at your restaurant?

CHAD: You think it's cute? You think it's not going to happen? There are some cost accountants and some professional architects from down at Memphis you should talk to.

DAN: The tourists are going to be flooding the place heavier than the lake, huh?

CHAD: You may know a hell of a lot about your grave robbing but you're really full of shit when it comes to commerce. I know you've had your nose stuck in the ground; it's not easy to see what's going on around you from that position, but this is the last trip you fellows are making down here—

DAN: —You don't seem to realize the importance of what's happening here today. Coordinating this site with the information we're going to be getting from the mounds—The information we have already will take years—

CHAD: (*Overlapping from "we have".*) You're just going to have to go on what you've got, buddy.

DAN: —It's a man's life work here—

<table>
<tr><td align="center">CHAD</td><td align="center">DAN</td></tr>
<tr><td>'Cause as it happens, I don't want you here. And there ain't going to be any mounds. The mounds are going to be fucking flat. The mounds are going to be under about forty tons of highway interchange. They're going to be under a tennis court.</td><td>I mean, it doesn't matter whether you understand or not, but I'd think you'd want to be part of that. God-damn! If you want tourists coming in here we're going to have to be digging around them.</td></tr>
</table>

DAN: I don't want to hear about your tennis courts.

CHAD: You people are dreaming! You might not like it, but there ain't no mounds next year. There's an interchange coming through you maybe don't know about.

DAN: I know all about it; the site is archaeologically too important to be superseded by—

CHAD: (*Overlapping from "to be superseded".*) They may be hot shit to you; Dad and me don't happen to want our property—

DAN: You don't realize how important a man like August Howe is. Jesus Christ, you talk like—

CHAD: —My land, baby! MY LAND! MY LAND! It don't belong to your Indian god. It don't belong to you. It's my land and there is an Interstate coming through. Now, if you want to sit in its way, every one of you, good, you're invited.

DAN: The Interstate isn't coming through your land.

AUGUST: That isn't necessary now.

CHAD: Hell, it isn't. You think they're going to build a motel where there isn't a highway?

DAN: (*Overlapping from "where there".*) Then they won't build it. What the hell difference does it make? You're talking about a goddamn Holiday Inn.

CHAD: They been here! I've seen the plans!

DAN: Goddamnit, there's a law since 1954—in this state—against public-funded construction defacing Indian monuments.

CHAD: (*Beat.*) Well, guys, I hate to disappoint you, but you're thinking about it a little late.

DAN: We thought about it two years ago. (*Pause.*) When did you last hear from your motel architects?

CHAD: What do you mean, two years ago?

AUGUST: —Not tonight. In the morning—

DAN: The highway isn't going to be anywhere near Blue Shoals. It's been rerouted to the other side of the goddamn lake! We got notice before we came down this summer.

(*A long pause.*)

CYNTHIA: When was this, August?

CHAD: Shit. "When"—Let on like—

DAN: Two years; after our first summer; after we heard about the highway.

CYNTHIA: It must have been a lot of trouble keeping me in the dark.

DELIA: We're a bad risk, Cynthia.

AUGUST: It was a matter of a brief report, a few pictures, and a phone call.

JEAN: You can't do that.

DAN: Old man Jasker wouldn't allow the land to become a national monument. How else could we protect them?

CYNTHIA: Them? Protect them or protect you?

CHAD: Boy, you're pretending to be my friend; you're listening to me talking about soul food and grilled bass out of the lake; what are you saying behind my back? Leading me on. Where do you get off thinking you're better than the people around here and can take over and take away everything we hope for—where—laughing about my goddamned island—what do you care. Millions! You're trying to steal from me!

JEAN: You don't know what it meant to him.

DAN: I know what it means to me; you should know what it means to me.

JEAN: I can't see one is more imporant than the other.

CYNTHIA: Using my photographs of the dig to surreptitiously—

DAN: Chad, I'm trying to make you see that you'd be better off—understand the value of what you have here, God, the place—

CHAD: (*A howling scream.*) NOOOOOOOOO! (*Silence. A pained plea.*) How can you treat people...?

(*Pause.*)

JEAN: Chad. I went down to the courthouse; I saw the model you told me to see, I ...

CHAD: (*Fiercely to* AUGUST)—you won't get it. I know what you want, Professor, but you might just have to stay up at State next summer with your whore and fuck her yourself. (*He exits.*)

CYNTHIA: Chad? (*Going out.*) Jasker, goddamnit, stay here. Talk to me! I didn't know.

DAN: What model at the courthouse?

JEAN: Of the motel and the resort; it isn't important.

DELIA: I may take you up, Dan, on writing that book.

AUGUST: I'm glad you're walking; I don't think it's necessary for you to stay.

DELIA: Not at all. Cynthia said Jasker'd be ripped off—I guess—

AUGUST: If I thought it were possible for you to write, I'd admonish against it.

DELIA: You always have. I never need either your approval or "admonishments"; Dad respected what I was doing, that was enough for me.

AUGUST: What you never realized was that Dad and I were close. You didn't want us to be, so you supposed it to be the way you wanted.

DELIA: (*Overlapping on "you supposed".*)—I was never interested in your opinion of anything I was—

AUGUST: —Thinking you were some kind of *Wunderkind* and assuming—

DELIA: —He respected what I was doing and that was—

AUGUST: —Dad never read a word you wrote. He quoted your reviews back to you verbatim and laughed behind your back because you never noticed. He thought you were a fool.

CYNTHIA: (*Re-enters, goes upstairs.*) I'm driving back to Urbana in the morning. If you think you've put one over on Jasker, you're a bigger ass than I thought you were.

AUGUST: (*To them.*) Dan, it's late, I hadn't thought we'd sleep much tonight, but maybe that's the best thing to do. We'll be getting up at five. (*Leaving.*)

DELIA: Dad's opinion was always too important to me. Thank you.

AUGUST: You're welcome.

(*He is gone, so is* DELIA; *the others begin to leave as the night sounds increase, along with a weirdly close screech owl, and the lights fade as tractor sounds are heard. As the stage becomes dark, we can hear someone moving about.*)

DAN'S VOICE: Hello? Jesus Christ. Is somebody down there? (*Pause. Flashlight.*) Delia? Hello?

(*The beam catches* CHAD *full in the face. He is wearing the God-King's mask, and has the knapsack in his arms. He stands perfectly still.*)

CHAD: The light's in my face.

DAN: (*The beam from the flashlight moves to* CHAD's *loaded arms.* DAN *stays on the stairs.*) Chad?

CHAD: Cynthia said you was a light sleeper.

(*Pause.*)

DAN: Yeah.

CHAD: I got something I want to show you.

(*Pause.*)

DAN: You . . . shouldn't handle . . .

(*Pause.*)

CHAD: It's only copper. They treasured it higher than gold.

DAN: What have you got in—what are you doing?

CHAD: There's something outside I want to show you.

DAN: What?

CHAD: Come outside. (*He moves to the door.*)

DAN: Don't go out with that . . .

CHAD: There's something I want to show you.

DAN: Chad? (*Light plays across the empty table.*) Chad? (*Back to the door through which* CHAD *has disappeared outside.*)

CHAD: (*Off*) I want to show you something.

(DAN *moves down the stairs and out. As a slow dawn begins, a girl's voice is hear calling, "Dr. Loggins?" Repeatedly, then another girl calling the same.* AUGUST, *barely awake, stumbles down, buckling his belt, yells out the window, "Yes, goddamnit," and goes off.* JEAN *follows him almost immediately, but stops at the bottom of the stairs as* DELIA, *fully dressed, enters.)*

JEAN: Good morning.

DELIA: Good morning.

(DELIA *takes a bottle of V8 from the refrigerator.)*

JEAN: My God, real clothes.

DELIA: The better to leave your enclave.

(The light continues to intensify.)

JEAN: Oh. Well, I guess you know what you need. Did Pollyandy sleep down here last night or did he even get home?

DELIA: I don't know.

JEAN: I woke up; then I managed to get pissed off enough to go back to sleep. It's gorgeous out.

(There are a few noises, girls' voices, AUGUST'S.)

CYNTHIA: *(Off)* What? *(Muffled answer.)* I'll be down—Said, I'll be down. *(She appears.)* The son of a bitch. I'll kill him.

DELIA: You'll kill whom?

CYNTHIA: Chad Jasker.

AUGUST: *(Off)* It's mad—He's a madman, it's crazy—

JEAN: *(Off)* August, where is—

AUGUST: *(Entering.)* Not now, damnit; not now. Everything's gone. He's carried everything off—the bulldozer's been run over the site—the bulldozer is out in the lake in six feet of water, apparently where it got stuck—

(CYNTHIA *goes out.)*

DELIA: Is Dan out there?

AUGUST: What's to do? There's nothing to do. Let him sleep it off.

JEAN: The girls are calling you.

DELIA: Jean, you'd better go in and call the county sheriff.

JEAN: Tell him he's wrecked the site.

DELIA: Tell him Dan is missing.

(JEAN *stands transfixed for a second. Turns and goes into the office.)*

AUGUST: Oh, God, no.

CYNTHIA: (*Entering.*) I tried to tell you last night that you didn't know what you were dealing with.

AUGUST: Cynthia—I want you to sit down. (*Takes her hands.*)

CYNTHIA: What? (*Breaks away.*) Oh, please.

AUGUST: Please.

CYNTHIA: What? What is it? Don't hold on to me, you know I don't like to be grabbed at. What on earth ... (*Freeze. Looks around.*) He's left. He's run off ...

AUGUST: No, no, no, no ...

CYNTHIA: Where?

AUGUST: There's the possiblity that—

CYNTHIA: Oh, damn your possibilities—

AUGUST: Dan hasn't—Dan isn't here. Did you talk to Jasker last night?

DELIA: Did he tell you anything?

CYNTHIA: I couldn't find him.

DELIA: What is Jasker capable of? I never looked at him twice until last night.

CYNTHIA: He'd do anything.

DELIA: You know what I'm talking about; I want to know if the madman is capable—

CYNTHIA: —Yes, yes! He's capable of anything—(DELIA *exits. Pause.*) You didn't tell me about the highway because you knew I'd tell him. I would have.

AUGUST: What matters is finding Dan.

CYNTHIA: We have nothing to show for our dig, August. We have nine pictures I took last night.

AUGUST: That isn't important to me.

CYNTHIA: What a stupid thing to lie about. (*As* AUGUST *starts to move away*) Well, I can do one thing for him. (*Takes up the camera, ejects the film, and begins unrolling it.*)

AUGUST: Stop it! CYNTHIA!

CYNTHIA: (*Throwing the unrolled film on the floor as he reaches her.*) There! There's your evidence.

JEAN: (*Entering.*) There are two police cars turning into the field if you want to go out. I'm trying to think where they might have ...

(*The light immediately confines* AUGUST *to his desk area.*)

AUGUST: At eleven that morning an oar from Chad Jasker's boat was found floating near the center of the lake. At nine that night townspeople turned their car headlights out across the water to assist the divers who had come down from Marion.

(*Car headlights swing across the room.* DELIA *turns on a lamp.*)

JEAN: Where the hell are all the people coming from? Why don't they stay away?

CYNTHIA: People from town, volunteers; there's almost no police force.

JEAN: They've got men with diving equipment. I can't help; I can't go outside; I'm swamped with commiserations. Keep those damn girls out of here; keep them all out.

CYNTHIA: August does that. They know better than to come here.

DELIA: Who's the old man?

CYNTHIA: Old man Jasker.

DELIA: What are all the goddamned people doing here; the cars keep turning into the area, there must be fifty cars.

CYNTHIA: They see the lights, they think we've discovered something.

DELIA: Can't they keep them away?

CYNTHIA: There's no law.

DELIA: All the laws are the wrong goddamned laws.

CYNTHIA: Someone heard we had discovered a monster in the lake. The sightseers will go away; the men will work all night.

JEAN: They've got a lot of machinery for a small town. (*Running to the screen door.*) THEY ARE NOT TO DRAG THE LAKE. THEY USE GRAPPLING HOOKS TO DRAG THE LAKE. THEY ARE NOT TO DRAG THE LAKE!

DELIA: Shut up!

JEAN: I'm going to be fine.

DELIA: You can't help. Shut up.

JEAN: Why did he go out? Why didn't someone hear him? Why did the girls stay at the motel? WHY DID HE HAVE TO HEAR NOISES IN THE NIGHT? WHY DID HE TRUST PEOPLE, WHY DID HE BELIEVE IN THINGS?

(*DELIA grabs her.*)

JEAN: I'm going to be fine.

(DELIA leads her to the swing. JEAN sits. DELIA sits beside her.)

JEAN: Morbid, morbid, stupid people. Vanished without a trace. I'm going to be fine. Cochise. Co. C-O-. Co. Vanished without a trace. I want the bone awl. I want the—

CYNTHIA: *(Going to her.)* Jean, please. Please. We don't have it. It's gone.

AUGUST: Dianne, Dianne . . . We left the house for the last time August 8. On December 31, Jean delivered a healthy daughter and the following morning, January 1, I went back to the house, only hoping to see the lake take it away. In my mind's eye the river's currents swept the house before it as a great brown flood bears off everything in its path. That was in my mind's eye. The lake had risen to half-cover the house. Much of the second level was above the water. The house looked more scuttled than inundated. The lake rises as a great long hand-shaped pond, slowly . . . *(Stops, turns the machine off. After a moment he turns it on again.)* Dianne . . . *(Turns the machine off, turns it on again.)* Dianne . . .

(AUGUST stares into the room. A long pause. As the lights begin to fade, DELIA's VOICE is heard.)

DELIA's VOICE: August stares out the window at the dark. The cassette continues to turn, recording the silence of the room.

Curtain

John Bishop

*The Great-Great Grandson
of Jedediah Kohler*

Of John Bishop's first play, *The Trip Back Down*, produced on Broadway in 1977, Douglas Watt wrote, "It is the goods, the genuine goods, and in John Bishop, who wrote it, Broadway has gained a talented new playwright with a voice that rings true."

Bishop subsequently became a playwright in residence and a member of the artistic staff, as Dramaturg, with the Circle Repertory Company. There his full-length plays—*Winter Signs, The Great-Great Grandson of Jedediah Kohler, The Harvesting* (published by Dramatists Play Service, 1985)—and his one-acts—*Cabin 12* (published by Dramatists Play Service and *Best Short Plays of 1979*) and *Confluence* (published by Dramatists Play Service and *Best Short Plays of 1983*)—were all first produced.

His one-act *Skirmishers* (also published by Dramatists Play Service) was produced originally at The New York Stageworks Festival, and his curtain-raiser, *How Women Break Bad News*, opened the Philadelphia Festival of New Plays in 1982.

His play *Borderline*, produced at Los Angeles' Skylight Theater in 1985, won a Dramalogue "Best Play" award and three L.A. Drama Critics Circle nominations.

Bishop was the recipient of an N.E.A. Literary Grant for 1979–80 and is a member of the Dramatists Guild Panel for awarding the CBS New Plays grants to regional theaters.

Columbia Pictures purchased *Trip Back Down*, and *The Harvesting* has recently been optioned by Hal Wallis productions.

In the summer of 1984, Bishop was one of a group of "core" writers from Broadway and Off-Broadway who were gathered by Nederlander TV Productions to write a limited run comedy series for CBS entitled *Comedy Zone*. Bishop, along with Jules Feiffer, Chris Durang, Wendy Wasserstein, and John Ford Noonan, wrote six shows which aired in August of that year. For the second show and for the remainder of the run, Bishop was also retained as one of the two head writers.

In addition to his work in theater and television, Bishop has written over 100 theatrical, film, and video presentations for many of the country's leading corporations. In just the period covering 1983 to 1984, Bishop wrote and directed shows for Ciba-Geigy, Squibb Pharmaceuticals, Arco Chemical, Control Data Corp, Campbell's, Coors, and Honeywell Int.

Bishop holds a BFA in Drama from Carnegie-Mellon University and is a member of The Dramatist's Guild, Writer's Guild of America, East, Society of Stage Directors and Choreographer's, and Actor's Equity.

The Great-Great Grandson of Jedediah Kohler previewed at The Circle Repertory Company on March 12, 1982 (Press Opening: March 21) under the direction of Marshall W. Mason and Jon Bard Manulis with the following cast:

DEATH	Jake Dengel
JED KOHLER	Michael Ayr
LEON	Ken Kliban
SHORTY RADABAUGH	Gary Berner
FATHER	Edward Seamon
MOTHER	Trish Hawkins
NANCY	Trish Hawkins
BOBBI	Katherine Cortez
BOB GRAHAM	Jonathan Bolt
JEDEDIAH KOHLER	Edward Seamon
BLAKE KOHLER	Ken Kliban
IKE MCKEE	William Hurt
DOC MCCULLOUGH	Gary Berner
JOHNNY TWO-DEUCE	Lou Liberatore
FRANK GRAHAM	Tim Morse
BROTHER	Jimmi Ray Weeks
JACK BECK	Jack Davidson
JOE GOLDMAN	Roger Chapman
WALLY SILVER	Charles T. Harper
PRESCOTT MAN	Jack Davidson
COACH FRANKIE TORSKI	Jack Davidson
RONALD HOERNER	Jonathon Bolt
HENRY JARVIS	William Hurt
COP	Edward Seamon

For information regarding stock and amateur production rights, including all other rights, contact: Flora Roberts, Inc., 157 West 57 Street, New York, NY 10019.

Notes About the Play

Size of Cast

This play was written so that it can be performed by a cast of eleven, nine men and two women. A producer could, if it was desired, cast a different actor for every role. A bit extravagant, perhaps, but the play will work equally as well. A middle-ground approach would be not to double the roles of WALLY and JOE with HOERNER and JARVIS. In any case the roles of MOTHER & FATHER should always be played by the actress and actor playing NANCY & JEDEDIAH. Following is a cast breakdown for the use of ELEVEN performers.

DON—no double
THE BROTHER—no double
JEDEDIAH—FATHER—JEREMIAH CRANDALL
NANCY—The MOTHER—JOHNNY-TWO-DEUCE
LEON—BLAKE KOHLER
SHORTY—DOC MCCULLOUGH
WALLY—BOB GRAHAM—RONALD HOERNER
JOE—IKE MCKEE—HENRY JARVIS
JACK BICK—FRANK GRAHAM—FRANKIE TORSKI
BOBBIE—no double
DEATH—BARTENDER, JERRY ZUTZENTHALER, DR. MACLAMORE, F.R. RILEY

The Set

Because the action of this play must flow swiftly from one scene to another, no time can be taken for setting of scenery or set dressing. Therefore use of sets and props must be minimal. A unit set that enables the action to segué from one area to another would serve this play best. Care must be taken also with the use of stage lighting. Over delineation of separate scenes by constantly and sharply changing lighting will have the effect of chopping the show into uneven segments. If one thinks of lighting ballet or dance, where the light shifts flow smoothly, almost imperceptibly, one into the other, then one would have a good approach to this play.

In case it might be of some help, I can tell you that at Circle Rep the "set" consisted of a small bar and stools down right . . . a weight bench down left . . . a cyclorama upstage. Castered chairs were used to set the large "businessmen" scenes, with the actors rolling onstage their own chairs. A sofa unit was pushed onstage from left for scenes in BOBBI's apartment or DON's home. In retrospect, I believe it would be interesting to make use of levels on stage to create different areas. But by no means do I think this is absolutely vital to the production. To sum up: the simpler this play is produced—the better.

Act One

(DEATH *enters in tuxedo and cape.*)

DEATH: Doesn't anyone dress for the theater anymore? *(Beat)* The house manager has informed me that we have had two walk-outs and the curtain isn't even up yet. Yes. Man looked at his program, noticed the first character was Death, and said to his wife, "The hell with this, Alice, I get enough of this at the office." He strode up the aisle exclaiming that for the price he paid he expected to see scenery and lights and girls! He did not expect to see death . . . or life. Nothing that grim. Not at these prices. *(Beat)* But don't worry. It's all here. Lights.

(LIGHTS *change color.*)

Girls . . .

(BOBBI *and* NANCY *enter.*)

Action . . .

(GUNFIGHTERS *enter.*)

Victims, villains . . . a Vice-President.

(The rest of the CAST *enter.*)

And . . . ah, yes . . . the hero.)

(DON KOHLER *enters. In his mid-to-late thirties, well-dressed, and with flair. Wearing steel-rimmed glasses and carrying an attaché case.*)

DEATH: Or, rather, the man about to become a hero. Well, to die a hero is, perhaps, a more accurate phrase. How long since you have witnessed an heroic death? A while, huh? A while since anyone has understood the significance of death . . . not just as an ending, but as the event by which a life acquires meaning. Instead, we seem to be in the midst of an epidemic of people accepting their fate! You can understand how this pisses me off! I who stood with Horatio at the bridge, Roland at the pass . . . who rode with Custer, charged with Cardigan . . . counseled Gordon at Khartoum and Travis at the Alamo. I, who was covered with glory at Thermopylae, Isandhlwana, Dien Bien Phu. I who once was courted and received as . . . *(He stops.)* Excuse me. I get rather emotional about this. Where was I? Oh yes . . . *(He snaps his fingers. A bar slides on down right. He removes his cloak and coat and puts on an apron as he continues.*) And so tonight I will produce upon this stage . . . before your very eyes . . . an heroic death! *(Refers to* DON.*)* I will take this seemingly ordinary man and alter his course away from a future meeting with me in some condominium in Florida . . . and toward a more heroic rendezvous. His name is . . .

DON: Don Kohler.

(Shaking hands with DEATH, *who has become a bartender.)*

DON: I'm Creative Director for "Show Biz For Big Biz Incorporated". We just moved into 481 across the street.

DEATH: "Show Biz For Big Biz"?

DON: We bring a touch of Broadway to industry. You know, when big corporations get all their people together to talk to them . . . the annual convention, a national sales conference, a new product intro meeting . . . we do the slides, the films, the music, the dance, the skits . . . whatever it takes to keep the audience from falling asleep.

*(*LEON *and* SHORTY *enter.* LEON *is in his early 40's . . . a touch of L.A in his apparel.* SHORTY *is* DON'S *age, quite tall, Ivy League in dress and manner.)*

LEON: Did we do it or did we do it?

SHORTY: We did it.

LEON: Right, Shorty. You realize we could bill around two million on this?

SHORTY: Closer to a mil five, Leon.

LEON: It'll take work. We'll need all noses on the grindstone.

SHORTY: It calls for a celebration.

LEON: Right! Bartender, drinks all across!

DEATH: What'll it be, gentlemen?

LEON: Perrier with lemon.

SHORTY: Club soda with bitters.

DON: Diet Pepsi.

LEON: How many companies were we competing with, Don?

DON: Six.

LEON: And thanks in no large part to your creativity, we got it! So . . . to the Monopoly Motors National Sales Meeting. Here's mud down your hatch!

DEATH: *(To audience)* So, there's our hero. And while he finishes his Diet Pepsi it's probably necessary that you know a bit more about him. This part always bores me in a play. The psychological background. However, everyone seems to want it, so . . .

*(*MUSIC: *50's Ballad.* MOTHER *and* FATHER *dance onstage.)*

MOTHER: The dinner was lovely, thank you. (FATHER *spins her. She laughs.*) You're a wonderful dancer.

DEATH: I think we went back too far. Although this is the most important night of Don's life ... the night he was conceived ... still, I don't think we needed to go back this far.

(MUSIC *ends.* MOTHER *calls toward offstage.*)

MOTHER: Don! Breakfast! (*To* FATHER) And I just mean that I don't see why you must put all those hours in at that factory when other men ...

FATHER: Grace, you don't know a goddamn thing about what determines what down at the plant and so ...

MOTHER: Fine, fine.

FATHER: Don't turn your back on me. Don't dismiss me like ...

MOTHER: I'm not dismissing you! I'm not anythinging you. Just drink your coffee and go to your damn plant and ...

FATHER: Jesus H. Christ!

MOTHER: (*Calling*) Don! Donald! (*To* FATHER) And don't swear at me!

FATHER: I'm not swearing at you for Christ's Sakes! But goddamn it ...

FATHER: ... if you start a god-damn conversation then don't turn a-goddamn-way in the middle of the goddamn thing!

MOTHER: I will not have ... the one ... one thing I will not stand for in this house is outhouse language from the streets and ...

(DON *crosses to them.*)

MOTHER: (*Sweetly*) Good morning, Don.

FATHER: Hi Champ, how's school?

DEATH: Okay, that's enough of the psychological background. You get the idea ... typical childhood, right? Let's jump to the present. Don is married. His wife's name is ...

DON: Nancy. You'll like her mom. Her dad runs a nice little auto supply store. Nice people.

MOTHER: Auto supplies?
DON: Yes.

MOTHER: Tires and things?
DON: Yes.

MOTHER: The kind of store where they have all those old tires stacked up in front?

DON: Yes, but neatly, Mom. They stack them very neatly.

DEATH: And they've been married nine years. Two boys . . . ages seven and five.

(MOTHER *has removed glasses and wig to become* NANCY.)

NANCY: Notice anything new?

DON. The hair?

NANCY: No.

DON: Skirt?

NANCY: I've had this for years.

DON: Shoes?

NANCY: The drapes.

DON: Oh . . . yeah. Nice, Nancy.

NANCY: I ordered slip covers to match. I was in the mall and I saw these cute tap pants. You know . . . sexy. But then I thought I've put on a little weight . . . so I went and bought the drapes. I'm a little worried about the fullness. What do you think?

DON: I don't know. Maybe a bit . . . around the hips.

NANCY: I meant the drapes, dammit! (*She runs off.*)

DON: What the hell?

FATHER: Your mother's just concerned son. I mean, you're just finishing college, maybe you don't have to rush right into marriage . . .

DON: I love her, Dad.

FATHER: There's plenty of fish in the sea.

DEATH: And here's one of them.

(BOBBI *enters. Young, pretty, with the lithe figure and tough manner of a Broadway dancer.*)

BOBBI: Open up, House Detective! You got a woman in your room?

DON: No sir.

BOBBI: Why not, everyone else has!

(DON *and* BOBBI *embrace.*)

DEATH: Her name is Bobbi. She's a dancer. He met her when she worked in his last industrial show. They had a liaison in Detroit. Not exactly the Isle of Capri. But they enjoyed each other's company.

BOBBI: Ready to go?

DON: I'm tryin' to find my necktie.

BOBBI: Hey, screw the necktie. You look gorgeous.

DON: We're going to a restaurant.

BOBBI: People eat in restaurants without neckties. Hell, in California they don't even button their shirts.

DON: This is Detroit.

BOBBI: Tell you what, let's forget the restaurant. I like you better without your clothes on anyhow.

DON: Should I order room service?

BOBBI: I'm it. (*She embraces him.*)

DEATH: On the airplane back . . . alone . . . he thought about her, as he leafed through *Sports Illustrated,* and he felt . . . a loss.

DON: Yeah, but what the hell. "I loved ya, but the show's over." Right? Just one of those things. (*Puts down money.*) See you tomorrow, gotta' catch a train.

DEATH: Take it easy, pal. (*To audience*) Yeah, I know, you're saying, "Hey, that's no hero. I see guys like him every day, waving an attaché case at a taxi cab." But don't worry, he's a hero. It's in his genes.

(*Four cowboys,* BOB *and* FRANK GRAHAM, IKE MCKEE *and* JOHNNY TWO-DEUCE *enter and hold stage right. Three Marshals,* JEDEDIAH KOHLER, BLAKE KOHLER, *and* DOC MCCULLOUGH *enter and hold left. The cowboys are dressed in "range" clothes. The Marshals are "city" dressed.* JEDEDIAH *wears a long black frock coat. He has a flowing black mustache.* BLAKE *and* DOC *are in black western cut suits and vests.* DOC *carries a shotgun.*)

BOB: What's this?

JED: You sons of bitches have been lookin' for a fight and now you can have it.

DEATH: For our hero is the great-great-grandson of Jedediah Kohler.

BLAKE: Put up your hands, boys.

IKE: You can go to hell!

FRANK: We are not armed. (*Reaches to pull back his coat.*)

BOB: No! Don't touch your coat!

(FREEZE *action.* DEATH *walks between the two groups.*)

DEATH: This is the famous gunfight at the Oak Street Corral. That's Don's great-great grandfather, the legendary frontier marshal. Jed's brother, Blake. And the infamous Doc McCullough. And over here. (*Indicating cowboys*) The Graham boys, Frank and Bob. Ike McKee. Young Johnny Miller . . . Johnny-Two-Deuce, they called him. I've no idea why. Frank Graham was indeed not carrying a weapon. But, when he reached to open his coat to prove it, well . . . Never reach for anything in front of a peace officer. For if you do, you're likely to be blown to pieces.

(*He snaps his fingers and the lights change so that only* DEATH *is lit. The others exit.*)

DEATH: Jedediah Kohler . . . born of a heroic age in American history. An age when men confirmed their status with deeds of resounding bravery. Sought out opportunities to exhibit exceptional strength or ability, regardless of consequences. (*Beat*) So, there you have them . . . the characters are in place. Now to . . .

(*The* BROTHER *enters. He is in his late 30's, strongly built, wearing a black sweat suit and sneakers. He carries a small athletic bag.*)

BROTHER: (*To* DEATH) Hi.

(DON *enters.*)

BROTHER: Hello Don.

DON: My God!

NANCY: (*Entering*) Who is it, Don?

DON: My brother.

DEATH: (*To audience*) I didn't know he had a brother. (*He crosses to his bar down right and begins searching through some index cards.*)

BROTHER: I need a place to stay for awhile, Don.

DON: Are you still . . . uh . . . well, you know . . . wanted?

BROTHER: I got no place to stay right now, Don.

DON: Well, I guess we could fix up a place in the fruit cellar.

NANCY: What?

BROTHER: I'll get my bag and iron.

NANCY: His iron? He's going to press something?

BROTHER: About 110 pounds. (*He exits.*)

DON: He lifts weights.

DEATH: (*Reading from index card*) Oh, here he is. Ten months in Viet

Nam. That must be how he knows me. Let's see . . . two purple hearts, Bronze Star . . . walks away from war. Captured by Viet Cong. Imprisoned . . . beaten severely . . . manages to escape, knocking out a guard in the process. Returns to own lines. Courtmartialed for desertion. Imprisoned . . . beaten severely . . . manages to escape, knocking out a guard in the process. (*Looking at audience.*) Patterns like that tend to distort your value system.

NANCY: But, he's a fugitive, isn't he? And he's going to live in our fruit cellar?

DON: I should tell you . . . he doesn't eat meat.

NANCY: Look, I have enough problems worrying about what you and the kids eat. I'm not about to worry about an escaped vegetarian. I'll do his laundry. That's it.

DON: He's no problem. All he wears are black sweatsuits.

NANCY: Black sweatsuits?

DON: I believe he thinks it makes him more inconspicuous.

NANCY: (*Exiting*) I don't know what the neighbors are going to think.

DON: (*Following her off*) He only goes out at night. To jog.

DEATH: Can we get on with my play!

BROTHER: (*Entering with weights*) Long time no see.

DEATH: Huh? Where was I? Oh yes . . . now, since heroics are a matter of choice . . .

BROTHER: (*Setting weights down left with loud clang.*) Sorry.

DEATH: . . . a matter of a road taken, we can skip to the day that Don begins his journey to Valhalla. That is the day he first realizes . . . as every man must . . . that he is "un epave" . . . floating.

(LEON, SHORTY, DON, JACK BICK, JOE GOLDMAN, *and* WALLY SILVER *enter.* JACK *is mid-40's, conservatively dressed, self-important.* JOE *and* WALLY *are a bit younger and dress quite casually.* DEATH *watches the scene from down right. The* BROTHER *works out quietly down left.*)

LEON: Come on in, Jack, and meet the team. Fellas, this is Jack Bick, Vice-President of Marketing for Monopoly Motors. (*Introducing him to others.*) This is Shorty Radabaugh, our account supervisor. He'll belong to you, Jack. Your man all the way. Perhaps you remember Shorty when he was an All-East split-end at Brown a few years back?

JACK: No, frankly I don't follow the Eastern schools all that much.

LEON: And Joe Goldman and Wally Silver, our writing team. Just free lance, of course. We have to share them with Broadway. Perhaps you saw their last effort . . .

JOE: *Zolaesque.*

JACK: No.

WALLY: It was a rock version of the Dreyfus case.

JOE: Would have run longer but there was a newspaper strike.

WALLY: Subway strike, Joe.

LEON: The boys got a git song out of it, though.

JOE: "Jaccuse Blues."

WALLY: Top 40's.

JOE: Solid Gold.

JACK: Perhaps my daughter . . .

LEON: And this is our creative director, Don Kohler. The guy who takes it off the wall and glues it together. Perhaps you saw his award-winning documentary for the AMA, *What To Do When Your Doctor Dies*?

JACK: I don't think so.

LEON: Okay, let's get to work. Oh, first of all and before we begin, let me remind everyone here that what we're working on is highly confidential. Right, Jack?

JACK: If competition smells what we're doing, we stand to lose a couple billion.

(SHORTY *whistles.*)

LEON: Right, Shorty. So let's rivet this to our heads. Top secret. Okay Jack, floor's yours.

JACK: Let me start by asking a question. What is America?

(*Pause. Others look at each other.*)

LEON: You . . . aah . . . want an answer to that, Jack?

JACK: Let me finish. America is the automobile (*All agree.*) Before the automobile, this country was nothing. People riding around in buggies. Nothing got done. The automobile pulled this country together. The car *is* America. Take your average American away from his car and you give him an inferiority complex the size of . . . well, of . . . (*Fails to find simile.*) . . . a big building.

(*After a stunned beat, ALL agree.*)

SHORTY	WALLY	JOE	LEON
That's true.	Good point.	I hear you.	I see what you mean, Jack.

JACK: So, you got the automobile. What else you got? What else is America?

LEON: (*After a beat.*) You . . . ah . . . want an answer to that, Jack?

JACK: Let me finish. America is vacations.

SHORTY	WALLY	JOE	LEON
I can see that.	Right on.	Good point.	Good observation.

JACK: Take an American away from his vacation and you'll make him as mad as a . . . well, as a . . . (*Again fails to find simile.*) . . . a really angry chicken.

SHORTY	WALLY	JOE	LEON
Good point.	True enough.	How right.	Yes, that would follow.

JACK: So, at Monopoly Motors we have put these two imperatives together. We asked, "How can we best serve the American public in the coming decade? They need a fuel-efficient car and they need to go on vacation." And we came up with the answer. (*Unrolls an artist's rendering of the car.*) It's a vehicle that lists for 15 grand, performs like our Super-90 on the highway and becomes the equivalent of a sub-compact yacht on the water!

(*Cries of astonishment from others.*)

JACK: That's right, it's a barn burner! Our market forecast people indicate to us that we will wipe out all competition in the recreational vehicle market inside of a year. Maybe . . . get this . . . maybe this baby'll shit-can the entire automotive industry. That's the Japs, that's the Eyeties, that's the Krauts . . . zip, zero, bankrupt! 'Cause this honey makes it a whole new ballgame out there. This sweetheart is a combo: camper, vacation car, pick-up truck, and luxury motor craft! The rivers and lakes of today will be the highways of tomorrow!

WALLY: Sensational!

JOE: What's it called, Jack?

JACK: The Esprey!

SHORTY: Wow!

LEON: Shorty's right, Jack. Great name!

JACK: We introduce a prototype model a year ahead of production this September. And we want a socko show. Can you meet that time frame?

LEON: We got the team that can do it, Jack. Right Shorty?

SHORTY: Right.

JACK: The audience will be our dealers, their wives or significant others ... and the press. And we need a show that really kicks this baby off.

LEON: We got the team. Right boys?

JOE & WALLY: Right!

JACK: We want to knock that audience on their collective asses!

LEON: We got the team. Right Don?

(DON *has risen and is crossing toward his* BROTHER, *down left.*)

DON: Remember during basketball practice ...

LEON: Don ... ?

(*As lights fade on* BUSINESSMEN, *and they exit.*)

DON: ... how it'd get dark around four-thirty ... and they'd turn the gym lights on? Outside, the snow would be falling and you could look up and see it beyond the big wirescreened windows. Inside, it was warm and bright and you were with a dozen other guys you cared about; and your mind was full of getting it right and the game coming up. And sometimes you'd look around at the guys you were with ... and you'd love them. 'Cause you were all there ... together.

(*He sits on the weight bench, lost in thought. After a moment the* BROTHER *speaks.*)

BROTHER: Sure I remember.

DON: Today I looked around that conference room and I said, "Why? Where's the promise? What's the point?"

BROTHER: I recall once in Nam, we were out on a Search and Destroy and Allen Tykodi, we called him "Trigger", 'cause he'd jerk it if a weed moved ... he's sittin on this paddy dike sayin', "What the hell we doin' here? What's the point?" "I don't know, Trigger," we said. "Does someone care if these slopes are communists? Is that the point?" "I don't know, Trigger," we said. "Does some conglomerate have investments here? Is that the point?" "I don't know, Trigger," we said. "Well, what is the point?" says Trigger. And just then the Lieutenant comes over and says, "We're movin' out. And Tykodi," he says, "you got the point." (*Laughs*)

DON: What's the point?

BROTHER: The point is the first guy out on patrol. The guy in front.

DON: No, I mean the point of the story.

BROTHER: That's it.

DON: What's it?

BROTHER: I could tell you a lot of funny stories about Viet Goddamn Nam. Lotta' funny stories, yessir. Nam made a man and a humorist of me. Only thing, it's hard to find work with those qualifications. I thought about the police force . . . but that's *too* funny.

(NANCY *enters.* DON *crosses to her as* DEATH *speaks to* BROTHER.)

DEATH: What are you doing in this play anyhow?

BROTHER: Hanging out.

DON: (*To* NANCY) I'm in trouble. Real trouble.

NANCY: What kind of trouble?

DON: At work.

NANCY: Trouble how?

DON: There's no promise. No point.

NANCY: No point to your work?

DON: To my life.

NANCY: (*After a beat.*) No point to me? Us?

DON: I don't feel worthy of us.

NANCY: What the hell does that mean?

DON: (*Crossing to* DEATH *at bar as* NANCY *exits.*) We're not a team.

DEATH: You and the little lady?

DON: Not together. With something in mind. Some . . . goal.

DEATH: Well a man's always got his work.

DON: Not there either.

DEATH: No team there either, huh?

DON: No.

DEATH: I guess the team concept's very big these days huh? Didn't used to be. In the old days men stood on their own.

DON: I don't know . . . maybe it's just me.

DEATH: Maybe you should just go with what you got. House, car, pretty wife, dog . . .

DON: No, I don't have a dog.

DEATH: ... smart kids, ...

DON: See right through me.

DEATH: Little kids?

DON: A silent jury.

DEATH: They got your number, huh?

DON: I have no career. I'm there. For the rest of my life, this is it. I been hustling ... scrambling ... and now that I'm here, where am I?

DEATH: Janis Joplin.

DON: Pardon?

DEATH: Janis Joplin said that. About New York.

DON: I just feel there's gotta' be something better than this.

DEATH: Gwen Verdon.

DON: Huh?

DEATH: Sang it.

DON: Well, I'm in real trouble.

DEATH: On the brink.

DON: What?

DEATH: Another drink?

DON: No, I've got a meeting.

DEATH: (*To audience*) On the brink. And to push him off ... all we need is for Don and me to become a little better acquainted.

(LEON, SHORTY, JACK, JOE *and* WALLY *enter.*)

LEON: Ahh, here's Don, we can start. Don, you remember Jack, of course.

DON: Of course.

LEON: (*Indicating* DEATH, *who has put on a sport coat and joined the group.*) And this is Jerry Zutzenthaler, from the agency.

(DEATH, *as Jerry, shakes* DON'S *hand, holding it a bit too long.*)

DEATH: (*Overly solicitous.*) How are you, Don?

DON: Uh ... fine, fine.

LEON: Okay, we know what the Esprey does. What's our show? Let's just barnstorm awhile.

JOE: Well, I've been thinking ...

LEON: Go ahead.

JOE: It's just a bare bones idea.

LEON: That's what we're doing here. This is a creative session. Say whatever comes to mind.

SHORTY: Freedom to create here, Joe.

JACK: No judgments being made here, Joe.

JOE: How about a circus motif?

LEON: That stinks.

SHORTY: Terrible idea.

JACK: That the best we can do here?

LEON: Don, you're creative director, let's hear from you.

DON: Well, the main thing is a car that drives on water. So perhaps we should go to the shore . . . build some grandstands . . .

WALLY: I got it! How about an aquacade? We rent a big sports arena in every city . . . put in an Olympic pool . . . and for the reveal of the Esprey, we drive the car right into the water.

JOE: Great!

JACK: I don't know, guys. The water sort of gives it away. I mean there'll be lots of talk when we start building swimming pools all over the country. Remember we want this to be a socko suprise for dealers and press.

WALLY: So we reveal the pool!

JOE: Right. Build a stage hiding the pool. Then on cue . . . Zap . . . there's the car! Zip . . . stage disappears, there's the water! Splash . . . car drives into it!

DON: How the hell are you gonna' disappear a stage?

LEON: Don, let's not get logged down in nuts and threads. This is a creative session.

DEATH: I don't know. You still give it away by installing pools all over the country.

WALLY: Couldn't we travel the pool?

JOE: What about those plastic pools like my kid has? Couldn't we travel a big one of those?

JACK: Maybe we should . . . right now, rule out a tour. Go for one big shot in Miami or Vegas.

LEON: Is that a decision, Jack?

JACK: I think I can make that one. Vegas.

SHORTY: Check. No tour . . . Vegas.

LEON: Get on the facilities out there right away will you Don?

JACK: I really need the suprise of the pool.

WALLY: What about Joe's kid's pool?

JOE: Oh it's not big enough, Wally. Besides the kid would . . .

WALLY: I don't mean *that* one. I mean one *like* that one.

DON: I doubt a plastic pool will hold the amount of water we need.

DEATH: How long does it have the hold it actually?

WALLY: Or else . . . we fill the pool as part of the action!

JOE: Fifty girls come out holding hoses all spraying different colored water.

JACK: Sounds a little suggestive.

WALLY: No. Great suspense. Everyone will wonder what's going to happen.

JOE: Why are those girls spraying water into that empty hole?

DON: Well, they'll have about 60 minutes to wonder while the pool fills up.

SHORTY: Too long.

LEON: Right, Shorty.

JOE: I've got it! A sliding stage! It moves back . . . there's the pool!

DON: A sliding stage!

JACK: I'm beginning to like this.

DON: That would cost a . . .

LEON: Don! Jack's beginning to like this.

WALLY: Then . . . the cyclorama flies!

DON: Don't have to fly it. It fell in the water when the stage moved back.

LEON: (*Warning*) Don!

WALLY: And there is revealed . . . the . . . (*Forgets name of car.*)

JOE: Esprey! And whoever is going to introduce the car . . .

JACK: Our president and chief operating officer, F.R. Riley, will handle this one himself.

WALLY: F.R. Riley walks to the center of the pool . . .

JACK: On water! (*To* DEATH, *worried.*) How do you think our stockholders will react to F.R. walking on water?

JOE: He walks to the center of the pool. Gives a short, powerfully dramatic speech . . .

WALLY: The Esprey fires its engine . . .

JOE: And speeds with an explosion of colored water into the pool!

DON: Soaking old F.R. to the bone.

LEON: (*Chastising*) Don!

JACK: Will F.R. get wet? He hates to get wet.

SHORTY: It's sensational!

LEON: Good thinking, Shorty.

JACK: And I'll want Shorty with me all the way on this. I like his head.

JOE: Then . . . as the car circles the pool . . . the 50 girls in red, white, and blue bikinis dive into the water singing "Try Tripping With Esprey" or something.

WALLY: Spotlights swirl! Laser curl! Flags unfurl!

JOE: The orchestra crescendos! The girls come up for air and a final note.

JACK: (*Shaking* SHORTY'S *hand.*) It's great, Shorty! Great!

JOE: Listen . . . Jesus! Could we finale with a tidal wave? A fake one . . . but Jesus, what a . . .

DON: (*Noticing* DEATH *slumped over in chair.*) Are you all right, Jerry?

LEON: Are you in pain, Jerry?

(LEON *touches* DEATH. DEATH *collapses on the floor.*)

LEON: Jesus! Do we need an ambulance here, or what?

(*All stand in stunned silence.* BOBBI *enters.* DON *crosses to her, carrying a bottle of wine. Others exit.* DEATH *crosses back to bar down right.*)

BOBBI: Hi.

DON: Hi.

BOBBI: Long time no see.

DON: Yeah. (*Beat*) So . . . how you been?

BOBBI: Okay. You?

DON: Okay.

BOBBI: You sounded kinda' weird on the phone just now.

DON: Well, a guy just died in my office.

BOBBI: Really? How awful. A friend?

DON: No. Agency guy. Heart.

BOBBI: (*After a beat, pointing to bottle.*) Frascati?

DON: (*Nodding*) I remembered. Got a corkscrew?

BOBBI: Yep. (*Exits with bottle.*)

DON: Nice apartment.

BOBBI: (*From offstage.*) Thank you.

DON: I wondered how you . . . what your apartment looked like. I mean when I thought about you. Well, I mean . . . lately I've been sort of thinking about you.

BOBBI: (*Offstage . . . amused*) Sort of thinking about me?

DON: Well, I mean . . . the time we spent together. The fun. You know.

(BOBBI *enters with opened bottle and glasses.*)

DON: So . . . here we are again.

BOBBI: Our second farewell concert.

DON: I really have missed you, Bobbi. Even though I didn't realize it. (*She laughs*) What I mean by that is that it feels good to be here. It feels right.

BOBBI: (*Handing him the bottle.*) Yeah?

DON: As if we're just picking up where we left off. (*Starts to pour her wine.*) Say when.

BOBBI: Probably after another drink.

(*He looks at her in surprise. She laughs.* NANCY *enters.* DON *crosses to* NANCY *as* BOBBI *exits.*)

NANCY: Not Leon or Shorty?

DON: Agency guy. Just . . . (*Makes diving gesture.*) . . . heart.

NANCY: You all right?

DON: Yes.

NANCY: You seem strange.

DON: Well . . .

NANCY: (*Waits a beat for him to say more . . . then . . .*) Well, we ate. There's meat loaf in the fridge. I'm going to my meeting. Mark and Scotty are next door.

DON: Meeting?

NANCY: Earthwatchers.

DON: What watchers?

NANCY: I joined an environmental group.

DON: When?

DON: Last week. After I bought the drapes. I was in the mall standing between Hickory Farms and Foxmore feeling a minor depression about the tap pants when this guy comes up and hands me a pamphlet and starts talking about resources and I was feeling out of those at that particular time so I accompanied him over to his booth between Chess King and Walden Books and signed up.

DON: Signed up to do what?

NANCY: I gotta' run, I'll be late.

DON: (*Crossing to his* BROTHER, *who is working out.*) Guy died in my office today.

BROTHER: Yeah? Why?

DON: Heart. Just . . . (*Makes diving gesture.*)

BROTHER: No, I mean why in the office? Why didn't he stay home? Or go out in the country?

DON: It was a sudden heart attack.

BROTHER: You always know when you're going to die. Believe me. Ever watch a dog who knows his number is up? He'll follow you around all day . . . wait till you sit . . . curl up on your feet and check out. Everyone, everything knows.

DON: Well, this guy didn't know.

BROTHER: Everybody knows. Once in Nam, Tony Delancy said to me, "I'm buyin' the farm today". Lurch, we called him. After that guy on TV, 'cause he walked like him. "I'm buyin' the farm," Lurch says.

DON: Buyin' the farm?

BROTHER: Some old-time expression. Sounds country. Which is strange since Lurch was from Pittsburgh. Probably heard it in a movie. "I'm buyin' the farm," he says. But the bullet missed him. Caught the kid behind him in the throat. Whitey Pearson, from Iowa somewhere. I said to Lurch, "You musta' lurched just right. The kid from Iowa bought your farm." "Well," says Lurch, "at least he'll know what to do with it." (*Chuckles.*)

DON: You think that's funny?

BROTHER: Sure.

DON: I don't. And anyhow the story is pointless. You said a guy always knows, but this guy was wrong.

BROTHER: So? Some days you get lucky.

DON: You don't give a damn about anything, do you? All you do is lift weights and jog.

BROTHER: I observe.

DON: What is there to observe in a fruit cellar?

BROTHER: You've got a fine life, Don. Fine home, fine wife, fine car, fine kids, fine dog.

DON: What dog? I don't have a dog?

BROTHER: Fine power saw.

(DON *crosses stage to bar.*)

DON: Guy died in my office yesterday.

DEATH: (*Pointing to newspaper he has been reading.*) Jerry Zutzenthaler. Young guy.

DON: Heart. Just . . . (*Makes diving motion.*)

DEATH: (*Reading obit in paper.*) Gerald Zutzenthaler. Born Mansfield, Ohio. Valedictorian, Phi Beta Kappa, Magna Cum Laude. World was his oyster at age 21. Published short story in *Kenyon Review* at age 22. Did nothing of importance for next 23 years. He is survived by pretty wife, nice kids, big home, nifty car.

DON: (*Grabbing paper.*) How old? 45! That's young! That's terrible! Jesus, I gotta' start doing something with my life. I gotta' make changes!

DEATH: Hey, you didn't finish your drink!

(JACK *and* SHORTY *enter.*)

JACK: Just what the hell is this slide supposed to be?

SHORTY: Beats me, Jack. Don, were there some changes made here?

DON: Yes, I re-did all the art work on the engineering section. I felt we needed to express . . .

JACK: No, no, it's too goddamn flowery. What are all these friggin' curlycues? When we talk the engine we want to see the engine, not a goddamn free love poster.

SHORTY: Doesn't work, Don.

DON: I think it does. I think we need something different. I was striving for something a bit more creative . . . more individual . . .

JACK: Strive to shoot detailed photos of the engine, okay?

DON: I really feel that . . .

SHORTY: (*Pulling* DON *aside.*) Don . . . him Tarzan, you Jane. Comprez vous?

(JACK *and* SHORTY *exit.* BOBBI *enters in bikini carrying bath sheet, sun tan lotion, spray bottle, can of soda, and eye shells. She spreads the towel on the floor and sits. Out of a dance bag she pulls magazines and a newspaper.* DON, *very agitated, crosses to her.*)

DON: Jesus Christ!

BOBBI: Take off your coat, you'll roast up here. What happened? You get off early?

DON: I left.

BOBBI: Take your shirt off too, get some sun.

DON: Hey, there's a guy over in that window with binoculars!

BOBBI: Yeah, he's a regular.

DON: Why don't you go to the park if you want sun?

BOBBI: In the park you get hit on. Here they can only look. Hey, don't get too near the edge.

DON: I'm okay. (*Looking down at street.*) Running around . . . running around . . . (*Shouts*) Do you know where you're going, any of you? (*Laughs*) Some guy looks up and waves. Like he knows me. (*Waving back*) Yes, yes, hello, you fucking idiot.

BOBBI: Why don't you come over and sit.

DON: I lied to you, Bobbi.

BOBBI: About what?

DON: Back when I first came back the second time.

BOBBI: Say again?

DON: When you ask me if I called because that guy died in my office? Well, I did. It scared the hell outa' me.

BOBBI: (*Handing him lotion.*) Do my back.

DON: Bobbi . . . I don't have a lot of time.

BOBBI: When do you have to be home?

DON: In my life!

BROTHER: (*From down left where he has been working out.*) There was a guy in Nam usta' dwell on time runnin' out.

DON: (*Still applying lotion to* BOBBI.) Look, I hope there's a point to this one.

BROTHER: His name was Gil Wilberton. "I think about death a lot," he'd say. "Shove it up your ass," we'd reply. We were a squad that enjoyed a metaphysical discussion. 'Bout a year later he spots me in a restaurant in Ghiradelli Square. Shouts at me across the room. "Hey, I'm still here," he says. "What the hell was I worried about?" "Careful, Wilberton," I says, "You might get run over by a cable car." And he laughs so hard he spills a bottle of steam beer all over some lady he picked up in North Beach. (*Chuckles.*)

DON: What's the point?

BROTHER: I don't know. Last I heard he was selling life insurance in Anderson, Indiana.

DON: That's the point.

BROTHER: I said I didn't know. Could be I guess.

DON: (*Agitated, he rises and crosses downstage.*) There was no point! Jesus Christ!

BOBBI: What? C'mon sit down. Relax. Wanna' smoke a joint?

DON: Bobbi, do you understand what's happening to me? I've suddenly realized that my life has no meaning. Stands for nothing. And I've got to make changes.

BOBBI: Just changes? You can do that by puttin' up wallpaper.

DON: What the hell does that mean? Jesus, my life is in turmoil and all I get are Zen punchlines!

BOBBI: Let's go to a flick. Here, pick us out a flick. (*Handing him newspaper.*)

DEATH: (*From his bar.*) There's a western film retrospective at Cinema 19. Tonight, *7 Guns to Tucson* and ...

DON: I need to move in a new direction.

DEATH: *Ride to Glory.*

DON: What?

DEATH: That's the second feature. With Burt Lancaster. He plays Jedediah Kohler.

DON: Jedediah Kohler?

DEATH: Yep.

DON: That's my great-great-grandfather!

DEATH: (*To audience, with a smile.*) N ... o ... o ... o ... o kidding?

(JEDEDIAH KOHLER *enters left.* BOB GRAHAM *and* IKE MCKEE *enter right and cross to bar.*)

JED: I hear you been askin' for me, Ike?

(IKE *continues to drink.*)

JED: Ike ... ?

BOB: We got no business with you, Kohler.

JED: (*With sudden anger*) Listen, that goddamn cur has been threatenin' my life and makin' gun talk against me everywhere but to my face, and it's about time to fetch that horseshit to a close. If you're anxious for a fight, Ike, jerk you gun and use it.

(IKE *whirls to face* JED. BOB *restrains him.*)

BOB: Kohler, damn you, we ain't heeled and you know it!

JED: Then he better stop flappin' his mouth or ...

IKE: An' you better stay the hell away from Sonita Wash or we will plant you under it.

JED: That land is the property of the Prescott Land and Cattle Company and as U.S. Marshal it's my duty to protect those interests.

BOB: We run our cattle there.

JED: From what I hear, Bob, they may not all be yours.

BOB: Listen ...

JED: No, you listen! The days of swinging a wide loop in these parts is over for you boys and ...

IKE: Kohler, that badge be dammed, you stay in our way and you will have to be got out!

JED: I will fight you godamn cow thieves anytime, anywhere!

(LIGHTS *shift, as action of* COWBOYS *freezes.* DEATH *leans across bar to* DON.)

DEATH: Yessir, Jedediah Kohler. Why there must be a dozen movies about him. John Wayne played him. And Charles Bronson. Bob Steele.

DON: Who?

DEATH: Imagine what it'd be like to have him around today.

(JACK *and* SHORTY *enter.*)

JACK: What the hell is this slide supposed to be?

SHORTY: Beats me, Jack.

JACK: It's too goddamn flowery. A friggin' free love poster. Who's responsible for this crap?

JED: I am.

JACK: (*Cowed*) Oh!

JED: Somethin' botherin' you boys?

JACK	SHORTY
No, no, everything's fine.	Hunky-dory with me, Jed.

JACK: Love the flowers.

SHORTY: Great idea.

JACK: Little curlycues and frilly crap . . . very effective.

SHORTY: Perhaps, if Jed likes, we could do more. All sorts of flowers.

JACK: Sure. Geraniums.

SHORTY: Philodendrons.

JACK: Pansies.

JED: PANSIES!

(JED *reaches for his gun.* JACK *and* SHORTY *back across stage in panic.*)

JACK	SHORTY
No . . . no . . . it's just a flower, Jed, a flower!	A flower, Jed. No offense!

JED: (*To* DON) You gotta' learn to take life into your own hands.

DON: But that's what I'm trying to do. Take my life in my hands. How's that done?

JED: Not your life, Sonny . . .

(*He fires twice.* JACK *and* SHORTY *fall to the floor.*)

JED: . . . other people's.

DEATH: So Jedediah Kohler was your great-great grandfather? You anything like him?

DON: I . . . I don't know.

(LEON, WALLY, *and* JOE *enter.*)

LEON: Don, a real problem. The meeting's going longer than anticipated and all the secretaries are tied down. So, since you're not particularly involved in this session, could you be a brick and take coffee orders?

DON: Coffee orders?

LEON: Thanks. Mine's black with sugar.

(LEON, WALLY, JOE, SHORTY, *and* JACK *go into conference.*)

IKE: (*At bar, to* BOB.) He ain't no more'n a pimp and a crimp artist anyhow.

JACK: (*To* DON.) I'll have light with sweetner.

DON	JED
Shorty, how about you?	What'd you say, Ike?

SHORTY: (*Annoyed*) What is it, Don?

DON: Your coffee order.

BOB: Back off, Kohler.

SHORTY: Oh . . . (*Mumbling*) Milk, no sugar. (*Back to conference*) So, I believe the engineering piece is . . .

JED: I asked Ike what he said.

DON: What?

SHORTY: What?

DON	JED
I didn't hear you.	Ike?

IKE: I said . . . you ain't nothin' but a crimp artist and a pimp, blacksmithin' for a . . .

SHORTY	IKE
(*Louder than necessary*)	
MILK . . . NO SUGAR . . . COM-PREZ VOUS?	. . . crowd of land sharks so's to feed your whores!

DON	JED
I'll comprez vous you, you son of a bitch!	Why you son of a bitch!

(*Two fights!* DON *goes for* SHORTY. LEON, WALLY, JOE *get in between. The whole thing resembles a hockey scuffle.*)

(JED *vs. the* COWBOYS, *however, is a deadly serious brawl.* JED *pulls his gun and slams it against* IKE'S *head. Blood spurts through* IKE'S *hands as he grabs his head and slumps to his knees.* JED *turns and levels his gun at* BOB.)

JED: C'mon you son of a bitch and I'll blow your ribs right out'n the back of your shirt!

(*The action freezes for a moment. Then the* BROTHER *speaks from down left.*)

BROTHER: What the hell you want to get into a fight for?

(DON *crosses to* BROTHER. *All others except* DEATH *exit.*)

DON: First of all, because that son of a bitch think's he's . . .

BROTHER: And in an office! How do you ask a guy on the 12th floor of a building to step outside? Imagine how stupid you'd feel riding down in the elevator together?

DON: I'm trying to establish changes in who I am. And I'm not a coffee order takerer.

BROTHER: There was a guy at Camp Pendleton always looking for a fight. Always found 'em, too. And won. Tough guy. Real tough. Went swimming off Solana Beach one afternoon . . . shark ate him.

DON: And I was thinking about Jedediah Kohler and . . .

BROTHER: Great-great grandpappy?

DON: . . . and how he brought law and order to the toughest town in the west.

BROTHER: I think he did that by leavin' it, actually.

DON: So I intend to live by *my* code from here on and . . .

BROTHER: What is it?

DON: What's what?

BROTHER: Your code?

DON: I don't know! How the hell can I know till I get rid of all the crap I'm walking around with? (*Pulls out notebook.*) See, I've made a list of changes. (*Reading*) Change job . . . get something creative. I'm signing with a head hunter tomorrow. Change relationships. That's Nancy. I'm going to speak to her about a separation. I know she's content with things as they are, but I'm not. Change environment. Maybe live on a farm. Get back to basics. Change oil and filter . . . no, that's . . .

NANCY: (*Entering*) Don, can we talk for a moment?

DON: Uh . . . sure.

NANCY: Don, how would you feel about a trial separation? I need to be on my own for awhile. We needn't say anything to the boys just yet. They're spending the summer with Mom and Dad anyhow.

DON: What?

NANCY: We're in a rut, Don. We're right out of the catalog . . . house, car, kids, dog . . .

DON: We don't have a dog, Nancy.

NANCY: Oh sure, there are days when I'm feeling wonderful. In the kitchen fixing dinner for all of us. And I think it's really going to work out. Then you come home and . . . Whap! . . . I'm depressed.

DON: But . . .

NANCY: Maybe it's all me. But I have to find out, don't I? Make changes. A new environment ... perhaps move to the city. Get back to the fast track. Get a job. (*Beat*) So ... (*Smiles and crosses to him.*) You understand that in one sense this isn't about us ... It isn't even in one sense about you. It's about me. So ... I'll stay in touch. (*Starts to go.*) Oh, here's the slip for the dry cleaning. And don't forget to get the oil changed in the Chevy. (*Starts to go.*)

DON: Nancy ...

NANCY: I've got to go, hon. They've got the car waiting.

DON: They?

NANCY: Earthwatchers. We're camping out in front of some bulldozers.

(*She exits.* BROTHER *chuckles.*)

DON: What's funny? You got another joke? Story about some guy in Viet Nam whose wife left him?

BROTHER: Oh, I got a hundred of those.

(LEON *and* SHORTY *enter.*)

LEON: Sorry to disturb you at home, Don, but Monopoly Motors is so damned concerned about security. Industrial strength espionage could really upset their tea cart, you know.

DON: So?

LEON: So when Shorty mentioned over drinks a lady friend you had in common. I did a little checking and ...

(DON *looks at* SHORTY.)

DON: What friend?

LEON: A dancer in our last show.

SHORTY: Bobbi.

LEON: Who, in college was a member of a radical group which ...

DON: Bobbi? C'mon, Bobbi was a ballet dancer in college. Ballet dancers don't join radical groups. *Folk* dancers, *maybe*, but ...

LEON: (*Reading from notes.*) A member of "The Classical Movement for a Democratic Society".

DON: Huh?

LEON: So when Shorty mentioned that he had had a brief liaison with her and that you were now ...

DON: (*To* BOBBI, *who is entering.*) Shorty Radabaugh!

SHORTY: (*To* DON) Great legs.

LEON: I don't want to be a thorn in your ass, Don, but radical groups are . . .

(*But* DON *is moving into scene with* BOBBI. *She wears a leotard and is doing a warm-up.* LEON *and* SHORTY *exit.*)

BOBBI: Shorty is . . . just one of those guys, you know. I mean it's just gonna' be fun and games, and you know it. Nothin' heavy.

DON: When was all this?

BOBBI: Couple months ago.

DON: While we were seeing each other?

BOBBI: Well, it sort of overlapped.

DON: Overlapped? Were you sleeping with both of us?

BOBBI: I didn't sleep with anybody. Everybody got up and went home.

DON: (*Unbelieving*) Shorty Radabaugh!

BOBBI: It was no big deal, for God's sake. A one-night stand.

DON: Where?

BOBBI: Shorty's office.

DON: His office.

BOBBI: It . . . I don't know why . . . seemed erotic. Being alone in that huge empty building. Outside his window the lights of hundreds of other offices. Some cleaning women across the street . . . a guy working late. It was sexy somehow and we'd been drinking. One thing led to another.

DON: What thing led to what other?

BOBBI: You want details?

DON: Yes.

BOBBI: Why?

DON: 'Cause I'm tryin' to understand *why!* Why you were with another guy at the same time you were with me!

BOBBI: Probably for the same reason you were with another woman at the same time you were with me.

DON: That's not the same at all!

BOBBI: (*Laughs*) You mean, "that was no woman, that was my wife"?

(DON *wheels, begins to pace, shaking his head, finally speaks.*)

DON: No, I can't . . . I can't get rid of the pictures.

BOBBI: What pictures?

DON: The two of you naked in Shorty's office!

BOBBI: Well, we weren't both naked if that helps you.

DON: What?

BOBBI: I don't think he ever did get undressed exactly.

DON: You were naked and he was dressed?

BOBBI: Yeah. So what?

DON: So what! You were naked and he was dressed! That makes it a . . . a whole other thing!

BOBBI: What the hell are you talking about?

DON: I don't know. This makes me crazy! See, you were a big change in my life. I came to you because I realized my life was going nowhere. I'm trying for some kind of authenticity. I want to do something and be something which feels new and exciting and has promise. And you're fuckin' some guy on a desk!

BOBBI: File cabinet.

DON: What?

BOBBI: (*Sarcastic*) Or maybe it was a photo copier. I remember he sent me some pictures later.

DON: Very funny.

BOBBI: See, the point here is not where, and not who, and not when, and not even that you were somewhere in the picture at the time. What you think I am and what I am, are beginning to sound like two different people, Don. I am certainly not a part of some master plan for the new Don Kohler.

DON: What the hell are you so angry about?

BOBBI: Because I liked what we had going. I thought we were two people who dug each other enough to hang around together and climb in the sack once in awhile. Instead I find you're making a movie about your life and I just happen to be one of the characters.

DON: I don't know what the hell you're talking about. All I know is that I thought you were someone . . . something else.

BOBBI: Something else?

DON: Other than the kind of woman who screws a guy in an office.

BOBBI: Well, that's the *kind* of woman I am, Don. I am also the kind who screws him in bed. And on the floor, which makes me the kind of woman who has carpet burns on her ass and has to cut you off for a couple days. Now, is that the *kind* of woman who fits into your movie? Is this a take?

(*She exits.* DON *slumps to the floor as if the wind has been knocked out of him.*)

DON: Jesus.

DEATH: As Margaret Hamilton said when Dorothy hit her with the water, "What a world. What a world." And we've probably shown Don enough of it for one act. So . . .

BROTHER: (*To* DON) Once when you were a little boy, maybe three, I took you climbing for the first time. It was a steep hill and hard work for you. When we reached the top you were smiling and talking to yourself. I leaned down to hear. "Donald," you were saying, "Me, Donald . . . Donald, me."

DEATH: Tell me, Punchinello, what is that all about?

BROTHER: Authenticity.

DEATH: You are definately not traveling with a full seabag. (*To audience*) As I was saying, we'll continue after an intermission. Oh . . . if you decide not to stay for the second act, of course I'll understand. But I'll be curious, so I'll drop by your place to discuss it with you. Say about four o'clock tomorrow morning? (*He chuckles and exits.*)

End of Act One

Act Two

(*The* BROTHER *is working out down left.* DEATH *enters.*)

DEATH: (*To the audience.*) How was the orange juice? Incidentally, I made note of all of you who were smoking. (*Chuckles*) Oh, and I heard someone out there say, "This play must be about reincarnation.' No, it is *not* about reincarnation. The play is about . . .

| DEATH | BROTHER |
| ... heroism and classic death. | Nuclear war. |

DEATH: What?

BROTHER: That's the guns your cowboys carry nowadays.

DEATH: No, this is not another play about nuclear war. I will explain it to you, though I am not sure it will penetrate the fog. For approximately one hour I have been presenting a play about heroism and ...

BROTHER: There was a guy in Nam used to say, "We're here because we've forgotten our history and are therefore condemned to repeat it."

DEATH: George Santayana said that.

BROTHER: I didn't think that was his name. He was Spanish, though. Maybe, Lopez ...

DEATH: Why don't you include some mind presses in your workout? You could use some strength there, believe me. Where were we ... ahh, yes ... gunfighters were walking the hot, dusty streets of an Arizona town.

(JED *enters left.* BOB *and* IKE *enter right.*)

JED: Bob, I hear tell you and your brother and Ike there and Johnny-Two-Deuce rode in this morning packin' more hardware'n a porcupine's got quills.

BOB: You mighta' heard wrong.

JED: (*Laughs*) Johnny-Two-Deuce don't even walk to the crapper without a six-shooter. Now, there's a law against carryin' firearms in this town, Bob. Certain people have elected me to this duty and I abide by their decisions in regard to the law.

IKE: (*Laughs*) Who the hell learned you that cowshit?

JED: I'm warnin' you boys I am plum fed up and if I see any guns I will not arrest you, but shoot you on sight.

BOB: Whatever guns we have are at the Oak Street Corral with our horses.

JED: Then get about your business here.

JED: You make a powerful lot of threats, Kohler. An' one day they'll get you flung plum to eternity.

DEATH: It is Ike, however, who will shortly become a piece of eternity.

(JED, IKE, BOB *exit as* LEON, JACK, *and* SHORTY *enter.*)

DEATH: And businessmen still sit making decisions which will have impact upon a nation's economy.

JACK: Anyone got any antacid? My kid had a birthday party last night and I musta' drank a gallon of "Fruit Powie".

LEON: "Fruit Powie"?

JACK: Never heard of it? My gals love it. It's sugar, fructose, corn syrup, sucrose, glucose, orange peels, and water.

SHORTY: How old are your girls, Jack?

JACK: Just six, the oldest. The youngest is five . . . or three? Here, I've got some shots I took at the shore last summer.

LEON: Great looking kids. Did I ever show you the portrait of Tilda we had done? I've got a photo copy here.

(*They all pull pictures out of wallets.*)

SHORTY: Beautiful! Listen, I'll give you a shot of my twins for one of your daughter.

JACK: How about my youngest for one of your twins?

LEON: I'll give you two Tilda's for one Chuck.

(DON *enters.*)

DEATH: As for our hero . . .

LEON: Oh, Don's here. We can start. Shorty, ball's in your floor.

SHORTY: This is hot! Frankie Torski is available to introduce the Esprey.

| LEON | JACK |
| This is incredible! | You're kidding me! |

SHORTY: How about that sports fans? Frankie Torski, the winningest coach in pro football. And we got him to appear at the convention and intro the car.

| LEON | JACK |
| Sensational! | Fantastic! |

DON: Did you say Frankie Torski?

SHORTY: Yep.

DON: He was my high-school football coach.

DEATH: (*As he puts on a baseball cap and picks up a clipboard.*) We have shown him the disappointing fact that external change only changes things . . . externally. Now we must push deeper. Take him to his core . . . his essence. Where he will find . . . nothing. (*Crosses to* DON) Coach Torski can see you now.

(DON *crosses to where* TORSKI *sits working at papers.*)

TORSKI: *(Not looking up)* You're from Monopoly Motors, right?

DON: Actually I'm from *Show Biz For Big Biz.*

TORSKI: What the fuck does that mean? Never mind, I got the letter. Here's the game plan . . . first, I don't write what?

DON: Uh . . . ?

TORSKI: Speeches. You do that. Two, I don't have time for what?

DON: Uh, Well . . .

TORSKI: Rehearsals. I arrive day of show, come to the hotel, you hand me what?

DON: Speech?

TORSKI: I read it. No problem.

DON: We were wondering about some film? Super Bowl stuff?

TORSKI: You'll be sent that. Comes with the fee. No sound, I talk it. You don't what?

DON: I don't *know.*

TORSKI: You don't write football. I write football. You write the car part. We straight? Have a car at the airport to meet me. Zip me to the hotel. I do my thing. Zip me back to the airport. Okay?

DON: Okay. (*Starts to go, stops.*) I guess . . . you probably wouldn't remember . . . I was a sophomore when you left. I played football for you. Mansfield High. Defensive back.

TORSKI: (*Without looking up, quickly and matter-of-factly.*) Yeah, I remember you. Toledo caught a touchdown behind you. Won the game.

DON: Uh . . . yeah.

TORSKI: (*Looks at* DON, *speaks without emotion.*) How ya' been?

DON: Fine.

TORSKI: (*Back to his papers.*) See ya in July.

(DON *crosses to bar.*)

DEATH: How's it going?

DON: Give me a double.

DEATH: That bad, huh?

DON: It's just that after my wife and girl friend left me, I ...

DEATH: Wait! Hold it! Wait a minute! Your wife and girlfriend left you?

DON: Yeah.

DEATH: Both at once?

DON: Yeah.

DEATH: Wow! Makes you feel terrible, huh?

DON: Yeah.

DEATH: Must make you think of yourself as a sexual zero, right?

DON: Well ... yeah ... I ...

DEATH: I should think so. (*Moving away*) Excuse me a minute, Champ.

DON: But then, everything has to end.

BROTHER: (*working out.*)We had a major who said that. "Everything ends," he'd say, "Everything has to end." He's still saying it.

DEATH: (*Returning to pour another drink.*) So ... you were saying?

DON: I went to see this guy I once played football for ... Frankie Torski.

DEATH: Yeah? I remember when he played linebacker for the Lions. One of the toughest ever was. You know him, huh?

DON: He coached me in high school. But he barely acknowledges it.

DEATH: No kiddin'? Wow, makes you feel pretty lousy, huh?

DON: Yeah.

DEATH: Must make you feel like a goose-egg in the macho column, right?

DON: Well ... yeah ... I ...

DEATH: I would think so. Excuse me a minute, slugger. (*Moves away*)

DON: Of course he's a professional athlete so I guess he sees things differently.

BROTHER: There was a jock with me in prison camp. Baseball player. When the Viet Cong asked him what he thought about the capitalistic system, he said he didn't know 'cause he was a free agent.

DEATH: (*Returning*) So you were saying?

DON: What?

DEATH: About your core, your essence, your ... nothingness.

DON: My what?

DEATH: (*Taking his glass.*) Can I give you a refill?

DON: It's just ... I feel I've written my life in sand. And the tide's coming in.

DEATH: Yeah? Must make you feel like a no-show in the game of life, huh?

DON: Yeah.

DEATH: I would think so. Well, drink up. Closin' early. Want to catch *Gun Stand At Apache Wells* on the late show. With Henry Fonda. Ever see it?

DON: I don't think so.

DEATH: It's about your great-great-grandfather.

DON: Jedediah Kohler? He ran a gun stand?

DEATH: (*A bit exasperated*) Took. Took a stand. It would have been against his code not to. Besides, takin' stands made him feel great!

DON: Yeah? Well, he was lucky. Nowadays it's pretty hard to find a stand to take.

DEATH: Is it?

(LEON, JACK, SHORTY, WALLY, *and* JOE *enter*)

LEON: Ah, here's Don, we can start.

JACK: Leon, I've been over your show and it's looking terrific.

LEON: Then we can assume a go-ahead?

JACK: In a word, yes and no.

SHORTY: Fine, Jack.

JACK: Firstly, the incentive program. We've revamped that.

WALLY: What's the new input?

JACK: Basically the same. Trip to Marrakech for any dealer who doubles his quota. But here's the new wrinkle . . . if he triples . . . the wife goes along!

(*Others mumur approval.*)

JACK: And every month we'll send his wife a graph showing her how her husband is doing, along with brochures about scenic spots and the hotel in Marrakesh. We figure, give or take a couple coronarys, to up the dealer quotas 29%!

(*Others respond.*)

JACK: Secondly, there's a problem on the film portion of the show. You'll have to postpone your shoot of the Esprey on Lake Chucumwa for at least three weeks.

SHORTY: Ouch!

LEON: Shorty's right, Jack, that'll put us in one hell of a quarry.

JACK: Sorry, but it can't be helped. Engineering's come up with a small problem.

DON: A problem?

LEON: Well, I'll tell you, Jack, our production people are already running around like bulls with their heads cut off. A delay now will . . .

DON: What kind of problem?

JACK: Small problem.

LEON: How's this gonna' impact the budget, Shorty? I mean the costs could get astrological!

DON: A problem with the car in water?

JACK: Small problem.

LEON: The budget is already so tight it's hard to make just one end meet.

DON: Jack, let me ask you a question. Is the Esprey safe?

LEON	SHORTY	WALLY	JOE
What?	Oh, for Christ's sake, Don!	Safe?	What's that got to do with it?

DON: Wait a minute! This is a question we have to ask. We've just heard there's an engineering problem with the Esprey on water. As responsible citizens who . . .

SHORTY: Hold on! We're not responsible citizens, we're in sales promotion.

LEON: I don't think we need pursue this line of . . .

DON: No, I'm taking a stand here and . . .

JACK: What the hell is going on here, Leon?

LEON: Fellows, I just recalled a little budget thing I need to go over with Don privately so . . .

SHORTY	WALLY
I've got to return a call.	I've got to call my agent.

JACK	JOE
I've got to call my office.	I've got to call my wife.

(*And in an instant* LEON *and* DON *are left alone.*)

LEON: Don, we've all been so damn busy there's been no time to lay any hands on, you know. Now you're a creative guy, maybe a little too innovative at times, but that's what you bring to the party. That little scrimmage with Shorty last week . . . (*A short laugh*) Well, let sleeping dogs live, as far as that goes. What's done is over. The show's the thing from here on. I guess what I'm asking . . . are you with us or for us?

DON: What?

LEON: Don, let me share this straight to your shoulder. We're all street guys here but we can only win as long as the team is interfacing, dig? Man, the old game plan is out the kazoo without synergism. The kind of synergism which created the heritage of excellence this company enjoys on a broad basis. So the bottom line is . . . when the going gets going, the tough get tougher. Pursuit of quality excellence, pal . . . that's the commitment I need from you. Am I right?

DON: The car may not be safe, Leon.

LEON: (*After a beat.*) So my thinking on this is that we let Shorty take over the creative and client relations. Leaving you free to handle tactics.

DON: Tactics?

LEON: Hotel accommodations, I.D. badges, pitches of ice water, that sort of thing. We'll move your stuff into your new office at lunch.

DON: New office?

LEON: Remember, Don, it's a team. No man lives in Iceland.

(DON *crosses to bar.*)

DON: Give me a drink.

DEATH: Double?

DON: Yeah. That's the last time I listen to you.

DEATH: Yeah?

DON: I took a stand. Whap! My career is over. They move me down the hall and nail the door shut.

DEATH: (*Returning with a martini.*) Want an olive in this?

DON: Fuck the olive! (*Beat*) Jesus, tomorrow I visit my sons. How can I face them. How can I be a role model? I'm their hero . . . me and Spider Man.

(WALLY *and* JOE *enter.*)

WALLY: Hey, Don, here you are! We were looking for you in your office, but you weren't there.

DON: Leon moved me. Give me another drink.

DEATH: With a twist?

DON: Fuck the twist.

JOE: Don, let me give you some advice on . . .

DON: Fuck that too. I been getting more help than I need lately. I got a brother who tells me shaggy war stories and a bartender who gives me advice he read off an embroidered pillow somewhere. And what's it all gotten me? My life is nowhere . . . career over . . . dead in the water.

WALLY: Geez, you're too young for that to happen.

JOE: You haven't even been promoted beyond your capabilities yet.

DEATH: A has-been before he ever was.

DON: Better give me another.

DEATH: Fuck the ice, right?

DON: And the napkin.

WALLY: Look, fall back on what you got left. House, car, dog . . .

DON: I don't have a dog, Wally.

JOE: I can get you a deal on a Dalmatian.

DON: In fact, I don't have anything. Christ, everything is gone! Everything I wanted to get rid of is gone!

WALLY: What?

(LIGHTS *change to dim bar and highlight* DON *and* JED *as he enters.*)

DON: What's left?

JED: A man's name is that which he lives by. So he must see to it that it stands for something.

DON: Don Kohler?

JED: There are them as has attempted to misuse or challenge my name, and in those circumstances I have had no choice but to send those hombres down the road to hell.

DON: That's easy for you to say. You were a legend. Me? I promote a car that terrifies ducks.

JOE: Who are you talking to, Don?

(JED *exits.*)

WALLY: You okay, Don?

DEATH: He's okay.

DON: I'm okay.

JOE: You want us to put you on the train?

DEATH: He's not drunk.

DON: I'm not drunk.

DEATH: He's depressed. (*Handing him pills.*) Here.

DON: What's this?

DEATH: Antidepressants. Take two after breakfast for the rest of your life.

DON: I'm going home.

DEATH: (*Giving him a light push toward stage left.*) Yes, you should. Last call, gentlemen, I've got a busy night ahead.

(DEATH *hustles* JOE *and* WALLY *out of the bar and quickly begins to change clothes.* DON *has crossed left. The* BROTHER *joins him.*)

BROTHER: He told you to take these pills?

DON: Yeah.

BROTHER: (*Tasting one*) Tastes sweet.

DON: You're not supposed to chew them.

BROTHER: I'm not chewing them. I'm tasting them. Probably some kind of antidepressant. I'll feed 'em to the cat. I notice he's been sittin' just starin' into space a lot.

DON: Cats always sit and stare into . . . oh, never mind.

BROTHER: They were scopin' this place out today.

DON: What?

BROTHER: Reconnoitering. Drivin' around the house in a black Chevy. Lookin' for me probably. Government people. I hid in the dirty clothes hamper.

DON: How do you know they were looking for you?

BROTHER: Put a used jock strap on top. Tends to discourage a thorough search.

DON: May have been burglars.

BROTHER: Nope. They wore hats.

DON: What?

BROTHER: Guy in Nam used to burgle for living. Told me he never wore a hat. Made him look like a burglar.

DON: You know, I don't remember you talking this way when we were kids.

(*DOORBELL*)

BROTHER: Government people! I'll be in the clothes hamper.

(BROTHER *runs offstage left as* NANCY *enters right.*)

NANCY: Jed, I'll come right the point. I need you.

DON: I've missed you too, Nancy, and . . .

NANCY: No, I said I *need* you. *We* need you.

DON: The kids?

NANCY: Are fine. The Earthwatchers.

DON: The who?

NANCY: Need you.

DON: Oh, that group you . . .

NANCY: And we need you.

DON: Were you driving around here earlier today? My brother . . .

NANCY: To stop the Esprey.

DON: What?

NANCY: We know a lot about that car, Don. The factory is like a military post . . . armed guards . . .

DON: They're concerned about industrial espionage and . . .

NANCY: That car is tied into the Defense Department . . . and big business.

DON: Isn't that the same thing?

NANCY: A member of the Rockamellon family has acquired a Monopoly Motors franchise for an entire city in Italy.

DON: What's so strange about that?

NANCY: A car dealership in Venice?

DON: Where are you hearing this stuff?

NANCY: Don, I want you to meet somebody. (*Calls*) Dr. MacLamore, could you come out of the bushes please!

(DEATH, *as* MACLAMORE, *enters, dressed in sport coat and carrying a pipe.*)

DON: He looks very familiar.

NANCY: Don, I want you to meet the President of the Earthwatchers, Dr. Henderson MacLamore. Dr. MacLamore chairs the Business and Ethics Department at the university.

DON: Business and ethics is a college major?

DEATH: No, you major in business. You minor in ethics.

NANCY: And someone else . . . (*Calling*) Ron, could you come out of the forsythia!

DON: Why are these people in the bushes?

NANCY: Don, this is Ronald Hoerner, our attorney. Ron wrote the book, *America, Clean Up Your Act, Or I'll Sue You!*

RON	DON
How do you do.	Hi.

NANCY: And finally . . . (*Calling*) Henry!

RON: He's behind the elm.

DON: Why is everyone hiding?

DEATH: Because, my uninvolved friend, we are challenging the power brokers of this country. And when . . .

(HENRY JARVIS *enters. His hair is tousled and he is wild-eyed and intense.*)

NANCY: Don, this is Henry Jarvis. Henry was a design engineer at Monopoly. He tried to speak out against the Esprey once he realized that the final product was monstrously dangerous. But he was silenced, fired, threatened, and hounded.

JARVIS: I'm a fugitive, mister. A fugitive. Broke and desperate. Those people want to kill me. Me, a graduate of Massachusetts Institute of Technology!

NANCY: The people he's referring to is Monopoly Motors, Don.

JARVIS: My son is bedridden with walking pneumonia.

DON: Wait . . . what . . . ?

JARVIS: My wife has become a hustler.

HOERNER: Henry, if we are to appeal to the integrity of the American people, we must be careful not to exaggerate. Your wife was always a hustler.

JARVIS: But now she's doing it for money!

NANCY: Tell him about the dangers, Henry.

JARVIS: Doors blow off.

DON: What?

JARVIS: At 35,000 feet the rear cargo hatch bolts snap like toothpicks and KA-BOW ... the ...

NANCY: No, no. (*To* DON) He worked for Bowmont Aircraft before he worked for Monopoly. (*To* JARVIS) Talk about the Esprey.

JARVIS: Oh that son of a bitch'll kill everybody. Incorrect ballast. Inadequate bilge pumps. Excessive steering angles. Water leakage in the axle house shields. Unbalanced by the power package. It'll drown everyone.

NANCY: And who's going to buy that car, Don? Families ... with kids. To go vacationing on a lake.

HOERNER: Your wife tells me you are related to Billy the Kid.

DON: Jedediah Kohler.

HOERNER: Whatever. It's the sort of courage needed for this job.

DON: What job?

NANCY: What we're doing is dangerous, Don.

DEATH: Because big money is at stake. Government contracts. Think about it a moment. Who'd be most interested in the development of a car that drives across water?

HOERNER: Well, anyone who lives in Sausalito or Staten Island or ...

DEATH: The military!

NANCY: We're taking a stand, Don.

DON: A stand?

NANCY: We need you to stand with us.

(LIGHTS *shift as* JEDEDIAH *enters.*)

JED: When it's time to stand ... you know. Something moves ... down in your gut. Creeps across the shoulders. Crawls into the back of your eyes. There's nothin' else then. Just you ... them you're against ... and the tiny patch of time you're standin' in. It's the clearest life'll ever be. And it's one moment before you reach for your gun.

(*A pause as all watch* DON.)

DEATH: Well?

DON: Aw, I don't know.

DEATH: (*Greatly frustrated*) Jeeesus!

DON: I mean, why don't you just do one of those TV editorials. Tell the facts. Monopoly will have to . . .

DEATH: Monopoly Motors doesn't *have* to do anything, son.

DON: Sure they do, if public pressure . . .

DEATH: Excuse me, I've got to make a phone call.

(DEATH *rushes to his bar and frantically changes into black business suit and homberg.*)

HOERNER: You have an opportunity, Mr. Kohler. An opportunity which comes to few and which fewer still respond to.

NANCY: The Vice-President of Engineering will be at your convention. With the engineering schematics. If we can get those we'll have the evidence we need to file a class action.

DON: I still think that TV . . .

HOERNER: Monopoly Motors will come back with hours of commercials featuring beautiful people wearing dark glasses and driving gloves. Who could believe *they'll* drown? No, we need the plans. And you have that opportunity, Mr. Kohler. An opportunity which comes to few and which fewer still respond to. Damn!

NANCY: You already said that, Ron.

HOERNER: I know. I was just trying to do it without ending with a preposition.

JARVIS: (*Pointing front*) Limousine in the driveway!

NANCY: What?

JARVIS: It's them! I've got to hide! Where's the cellar? (*He runs offstage.*)

DON: (*Shouting after him.*) Don't jump in the clothes hamper!

HOERNER: Kohler, a very heavy hitter is sitting in your driveway.

DON: Sitting in my driveway?

HOERNER: In a car, of course. That's F.R. Riley, himself. The President and Chief Executive Officer of Monopoly Motors.

DON: (*A bit stunned, he begins to walk toward down right.*) Jesus! What's he doing here?

NANCY: Be careful, Don.

(DEATH, *as* F.R. RILEY, *sits as if in the back seat of a car. He leans over and pantomimes opening a door.*)

DEATH: (*Holding out hand.*) F.R. Riley.

DON: (*Leaning down to shake.*) Don Kohler.

DEATH: Sit down.

(DON *sits next to him.*)

DEATH: I understand you expressed some concern at a meeting the other day regarding the safety of our new motor vehicle.

DON: Well, yes . . .

DEATH: You don't know about our safety complex at Monopoly?

DON: Well . . .

DEATH: You don't think we understand our responsibility to the American consumer?

DON: Well, yeah, probably. But . . .

DEATH: No *probably.* No *but.* We do. The Esprey has passed every government standard that is currently being enforced. Do you know our motto?

DON: Ahh . . . I'm not real sure.

DEATH: Monopoly . . . Where the heritage of excellence meets the quality of today, tomorrow.

DON: Oh.

DEATH: The Esprey is, I can assure you, as safe as any other car on the road.

DON: Well, that's what some people are afraid of.

DEATH: What are you, a comedian?

DON: No, but the car is going into water and some people . . .

DEATH: What people?

DON: (*Stalling*) Huh?

DEATH: You said "some people". Who?

(DON *doesn't answer, sensing trouble.*)

DEATH: Tell your "some people" to go help the baby seals and the grizzly bears, 'cause if they start screwin' with us they're gonna' quickly become an endangered species themselves. (*Beat as he studies* DON.) Let me make one thing real clear. Monopoly Motors is a financial company. We make product, but we are a financial company. We have over 500 million dollars in the Esprey. Now, let me give you a lesson in economics. We are the sixth largest company in the world. And size does not easily equate with flexibility. Once you get a dinosaur moving in one direction, he ain't easy to turn around. Some little fart like you can go kick the dinosaur, but it wont't make a hell of a lot of difference. It'll not stop him. It'll not turn him. It'll just make him angry. And he will piss all over you. Do I make myself clear?

DON: Hey, wait a minute. Who do you think . . .

DEATH: And when a dinosaur pisses it's a torrent. We're talkin' a torrent of piss here, friend. Get my point?

DON: (*Pantomining getting out of car.*) You go to hell.

DEATH: One person does not . . . nay, cannot make any difference in the commerical enterprise of this nation. When's the last time one person made a difference in anything in this country?

DON: Jedediah Kohler cleaned up a town that . . .

DEATH: (*Laughs*) A cowboy? Are you a cowboy? A gunfighter? (*Laughs*) You sir, are a wimp. Haven't you found that out by now? (*Laughs*) A nothing. (*Pantomimes a speaker tube.*) Hotel, Bruno. (*To* DON) Adiós, pardner! (*Laughs*) This town ain't big enough for both of us! (*Laughs uproariously.*)

(DON *watchs as if car is moving toward stage left and yells.*)

DON: You son of a bitch!

(JEDEDIAH *enters. He and* DON *finish speech together.*)

DON *and* JED: You been looking for a fight and now you can have it!

DEATH: (*Quietly, to audience.*) Got him!

DON: (*Calling*) Nancy!

JED: The whole thing only took thirty seconds.

DEATH: I'll admit there was a time . . . because of that looney brother . . .

DON: (*To* NANCY) I'll get you those plans!

DEATH: But I got him!

NANCY: Oh, that's wonderful!

DEATH: (*Doing a little jig.*) I got him! I got him! I got . . .

NANCY: Isn't it Professor?

DEATH: (*Quickly recovers, jamming pipe in mouth.*) Yes, wonderful. How do you propose to do it?

DON: I'm not sure.

JED: Johnny-Two-Deuce was the last to die.

DON: I'll need help. Someone who can get into the Vice-President's room.

DEATH: He's a tough cookie. All business. But we've learned he's secretly obsessed with ballet dancers. Perhaps . . .

DON: Bobbi! Of course! I'll call her. Offer her the starring role in the show. She's been talking about moving West. This'll be her chance. C'mon we'll go see her. (*Remembering* NANCY) No, I'll go see her. We'll stop that son of a bitch and his goddamn dinosaur! (*Runs off*)

NANCY: We'll see you in Las Vegas, Don!

(HOERNER *and* NANCY *exit.* DEATH *rushes to his bar to change again.* LIGHTS *come down to highlight* JED.)

JED: He sat there on the brown grass tryin' to level his six gun at me, though he was shot to pieces. He was screamin' at me . . . great globs of blood sprayin' out of his mouth.

DEATH: And the inevitable conclusion approaches!

JED: Both the Graham brothers were dead. Ike McKee was dead. My brother Blake was dead. A bullet tore the top of his head off. Doc was dyin'. Shot in both legs and through the stomach. Pieces of which were blown out the back of his shirt. He knelt on one knee for awhile . . . staring at his boot. Then he toppled over.

DEATH: Yes, yes that's fine, old timer. We have no more need of you.

JED: Thirty seconds of guns . . . and then . . . dead silent. I walked to the street. A mongrel dog followed along barkin' at me. It was the only sound in the whole town. (*Beat*) I had been hit three times. I carried the lead the rest of my life. Most days . . . especially when it was cold or damp it hurt so bad I wished I'd died with the rest of them. In the end . . . they got me anyhow. It just took a while longer.

DEATH: Thank you Jedediah Kohler. Stick around for the curtain calls if you want to. And now . . . Las Vegas!

(*Banners fly in reading* "WELCOME MONOPOLY MOTORS.")

DEATH: This is the ballroom of the Las Vegas Hilerton. Where for three days Don's group has been preparing for the convention.

(JOE, WALLY, LEON, *and* SHORTY *are crossing stage and conferring, all carry yellow legal note pads.* DON *enters and meets with them. Much pointing . . . up at grid, at wings, etc.*)

DEATH: A stage has been built. A set erected. The ballrom festooned with Monopoly banners and logos. Last night 6,000 Monoply Motors dealers and wives arrived. At a gala reception they were given cowboy hats ... (*Puts on a cowboy hat.*) name badges ... you know the kind. They say "Hello, I'm ... " and then you marker in the name. (*Puts on a badge.*) Hello, I'm Death. That should get some interesting reaction.

LEON: Has anyone seen Jack Bick?

WALLY: Leon, Jack was so goddamn nervous about the show he chewed up a valium instead of a Maalox and he's up in his room tossing his cookies.

JOE: Don, I've got last-minute revisions on the marketing speech.

DON: Get them to the stage manager. And make sure the slide director sees them.

(WALLY *and* JOE *exit.*)

SHORTY: Frankie Torski arrived yet? I've written his speech about the car.

DON: No.

SHORTY: I must say it's a minor little masterpiece. Rhapsodic, but macho.

DON: Sounds great. (*Seeing* NANCY, *who has just entered.*) Excuse me, I have to talk with the banquet manager.

(DON *crosses to* NANCY *at down right.*)

NANCY: Have you got the plans?

DON: Any minute now. Here ... (*Handing her a large shopping bag.*) I got you all hats and badges. Put them on so you'll look like conventioneers. The place is crawling with Monopoly Motors security people.

NANCY: Where shall we meet?

DON: Outside. The parking lot. Go. I'll be right there.

(NANCY *hurries off right.* JACK *enters left.*)

LEON: Here's Jack. How you feeling, buddy?

JACK: Not bad. I was going to go for a swim but there's some weirdo in a black sweatsuit chinning himself on the high diving board.

LEON: Come see the command center, Jack. From now on we're going to be busier than one-armed beavers.

(JACK, LEON, *and* SHORTY *exit left, passing* BOBBI *who enters left carrying a dance bag.*)

JACK: Don't forget, when our VP Sales speaks ... turn up the house lights. He wants to see the men he's going to fire.

BOBBI: (*To* DON) Okay, you got 'em.

DON: You're wonderful, Bobbi.

(*Taking dance bag which has blueprints sticking out from it.*)

BOBBI: They must really be hot. As I was comin' out of the room I was stopped by three Japanese guys who said if I let them photocopy the stuff they'd set me up with a sushi bar in Burbank.

DON: Any difficulty getting in the room?

BOBBI: Naw, fun. He was cute.

DON: Cute? That Vice-President of Engineering has a face like a prune.

BOB: What Vice-President? I'm talking about the room clerk. (*Hands key to* DON.) Turn in the key for me, will you? I gotta' warm up for the opening number. (*She starts to go.*)

DON: Bobbi, I owe you a ticket to L.A. for this.

BOBBI: Thanks.

DON: And a apology.

BOBBI: For what?

DON: Some things I once said.

BOBBI: I'll settle for first class.

(BOBBI *exits up left as* SHORTY *enters down left.*)

SHORTY: Don! Command center! Last-minute briefing.

DON: Be right there, Shorty. Gotta' deliver the dinner menu to the banquet department.

(SHORTY *exits as* DON *crosses right.* NANCY, HOERNER, JARVIS, *and* DEATH, *as* MacLamore, *enter down right. All wear cowboy hats.*)

DEATH: Have you got the blueprints?

DON: Yes.

JARVIS: Hurry, I can't stay here much longer.

DON: Have you been spotted?

JARVIS: No, but I'm losing what money I have on the slots.

HOERNER: Just give us the schematics and we're on our . . . My God!

(JED, BLAKE, *and* DOC *enter. All wear sunglasses and the black coats are of a modern cut but they strongly resemble the "Marshals" from Act One. In fact, the stage picture, with* DEATH, NANCY, HOERNER, *and* JARVIS *down right and the "MARSHALS" up left is exactly that of the Oak Street Corral. The exception, this time, is that* DON *is caught right in the middle, center stage.*)

JED: I'm Captain Jeremiah Crandall, head of security for Monopoly Motors. These men are from the Las Vegas Police Department and the Federal Bureau of Investigation.

JARVIS: They're CIA, that's what they are! All of 'em!

JED: Henry Jarvis, you pea-brained son of a bitch, I been huntin' you and . . .

JARVIS: I warn you, Crandall, I'm armed and will fire at you if you attempt anything!

JED: If you sons of bitches are lookin' for a fight, you can have it!

DON: Jesus Christ, it's the Oak Street Corral!

DEATH: Quick, Don, give us the blueprints!

JED: One step, sonny, and I'll blow your ribs out the back of your shirt!

DEATH: This is it, Don! This is your moment! Your chance for immortality! You are one step away from being a hero!

(DON *takes a step toward* DEATH. JED *pulls a gun. Almost simultaneously* JARVIS, BLAKE, *and* DOC *pull guns.* NANCY *screams.*)

JED	BLAKE	DOC	JARVIS
Freeze!	Hold it!	Reach!	I'll blow your
			brains out!

DON: No wait! Oh, Jesus! *Everyone* . . . this is a very dangerous situation. Please, don't you realize how dangerous this is? We can all be killed. All of us! (*Beat, then a bit quieter.*) Nancy, don't touch your coat.

NANCY: I'm not wearing a coat.

DON: No one move . . . please. We can work this out . . . if we all just, give some slack. (*Takes a deep breath.*) Boy, Jed, you sure were right about this being the clearest life would ever be. It is very fucking vivid here. You have a trickle of sweat rolling past your ear. Please don't reach to wipe it off, okay? (*To* JARVIS) And Henry, you're hyperventilating. (*Beat*) So . . . let's all ease off. And I will . . . slowly . . . reach into this bag. For the plans, Jedediah.

JED: Jeremiah.

DON: There is nothing in this bag . . . *except* the plans. Which I am now . . . slowly . . . removing. (*Pulls out plans and hands them to* JED.) Here.

DEATH: NO! NO! NO! NO!

JARVIS: You won't get me that easy! (*He runs offstage.*)

JED: C'mon boys, we'll head him off at the Sands!

(JED, BLAKE, KOC *exit.*)

DEATH: No, wait! Come back here! Come back! (*He wheels on* DON. DEATH *has completely lost his composure.*) You ruined everything! You blew it! Ever hear of Valhalla? Well that's where you could'a been. But you blew it!

BROTHER: (*Enters, carrying a carton of Chinese food.*) Blew what, Don?

DEATH: You! You get the hell out of this play . . . or else!

BROTHER: Or else, what?

DEATH: You know, at one point I suspected you knew who I was. But obviously you don't or . . .

BROTHER: Aw hell, I know who you are. You're that son-of-a-bitch I met in Viet Nam.

DON: What?

DEATH: You got it, pal. So you better . . .

BROTHER: (*Offering him food carton.*)]Like bean curd? With oyster sauce?

DEATH: What? No! (*Spins and points at* DON.) This is not over yet! (*Runs offstage.*)

BROTHER: Temperamental son of a bitch, isn't he?

NANCY: What on Earth has gotten into Doctor MacLamore?

DON: (*To the* BROTHER) Death. I was looking at Death, right?

BROTHER: That's him.

DON: Nancy, they'd have killed us all. That's what happened before and it would've happened again.

NANCY: I'm just glad you're alive, Don. There must be something else we can do, isn't there, Ron?

HOERNER: Well first, we've got to get to that phone booth over there and cancel the *60 Minutes* shoot. Got a quarter?

NANCY: (*As she and* HOERNER *exit.*) What about *Entertainment Tonight*?

DON: Death. What'd he want? Just to see us all die?

BROTHER: You in particular, I suspect.

DON: Why?

BROTHER: (*Shrugs*) Bored, I guess.

DON: Funny, here I am tryin' to be Jedediah Kohler and Jedediah Kohler turns up on the wrong side. What happened?

BROTHER: 'Bout a hundred years happened.

DON: Huh?

BROTHER: I recall once in Nam, we were sitting in this village when Bob Sowash, we called him "Sody", says, "Do you realize we've pushed the American frontier so far west we are now east? And do you further realize that if we continue this procedure we will be attacking Atlantic City in August, 1989?" And we all thought about that awhile. "Not me," says Trigger Tykodi. You met him in an earlier story.

DON: Yes, I remember.

BROTHER: "Not me," says Trigger, "I am done with corrupted legacies." And he picked up his rifle and he left the war. And then Lurch ... you remember ... ?

DON: Yeah.

BROTHER: Lurch stood, stretched, and said, "Certain aspects of our myths are not doin' us much good these days." And he also left the war. One by one they all, the whole company, walked out of that ville. Only the captain was left. I went over to him and said, "Sir, the company has ... well, sort of evaporated." "Well," he said, "you'd better get going then." So I started walking and just as I stepped out of the ville I heard him shout, "Kohler, stay off the roads. Because here, in country, or back in the world, the shortest distance between life and death is a straight road.

DON: That's strange.

BROTHER: What?

DON: I got the point of that one.

(JARVIS *runs across upstage, followed by* JED.)

JED: Freeze, damn you!

(HOERNER *and* NANCY *enter.*)

HOERNER: Well, that's that. I guess we should gather up the rest of our people and head for home.

(JARVIS *runs back the other way.*)

HOERNER: Oh, Henry ...

JARVIS: I can't stop now!

HOERNER: (*Calling after him.*) Henry, check-out is 12 o'clock. We don't want to get into an extra day!

(JED *runs on.*)

JED: Which way'd he go?

(*They all point opposite to where* HENRY *left.* JED *runs off.*)

NANCY: Ron, what about Mr. Torski?

HOERNER: Oh, that's right.

DON: Coach Torski?

NANCY: Some of our people represented themselves as being from Monopoly Motors and picked the coach up at the airport. They're driving him out into the desert. We didn't want him lending his prestige to the Esprey.

DON: (*Ecstatic*) Wait a minute! You've got Torski! (*Starts to laugh.*) You've got Torski and he's supposed to introduce the Esprey in ... (*Looks at watch.*) Jesus, the show's started. We don't have much time. (*Looks around.*) Quick, over to that drugstore.

NANCY: What for?

DON: C'mon!

(*As they all start to go,* SHORTY *runs on.*)

SHORTY: Don, Don, we've been looking all over for you! The show is on and Frankie Torski isn't here yet! This your ass, Kohler, comprez vous? If Torski isn't ...

DON: Relax Shorty. He's here. He's over at that drugstore buying some sunglasses. In fact, this ... (*Pushing the* BROTHER *forward.*) ... is his line coach, the famous Elbows Bradashevski. You've heard of him, of course.

SHORTY: Oh, of course. Nice to meet you Mr. Bradashevski.

BROTHER: You can call me Elbows.

DON: I'll get Torski.

(DON NANCY *and* HOERNER *run offstage as* LEON *enters from the opposite side.*)

LEON: Don, Don! We don't have Torski!

SHORTY: Leon, this is Coach Torski's assistant, Elbows ... ah ...

LEON: Mr. Elbows, you've got to understand my dilemma. We are, at this moment, running the Super Bowl film that introduces Frankie Torski.

BROTHER: No shitski?

LEON: What?

SHORTY: Leon, it's okay. Torski is here. Don went to get him.

LEON: Thank God! Then we're go?

SHORTY: It's a lift-off!

LEON: We're ready with the socko Esprey reveal?

SHORTY: Ready.

LEON: Balloons ready?

SHORTY: Ready.

LEON: Turntable?

SHORTY: Ready.

LEON: Pigeons?

SHORTY: All ready.

LEON: As soon as Torski says, "And here's the Esprey!", we go everything. We shoot the whirlpool, right, Shorty?

SHORTY: You got it!

LEON: (*Unable to contain himself, grabs* SHORTY'S *arm and begins to jig.*) It's the big one, Babe! The big one!

SHORTY: The biggest! (*As they dance.*) We better get inside, Leon, it must be getting close!

LEON: Right on! Stand by to knock that audience on their friggin' toes!

(*They run off and* BROTHER *exits opposite side as we hear a voice over announcement.* DON, *wearing dark glasses, baseball cap, and carrying a clip board, strides to center stage.*)

VOICE OVER: And here to introduce the car you've all been waiting to see . . . American's super coach . . . Frankie . . . Tooooooor . . . ski!!!

DON: Well you saw the film of the Super Bowl. And it was a what? A victory! And now victory for you dealers out there in the audience. And victory for the American people as they discover a new world of leisure with Monopoly's revolutionary land-sea vehicle, the what? The Esprey! Sure you've heard a lot about it here today. But let me say that I have seen it in action. Yeah, I saw it test driven along the highway and into the blue waters of Lake Chucumwa. I saw the Esprey gliding there on that lake. The sun flashing off its lovely chrome trim. A monument to man's genius. Floating like a lovely jewel for a good three and a half minutes before it sank like a what? A stone, right! No, the Esprey is not safe.

LEON: (*Rushing on.*) Wait! Coach Torski, wait! There must be a mistake. You . . .

(DON *straight-arms* LEON, *laying him out flat.*)

DON: Incorrect ballast ... inadequate bilge pumps ...

LEON: (*From the floor.*) Pull the lights! Kill the curtain!

DON: Excessive steering angles ...

(*Now* SHORTY *joins* LEON *in trying to stop* DON. *[NOTE: IF WALLY AND JOE ARE NOT DOUBLED USE THEM IN THIS MELEE ALSO.]* DON, *like a good runningback, head fakes both* SHORTY *and* LEON *and keeps talking till they finally manage to wrestle him to the floor.*)

DON	SHORTY *and* LEON
Water leakage in the axle house shields ... unbalanced by the power package ...	Coach, stop! Wait, don't! A horrible mistake's being made!

(NANCY *and* HOERNER *run on.*)

NANCY: Everyone, please ... listen! Keep your seats and listen! Quiet down! Please, listen. The car is a killer!

(*Everyone is now talking at once.*)

LEON	NANCY
(*Discovering* TORSKI *is* DON.)Don! What are you doing?	We are the Earthwatchers and we have seen the plans. This is Ronald Hoerner, attorney and author ...

SHORTY	HOERNER
Someone shut her up!	*America, Clean Up Your Act Or I'll Sue You!*

LEON	NANCY
Oh my God, they've released the pigeons! Get the goddamn pigeons back!	The Esprey will sink. Yes, sink! It is horribly unsafe. It will drown anyone in it!

SHORTY: Leon, come back here! Leon we've got to come up with a cover story! Leon, forget the fucking pigeons!

(*As* LEON *is running off left, followed by* SHORTY, JARVIS *steps onstage left, brandishing a revolver.* LEON *and* SHORTY *screech to a halt at his voice.*)

JARVIS: Freeze! (*To audience*) Everybody freeze! Out there ... sit down! You're going to hear how dangerous this car is or I'll kill all of you!

(JEDEDIAH: *runs on from right with gun drawn.*)

JEDEDIAH: Drop that gun, Jarvis, or you're a dead man!

(*The stage is momentarily frozen as the two gunmen face each other, with* DON *right smack in the middle. At this point,* DEATH *enters and strolls center stage to* DON.)

DEATH: Right in the line of fire, are you Don? (*Chuckles.*) How unlucky. So you will die . . . not as a hero . . . but just as some schmuck who was in the wrong place at the wrong time. (*Laughs again and turns toward left.*)

JARVIS: (*When* DEATH *faces him.*) F.R. Riley, you son of a bitch! You're the reason my wife is a hooker and my son is bedridden with walking pneumonia!

DEATH: Wait a minute! I'm not F.R. Riley. I'm . . .

JARVIS: Riley, it is men like you who have hounded men like me till we froze to death in the icy winter of our isolation!

JED: Jesus, what a metaphor! Lemme' shoot that pea brain before he comes up with another!

JARVIS: And so, Riley, you are going to die!

(*Pulls trigger . . . misfire.* HOERNER *grabs the gun away from him.*)

HOERNER: Christ, can't they manufacture anything that works anymore?

(*The real* COACH TORSKI *now enters, right.*)

TORSKI: Sorry I'm late but those jerks you sent to pick me up got lost and drove me out into the godamn what?

JED: (*Pushing him.*) Out of my line of fire you lame-brained son-of-a-bitch!

(*POW!* TORSKI *decks him.*)

TORSKI: (*Crosses to* DON) Who the fuck is that clown?

DEATH: (*Rushing to* JEDEDIAH.) Get up! Get up! Shoot him! Shoot him!

BROTHER: Naw, it's over. You never did know when you were beaten.

DEATH: I am never beaten.

BROTHER: Aw hell, some one beats you every day.

DON: (*To* TORSKI) Coach, the show's over. We don't need your speech.

TORSKI: Fine with me. Just don't forget to send me my what?

DON: Your check.

TORSKI: (*As he exits.*) Right.

BROTHER: (*Crossing to* DON.) You did it, old buddy. The ballroom's a madhouse, look! People tearin' down the banners. TV getting it all.

DON: It's the end of the Esprey.

NANCY: Don, I'm so proud of you.

HOERNER: You pulled it off, fella!

JARVIS: Nice work. I'd stay for the celebration but I gotta' go dynamite a chemical company. (*He runs off.*)

JED: (*Staggering to his feet.*) Which way'd he go?

LEON: Who?

JED: (*As he runs off.*) Anybody.

DEATH: (*Following* JED) Come back here with that gun!

LEON: Don, do you realize this could be the end of *Show Biz For Big Biz*? This could be our Agamemnon!

DON: I'm sorry, Leon, but . . .

LEON: Don, Don, how could this happen. That Torski speech you . . .

DON: Gee don't ask me Leon. I just read it. Shorty wrote it. Comprez vous, Shorty?

SHORTY: What! Jesus! (*He runs out into the audience.*)

LEON: Shorty, wait! Don't leave me to face the musicians! Shorty, I thought we were all for one and two to make ready! Shorty! (*Chases* SHORTY *into the audience.*)

HOERNER: Well, Nancy, I guess the Earthwatchers are finished here, so . . .

DON: (*As* NANCY *starts to go.*) Nancy! If . . . well, if a guy wanted to get back together with a woman. That is, a woman he hadn't appreciated the way he should. And since that woman was with him in a hotel and the kids were with her folks, would that woman consider moving her bags into his room?

NANCY: Is that a syllogism or a proposition?

(*They embrace. As they do,* HOERNER *shakes hands with the* BROTHER.)

HOERNER: Well, I'll be going then. See you next Monday, right?

BROTHER: I'll be there.

(HOERNER *exits.*)

DON: What's Monday?

BROTHER: He's on the board of a college, back East. Hired me. I'm gonna' teach mythology.

BOBBI: (*Entering*) One helluva' finale, huh? Place is full of balloons and pigeon shit and somebody just drove the Esprey into the orchestra pit. (*Sees* BROTHER) How ya' doin'?

BROTHER: You know each other?

BOBBI: I was running away from a conventioneer when this guy trots up and asks me how many miles I'm doin'. Next thing I know is I'm in this incredibly complex conversation and doing laps 'round Caesar's Palace.

DON: Well, Bobbi, I'd like you to meet my wife, Nancy.

BOBBI: (*Sincerely, as she shakes* NANCY'S *hand.*) Hi, I've heard so much about you.

DON: What do you say we all celebrate by having dinner? Maybe champagne.

(*They start to exit right.* DEATH *stands there. He is dressed in a long black cloak and hood. He holds a scythe. In other words, he has become the faceless spectre we all know and dread.*)

DEATH: Hold! You're not going anywhere. The play is not over. The curtain is not down. The lights have not faded to black. Total, unending, black. I do that.

DON: (*To others*) Excuse me a moment. (*Crosses to* DEATH) Listen, you're scaring the two ladies and . . .

DEATH: They're about to watch you die.

DON: Jesus, don't you ever give up? Look, it's been a really interesting experience meeting you, but . . .

DEATH: Oh very blithe! But you haven't met me, Buster. Not really. You haven't felt the steel grip of my fingers on your heart. Tasted the cold, bitter . . .

DON: Yes, yes. You've got a lock on scariness, no doubt about it. (*Confidentially*) But see, what I've noticed is . . . you can't get anyone by yourself. You need help. And since I'm no longer your partner in my destruction . . . well, there's not a hell of a lot you can do till the clock runs out. And that's not going to be tonight. (*Beat*) Now, you're welcome to join us for dinner if you promise not to bully the waiters . . . ? No? (*Shrugs and crosses back to others.*) Let's go.

BOBBI: (*As they start off.*) Who was that guy you were talking to?

DON: A bartender.

BOBBI: Yeah? Looks just like a choreographer I once knew.

BROTHER: I knew a choreographer in Viet Nam. Name was Howard Sycamore. We called him "Twinkle Toes". Well, he wasn't actually a choreographer, but one day he sat on a scorpion and . . .

(*And they are offstage.*)

(DEATH *has not moved. He flicks off his hood and strides toward the audience. His manner is a bit fierce.*)

DEATH: No problem. I had the wrong man, that's all. Come back next week. I'll give you a heroic death. No problem. I'll find someone made of steel. Someone who'll follow the road to glory. Not some shilly-shallying fool who bends and retreats and wanders aimlessly like a stream dodging around rocks. I'll find someone unafraid to reach for the gun. I'll find a star for my show! Perhaps . . . one of you?

(*He is peering into the audience as the* LIGHTS *fade to black.*)

End of Play

Jim Leonard, Jr.

The Diviners

JIM LEONARD, JR. is also the author of *And They Dance Real Slow in Jackson*, which was performed at the Hudson Guild Theatre in 1985. After completing *The Diviners*, he spent the next several years writing screenplays for Robert Altman. Jim is currently putting the finishing touches on a new play called *A Civil War*. He received a Villager Award for playwrighting, the Midland Writers Award, and the American College Theatre Festival Playwrighting Award.

For information regarding stock and amateur production rights, contact: Samuel French, Inc., 25 West 45 Street, New York, NY 10036. For information regarding all other rights, contact: William Morris Agency, Inc., 1350 Avenue of the Americas, New York, NY 10019.

THE DIVINERS was first developed and performed by the Hanover College Theatre Group under the direction of Tom Evans and with the support of the American College Theatre Festival. The set was designed by Tom Evans. Tracy Dedrickson designed the lighting. Costumes were designed by Katy Matson, and Robert Padgett designed the sound.

BUDDY LAYMAN	John Geter
JENNIE MAE LAYMAN	Dee Meyers
FERRIS LAYMAN	Keith White
C.C. SHOWERS	Doug Rogers
NORMA HENSHAW	Susan Leis
DARLENE HENSHAW	Valerie Sherwood
BASIL BENNETT	Mark Fearnow
LUELLA BENNETT	Shannon Robinson
GOLDIE SHORT	Liz Hans
MELVIN WILDER	Mark Bock
DEWEY MAPLES	Clint Allen

THE DIVINERS was first professionally produced by the Circle Repertory Company in 1980 under the direction of Tom Evans. The set was designed by John Lee Beatty. Jennifer von Mayrhauser designed the costumes. Areden Fingerhut created the lighting. James M. Arnemann was the stage manager.

BUDDY LAYMAN	Robert MacNaughton
JENNIE MAE LAYMAN	Lisa Pelikan
FERRIS LAYMAN	Jimmie Ray Weeks
C.C. SHOWERS	Timothy Shelton
NORMA HENSHAW	Jacqueline Brookes
DARLENE HENSHAW	Laura Hughes
BASIL BENNETT	Jack Davidson
LUELLA BENNETT	Elizabeth Sturges
GOLDIE SHORT	Mollie Collison
MELVIN WILDER	Ben Siegler
DEWEY MAPLES	John Dossett

Setting

The play takes place in the homes, fields, and public gathering places of the mythical southern Indiana town of Zion, population forty. A small and rural community with a few houses and farms along the river.

The entire play takes place on one set without any carry-on tables or chairs, etc. The set should be raked and smooth enough for an actor to pull himself over it on his belly. The starting point for the design should be the final scene.

Lighting

Lights should convey time, place and mood. A sky would be nice.

All the night scenes, and there are several, happen during full moon. So the night light can be fairly bright and still believable.

The river light must be an absolutely solid swash of color with a definite depth line. The well light, which attunes us to the use of light as water, should probably be a lighter shade of river-color.

Props

The Cafe can be dealt with by simply giving the proprietor a tray with several coffee cups, etc. All the Dry-Goods needs is a jar of jelly beans and a small sack of healing salts. There's no need for line on the fishing poles.

Anything live, such as the birds, worms, etc., should simply be assumed and seen in the eye of the actor.

Style

These are good and simple people. They have nothing but the best of intentions.

First Elegy

(*A dulcimer plays "Amazing Grace" as the lights rise. There are two pin spots: one is isolating* BASIL *and the other on* DEWEY. *The farmer and farmhand speak directly to the audience but not to each other; they speak as if they know the people in the theatre the way a man knows his neighbors. The dulcimer fades into the story.*)

BASIL: Now. Just before Buddy Layman passed beyond us there was a storm to the sky like no other. I was workin out to the back fields, down along the crick there, when I first felt the air start to changin. I looked at the clouds. I heard the wind blowin. And I says to myself, "Basil," I says, "Don't stand out here like a fool to the field. Get the tools to the barn fore the storm hits!"

DEWEY: And I run like the wind right after the boy died. Callin all over town for his father. I fly by the Dry-Goods and on through the Diner, looking clean over Zion to find him.

BASIL: So I set the tools down and I turned my head to see the air all in motion above me. I'm standin there, near the barn there for shelter, and the clouds're as dark as the land is long—circlin and swirlin like a fire to the sky!

DEWEY: And I looked!

BASIL: And I seen it!

DEWEY: And I hollered!

BASIL: And I knew!

DEWEY: I says, "Ferris! Ferris! He's dead now for certain." (*A moment. Then quietly:*) Buddy Layman . . . he's passed on beyond us.

BASIL: (*Softly*) And like a slate wiped clean or a fever washed away where there was fire to the sky now there's nothin. Where there was clouds there's just blue and the sun.

DEWEY: His only son gone and it's me who brings the word when Ferris comes to his door in the mornin. I seen him there like he's a wood stick carvin in the wood frame door and they're welded together in grievin. I says, "Ferris . . . I'm sorry." And he don't move and don't speak. I says, "Yor son, he's passed on beyond us." (DEWEY's *light fades. He exits. Moonlit night as* BASIL *speaks:*)

BASIL: The idiot boy is dead, don't you see? Buddy Layman's gone. There's no tellin the weather. When he said it would rain we layed our fields in rows and we knew it would be a good season. You see, a man works, a man waits, and he hopes and he plans, but it was the boy who told us the weather. And that boy . . . he was somethin. Somethin else for a fact. He couldn't talk for two cents or take the time to tie his shoes, but he seemed to know things you figured nobody knew. Without drillin rigs or men with machines—without nothin but a willow rod in his hands—Buddy Layman came onto my land in late spring and he set himself to witchin a well. Call it vein-findin, water-witchin, smellin, seekin or divinin, . . . the body had a touch and a feel for water.

Act One

The Earth and the Water

(The boy searches for water with a long forked stick. He overlaps and repeats the word "water" three times whenever it is mentioned during the dowsing. His head is turned up and his eyes are nearly closed as he follows the sense of the stick. DEWEY, MELVIN, and LUELLA enter and are immediately involved in the scene:)

BUDDY: Water water water . . .

BASIL: Come on, boy. You'll find her.

DEWEY: (*To* MELVIN) Would you look at him go?

MELVIN: Witchin ain't nothin. It's that stick there that does all the work, Dew.

DEWEY: Like hell it's the stick.

MELVIN: Like hell if it ain't.

DEWEY: Bud knows what he's doin.

MELVIN: He knows next to nothin.

DEWEY: Hell if he don't.

MELVIN: Hell if he does.

BASIL: If you fellas keep up this ruckus you'll throw the boy off! Now how many times have I told you tonight this dowsin's a delicate business.

LUELLA: I doubt he's gonna find any water.

BASIL: Luella, the signs're all right on the money. It's a full moon, it's May, not to mention a wind from the east.

LUELLA: The signs don't find water. You want water you hire a drill rig.

BASIL: Luella.

LUELLA: We've been chasin around through the fields half the night and there's no sign of nothin at all.

BASIL: Just give the boy time.

LUELLA: How's he gonna find any water whin he won't even touch it? He don't wash, he don't bathe. The boy's dirt head to toe. I mean, Basil, he's not even baptized.

BASIL: That's cause he feels it right to the bone, don't you see?

BUDDY: (*Sudden*) Water. He feels water!

DEWEY: He's on it now, Basil!

MELVIN: He's on it but good!

BUDDY: He's on it!

DEWEY: You'll find her!

BUDDY: He'll find her!

MELVIN: Let the stick show you!

BASIL: Come on, boy!

DEWEY: Water!

BUDDY: Find water!

MELVIN: Water, boy!

BUDDY: Water!

LUELLA: Lord, Basil!

BUDDY: Water!

BASIL: You'll find her!

(*The* WELL-DIGGERS *coach the boy on, building on the suggested lines for them below, as the stick reaches higher and higher.* BUDDY's *entire frame tenses as he comes closer and closer:*)

BUDDY	WELL-DIGGERS
Water! Find Water! Ground, you got to give water! Water, ground! Water! He's got to find water! Now, ground! Give water! Water! Water, ground! Now!	Come on, Bud! You'll find her! Dowse it, boy! Water!

(*The stick suddenly begins to bend. Everyone falls silent. The stick bends nearly in half:*)

LUELLA: (*Softly*) Sweet Jesus in Heaven would you look at that?

(BUDDY *drops the stick and drops to his knees, exhausted:*)

BUDDY: He got you some water . . . he got you some.

BASIL: You done just fine, boy. You done fine by me.

BUDDY: He's a good guy, Basil?

BASIL: You're a good guy, Buddy Layman.

BUDDY: Wooboy!

MELVIN: (*Shaking the boy's hand.*) You hit her right on the money!

DEWEY: (*Shaking the other hand.*) You done real good Bud.

MELVIN: Done a damn fine job. Damn fine.

BASIL: (*Partial overlap*) Let's get to work—

DEWEY: I never saw such a job.

MELVIN: It's a hell of a job.

BASIL: (*Taking charge*) I'm not paying you boys to stand around cussin and shakin hands half the night. Now run up the barn and get the shovels.

(MELVIN *and* DEWEY *run off.* BUDDY *starts to follow:*)

BUDDY: You want him to help you?

BASIL: (*Stopping the boy.*) You done your fair share, Bud. Now you can tell your Dad I'll be sendin over a dozen or so bushels a corn and wax beans come this fall. You remember to tell him I thank you.

BUDDY: You thank him?

BASIL: I thank you, my friend. (BASIL *exits to the barn.* LUELLA *has the stick:*)

LUELLA: Hey, honey? You wouldn't want a show Luella how to work thes thing would you?

BUDDY: How to work it?

LUELLA: How to make her find water.

BUDDY: (*Demonstrates*) Well . . . he shuts his eyes.

LUELLA: (*Holds the stick out and does so.*) Yeah?

BUDDY: And he thinks on his Mama.

JENNIE MAE: (*Calling from off-stage, as if the boy's in the distance.*) Buddy—?

LUELLA: Your Mama?

JENNIE MAE: Buddy—?

LUELLA: You think a her whin you try to find water?

(BUDDY *crosses to his sister as she enters. The two scenes, one at the well and one at the Layman's happen on opposite sides to the stage. The sun's beginning to rise:*)

JENNIE MAE: I can't take my eyes off you for two seconds, little brother, without you're runnin off all over the fields.

BUDDY: Well, he's playin, Jennie Mae.

JENNIE MAE: (*Holds the broom out.*) And you're supposed to be sweepin.

BUDDY: What're we gonna do with that boy? He can't do nothin right,

Jennie Mae. See that broom right there? He couldn't make it get to workin. And you seen how he done with his shoes.

JENNIE MAE: Buddy.

BUDDY: (*Pulling his shoes out from under the set.*) His sister says, "Buddy, you keep them shoes on your dogs. Them feet ain't supposed to get naked." And would you look how he does like he's dumber than dirt?

(MELVIN *and* DEWEY *enter with a post hole digger and a shovel. There should be a trap where the boy divined water. As the farmworkers dig they step into it, working their way deeper and deeper:*)

JENNIE MAE: Don't call yourself names.

BUDDY: He can't help it he's daffy.

JENNIE MAE: Now Bud.

BUDDY: He's a looney little coot for sure.

DEWEY: Let's get to workin.

JENNIE MAE: Let's get your boots on.

BUDDY: He don't want to wear boots.

JENNIE MAE: Buddy.

MELVIN: Let's get some dirt into it, Dewey.

DEWEY: (*Referring to a shovelful.*) It's a good chunk a diggin.

MELVIN: There ain't enought dirt there to hide a worm, Dewey.

DEWEY: Listen, Melvin. I'm at thes hole workin. I'm standin here sweatin and you're doin nothin but lean on that post holer.

MELVIN: You tryin' to say I don't know how to dig, huh? You tryin' to tell me what's what with a shovel? Will listen, Dewey, I been through the best damn trainin Uncle Sam's got to offer. Got sent through basic trainin two times in a row. Now I may not know much but I know what's what with a shovel.

DEWEY: Then why don't you use it?

MELVIN: Why don't you give me a little room, Dew? Give me a little room, pal, I'll tear this hole up.

(BASIL *enters with another shovel. He takes charge immediately:*)

BASIL: Would you fellas shut up and get diggin for water?

LUELLA: You're not gonna find us a well out here, Basil. There's nothin but mud in that hole.

BASIL: Luella.

LUELLA: I tried this stick, Basil. I give her a shake and it's worth next to nothin. You're wastin your time on that hole.

JENNIE MAE: Take your time with those laces.

BUDDY: Well he can't make 'em tie.

LUELLA: Buddy Layman's not crazy. He's just smart enough to fool with you, Basil. Leave you diggin out here after nothin. When a farm needs a well you got to use a machine.

(DEWEY *is in the trap. They pass him tools as if in delicate surgery:*)

DEWEY: Shovel.

MELVIN: Shovel.

LUELLA: Even a fool knows that folks need a drill-rig for water. Sticks and shovels get you nowhere in this land.

DEWEY: Post holer.

MELVIN: Post holer.

LUELLA: Indiana is nothin but rocks and mud, Basil. Clean down to China it's rocks and mud and mud and rocks and it takes a full-sized drill rig to dig down to water.

BASIL: Put your back at it, Dew.

LUELLA: But no, you wouldn d listen. You won't use a machine. And there you all sit to your elbows in mud and plain to see you're gettin nowhere but dirty.

BASIL: Lean into it, Dew. Heave some weight on it, boy—

DEWEY: (*Partial overlap*) Basil, hold it! Hold on . . .

(DEWEY *lowers himself completely into the well as* SHOWERS *enters on the other side of the stage. He carries two beat up old suitcases. He's worn out.*)

BASIL: Water . . . ?

SHOWERS: (*Looking at the sky.*) Lord God A'mighty.

(*A light shines up from the well:*)

DEWEY: (*Amazed*) My feet're gettin wet . . . !

BASIL: Water! Luella, there's water!

LUELLA: Water.

BUDDY: He did it! He tied em! BUDDY *jumps up and there is simultaneous celebration at the well and at the Layman's.* SHOWERS *remains where he is:*)

BASIL	BUDDY
Water. I told you he'd find it.	Tied his shoes by his self!
MELVIN	JENNIE MAE
Waaaooo!	You're a good boy.
BASIL	BUDDY
We hit the vein!	He tied em!
DEWEY	JENNIE MAE
Water!	You sure did!
MELVIN AND DEWEY	BUDDY
Waaaaooooo!	He's a good guy!

BASIL: Grab the shovels, boys! Let's get a drunk on!

(*The* WELL-DIGGERS *exit and* BUDDY *grabs the broom. He sweeps enthusiastically as* SHOWERS *crosses to the Layman's:*)

SHOWERS: Lord God in Heaven I'm tired.

BUDDY: Tied his shoes by his self, he's gonna sweep by his self! He's sweepin and sweepin—

JENNIE MAE: Buddy, stay on the porch.

BUDDY: He's cleanin his yard, Jennie Mae.

JENNIE MAE: Buddy.

BUDDY: He's sweepin and sweepin . . . (BUDDY *sweeps into* SHOWERS.)

SHOWERS: Hi.

BUDDY: Hi . . .

JENNIE MAE: Can I help you with somethin?

SHOWERS: Well, to tell you the truth, Ma'am, I'm lost.

JENNIE MAE: What you lookin for?

SHOWERS: I'm not lookin for nothin too special here, Ma'am. I'm just kinda curious where I am at the moment. (SHOWERS *is a bit of a fast-talker:*) I had me a fitful night a dreamin, you see, got myself all turned around in my sleep. And when I woke up this mornin I looked at the road one way there and then I turned and took a look up the other—and what do you think I said?

BUDDY: What?

SHOWERS: I says, well, I'm fit to be tied if Indiana don't look at all the same no matter which way you turn! I says to myself, "C.C. Showers," I says, "You're about as lost on this road as a small ball in tall grass. Just stuck up like a boot in the mud." Couldn't tell comin from goin or which end was up—till I seen my friend over here given the grass the once over. And I says, "Now there's a man who cares about the land that he stands on." I says, "Here's a fella who can tell me where I am."

BUDDY: (*Proud*) You're at Buddy Layman's house.

SHOWERS: I had a sneakin suspicion I might be.

BUDDY: Yeah. It's his house all right. Them's his windows, his door, his porch. And this girl right here? She's his sister.

JENNIE MAE: Buddy.

BUDDY: You gonna sweet talk her, Mr.? You want him to maybe get lost?

JENNIE MAE: You just get back to sweepin.

BUDDY: Aw, he's tired a sweepin.

SHOWERS: You know you can't be too clean, pal.

BUDDY: Huh?

SHOWERS: I says a fine and upstandin young fella like yourself ought to love keepin clean.

BUDDY: You ain't gonna wash him?

JENNIE MAE: Are you sellin soap or something, Mister?

SHOWERS: No, Ma'am.

BUDDY: You ain't gonna put him in water?

SHOWERS: In water?

BUDDY: Jennie Mae, don't let that guy wash him!

JENNIE MAE: Now what do you want a go scarin him for? He never done nothin to you!

SHOWERS: Now wait a minute—

JENNIE MAE: You just come walkin up here out of a clear blue and go teasin folks you don't hardly know!

SHOWERS: Now hold the boat, Ma'am! I only stopped cause I'm lookin to help folks!

JENNIE MAE: Are you one a them Mormons?

SHOWERS: To put it real plain, Ma'am—I'm in need of a job.

JENNIE MAE: Well, we're not givin handouts.

SHOWERS: I'm not wantin a handout, I'm wantin to work! You name it, I'll do it. Yard work, house work, cleanin or mowin. I'll milk the chickens, I'll pluck the cows. (*Pause.*) I'm willin to work the whole day for just food. I'm not a big eater. Little tiny portions. To look at me eat you'd think I was raised by the birds. A crumb here, a crumb there.

BUDDY: (*Concerned*) Ain't you had you some breakfast?

SHOWERS: Not lately, my friend . . .

JENNIE MAE: Maybe you better talk to my Daddy.

SHOWERS: If it wouldn't put you to no trouble.

JENNIE MAE: (*Exiting*) S'no trouble at'all, Mister.

BUDDY: What's your name, Mister?

JENNIE MAE: (*Calling, on her way offstage.*) Daddy?

SHOWERS: C.C.

BUDDY: You think you're maybe gonna stick around awhile, C.C.?

SHOWERS: It all depends, Bud.

BUDDY: They's lots a stuff here you know?

SHOWERS: There is, huh?

BUDDY: Yeah! They's lots a good stuff. You see the woods over ther don't you?

SHOWERS: Bud, I sure do.

BUDDY: Well that's where the birds live.

SHOWERS: Do they, now?

BUDDY: Yeah! Way up the trees they do. Way up the leafs.

SHOWERS: Now that's a good thing to know.

BUDDY: You see the ground right there don't you?

SHOWERS: Mr. Layman, I do.

BUDDY: Well that's where the doddle bugs are.

SHOWERS: Well, you're just chock-full a knowledge, my friend.

BUDDY: He thunk he might be.

SHOWERS: (*As if he didn't hear right.*) I beg your pardon?

BUDDY: He says he thunk he might be.

SHOWERS: (*Unsure*) Now you're talkin about you?

BUDDY: Yeah. Can't you hear him?

SHOWERS: Yeah. Yeah, pal, I hear you.

BUDDY: You see the sky up there, pal?

SHOWERS: Bud, I'm looking right at it.

BUDDY: You know who lives up there?

SHOWERS: Who?

BUDDY: (*Amazed*) Jesus.

SHOWERS: Way up there?

BUDDY: Jesus Son a God does.

SHOWERS: What do you figure he does up there, Bud?

BUDDY: (*Thinks this over.*) Well . . . he's maybe got him a little house.

SHOWERS: (*Interested*) Yeah?

BUDDY: Yeah. Maybe got him a runnin toilet inside.

SHOWERS: Now that's a good thing to have.

BUDDY: He thunk it might be.

SHOWERS: Mr Layman, it does my heart good to meet a man who knows his way around the Church.

BUDDY: We ain't got no Church, C.C. Don't you know nothin?

SHOWERS: Your Mama taught you the Gospel at home, huh?

BUDDY: His mama?

SHOWERS: Yeah.

BUDDY: (*Concerned*) You ain't seen her?

SHOWERS: No . . .

BUDDY: He can't find her nowhere, C.C.

SHOWERS: (*Gentle concern*) How long she's been gone?

BUDDY: Well he ain't sure no more. He looks in his house and his yard and the woods and he can't find her nowhere.

SHOWERS: Well, I'd imagine she'll be home before long, don't you think?

BUDDY: Sometimes he hears her. Sometimes at night he hears her right there . . . and her voice is right there . . . like he can touch her almost, when he's sleepin . . .

SHOWERS: (*Gentle*) You mean your Mama's passed away, Bud?

BUDDY: You know where she is?

SHOWERS: Well, . . . I'd imagine she's livin in Heaven. You know what angels are, don't you?

BUDDY: What?

SHOWERS: Angels're what we call the people in Heaven. The folks on beyond us, you see?

BUDDY: What's angels do?

SHOWERS: For the most part they all tend to fly around singin.

BASIL: (*Likes this idea.*) Angels can fly?

SHOWERS: That's what they say.

BUDDY: Like the birds?

SHOWERS: Like the birds.

(FERRIS *enters. He's a greasy mechanic.* BUDDY *runs to him:*)

BUDDY: Hey, Dad, she's up to the sky! His Mama's flyin with Jesus!

(FERRIS *might swing his son around some. He enjoys playing with the boy. Likes teasing him:*)

FERRIS: You're gonna be up to the sky like to never come down, you don't finish your chores before noon, boy.

BUDDY: Well he's talkin to C.C.

FERRIS: You made you a friend, huh?

BUDDY: (*A secret*) That guy ain't had nothin to eat, Dad.

FERRIS: (*Eyes him over.*) So you're the fella that's lookin to work, huh?

SHOWERS: (*Crosses to* FERRIS, *hand out to shake.*) C.C. Showers, sir.

FERRIS: Ferris Layman, Mr. Showers. Chew tobacco?

SHOWERS: No, sir.

FERRIS: (*Taking a plug out.*) Well, you oughta! A man wants to work in a garage then he's gotta chew somethin. Can't hire a fella that's prissy.

SHOWERS: (*Takes the plug.*) Thank you kindly.

FERRIS: It's a good tastin' plug, huh?

SHOWERS: (*It tastes awful.*) Real tasty.

FERRIS: Don't swaller it, Mister! Hell, the whole point's to spit!

SHOWERS: Beg your pardon.

FERRIS: Too late, huh? Can I get you some water?

SHOWERS: I'm fine. Just fine.

FERRIS: I'd offer you more but with Hoover in office there ain't a lot more to be had, huh?

SHOWERS: I hear you.

FERRIS: (*Making sure*) You're a democrat, ain't you? Not votin for Hoover?

SHOWERS: Not by a long shot.

FERRIS: I don't mean to be nosy but no man votin' for Hoover is working for me.

SHOWERS: Folks vote for Hoover there'll be nobody workin.

FERRIS: Damn Hoover. Those government guys don't know shit from shine-ola.

SHOWERS: Nope.

FERRIS: Here we sit with half the damn country wound up as tight as a shock spring and Hoover won't let a man drink.

(BUDDY *has found his way to the two suitcases. He is sitting between them:*)

BUDDY: Ain't you figure they's maybe somethin to drink in these boxes?

SHOWERS: Well, they're mainly full a nothin, my friend.

BUDDY: Ain't you figure they's maybe a little rootbeer down in em?

FERRIS: Don't be so darn nosy.

BUDDY: He ain't gonna hurt nothin, Dad. He's gonna haul em around some. Like he's a helper, you know? Like C.C.

SHOWERS: Make a deal, my friend?

BUDDY: Word a Honor, C.C.?

SHOWERS: You can haul these cases around town for awhile if you promise to bring 'em right back.

BUDDY: (*Serious*) Lick your hand, C.C. (BUDDY *licks his palm and holds it out.* SHOWERS *understands, does the same, and they rub palms together in a solemn vow of sorts.* BUDDY *then walks and talks his way offstage with the cases:*) Ain't gonna drop these boxes for nothin. No sir. Ain't gonna nose down inside em or bang em up nohow. He knows they ain't no rootbeer down in em. He's a good guy, that Buddy. Word a honor, he is.

SHOWERS: (*Smiles*) I'd imagine bein a Daddy gets to be a full time business.

FERRIS: Hell, there ain't nothin to it. I raise em like weeds.

SHOWERS: Like weeds, Mr. Layman?

FERRIS: You can pull em or trim em or hedge em on back some, but you're best off to just leave em go. You ever seen a weed that ain't healthy?

SHOWERS: No.

FERRIS: Same way with kids. If a car breaks, you fix it—if a tire's flat, patch it. But kids're just fine on their own.

SHOWERS: Mr. Layman, I take it you like cars.

FERRIS: Mr. Showers, I love em. Nash, Buicks, DeSotos—you name it. Plus there's a whole world a tractors. Your John Deere, Farm-All, Fords a course.

SHOWERS: Yeah—

FERRIS: Nothin like a good solid engine.

SHOWERS: No sir.

FERRIS: You ever tear down a six banger?

SHOWERS: That's quite an engine.

FERRIS: Hell of an engine. Course a flathead'll put it to shame.

SHOWERS: I'd imagine.

FERRIS: Can you rebuild a flathead?

SHOWERS: Is that a car or a tractor? *Pause)*

FERRIS: Never heard of a flathead tractor.

SHOWERS: It's a car, huh?

FERRIS: (*Suspicious*) Can you at least tear down a carburetor?

(SHOWERS *shakes his head.*)

FERRIS: Fuel pump? Ignition?

SHOWERS: Well—

FERRIS: Steerin or tires?

(SHOWERS *shakes his head.*)

FERRIS: You can't patch a damn tire? Where the hell a you been?

SHOWERS: I been walkin, Mr. Layman, for close to three months. I hardly rode in a car, let alone try to fix one. But I'm needin a job awful bad, see? Just enough work to feed me.

FERRIS: If I knew what you did it might be I could help you.

SHOWERS: Well there wasn't much work back in Hazard, Kentucky. I mean, I quit what I did, see?

FERRIS: Quit a good job for nothin?

SHOWERS: I couldn't do it no more.

FERRIS: You walked off the job when there's no work for miles?

SHOWERS: I had to leave.

FERRIS: (*Pushing*) Did they fire you?

SHOWERS: No—

FERRIS: Did you run in the law?

SHOWERS: I just couldn't keep workin.

FERRIS: What the hell'd you do?

SHOWERS: (*Nearly angry*) It don't matter no more!

FERRIS: (*Starts to walk away.*) I can't hire a man don't know what he does,

SHOWERS: I'm lookin to start all again, don't you see? I been lookin to work the whole time I been walkin.

FERRIS: You're wastin my time, mister. (*Starts to exit.*)

SHOWERS: Listen, Mr. Layman. To tell you the truth . . . I's a preacher.

FERRIS: Teacher?

SHOWERS: No. A Bible-totin preacher. (*Pause.* FERRIS *smiles:*)

FERRIS: Aw now, you're full a shit.

SHOWERS: I ain't preachin no more though—

FERRIS: You full a shit, ain't you?

SHOWERS: I quit! I give it up altogether! (FERRIS *smiles.*) I ain't preached for three months in a row, Mr. Layman. Went close to twelve years then I quit, now I'm done.

FERRIS: You really a preacher?

(JENNIE MAE *enters with her brother in tow. The boy has both suitcases, but they're significantly lighter:*)

SHOWERS: I was! I ain't preachin no more, though.

BUDDY: (*Protesting*) Word of honor, Jennie Mae! Word a honor!

FERRIS: A Bible bangin, Jesus jumpin, Heaven and hellfire preacher!

JENNIE MAE: You tell Mr. Showers the truth Buddy Layman!

BUDDY: He ain't done nothin wrong!

JENNIE MAE: (*Gives her brother a whack on the tail.*) Just you tell him.

BUDDY: (*Demonstrating*) Well . . . He was just walkin, see, C. . . . C? Till his arms get to feelin kinda lousy, see. So he says, maybe he'll feel better, he gets him some rootbeer. On account a them boxes're heavy and his arm's hurtin somethin awful . . .

FERRIS: You didn't take somethin outta those cases now, boy?

BASIL: (*Innocent*) No siree, Dad. They ain't nothin in em.

FERRIS: Nothin in em?

BUDDY: Nope. Not no rootbeer nor nothin. (*He sets the luggage by* SHOWERS *and holds up his hand in the sign of the pledge.*) Word a honor, C.C.

(SHOWERS *open the suitcases. They are empty.*)

FERRIS: You mean the boy dumped all you stuff out?

SHOWERS: They're a little easier to carry now, yeah.

FERRIS: All your clothes?

JENNIE MAE: Your blankets—

SHOWERS: My bedroll—

BUDDY: Your Bible—

SHOWERS: My Bible.

FERRIS: Everything?

SHOWERS: Seems to be the case. (*Slight pause*)

BUDDY: (*Innocently*) Well . . . he figures he better take him a little walk for now, Dad.

FERRIS: (*Grabs the boy's arm.*) Hold still a minute, Bud.

BUDDY: He don't want a sit still!

FERRIS: Well you're gonna sit still till you tell us what you did with his things, boy.

SHOWERS: Now Mr. Layman.

FERRIS: Now some things don't irk me, Mr. Showers, but stealin the clothes off the back of a preacher ain't quite on my list a sittin still for.

JENNIE MAE: A preacher!

FERRIS: A marryin-buryin, readin-revivin, devil and damnation preacher, Jennier Mae. And your little brother, who somebody was supposed to be watchin, just stole everything the man owns!

JENNIE MAE: I can't be watchin him all the time, Daddy.

FERRIS: I can't be watchin him either.

JENNIE MAE: I dress him, I feed him, I walk him all over the place—

BUDDY: He don't want a sit still!

JENNIE MAE: I need time to spend with my friends, damnit!

FERRIS: Would you knock off the cussin? He's a preacher I told you.

JENNIE MAE: I don't care if he preaches!

BUDDY: Stop screamin!

JENNIE MAE: I'm not screamin!

FERRIS: This man's a preacher!

SHOWERS: Now hold it! Hold the boat, will you? (*All commotion stops. He preaches:*) I was a preacher, but I ain't preachin now. I don't do prayers or lead songs and I give up on sermons. It's no sin to change and I've changed! (*Slight pause.*) I give it up. (SHOWERS *picks up his luggage and starts to exit:*)

BUDDY: Ain't you gonna stick around here some?

SHOWERS: I come this far. I'll get by just fine.

JENNIE MAE: With no clothes?

FERRIS: Without nothin?

BUDDY: Aw, C.C., don't leave him.

SHOWERS: (*Stops*) Aw now, Bud.

JENNIE MAE: He could sleep in the barn, Daddy.

SHOWERS: No, I don't mean to burden.

FERRIS: I don't mean to take offense, but my barn ought to be good enough for a good man to sleep in.

JENNIE MAE: (*Exiting*) I'll get you some blankets.

SHOWERS: (*Crossing back to* FERRIS *and the boy.*) Now listen, Mr. Layman. I'm willin to work for my keep, see?

FERRIS: And I'm willin to make you keep workin, C.C. (FERRIS *takes one of the suitcases and exits to the barn.* BUDDY *starts to follow:*)

BUDDY: Come on, C.C.

SHOWERS: Hey, Bud. You don't happen to have any idea where you might a walked with my things do you?

BUDDY: Nope. How bout you?

SHOWERS: You sure you don't know?

BUDDY: He knows where theys birds at though C.C. Out the barn—way up the roofters. Theys big birds and little birds, baby birds and mamma birds—theys flyin all over like angels.

SHOWERS: (*Exiting with the boy.*) No, now the angels're way up in Heaven there, Bud, and the birds're here in Indiana.

(NORMA *enters singing "Rock of Ages." She mops the floor in her store as she sings.* LUELLA *enters and watches* NORMA *mop.* NORMA *should stop singing abruptly as* LUELLA *finishes her speech:*)

SHOWERS: (*Continued*) It's a whole world a difference, my friend.

NORMA: "Rock of Ages, cleft for me,
Let me hid myself in Thee;
Let the water and the blood,
From Thy wounded side which flowed
Be of sin the double cure,
Cleanse me from its guilt and power—"

LUELLA: (*Overlapping*) I know why you're singin, Norma Henshaw. You're singin and cleaning the whole Dry-Goods top to bottom on account a that new slick-talking preacher.

NORMA: Luella.

LUELLA: Now, Norma, for all we know this guy is a smooth-talkin con man. We don't know nothin about him.

NORMA: We know he's a preacher.

LUELLA: What Church is he with?

NORMA: Why Luella, he's a Christian a course.

LUELLA: Well that doesn't mean you can trust him you know.

NORMA: I been prayin for this for ten years in a row. I don't ask the Lord much, I don't pester him, see? But I have made a few small requests. The Lord knows how the town needs a preacher, Luella.

LUELLA: But what kind a preacher'd work in a garage?

NORMA: Well we can't afford to be picky.

LUELLA: By picky!

NORMA: We been ten solid years without singin or savin or baptizin, period. The Lord's answered our prayers, don't you see?

LUELLA: Well I don't know, Norma.

NORMA: Don't be so darn doubtful, Leulla. So down in the mouth. Why, just look at Goldie next door. She's been spickin and spannin for days in a row just to let that man know how he's welcome.

(SHOWERS, BUDDY, *and* FERRIS *enter:*)

GOLDIE: Why you fellas're just as welcome as welcome can be.

BUDDY: Got any rootbeer here, Goldie?

GOLDIE: What kind a Diner'd I run without rootbeer?

BUDDY: Pretty lousy.

GOLDIE: (*Handing him one.*) Well it wouldn't be the Dine-Away-Cafe. Just made some fresh coffee, boys.

FERRIS: Coffee sounds fine.

GOLDIE: I'd expect you been showin our new friend around town, huh?

FERRIS: Ain't much to see.

GOLDIE: Why there's the Dry-Goods and the Diner and the view a the river. Not to mention the place where the Church was. You seen the Church ain't you?

SHOWERS: Guess it must a slipped by me.

FERRIS: Ain't nothin left but the foundation, Goldie.

GOLDIE: (*To* SHOWERS) Well before she burned down, it was somethin I tell you. That Church had a steeple so high it put the tree tops to shame. And people? There was people all over. Those bells got to ringin and the whole town was full. Did a real good business on Sunday.

SHOWERS: You don't say?

GOLDIE: Fed more people on Sunday than the whole week together. Those Church folks're real big eaters. You want some pie with that coffee.

SHOWERS: No thanks, Ma'am. I'm fine.

GOLDIE: Apple pie, peach pie, rhubarb and cherry—whatever you wants on the house.

FERRIS: Well I'd like a donut.

GOLDIE: Plain donut's a penny, Ferris. Glazed're two cents.

FERRIS: Plain, thank you.

BUDDY: How bout you get him a rootbeer?

GOLDIE: (*A little surprised.*) You're not done with that last one?

BUDDY: Ain't no more down in it.

GOLDIE: You're gonna throw off your whole constitution, you know that? You drink and drink and drink and drink—you will make yourself irregular. (*She hands him a rootbeer.*)

BUDDY: You regular, Dad?

FERRIS: Hell I'm fine.

GOLDIE: (*Crossing off to get a donut.*) No cussin.

SHOWERS: That Goldie's quite a woman.

FERRIS: Well she's pretty but she's pushy.

SHOWERS: I noticed.

FERRIS: Ain't nothin worse'n a damn woman gets pushy.

GOLDIE: (*Entering with a donut.*) You're gonna cuss you can eat this outside, Ferris.

FERRIS: It's a awful good-lookin donut.

GOLDIE: Don't you dare bite that donut.

FERRIS: I'm gonna pay you.

GOLDIE: You know the rules just as well as I do "No drinkin—"

FERRIS AND GOLDIE: "No Cussin" and "You Pray Before You Eat—"

FERRIS: (*To* SHOWERS) Keeps em posted right there on the sign.

GOLDIE: Care to pray?

SHOWERS: I beg pardon?

GOLDIE: It's only right for the guest to say grace over meals.

SHOWERS: Well, Ma'am this ain't exactly a meal.

GOLDIE: Well you're still the guest.

FERRIS: Just give her the grace, huh?

SHOWERS: You give her the grace.

FERRIS: I'm no good at prayin.

SHOWERS: It's your donut, Ferris.

GOLDIE: It's my Diner. I'd like for our guest to say grace.

SHOWERS: Ma'am, you don't understand—

GOLDIE: You don't pray, he don't eat. (*Slight pause.*)

FERRIS: Listen C.C. I'm really kind a hungry.

SHOWERS: I know.

FERRIS: Well just run off a quick one.

SHOWERS: Aw, Ferris—

FERRIS: It's just a donut, C.C.—won't take you but a second.

GOLDIE: Bow your heads. Shut your eyes, Buddy. Pastor Showers? (*All heads are bowed but for Showers. Buddy's eyes are closed, no real semblance of prayer.* SHOWERS *looks straight ahead, eyes open. After a moment he says quite simply.*)

SHOWERS: Thanks for the donut.

FERRIS: Amen. (*Slight pause. Suspiciously:*)

GOLDIE: What Church're you with?

FERRIS: Goldie, the man means to give up on preachin.

GOLDIE: Give it up?

SHOWERS: Yes, Ma'am.

SHOWERS: I mean to stop altogether! (*Slight pause.*)

GOLDIE: In that case the coffee'll cost you a nickel.

SHOWERS: It's a good cup coffee.

FERRIS: I got her.

SHOWERS: (*To* BUDDY) You bout ready to go, pal?

(BUDDY *has taken one of his shoes off:*)

BUDDY: He ain't goin nowheres till his dogs feel better.

SHOWERS: What's a matter?

BUDDY: He's itchin.

SHOWERS: (*Looking at the boy's foot.*) Looks like a touch a the ivy.

BUDDY: Itchin like crazy, C.C.!

GOLDIE: All the boy needs is a tub a hot water. I been sayin that much for years.

BUDDY: Huh?

GOLDIE: Fever weed, salts, and a hot tub a water.

BUDDY: (*Lying*) He ain't itchin no more.

GOLDIE: You'll be itchin all over, you don't soak those feet.

FERRIS: Hell, I'm dirt head to toe and I'm fine.

GOLDIE: It ain't right not to wash.

FERRIS: Does he smell? Does he stink?

GOLDIE: That ain't the point, Ferris.

FERRIS: Half the world's made a dirt and it ain't hurtin nothin. The damn roads're all dirt, the fields're dirt. Even Hoover's got a mud pie for brains.

GOLDIE: Don't make fun a Mr. Hoover in my Diner, Ferris. Badmouthin the president's the same thing as cussin. Same exact thing to a T.

SHOWERS: Kind a fond of him, are you?

GOLDIE: I couldn't care less if Herb Hoover got hit by a truck in his sleep. But he's still the president and I won't have him badmouthed.

FERRIS: Now what'd I say that's so awful, Goldie?

GOLDIE: I'm not about to repeat it.

BUDDY: Said hell, said damn, said Hoover—

GOLDIE: You see ther! You see what it leads to?

FERRIS: Bud can cuss if he wants.

GOLDIE: He's just a boy, Ferris.

FERRIS: When I was his age I cussed all the time.

GOLDIE: He's only 14.

FERRIS: And I'll tell you what else, I'm a better man for it.

GOLDIE: You are the most bull-headed man in the world, Ferris Layman.

FERRIS: A man can't cuss, he can't hardly talk.

GOLDIE: What would your wife say? (*Pause. With true concern:*) The way you raise the boy, Ferris . . . it ain't right for him.

FERRIS: (*Softly*) Well Sara ain't here no more, Goldie.

BUDDY: (*Softly*) Dad?

FERRIS: What you need, son?

BUDDY: Dad? S'gonna rain.

FERRIS: (*Gentle*) Change a the weather'd be nice, Bud.

BUDDY: They's clouds up there, Dad. S'gonna rain somethin awful.

SHOWERS: Bud, the sky's awful blue.

FERRIS: (*Softly*) It'll rain.

BUDDY: Can't you feel the clouds? It's gonna storm somethin awful.

GOLDIE: Lord knows we could use it.

(DEWEY *and* BASIL *enter with hoes as the others exit:*)

SHOWERS: Not a cloud in the sky.

DEWEY: Rain, Basil.

BASIL: Rain, huh?

BUDDY: Can't you feel the clouds?

DEWEY: It's what the boy says.

BUDDY: (*Exiting*) Gonna rain.

BASIL: How'd he look when he said it?

SHOWERS: Well. He was scratchin his feet somethin awful.

BASIL: Seemed pretty sure did he?

DEWEY: I come walkin up the garage, I says, "How you doin, Bud?" He says, "It's gonna rain."

BASIL: Well . . . the alfalfa's in at least.

DEWEY: Yeah.

BASIL: But the rutabaga's not near.

DEWEY: It ain't even close.

BASIL: Figure you boys can get that highland turned?

DEWEY: S'awful rocky.

BASIL: I know.

DEWEY: Full a rocks.

BASIL: Get her turned before the rain comes, give you eighty cents a day.

DEWEY: Damn.

BASIL: A little rain'll be nice, huh?

DEWEY: I guess.

BASIL: Yeah.

DEWEY: Hey, Basil. Look at the sky, will you?

BASIL: Pretty.

DEWEY: There's no clouds for miles.

BASIL: It'll rain soon enough, Dew. The boy knows.

DEWEY: How you figure that is? What's that?

BASIL: I mean, you done your fair share a doctorin, Basil.

BASIL: I'm no doctor, son. Most things'll heal alone.

DEWEY: But how do you figure the boy knows like he does?

BASIL: He just feels, I guess.

DEWEY: Feels the weather?

BASIL: Close as I can figure it, yeah.

DEWEY: It's that drownin, you figure? I mean, a fella falls in the water so young like he did—

BASIL: Don't take long underwater to change you.

DEWEY: I guess.

BASIL: He was under awhile, you know. The boy was only three, maybe four, and he was under that water some time.

DEWEY: Jesus.

BASIL: It was his mother that kept him from drownin, you know . . . she died in the water. It's a strange kind a thing.

DEWEY: It's kind a scary almost. I mean, Basil, the way the boy is now—

BASIL: Listen, Dewey, you can't think like that, son. Sometimes things happen—there's no way to stop em or change em, nothin better for tryin. If a boy knows the weather you got to call it a blessin. It's a blessin.

DEWEY: Yeah. Yeah . . . the place'll look awful nice, a little rain on the fields.

BASIL: We get that highland seeded she will.

(JENNIE MAE, SHOWERS, *and* BUDDY *enter.*)

DEWEY: It's good land on the rise there.

BASIL: Yeah, the farm's lookin fine.

SHOWERS: There's nothin so fine as the woods in the summer.

BUDDY: You see all the birds?

JENNIE MAE: Yeah, I see em.

BUDDY: You see that one there?

SHOWERS: That's a blue bird, my friend.

BUDDY: How come he's flyin?

SHOWERS: We scared him, I guess.

BUDDY: Hey, bird. Where you goin? Don't hide in them trees.

SHOWERS: Whoa now—

(BUDDY *follows his bird offstage:*)

BUDDY: Hey, you bird! Come on back here! Why you flyin from Buddy?

SHOWERS: Hey, Bud—

JENNIE MAE: Oh, Buddy's all right.

SHOWERS: Bud—?

JENNIE MAE: Buddy gets in the woods he's not about to sit still.

SHOWERS: Well . . . this old back a mine ain't about to go chase him.

JENNIE MAE: Oh, you're not that old, Mr. Showers.

SHOWERS: I been feelin it lately.

JENNIE MAE: Well, come here. I'll rub your back some.

SHOWERS: (*A little embarrassed.*) Oh . . .

JENNIE MAE: Now stop moanin and groanin and sit yourself down. Come on. It'll do you some good to sit still. (SHOWERS *sits. She rubs his shoulders:*) There you go. How's that now? A little better maybe?

SHOWERS: Oh . . . I'm dead and in Heaven.

JENNIE MAE: You just been workin too hard.

SHOWERS: Naw—

JENNIE MAE: Yeah, you have.

SHOWERS: Oh—

JENNIE MAE: You're like to work all the time, Mr. Showers.

SHOWERS: (*Softly, dismissing the idea.*) Shit.

JENNIE MAE: What?

SHOWERS: Little work never hurt nothin.

JENNIE MAE: I never heard you talk like you been today.

SHOWERS: Use those kind a words all the time when I'm thinkin.

JENNIE MAE: You think in swear words?

SHOWERS: I think worse things'n that.

JENNIE MAE: Is that why you give up on preachin?

SHOWERS: That ain't quite how I'd put it.

JENNIE MAE: Don't you believe in the Bible?

SHOWERS: I was raised on the Bible, Miss Layman. My Daddy's a preacher and his Daddy before and his Grandad and right down the line. Boy comes to be seventeen or eighteen there's no questions asked—hand him a Bible, turn him loose on the world. He'll make his way fine. Be an awful fine preacher. (*Slight pause. To himself:*) Be just like his Daddy I guess . . . (*He begins to preach as the memory builds:*) My Daddy . . . now he was a preacher. He had folks up on their feet and out a their seats and singin and stompin and life was just fine. Man took to a Bible like he was there just to shout it. Gonna tell everybody! Everybody about the wonder and the miracle and the sweet love a Jesus! He'd say now you there, Miss Layman, don't you love that sweet Jesus? Don't you love him so much you could cry? Well sure you do! I said sure you do! I said come on up front here and tell us about it! Tell the whole Church how you love that sweet story! Bring em all up front! Let em all tell the story! No sin's a great sin cause all men are sinners! Yes, Ma'am! That's all men! I said all men! I said every last man is a sinner! (*He catches himself. Slight pause:*) Then there's me . . . I'm up front the Church and I'd shout somethin out and they'd "Amen!" right to me. I'd shout and they'd shout and then all a sudden . . . it's dead quiet. I mean they're lookin and waitin and all ready to holler. And there's me up there . . . thinkin! Plain forgot I was preachin.

JENNIE MAE: No—

SHOWERS: Yeah! Plum forgot where I was. Sometimes two or three minutes at once. I tell you, Miss Layman, I think too much.

JENNIE MAE: Think too much?

SHOWERS: I am all the time thinkin! And thinkin and preachin don't mix too well, Ma'am.

JENNIE MAE: Well I never read too much Bible, but you surely can fire it up, Mr. Showers.

SHOWERS: I'm thirty years old, I never done nothin else! All I'm good for is talkin, Miss Layman. Runnin on at the mouth, just jawin away . . .

JENNIE MAE: I think you talk real nice.

SHOWERS: The whole time I was preachin you know what I felt? Nothin.

JENNIE MAE: Mr. Showers—

SHOWERS: I felt nothin, you see?

JENNIE MAE: You still sound awful nice.

SHOWERS: Aw, I need to learn to shut up. (*Pause. Then quietly:*) Well, damn it.

JENNIE MAE: What's a matter?

SHOWERS: I just can't shut up! I guess you're just too nice to talk to.

JENNIE MAE: Now don't tease me.

SHOWERS: Miss Layman—

JENNIE MAE: You make me feel like an old maid when you call me "Miss Layman."

SHOWERS: Well you're awful formal yourself, ain't you?

JENNIE MAE: I'm younger'n you. I'm suppose to.

SHOWERS: Here we are in this day and age—with tractors and light bulbs and Singer Sewin Machines—and you're talkin like any man older'n you's automatic a Mister right off the bat!

JENNIE MAE: Now don't be rilin me up, Mr. Showers. Girls sixteen years old can't call men by first name. Least not in Indiana they don't.

SHOWERS: Then let's just pretend it's Kentucky.

JENNIE MAE: Mr. Showers, I can't!

SHOWERS: We'll say that old beech tree down the way's the door to a mine shaft, and that gulley right there's an old coal train.

JENNIE MAE: Oh, Mr. Showers.

SHOWERS: Come on now.

JENNIE MAE: I can't.

SHOWERS: Sure you can.

JENNIE MAE: No I can't.

SHOWERS: Well, I don't see why not. (*Pause. She looks in his eyes:*)

JENNIE MAE: You want me to?

SHOWERS: I want you to call me by name. (*Light sound of thunder.*) Did you just feel somethin?

JENNIE MAE: Yeah. Yeah, I felt somethin . . .

SHOWERS: Was that rain drop you figure?

JENNIE MAE: What's that?

SHOWERS: Would you look at those clouds, Jennie Mae? Right up through the break in the trees there.

JENNIE MAE: Oh, my Lord.

SHOWERS: We best find your brother fore the sky splits wide open.

JENNIE MAE: He's on his way home.

SHOWERS: (*Calling Loudly.*) Buddy—?

JENNIE MAE: He's not gonna stay in the woods if it's stormin.

SHOWERS: Buddy—?

JENNIE MAE: C.C., come on! If he's home alone he'll be scared half to death!

(*They run off-stage as the thunder builds and the lights change. The thunder grows louder and louder. BUDDY enters, calling frantically for his family:*)

BUDDY: It's rainin! Hey, Dad, it's rainin! Ain't they nobody here? Ain't they nobody hear him? Dad? Jennie Mae? It's rainin outside! He can't breathe right no more. It's rainin! (*He wraps himself up in a blanket and lies down, struggling for breath. He should be completely covered by the blanket:*) It's rainin it's rainin it's rainin . . .

(SHOWERS *and* JENNIE MAE *run on as if coming in from the storm:*)

SHOWERS: Woooeee! Never saw such a storm! Like to split the sky open!

JENNIE MAE: Buddy?

FERRIS: (*Entering on the other side of the stage.*) I tell you, it's wild out there!

JENNIE MAE: Buddy?

FERRIS: (*To* SHOWERS) Wind's blowin like crazy.

JENNIE MAE: (*Sees him and goes to him.*) Buddy, look at you. You must be scared half to death. It's all right. We're here now.

(FERRIS *crosses to the boy, concerned.*)

FERRIS: Hey, Bud.

JENNIE MAE: You're fine now. We're here.

BUDDY: Mama . . . ?

JENNIE MAE: You're all right.

BUDDY: Mama . . . ?

JENNIE MAE: It's Jennie Mae.

SHOWERS: (*Crossing to them.*) Is he all right?

BUDDY: It's rainin.

FERRIS: You're fine son.

BUDDY: It's rainin.

(*The three of them are grouped around the boy.* BASIL *and* LUELLA *enter on the other side of the stage. As if watching the storm from their porch:*)

LUELLA: Lord knows how we need this.

BASIL: It's an awful fine rain.

FERRIS: Go to sleep, son.

(NORMA *and* DARLENE *enter. As if watching the rain from their window:*)

NORMA: (*Reading from a Bible.*) "And the Spirit of God moved on the face of the waters."

DARLENE: And the Spirit of God was there in the waters.

BASIL: You see there? The way the ground soaks in the water.

FERRIS: Just relax now.

JENNIE MAE: Go to sleep.

NORMA: "And God said, Let the waters under the Heavens be gathered together."

DARLENE: And God said let the waters be together.

BASIL: The highland's all turned and the seeds're all in.

LUELLA: It's bound to be a good season.

SHOWERS: He's asleep now?

JENNIE MAE: He's asleep.

BASIL: Yeah, the farm's lookin fine.

LUELLA: Be a real good summer.

NORMA: "And God saw it was good."

DARLENE: And God saw it was good. Aunt Norma?

NORMA: Darlene?

DARLENE: I thought we already did that one.

NORMA: That was for light.

DARLENE: God thought all of this stuff was pretty good, huh?

NORMA: In the beginning, yeah.

(BUDDY *wakes up as the women exit. He's alone on stage, middle of the night, and realizes he's itching:*)

BUDDY: Hey...he ain't sleepin...ain't sleepin no more, he's itchin, hey, hey he's itchin all over. Dad? He ain't sleepin! His foots are itchin awful! Jennie Mae? C.C.? Get up!

(JENNIE MAE *and* SHOWERS *enter from opposite sides of the stage. She might be in a night shirt.* SHOWERS *might carry his shoes and have his shirt unbuttoned:*)

JENNIE MAE: Hey now, Buddy!

BUDDY: He's itchin like crazy!

SHOWERS: Calm down, now.

JENNIE MAE: Hush now. You're gonna wake Daddy.

BUDDY: He's itchin!

FERRIS: What the hell's all this belly aching, boy?

BUDDY: Can't you hear him? He's itchin his head off!

FERRIS: And you're makin more noise then a half-blowed out Buick. Now settle down, will you?

BUDDY: Can't you make him all better?

FERRIS: Bud, you'll be fine if you just get some shut eye.

BUDDY: He ain't lyin down, Dad.

FERRIS: You're gonna do like I tell you.

BUDDY: He ain't tired a bit!

FERRIS: Now don't back-talk me, boy.

BUDDY: He ain't gonna sleep. You can't make him.

FERRIS: I'm gonna give you to ten, Bud. You hear me?

BUDDY: Aw, Dad.

FERRIS: I says, One. Two.

(JENNIE MAE *takes* BUDDY *back to his quilt and tries to talk him into lying down. The boy hits the hay just short of the ten count:*)

FERRIS	J.M.
Three. Four. Five, Six. Seven. Eight's awful close. Nine! Nine and a quarter. Nine and a half! Nine and three quarters!	Come on, Little brother.

J.M.

Come on, Little brother.

BUDDY

Aw, he's itchin just awful.

J.M.

Just lie yourself down.

BUDDY

He ain't tired a bit!

J.M.

He's almost to ten, Bud!

BUDDY: He's sleepin, he's sleepin!

(*Slight pause.*)

SHOWERS: You drive a hard bargain, Ferris.

FERRIS: Aw, I don't know, C.C. You gotta be headstrong when you're dealin with Bud.

(JENNIE MAE *stays with her brother. The men cross away.*)

FERRIS: (*Continued*) You never had you no kids.

SHOWERS: Naw.

FERRIS: Never had you a wife.

SHOWERS: Ferris, I'm all I can handle.

FERRIS: Don't you like women much?

SHOWERS: All the women I courted were in church, Ferris. You can't sweet-talk em one night and preach at em next.

FERRIS: Well there's plenty a time, huh? Used to be I didn't know nothin either. I mean, when I went to marry I didn't know a damn thing. I can tell you that now cause I'm older, you see, but at the time I thought I was a genius. Women or horses or cars or what have you. I's the firs one to tell you what's what. You know how I asked her to marry? How I married the wife? I says "I love you. I want you. Let's go." I didn't know the first thing about women, C.C.

SHOWERS: Were you sure that you loved her?

FERRIS: Was I sure that I loved her?

SHOWERS: I mean, bein so young...

FERRIS: I was crazy about her. Ain't a day that goes by I don't think a that woman. Lie to bed in the mornin, I think how she was. See the house, see the kids, you can't help but remember. I was head over heels in love . . . (*Pause*) Never came cross my mind I could lose her, I guess. You wake up one mornin and she ain't there no more . . . but you still keep on lovin, you see? I mean, she made me so happy. She's my darlin, my Sara. And nothin on earth gonna change it. (*Pause*) Course now bein a husband was a piece a damn cake compared to bein a Daddy full time. I wasn't married a year and she give me a daughter. I was just gettin used to a wife.

BUDDY: Hey, Dad?

FERRIS: Then the boy came along.

JENNIE MAE: He's not gonna sleep, Dad.

BUDDY: Dad, he's still itchin. His footbones, his anklers, he's itchin all over.

SHOWERS: You know it could be those salts're the thing the boy needs.

FERRIS: We go soakin his feet, he'll be screamin for days.

SHOWERS: We can't leave the kid go.

FERRIS: Look I know he needs washin, but there's no way in hell you're gonna get him near water.

SHOWERS: Well it's worth a try ain't it?

FERRIS: You can try all day long but you're not gonna change him!

BUDDY: Hey, Dad! He's still itchin!

FERRIS: This hollerin here's like a whisper, you see?

BUDDY: He's itchin just awful.

FERRIS: Would you quiet down, Bud?

BUDDY: Well it hurts him. (BUDDY *quiets down.* FERRIS *kneels beside the boy.*)

FERRIS: (*Softly:*) Lay back down now and try to get some shuteye. We'll talk in the mornin. All right? (FERRIS *tousles the boy's hair. He exits.*)

JENNIE MAE: Goodnight, now.

SHOWERS: Goodnight.

BUDDY: (*Itching*) You guys ain't gonna sleep!

SHOWERS: Aw, Bud. What say we have us a walk and a talk, pal? Keep you mind off your dogs a while.

BUDDY: Where you want a walk at, C.C.? (BUDDY *climbs on Showers's back.* JENNIE MAE *folds the blanket.*)

SHOWERS: Just outside a while.

JENNIE MAE: You two be careful out there in the dark now.

SHOWERS: Goodnight.

(DARLENE *enters. A bit flirty:*)

DARLENE: Evenin, Pastor Showers.

SHOWERS: Evenin, Darlene.

DARLENE: I can't sleep for nothin when the moon's shinin down.

SHOWERS: (*Exiting with the boy.*) It's warm weather for sleep.

DARLENE: (*Watching him go.*) Don't I know it?

JENNIE MAE: (*Crossing to* DARLENE) Did you sneak out a the house?

DARLENE: (*Innocent*) I'm just lookin for trouble.

JENNIE MAE: At this time a night?

DARLENE: It's the best time I know to find trouble. I seen the preacher man standin out here on the porch. He couldn't be no better lookin, Jennie Mae.

JENNIE MAE: Oh, Darlene.

DARLENE: I'd be up all night long if that guy lived at my house. Be walkin in the stars so bad I'd bump into walls. I tell you, for a preacher he sure is good lookin.

JENNIE MAE: His eyes sure are somethin. It's like they change colors sometimes when he sees you.

DARLENE: (*Impressed*) Jesus. There's just somethin about an older type man.

JENNIE MAE: (*Worldly*) Yeah, he's pretty mature.

DARLENE: Not like these boys around here.

JENNIE MAE: Who you courtin, Darlene?

DARLENE: Just these boys around here.

JENNIE MAE: Not Melvin Wilder?

DARLENE: (*Coy*) I might be.

JENNIE MAE: Dewey Maples?

DARLENE: I could be. Why don't you come see?

JENNIE MAE: I'm awful tired, Darlene.

DARLENE: Well you don't have to be so darn prissy about it.

JENNIE MAE: (*Exiting back into the house.*) I been up half the night.

(MELVIN *and* DEWEY *enter.* DARLENE *turns and imitates her friend's words to them in Scarlet O'Hara style:*)

DARLENE: "I been up half the night." She just got eyes for the preacher.

DEWEY: Jennie Mae likes the preacher?

DARLENE: Listen, Dewey, she doesn't just like him—she likes him. But don't tell her I told you, okay?

MELVIN: What, do you think Dewey here can't keep a secret, Darlene? You think Dewey's gonna go blabbin all over?

DEWEY: I won't tell her, Darlene.

MELVIN: (*Hands him a flask.*) Have a drink, Dew.

DEWEY: All right.

DARLENE: Ain't you guys never heard a the Dry-Laws?

MELVIN: Darlene, you're talkin to a veteran a the Army a the U.S. of A. and I'm telling you the Dry-Laws mean next to nothin. I mean a drink's just a drink, huh? Give her the hootch. Dew.

DARLENE: I'm not touchin that hootch.

MELVIN: (*Challenging*) What're you scared of a drink?

DARLENE: (*Takes the bottle.*) I ain't scared a nothin.

(MELVIN *pulls* DEWEY *aside as she drinks.*)

MELVIN: Now, you see how that is, Dew? Girls're tricky business. Real tricky business. But you gotta let em know how you stand, see? Now you want a take this girl dancin. You want to take Darlene to the dance.

DEWEY: I'm not sayin I love her or nothin.

MELVIN: But you gotta let her know what you're thinkin.

DARLENE: Hey, Melvin?

MELVIN: We're tryin to talk man to man. You understand?

DARLENE: What're you takin about Melvin?

MELVIN: We're talkin on how nice you're lookin, Darlene. My pal Dewey, he can't hardly stand it. Now you see how that is, Dew?

DARLENE: You really think I look nice, Dewey?

MELVIN: Tell her how it is, pal. Tell her you mean business.

(DEWEY *crosses to* DARLENE, *very shy:*)

DEWEY: Hey, Darlene.

DARLENE: Hey, Dewey.

DEWEY: I don't love you or nothin.

MELVIN: Dewey, what're you sayin?! That's not what he's meaning, Darlene.

DARLENE: (*A little upset.*) Well what are you meanin?

DEWEY: I guess I'm kind a wonderin what you might think about dancin.

DARLENE: (*Warming*) I like dancin just fine.

DEWEY: Me too. I don't know how or nothin but I sure like to watch.

MELVIN: This guy puts the dance floor to shame.

DARLENE: Maybe you could teach me a step or two, Dewey.

MELVIN: (*Referring to* DEWEY) Hell of a dancer.

DEWEY: Well, my feet're kind a sore. I got planters warts, see?

MELVIN: Now, Dewey that ain't the way to her heart.

DEWEY: (*Exiting*) I can't dance if my feet hurt.

(BASIL *enters with the bike.* FERRIS *has the pump.*)

BASIL: My damn dogs're dyin.

MELVIN: (*To* DARLENE *as they exit.*) His feet will be fine fore you know it.

BASIL: I bought the damn bike to ride for a change and I end up walkin all over.

FERRIS: Now settle down, Basil.

BASIL: I'm not settlin for nothin! Every time I go to ride the thing, Ferris, the tire goes flat fore you know it.

FERRIS: Now, Basil, . . .

BASIL: Damn bike.

FERRIS: You're gonna upset your system.

BASIL: I've doctored half the cows and kids in the county here, Ferris. I ought to know my own system and my system's piss mad at this tire!

FERRIS: Well, we'll pump her up some and see how she does.

BASIL: Just look at that, will you? A man works his tail off to pay for a thing and just look at it!

FERRIS: Well, the rubber's still good.

BASIL: I tell you, Ferris, I've had it up to here with these Schwinns.

FERRIS: Spokes're all right.

BASIL: Spokes're okay, huh? Well, if it ain't the spokes, it's the rim.

FERRIS: Naw, the rims' lookin fine. If she's not holdin air, it's the tube or your valve.

BASIL: Tubes're pretty costly?

FERRIS: Yeah, but patches're cheap. She needs any work I'll get C.C. right on her.

BASIL: Good worker, is he?

FERRIS: Well, he's new yet, you know.

BASIL: Kind a wet behind the ears, yeah.

FERRIS: And there's two strikes against him, bein born in Kentucky.

BASIL: I'd a thought he's a Hoosier!

FERRIS: Naw.

BASIL: Acts like a Hoosier.

FERRIS: Well, I wasn't too sure when he got here. Hell, I'd hand him a wrench and he'd call it a pliers. Plus, you know he's good lookin.

BASIL: (*Not too happy about the fact.*) Yeah, that's what the wife tells me.

FERRIS: And if there's one thing I've learned in life, Basil, it's that good-looking guys make damn awful workers. Back when Bud was just born and the wife was still with us I hired a good-lookin kid for a while. Go to put on a headlight, he'd comb his hair in the chrome! Wouldn't get dirty or crawl up under a car.

BASIL: Yeah, those good-lookin guys.

FERRIS: They just ain't for shit.

BASIL: Nope.

FERRIS: Course, now C.C. ain't like that. You give him a grease gun you'd think he's in Heaven.

BASIL: I though those preacher types loved to keep clean.

FERRIS: Well, he does want a wash down the boy.

BASIL: Yeah, the're all the time a dippin, all the time dunkin. Preacher's like a duck around water.

FERRIS: Well he's got another think comin he thinks Bud'll sit still.

BASIL: Who knows? He might do it Ferris. Wouldn't hurt nothin, would it? The boy needs a washin. Will be a hell of a job though.

FERRIS: I know.

BASIL: But if this preacher guy's foursquare you're lucky to have him. What with all the men out a work, you'd think there'd be more half de-

cent help than there is. Not that Dewey and Melvin don't work hard
you know.

FERRIS: But they're lazy.

BASIL: They're young yet.

FERRIS: I know.

BASIL: Since the bank's took my tractor I ain't got much choice, Ferris. I
need hired help just to keep above water.

FERRIS: Aw, now, Basil, you're fulla shit.

BASIL: Well, I like workin with workers.

FERRIS: (*Handing him the tire pump.*) Then work me this tire why
don't you?

(BASIL *pumps the front tires while* FERRIS *tightens the spokes on the
back one.*)

BASIL: I never could run that tractor for nothin you know. The damn
thing had too many knobs on it. Too many levers.

FERRIS: You shoulda pulled one and started her up.

BASIL: Naw, tractor's too noisy. Sides, it left big old ruts in my fields.

FERRIS: Never got to your fields.

BASIL: Never got any gas in it. Only bought her cause the wife liked
the color.

FERRIS: Least it never got dirty.

BASIL: Nope. The bank took her back. You ask me, they cause all the
trouble.

FERRIS: Never had use for a bank.

BASIL: No, the tractors, I mean. Banks can't hurt nothin—they're
folded.

FERRIS: Now what's wrong with tractors?

BASIL: Well for starters I hate em. You see, to build the damn things they
go rippin the ground up. It's worse'n coal, they go diggin for ore. And to
rip out that ore they build more machines—till there's more metal
diggin the ground up than men. Then the next thing you know those
machines get like rabbits and start makin babies. Little lawn mower
machines and hole diggin jobbers. Trench makers . . .

FERRIS: Well diggers . . .

BASIL: Cow milkers . . .

FERRIS: Gets kinda crazy.

BASIL: It gets so a man touches nothin but metal. And metal just don't feel so good to my hands . . . leastways not the way that the earth does.

FERRIS: (*Softly*) Times ain't what they used to.

BASIL: Well it makes me mad that there's men out of work and they keep right on buildin machines. A man don't work, he can't hold up his head—look his kids in the eye. You take a man's work and you take half the man.

FERRIS: Listen Basil, things're bound to come around, huh?

BASIL: (*Not believing it.*) Yeah.

FERRIS: I'm sayin you gotta want things better or they only get worse, huh?

BASIL: Yeah, Ferris. Yeah, maybe good times're comin. You know they got some fancy kind a manure spreader now. It's in all a them Farm Bureau News things. Biggest damn machine you could dream of. You pull it around, see—and it shits on your fields. (*Pause*)

FERRIS: Basil, hand me that valve cap, why don't you?

BASIL: The what?

FERRIS: I need the little cap here that fits to your valve. The stem's kind a worn, but if you keep the cap on her you might keep some air in it, Basil.

BASIL: That little cap thing's a part a the tire?

FERRIS: A course it's a part a the tire.

BASIL: Well, I didn't know. I thought it was just there for looks.

FERRIS: Took it off, huh?

BASIL: Can't stand a thing just for looks.

FERRIS: Did you toss it?

BASIL: No, I didn't toss it. I never toss a damn thing. I set it to the shelf of my barn.

FERRIS: Well, take it off a the shelf, put it back on the Schwinn and you'll stop losin air all the time.

BASIL: It ain't just for looks, huh?

FERRIS: Basil, if it's on a Schwinn it's there for a reason.

BASIL: Yeah. Schwinn's a good bike.

FERRIS: Don't make em much better. (BASIL *starts to get on the bike.*) But I wouldn't ride the thing, Basil, till you get the cap on her.

BASIL: Well the sun's full up now. It's a good mornin for walkin.

FERRIS: (*Looking at the sky.*) Looks to be a real nice day.

BASIL: The whole lay a the land looks nice in the mornin.

FERRIS: Yeah.

BASIL: Yep.

FERRIS: Well you stay on those dogs now and walk 'em.

BASIL: Will do.

(BUDDY *and* SHOWERS *enter as* BASIL *walks the bike offstage and* FERRIS *exits up to the garage.*)

BUDDY: Your foots itchin awful?

SHOWERS: No, they kind a smell bad though.

BUDDY: Itchin like crazy, C.C.

SHOWERS: Life's awful tough, ain't it.

(NORMA *enters with a colorful jar of jellybeans.*)

BUDDY: He'll feel better he gets him some jelly beans.

NORMA: Sorry. These beans ain't for sale. You can shop around the Dry Goods all you like, honey, but this candy's stayin right here.

BUDDY: Well he's sick you know, Norma.

NORMA: (*Concerned*) Oh, what's the matter with you, honey?

BUDDY: (*Sticking his feet up.*) Itchin like nuts. How bout you?

NORMA: Oh, Bud.

SHOWERS: We're hopin you might have some healin salts, ma'am.

NORMA: Best salts in the county. Little fever, little epsom might help you some. A bad rash is a tough thing to shake.

BUDDY: How bout you just give him them jellybeans?

NORMA: Buddy, those beans ain't for sale. This jar a candy means business.

BUDDY: (*Impressed*) Them're business beans, Norma?

NORMA: The fella that guesses how many're in here gets to take the whole jar home scott free.

SHOWERS: Lucky fella.

NORMA: You wouldn't care to take a guess for yourself? Would you, Mr?

BUDDY: (*Grabs the jar.*) Yeah. Come on, C.C.

SHOWERS: Let me confer with my friend here a moment.

NORMA: It ain't so easy like it looks, I'll tell you that much right off. I did her once before, but with peanuts. My niece Darlene, she says, "Oh, Aunt Norma that's silly," she says, "I could guess how many in a minute." But I'll tell you those goobers sat here on the counter for a whole solid year.

SHOWERS: I hear you.

NORMA: You bout ready?

SHOWERS: I think we are, Ma'am.

NORMA: It's a whole lot more that she looks. I had those goobers just sit here all year.

(SHOWERS *and* BUDDY *guess with no consultation between them.* SHOWERS *just makes a random estimate and* BUDDY *throws out the highest number he knows.*)

SHOWERS: Well, we'd say ther's about . . . seven hundred and . . .

BUDDY: Two.

(*Pause.* NORMA *looks like she's just seen a ghost. Very quiet:*)

NORMA: Come again?

SHOWERS: (*Slight pause. Then quietly:*) Seven hundred and two, Ma'am . . .

(*Pause. Then with full conviction of the miracle in her presence.*)

NORMA: Why, you're that new preacher fella, ain't you?

BUDDY: Want some candy, C.C.?

NORMA: I been wantin to meet you the whole summer, Pastor! Lord am I glad that you're here. You should a dropped by the Dry Goods and saw me before. There's all kinds a work to be done. There are back slidin sinners all over this town.

SHOWERS: Ma'am, I just work down the garage.

NORMA: I can see how the Lord's workin through you.

BUDDY: Ain't you hungry, C.C.?

NORMA: You're gonna heal the boy, ain't you? Gonna stop his affliction? (*Covering* BUDDY'S *ears.*) Lord knows it ain't gonna be easy.

BUDDY: What?

NORMA: Lord know he could use it.

BUDDY: (*Shaking his head.*) Hey he can't hear.

SHOWERS: Ma'am you're just a little mixed up here.

NORMA: I know just what you're doin. You're healin the boy.

SHOWERS: (*Taking charge.*) Here's a dime for the salts, Ma'am, you keep the candy. I got work to do now, so we'll see you.

NORMA: But Pastor...

SHOWERS: Come on, Bud.

NORMA: (*Calling after them as they exit.*) If you need any help, Pastor, just turn to me. I been prayin for this for years and years now. I've said all along this is what the boy needs.

(GOLDIE *and* LUELLA *enter as if walking down the street or leaving the cafe or something.*)

NORMA: (*Continued*) The beans—these beans're a sign.

LUELLA: Tastes like plain old candy to me, Norma.

NORMA: Those beans're a sign if ever there was one. That man's got the spirit clean through him.

GOLDIE: But he told me right to my face that he gave up on preachin.

NORMA: You can't toss off the spirit like you toss off a coat. When the Lord sends a sign he means business. It's a blessin, you see. It's a gift the man has.

LUELLA: Now, Norma...

NORMA: Don't you "Now, Norma" me. I never seen nothin like it.

GOLDIE: You best rest yourself some.

GOLDIE: I'm tellin you, Goldie, that man is amazin. He'll bring the whole town to the Lord.

(BUDDY *and* SHOWERS *enter as the women walk* NORMA *offstage. The moon rises during the scene.*)

BUDDY: How come he can't find him no angels, C.C.?

SHOWERS: You been lookin for angels?

BUDDY: Been lookin all over and he can't find em nowheres. You think maybe they's hidin, C.C.?

SHOWERS: Well there's lots of things around you can't lay your eyes on. Now you see the moon risin, don't you?

BUDDY: Yeah.

SHOWERS: Well where do you figure the moon goes in the daytime?

BUDDY: Well he don't recollect it C.C.

SHOWERS: Just because you can't see it doesn't mean it's not there. There's all kinds a things you can't see.

BUDDY: You know who lives up there, don't you? The moon man.

SHOWERS: Does he now?

(JENNIE MAE *enters with a tub of hot water.*)

JENNIE MAE: Sure, he' up there eatin green cheese.

SHOWERS: (*Smiles*) Kind a hungry now, is he?

BUDDY: Yeah. What do you got in that soup?

JENNIE MAE: Well, it's mainly just salts.

BUDDY: Can he taste it?

JENNIE MAE: I wouldn't taste the stuff, Bud.

SHOWERS: But you're sure more than welcome to touch it.

BUDDY: (*Sensing something is not right.*) You gonna make him?

SHOWERS: No.

BUDDY: He don't wanna touch nothin.

SHOWERS: Well, I'll tell you, my friend, I never seen nothin like it. What we're onto right here is amazin.

BUDDY: Don't make him get wet.

SHOWERS: This ain't just your run a the mill here, my friend.

BUDDY: He ain't gonna go in no water!

JENNIE MAE: Now Buddy...

SHOWERS: (*Overlapping*) This stuff ain't just water.

BUDDY: He can't breathe if you wash him, C.C.!

JENNIE MAE: Just relax...

BUDDY: Gonna scream! He's gonna holler!

SHOWERS: (*Forceful*) Now calm down a little! Just look at this for a second!

BUDDY: He don't need him no bath!

SHOWERS: (*More forceful.*) Now water's usually cold, ain't it, Bud?

BUDDY: He can't breathe in a water!

SHOWERS: Don't go away! I asked you a question! Now answer me, Buddy! I said, ain't water cold? Buddy, ain't water freezin? I always thought that water was cold.

BUDDY: (*Reluctant, keeping his distance.*) Yeah...

SHOWERS: Well, I know for a fact that this sure ain't near cold. It ain't cold cause it's warm! This ain't just plain water.

JENNIE MAE: Just look at it, Bud.

SHOWERS: I tell you, my friend, I am absolutely astounded by what's in this bucket.

BUDDY: (*Still keeping his distance.*) What is it!

SHOWERS: What we're onto right here is called . . . itch-juice.

BUDDY: Itch-juice?

SHOWERS: In a manner of speakin.

BUDDY: (*Moving closer.*) What's it do to him, C.C.?

SHOWERS: Well, the wonderful thing about itch-juice, my friend, is it takes the itchin right out a your feet.

BUDDY: Will it hurt him, Jennie Mae?

JENNIE MAE: Folks say it makes you feel better.

SHOWERS: Sure does. I knew a fella way back in Hazard, in fact—had him a horrible case a the rash. Scratchin and itchin, like to drive himself crazy. Till the day he stumbled onto this itch-juice.

BUDDY: It ain't gonna hurt him?

SHOWERS: Bud, there's nothin on earth gonna hurt you.

BUDDY: (*Moving closer, looking in the bucket.*) Kinda gives him the willies all over, Jennie Mae. Got the willies somethin awful, C.C.

SHOWERS: Now, Bud . . .

JENNIE MAE: I'd say Mr. Showers knows just what he's doing.

BUDDY: He ain't feelin so sure he can breathe right no more. (BUDDY *is directly above the bucket. He pulls into himself, very scared. Starting to move away.*) He ain't gonna touch it!

SHOWERS: (*Taking charge.*) Now hold the boat, Bud! What say you and me make a deal here, pal.

BUDDY: (*Scared to give his word.*) Word a honor C.C.?

(SHOWERS *licks his palm and holds it out. The boy hesitates, decides, they bring their hands together.* BUDDY *grabs onto* SHOWERS' *hand very tightly— possibly using both hands. As if the preacher can keep him from harm:*)

SHOWERS: Now. There's nothin like singin to put a good man at ease. Lets you forget about anything might be at you, you see, and it settles your insides right down.

(JENNIE MAE *is rolling the boy's pants legs up.*)

BUDDY: You want him to sing, C.C.?

SHOWERS: And by the time you finish we'll have this itchin right out a your feet.

JENNIE MAE: Just relax now ...

(BUDDY *lets go of* SHOWERS' *hand and leans back, looking straight up at the sky so as not to see the bucket. When he begins to sing his voice is full of nervous energy. He's as tense and anxious as a child can be, knowing that something is sure to cause him great pain. They begin to wash his feet during the second line of the song. As the water touches him, everything in his voice and body suddenly tense and take on all the fear and terror of the water, as if in great pain.* JENNIE MAE *washes one foot and* SHOWERS *the other.*)

BUDDY: "You are his sunshine, his only sunshine,
You make him happy when skies are grey.
You'll never know, dear, how much he loves you
Please don't take his sunshine away ... "

(SHOWERS *immediately leads the boy into the second verse and* JENNIE MAE *joins in after a moment. They sing softly, gently, with reassurance.* BUDDY'S *voice is most prominent still as if in great pain.*)

FOOT WASHERS: "The other night dear, as he was sleepin,
He dreamt he held you in his arms.
But when he woke, dear, he was mistaken,
So he hung his head and cried ... "

(*As they sing the final verse the boy's voice relaxes just a bit. Growing softer. The lights are changing, forming a circle around them and framing them—its center is the boy's face.*)

FOOT WASHERS: "You are his sunshine, his only sunshine,
You make him happy when skies are grey.
You'll never know, dear, how much he loves you.
Please don't take his sunshine away ... "

(*The lights are fading, the singing has grown gentle. The last sound we hear, and we should hear several moments of it before the lights go to black, is the unamplified sound of water washing again and again over the boy's feet.*)

End of Act One

Act Two

The Sky and the Water

(Morning. Faint sounds of birds. As the light rises we see BUDDY *creeping onto the stage, bent low with one hand held out as he tries to befriend a small bird:)*

BUDDY: Ain't you so pretty, huh? Ain't you so pretty. You're the color a the sky. Yes, you are. You want a be up there, now, don't you? In the sun and the wind. Well, hold still, now. Hold still. He ain't gonna hurt you. (SHOWERS *enters as the boy catches the bird.*) You're too little to fly. Shhh, you're all right.

SHOWERS: Is he hurt?

BUDDY: Look at him, C.C. He's little.

SHOWERS: It's an awful pretty bird.

BUDDY: See his feathers?

SHOWERS: Those're blue.

BUDDY: Blue?

SHOWERS: Blue like your eyes.

BUDDY: His eyes is blue?

SHOWERS: Like the bird, like the sky—that's all blue.

BUDDY: Boy. You want a lift him, C.C.? Put him back to his Mama? (BUDDY *climbs on* SHOWERS's *shoulders and they move downstage to the edge of the stage.*)

SHOWERS: Careful, now, pal. You all right?

BUDDY: Yeah. How bout you?

SHOWERS: Oh, you're awful heavy! Now watch yourself up there. You got him?

BUDDY: (*As he places the bird in the tree.*) What color's that?

SHOWERS: That's green.

BUDDY: Green? Trees is green. Weeds is green. Grass is green. And birds're blue.

SHOWERS: (*Letting the boy down.*) You're awful smart first thing in the mornin.

(BUDDY *lies on the stage floor looking up at the trees.*)

BUDDY: Like to live up there with him. His arms turn to wings and his wings turn to feathers.

SHOWERS: How'd you get down?

BUDDY: He'd just fly down, C.C.

SHOWERS: Well, if you're gonna be barnstormin you'd best get your wings out.

BUDDY: Like a bird?

(SHOWERS *holds onto the boy's arms, slowly lifting his upper body until the boy stands on his toes with his arms extended.*)

SHOWERS: Like a bird.

BUDDY: Is he flyin?

SHOWERS: Shut your eyes, now.

BUDDY: Is he flyin?

SHOWERS: If you're willin to fly, pal, I'm willin to witness.

BUDDY: Lift him higher.

SHOWERS: Higher?

BUDDY: Lift him way up the sky! Clear up the sky!

SHOWERS: Higher?

BUDDY: Higher! (BUDDY *runs to a high platform.*)

SHOWERS: (*As if calling a great distance.*) How's the air up there?

BUDDY: Blue!

SHOWERS: Where's Buddy Layman?

BUDDY: He's flyin!

SHOWERS: Flyin!

BUDDY: Flyin clear up the sky! Way up the sky!

SHOWERS: Have you seen Mr. Lindbergh? Any word from Mr. Lindbergh?

BUDDY: Mr. Who?

SHOWERS: Mr. Lindbergh!

BUDDY: Ain't nobody flyin but birds.

SHOWERS: Any sign a Buddy Layman?

BUDDY: Who's Buddy Layman!

SHOWERS: He's a good boy.

BUDDY: (*Pleased*) He is?

SHOWERS: He's a smart boy. I know him.

BUDDY: Have you seen Mr. C.C.?

SHOWERS: Mr. Who?

BUDDY: Mr. C.C.?

SHOWERS: Who's Mr. C.C.?

BUDDY: He's a bird!

(SHOWERS *has spread his arms and moved up behind the boy. The distance games with their voices stop.*)

SHOWERS: A bird brain, you mean.

BUDDY: Hey, C.C.? You flyin?

SHOWERS: Keep your eyes closed.

BUDDY: (*Amazed*) You're flyin.

SHOWERS: Want a go higher?

BUDDY: He wants to go where you go, C.C.

SHOWERS: I'm stayin right here with you.

BUDDY: You like it here?

SHOWERS: I like it just fine.

BUDDY: (*Softly*) You like the wind?

SHOWERS: Feels nice . . .

BUDDY: Feels soft . . .

SHOWERS: That's a nice sort of feelin.

BUDDY: His Mama's soft like the wind. Her voice's soft when he's sleepin.

SHOWERS: That's a dream, my friend.

BUDDY: (*Concerned*) Is angels a dream?

SHOWERS: Buddy.

BUDDY: How come he can't find her?

SHOWERS: Your Mama's been gone a long time now.

BUDDY: He wants her so bad.

SHOWERS: I know.

BUDDY: If his arms turn to wings and his wings turn to feathers he could find her in the sky, maybe, C.C. (*The boy moves away from* SHOWERS.) If he's flyin he could be with his Mama.

SHOWERS: Buddy, listen to me . . .

BUDDY: (*Overlapping*) They could fly in the sky, in the wind, in the sun! He could be with his Mama! They could fly and they fly and they fly!

SHOWERS: (*Overlapping from the next to last "fly".*) Your Mama's not here anymore!

BUDDY: He has to find her!

SHOWERS: (*Forceful*) No! You have to remember! She's left you a father and a sister and there's friends here for Buddy! And they want him and need him and love him! And he isn't a bird—he's a boy! You're a boy. You're a son. You're a brother. And you're a friend.

BUDDY: (*Moved*) And you like him?

SHOWERS: I like him a lot.

BUDDY: That's somethin, huh?

SHOWERS: You know it is.

BUDDY: Hey C.C.? You know what?

SHOWERS: What?

BUDDY: (*Shakes his hand.*) You're a good guy.

SHOWERS: I am, huh? Well you too!

BUDDY: Buddy is?

SHOWERS: Sure you are.

BUDDY: You know what else he is, C.C.? He's itchin.

SHOWERS: Still itchin?

BUDDY: Right there, C.C. Itchin right there.

SHOWERS: Well, the skin looks a little red yet.

BUDDY: He don't want no more itch-juice.

SHOWERS: You'll never get better if you keep scratchin, Bud.

BUDDY: Well it itches!

SHOWERS: I know—but anytime your legs start to get at you, you say "I'm gonna save this scratch for another time." (SHOWERS *starts to cross away.*)

BUDDY: Hey, C.C.? When's it gonna be another time?

SHOWERS: After you're better.

BUDDY: Is he better now?

SHOWERS: Nope.

BUDDY: Not yet?

SHOWERS: Not quite.

(MELVIN *and* DEWEY *come on left.* DEWEY *is dancing.* BUDDY *and* SHOWERS *leave right.*)

MELVIN: You're lookin better.

BUDDY: After while?

SHOWERS: After a while.

DEWEY: After the right foot then the left foot. It's a long step and then a short step. Long step and a short step . . .

MELVIN: Now you're not lookin bad, Dew. But you can't be tippy toe dancin with a girl like Darlene. A girl likes a man to be leadin.

DEWEY: So maybe I want a spin her around, huh? A little razzamatazz?

MELVIN: Dewey, you go tippy toein around her and you're nowhere, you see? Dancin's a damn serious business.

DEWEY: Well, I don't want a be fancy-dancin and get her in trouble.

MELVIN: Now Dewey.

DEWEY: You know what I mean.

MELVIN: Have you been hangin around to the Dry Goods again, Dew? Hey, Dewey.

DEWEY: Yeah, I guess.

MELVIN: What's Norma Henshaw been tellin you?

DEWEY: Nothin much.

MELVIN: Oh, come on, Dew. Dewey?

DEWEY: (*Sudden*) Says dancin's a sin.

MELVIN: What!

DEWEY: She says it's a sin.

MELVIN: Naw.

DEWEY: Darlene's Aunt says it's right in the Bible. Plain as the day is long! Dancin is sin. S-I-N, sin!

MELVIN: Dancin's just dancin, Dew! It's got nothin to do with the Bible!

DEWEY: I'm on a one-way road to you know where, Melvin.

MELVIN: If you want to know about the Bible then go out the garage and have a talk with the Preacher! But you want a know about dancin or drinkin or girls—you stick right here and ask me.

DEWEY: Yeah?

MELVIN: Dew, you name it, I know it. There ain't much I ain't seen.

DEWEY: Well, I'll be.

MELVIN: Listen, Dew. I been around. Here now, you be you, and I'll be Darlene. Put your arm around me. Hey. Would you knock it off, Dewey? I'm tryin to teach you.

DEWEY: Sorry.

MELVIN: All right. Now the first rule a dancin is girls're flesh and blood.

DEWEY: I got that much down pretty good.

MELVIN: So you want to keep her close to you. And you don't want a be steppin on her feet, Dew.

DEWEY: Sorry.

MELVIN: All right. (*They dance across the stage.* MELVIN *calls out the steps like a drill sergeant in a military cadence. Neither of them notice when* BASIL *enters with a pitch fork.*)

MELVIN: Left! Right! Left! Right! Left! Right! Left! Right!

BASIL: (*Overlapping with the last "left!"*) I'm not gonna say you boys're dawdlin around, or goof-offs or do-nothins. And I'm not gonna tell you that you're tryin to cheat me out a the seventy some cents a day that I'm good enough to pay you. I'm just gonna point to that mound a hay over there that somebody, some poor old farmer, spent half his day stackin. And if that hay ain't loaded to the flatbed and hauled to the barn inside an hour—I am more than like to go out and buy me a damn tractor! (BASIL *hands* MELVIN *the pitch fork and stomps off.*)

MELVIN: You know if Basil ever fires us, Dewey, we're gonna have to go find us a job.

DEWEY: I can't hardly breathe without gettin in trouble. I can't romance or dance and now I can't even work right.

(DARLENE, JENNIE MAE, *and* BUDDY *enter. The boy and his sister each have a spoon. They dig for "worms" and put them in a tin can.*)

DARLENE: Don't let 'em near me.

MELVIN: (*As he and* DEWEY *exit.*) Don't let it get to you, Dew.

JENNIE MAE: Don't be so prissy, Darlene.

DEWEY: (*Exiting.*) I don't mean to be gettin in trouble.

DARLENE: I'm not about to let em touch me.

BUDDY: How come?

DARLENE: Cause I don't like worms. That's how come.

JENNIE MAE: Just put em in the can, Buddy.

BUDDY: He is.

DARLENE: It was me, I'd make that preacher dig em himself.

JENNIE MAE: I don't mind.

DARLENE: Who ever heard of a man askin you out and then makin you do all the work?

JENNIE MAE: Mr. Showers isn't askin me nowhere, Darlene. He just said it might be nice to go fishin.

DARLENE: Same thing, Jennie Mae.

BUDDY: (*Dangling a "worm".*) Hey, Darlene.

DARLENE: Jennie Mae!

JENNIE MAE: Buddy!

BUDDY: Just put em in a can.

JENNIE MAE: Just keep diggin and mind your own business.

DARLENE: It wouldn't bother me so much, see? But they used to be able to walk.

JENNIE MAE: Worms?

DARLENE: Sure. Worms and snakes both. They could talk too.

JENNIE MAE: Oh come on.

DARLENE: It's true, Jennie Mae. Don't you guys read the Bible?

BUDDY: Nope. How bout you?

DARLENE: (*Not too happy about the fact.*) Yeah, I gotta learn the whole thing. Like, say I'm sittin at the table and I want seconds on dessert, Aunt Norma says, "Give me a verse first, Darlene." If I didn't know the Bible I'd starve to death, see?

JENNIE MAE: You Aunt's awful strict.

DARLENE: But I been learnin who Adam and Eve are. You heard a them, ain't you?

BUDDY: Nope.

JENNIE MAE: The first people.

DARLENE: And they're livin in this great big old garden in Europe. And the thing about Eve is she's walkin around pickin berries and junk with no clothes on.

JENNIE MAE: She was naked?

DARLENE: Listen, Jennie Mae, they were like doin it all the time.

JENNIE MAE: They were doin it?

DARLENE: All the time, Jennie Mae.

BUDDY: What're they doin?

JENNIE MAE: Nothin.

BUDDY: Nothin?

DARLENE: All the time, Jennie Mae. That kind a stuff happens in Europe. But like I'm saying, this snake comes strollin up, see? And he tells her how she's sittin there jaybird stark naked.

BUDDY: She's neked?

JENNIE MAE: Oh, that's crazy, Darlene.

DARLENE: Oh, there's lots crazier stuff'n that in the Bible. Like there's people turnin to stone. One minute they're sittin there just shootin the breeze—and the next thing you know they're all rocks! Lots of weird stuff.

BUDDY: How come they's rocks?

DARLENE: Cause they ask too many dumb questions.

JENNIE MAE: (*Watching out for her brother.*) Darlene.

DARLENE: So anyway, this business a bein naked really sets God off at the snake, see? Cause with Eve bein so dumb she didn't get in any trouble, but now it's like a whole nother ball game. And God wasn't just mad at this one snake either—he was mad at all a the snakes and all a the worms in the world. So he tells em "From now on you guys're gonna crawl around in the dirt!" God says, "From now on nobody likes you."

JENNIE MAE: God really said that?

DARLENE: Right in the Bible. Later on he gets really mad and floods the whole world out.

JENNIE MAE: You mean he kills em?

BUDDY: With water?

DARLENE: Floods em right under.

BUDDY: Under water?

DARLENE: He makes it keep rainin, see?

BUDDY: God makes it rain? He can't breathe in a water...

JENNIE MAE: It's only a story.

DARLENE: It's in the Bible—it's true.

BUDDY: How come God's mad? He ain't done nothin wrong. (BUDDY *runs across stage as* FERRIS *and* SHOWERS *come out of the garage.*)

JENNIE MAE: It's only a story, Buddy! Wait!

BUDDY: It's gonna rain, C.C.! Gonna rain and it ain't gonna quit, Dad!

FERRIS: Now, slow down—

SHOWERS: Whats a matter?

JENNIE MAE: (*Exiting*) Why'd you scare him so bad?

DARLENE: (*Following her off.*) I didn't mean to.

BUDDY: Ain't nobody gonna be breathin no more!

FERRIS: Now, Bud—

BUDDY: Gonna rain and it ain't gonna quit! God's makin it rain! Can't you hear him?

SHOWERS: You're all right.

BUDDY: Come on! We gotta hide!

FERRIS: Calm down...

BUDDY: We gotta hide!

FERRIS: (*Taking charge, forceful:*) I said calm down a minute and hold your horses, Bud! (*Slight pause. Then gently.*) Now catch your breath, son.

SHOWERS: Nothin's gonna hurt you.

BUDDY: God is!

FERRIS: If God ain't struck down the likes a Herbert Hoover by now, I'd imagine that you're in the clear, Bud.

BUDDY: He is?

FERRIS: (*Exiting*) I wouldn't worry yourself any.

(BUDDY *is crouched low to the ground rocking back and forth.* SHOWERS *kneels beside him. There is a quiet moment between them as* NORMA *enters with her jar of jellybeans. From her perspective it looks like they are praying.*)

SHOWERS: You all right?

BUDDY: He thinks so.

SHOWERS: Just breathe real easy. There you go. That's a boy.

NORMA: (*To herself.*) Sweet Jesus in Heaven.

SHOWERS: You need to calm down a little.

NORMA: (*Making herself known.*) I knew you could do it! I told the whole town so.

SHOWERS: Beg pardon?

NORMA: I knew that you'd bring that boy to the Lord. I told the Browns and the Bennetts, the Jones and the Seemores—they all know the Lord's workin through you.

SHOWERS: Miz Henshaw . . .

NORMA: Folks come in for miles just to look at this jar! We could set to revivin in no time at'all. Run a real good service.

SHOWERS: Now hold the boat, Ma'am.

NORMA: (*Charging on.*) There'll be singin and savin.

SHOWERS: Would you listen a second?

NORMA: (*Still charging.*) Readin, revivin. You could witness all over the country!

SHOWERS: There's nothin to witness!

NORMA: (*Setting the candy down.*) You don't need to be humble. You can quit at the garage here and take up your Bible—you can do what the Lord wants full time. (*Singing as she exits.*) "What a fellowship, what a joy divine. Leaning on the everlasting arms . . . "

SHOWERS: I like what I'm doin! I don't want to preach! (SHOWERS *calls after her. She should continue to sing once off-stage as if moving farther down the way.*) I spent my whole life tryin to do what the Lord wants! I'm doin for me now, you see?

BUDDY: Hey, C.C.?

SHOWERS: (*Still calling.*) Miz Henshaw!

BUDDY: Whatsa matter?

SHOWERS: God . . . damn her!

BUDDY: (*A little worried.*) Ain't you feelin okay?

SHOWERS: (*Trying to control his anger.*) Just leave me alone, Bud.

(BUDDY *takes a jellybean from the jar and holds it up to* SHOWERS)

BUDDY: Maybe you'll feel better you eat somethin.

SHOWERS: (*Lashing out, knocks the boy's arm away.*) I said leave me alone!

BUDDY: (*As* SHOWERS *exits.*) What's a matter, C.C.

(NORMA *and* LUELLA *enter with umbrellas as the boy exits. Light sound of a very gentle summer rain. The women set their umbrellas out to dry.* GOLDIE *enters with her tray.*)

NORMA: Just wait'll you hear.

BUDDY: (*Upset*) Did he do somethin wrong?

LUELLA: That man is amazin.

BUDDY: (*Exiting*) Hey, C.C.?

NORMA: When you hear what happened not half an hour ago you'll say it's just like I told you all summer.

LUELLA: I'd just as soon tell her myself.

GOLDIE: Let me get you some coffee.

LUELLA: Just half a cup, Goldie. Too much'll give me the skitters.

NORMA: After what she's just been through.

LUELLA: (*Quickly*)I can tell her myself!

NORMA: She fell right off her bike in the road!

LUELLA: I was maybe half way to Zion when it started to rain, see? So I says to myself as I'm pedalin along—I says, "Luella, the thing to do here is use your umbrella." But to hold the thing up and ride the bike all at once I had to steer with just my left hand, see?

GOLDIE: No wonder you fell.

NORMA: Right down in the road.

LUELLA: And when I go to get up, I can't move!

NORMA: She can't move . . .

LUELLA: First I'd wiggle at my left side and then give a shake at the right. Tried her backwards and forwards and I can't budge an inch!

NORMA: Now, this is the part that's amazin . . .

LUELLA: There I am on my rump in the road, and I've just about given up hope—

NORMA: The part where she meets him.

GOLDIE: Meets who?

NORMA: You know!

GOLDIE: I don't know!

LUELLA: I look up through the rain, Goldie, and who do you think I see comin?

NORMA AND LUELLA: The new preacher!

NORMA: (*Charging on*) Ain't it amazin, Goldie? Ain't it just like I told you? (*Pause. Quietly:*) You go on, Luella.

LUELLA: So he says to me, "Mrs. Bennett," he says, "Get up off the road, you're just fine." So I says, "I'm not fine—I can't budge, I fell off my blame bike." I says, "if you want a help me, you go get my husband."

GOLDIE: You must a hurt somethin awful.

LUELLA: But the longer I'm talkin the more the preacher keeps starin, till I seen he's starin right in my eyes.

NORMA: Lookin right in her eyes, Goldie—

LUELLA: And it was the funniest sort of a feelin, I tell you—like when he looked in my eyes he saw way down deep inside em. Like he's lookin and seein clean through me.

NORMA: Lookin clean through her, Goldie . . .

GOLDIE: Did he "touch" you?

LUELLA: He says, "I'm gonna hold my hand out here, Ma'am, and I want you to take it. Just grab hold and we'll boost you right up." And his voice is real quiet and his eyes're real calm, and he says, "Mrs. Bennett, get up." And I'm up . . . !

GOLDIE: (*Amazed*) And your back was all right?

LUELLA: I tell you, I never felt better. I might a been a little lightheaded, but—

NORMA: Bein lightheaded's a good sign, don't you think?

GOLDIE: You say the pain was all gone?

LUELLA: Goldie I'm as fit as a fiddle. Course now the Schwinn's quite a mess . . .

NORMA: Folks can give up farmin or minin or schoolin or what have you, but a man can't just toss off the spirit. Like a doctor with healin or a singer with singin—when a man's born to preach then he'll preach. I know he don't have a Church and he's not givin sermons but the spirits within him, you see? Don't you remember the Wednesday night meetins and the singins on Sundays—times when the whole town came together. Nearly thirty or forty people together and all singin with one voice on a Sunday. Without a Church here in Zion I don't know where we're goin . . . one day's the same as the days all before . . . but that's gonna change . . . with him layin on hands now and healin folks, ladies—he knows the Lord's with him, you see? We could build us a new Church in no time at'all. The Lord's brought him to town for a reason.

LUELLA: Well, Norma, you surely can witness.

GOLDIE: A Church back in town'd be darn good for business.

NORMA: Be good for us all, don't you think?

LUELLA: I think the sky's gonna clear.

NORMA: I beg pardon?

LUELLA: I says the sky's clearin up some. The sun's pokin through.

NORMA: Now you see there? You see? That's a good sign if ever there was one.

LUELLA: (*Exiting, to herself.*) Zion looks awful nice after a good summer rain.

GOLDIE: (*Same*) It's a nice town.

NORMA: (*Same*) And when you think how long we been with no preacher.

(SHOWERS *and* JENNIE MAE *enter with cane poles, a worm can, etc. A solid green light washes across the stage; the river.*)

JENNIE MAE: How long?

SHOWERS: This long at least.

JENNIE MAE: Oh, C.C.

SHOWERS: Well maybe this long. But I'll tell you that fish was a fighter. By the time we got him to shore and netted all right he liked to bruise up a good dozen men.

JENNIE MAE: Well little sunfish and bluegills about all you can catch here. Fish bottom you might find a carp.

SHOWERS: Sure looks awful pretty.

JENNIE MAE: It's a nice spot for fishing.

SHOWERS: Now look at this, will you? I just here touch bottom. Must get to ten or twelve foot just a couple yards out there.

JENNIE MAE: It gets awful deep towards the middle. Lot a the boys like to come here and swim.

SHOWERS: Now if boys in Indiana are halfway like the boys in Kentucky I wouldn't imagine they bother too much with swim suits.

JENNIE MAE: Yeah, they're the same then.

SHOWERS: (*Smiles*) I had a feelin they might be. When it comes to swimmin I'm lucky to float. Do a little dog paddlin—that's about it.

JENNIE MAE: I stick to wadin, myself.

SHOWERS: Be happy just dangling my toes in the water. Been a while, I tell you. Too long, I figure.

JENNIE MAE: I thought you fished all the time.

SHOWERS: Well, I used to when I was a kid anyway. But when I had a church I was so full a worry. I never found time to do nothin.

JENNIE MAE: What'd you worry about?

SHOWERS: Everything.

JENNIE MAE: Oh . . .

SHOWERS: You name it, I worried over it. Like I'd see a family loadin down and takin off for California—they'd say, "Pastor, we ain't got no room for the dog." Well, I'd worry a while, then I'd take the dog. Must had near to a dozen old hounds at once for a while. Good dogs, though. I'd line em all up in the front room and practice my preachin on em. Dogs kinds like bein talked at.

JENNIE MAE: Well you talk real nice.

SHOWERS: I talk too damn much, Jennie Mae.

JENNIE MAE: It's not your fault, C.C. It's the river. My Mama used to say people sit by the water they can't help but be talkin. River's kind a magic like that.

SHOWERS: Your Mama was right.

JENNIE MAE: I don't think she ever liked any place so much as the river. Be down here every other day through the summer. And come fall— well you never been here in the fall, but when the leaves start to changin and the air's gettin cooler . . .

SHOWERS: Won't be too long now . . .

JENNIE MAE: And as long as you're here you might as well stay on through winter. Everythin's nice in the spring.

SHOWERS: Sounds like I might have to stay.

JENNIE MAE: Less you're missin Kentucky.

SHOWERS: Naw. I tell you what I miss, though, is them dogs.

JENNIE MAE: What'd you do with em all?

SHOWERS: Well, right before I left I gave em all to my kids.

JENNIE MAE: You have kids in Kentucky?

SHOWERS: Oh yeah. Must a had a good couple dozen spread clear cross the county.

JENNIE MAE: Couple dozen?

SHOWERS: Don't get so darned riled, Jennie Mae. They were church kids.

JENNIE MAE: Well I ought to use you for bait, C.C. Showers, but I can't be so mean to the fish.

SHOWERS: You know what those bubbles are on the water there, don't you?

JENNIE MAE: Air, I imagine.

SHOWERS: Those bubbles right there?

JENNIE MAE: Yeah?

SHOWERS: All those millions and trillions of bubbles?

JENNIE MAE: What?

SHOWERS: Fish farts.

JENNIE MAE: Fish farts!

SHOWERS: Jennie Mae, there must be more fish in this river than stars in the sky and we still ain't had a nibble worth a notice.

JENNIE MAE: Well you'll never get a bite with no worm on your hook. Here. Let me put one on for you.

SHOWERS: Naw . . .

JENNIE MAE: I don't mind.

SHOWERS: No, then I'd end up havin to take a fish off. And don't tell me you'd do that for me too.

JENNIE MAE: All right, I won't tell you.

SHOWERS: But you would, huh?

JENNIE MAE: If you want.

SHOWERS: (*Setting his pole down.*) Well . . . I'm happy just to sit by the water.

JENNIE MAE: (*Setting her pole down.*) All right. (*Pause*)

SHOWERS: You know, Jennie Mae, . . . you know you're awful nice.

JENNIE MAE: Oh . . .

SHOWERS: Yeah you are, and I been meanin to tell you.

JENNIE MAE: You have?

SHOWERS: I sure have. You're real nice, Jennie Mae . . . and you're also . . . (*They are both about ready to kiss.*) . . . real young.

JENNIE MAE: I'm sixteen.

SHOWERS: I know. That's awful young, don't you think?

JENNIE MAE: I don't feel real young.

SHOWERS: Well you are. You don't know how young, Jennie Mae, let me tell you.

JENNIE MAE: My mother was only seventeen when she got married.

SHOWERS: Got married?

JENNIE MAE: Yeah.

SHOWERS: Listen, I think we better head back to the house now.

JENNIE MAE: But we just got here.

SHOWERS: I know, but it's gonna be dark before long and I think we best get home before . . .

JENNIE MAE: Are you tired or somethin?

SHOWERS: Miss Layman, I'm worn to a T.

JENNIE MAE: You want your back rubbed?

SHOWERS: No. No, here now. Let me help you. (*He gives her his hand and helps her stand. They carry their shoes and poles off, etc.*)

JENNIE MAE: (*As he touches her.*) Do you know much about Adam and Eve?

SHOWERS: Yeah . . . yeah I've run into that story before.

JENNIE MAE: You have?

SHOWERS: Yeah, it's a good one all right. But I'm a little more partial to what comes right before. I kind a like all the light the whole story starts out with.

(BUDDY *enters with a lit candle. It is late at night.*)

BUDDY: Ain't they nobody? Ain't they nobody not sleepin? Hey, C.C.? You sleepin? How bout you want a get up? Hey, C.C.? You hear?

SHOWERS: (*Very tired.*) I'm here.

BUDDY: You sleepin?

SHOWERS: Nope.

BUDDY: You awake?

SHOWERS: Nope.

BUDDY: You been sleepin?

SHOWERS: I been tryin, pal.

BUDDY: So's Buddy. He's itchin like nuts. How bout you?

SHOWERS: Bud, there's got to be a cure to all a this itchin . . . (*Yawn*) . . . and I'll be a happier man when we find her.

BUDDY: How bout you want a rub some goop on him, C.C.?

SHOWERS: Bud, what you got here?

BUDDY: Well, he ain't so sure.

SHOWERS: Bud, this is Wildroot Cream oil. You got your Daddy's hair tonic, pal.

BUDDY: Well, he's itchin.

SHOWERS: Bud, this isn't going to help.

BUDDY: Well it smells good.

SHOWERS: You think maybe you'll get back to sleep if I dab a little on you?

BUDDY: Rub it around his backbones.

SHOWERS: Your back's itchin, huh?

BUDDY: His backbones, his elbones. Itchin like he can't sleep for nothin, C.C.

SHOWERS: Yeah, I know the feelin.

BUDDY: Hey, C.C.? You got one a these? You got a belly buttoner?

SHOWERS: Last time I looked I did.

BUDDY: What's it for?

SHOWERS: As far as I know you're born with it, pal. It's part a the package.

BUDDY: (*Amazed*) When he's a baby, C.C.? Babies got belly buttoners?

SHOWERS: You're born with all kinds of amazin things. (*Pause*)

BUDDY: (*Softly*) Wheres babies come from?

SHOWERS: Well, . . . their Mamas have em.

BUDDY: How come?

SHOWERS: Cause Mamas like having babies, I guess. (*Pause*)

BUDDY: Hey, C.C.?

SHOWERS: Yeah?

BUDDY: How come she's with Jesus?

SHOWERS: Cause your Mama's in Heaven.

BUDDY: (*Near tears.*) How come he won't give her back?

SHOWERS: Aw, Bud, it just doesn't work that way, is all . . .

BUDDY: Did he do somethin wrong?

SHOWERS: Well, I wouldn't worry yourself too much.

BUDDY: How come?

SHOWERS: Cause we got enough worry with you losin sleep all the time. Now, what do you say we get you Daddy's hair tonic back where it belongs and get you back on into bed, huh?

BUDDY: (*Yawning*) He ain't so tired, C.C.

SHOWERS: Come on, my friend. It's nearly sunrise. You see in the east there?

(BASIL *and* FERRIS *cross the stage.* FERRIS *has the bike wheel.*)

BASIL: You're yawnin, there, Ferris.

SHOWERS: We're not far from mornin.

BUDDY: Time for breakfast.

SHOWERS: (*Chasing after the boy.*) Time for bed, my friend. Time for sleep.

BASIL: I was wide awake 'fore the sun's in the sky. Lying to bed and the first thing I thought was, "Today's the day." I rolled over to Luella and I says, "Sugar, I'm gonna pick up the Schwinn."

FERRIS: How's she doin?

BASIL: I don't know. I ain't rode her in two weeks.

FERRIS: No, the wife. I mean the wife.

BASIL: Oh. She's fine. Just fine. How's the boy doin, Ferris?

FERRIS: Bout the same, I guess, Basil.

BASIL: Not still itchin, is he? I better look him over again. I was out along the river tryin to doctor the Simpson boy last week. They had him layed up to bed and takin pills right and left.

FERRIS: What's the boy got the flu?

BASIL: No, he's lovesick. Turns out I walked all the way out there just to have him cry on my shoulder and tell me all about how his dog died. Boy loses a dog it does that sometimes.

FERRIS: Felt the same way when I wrecked my first car.

BASIL: Yeah.

FERRIS: He'll get over it.

BASIL: Well he gets back to the fields and starts bringin in the crops he won't have time to be grievin.

FERRIS: Little hard work'll take care of most things, I guess.

BASIL: What you doin to my tire there, Ferris?

FERRIS: Just workin the spokes.

BASIL: That rim's all right, ain't it?

FERRIS: Yeah, C.C.'s pounded her out pretty nice, pretty even. Move on down there and we'll see how she does. (FERRIS *rolls the tire to* BASIL.)

BASIL: Damn thing's always had a wobble to it.

FERRIS: Not bad, though.

BASIL: It'll do. It'll do. I know I'm gettin old fashioned, Ferris, but I look at these damn cars on the road and they're so fast and so noisy . . . I'm like to wish em all away and be done with em. Good for nothin but scarin cattle and kickin the dust up, you ask me. But a bike . . . a bike's a whole nother story. A man gets on his Schwinn and there's no questions asked. Anywhere you want . . . you just peddle along and you're there.

(SHOWERS *and* BUDDY *enter with the rest of the bike.*)

BUDDY: He helped fix her up, Dad. Him and C.C. was workin.

SHOWERS: Bud was in charge a the horses.

FERRIS: The what?

SHOWERS: In charge a holdin his horses.

BASIL: Tough job, huh?

SHOWERS: Oh yeah.

BUDDY: You gonna ride this thing, Basil?

BASIL: You hold your horses, I will. Looks real nice, fellas.

FERRIS: Get this tire on, you're ready to roll. She's got a few miles left in her.

(BUDDY *smears grease on his chest.*)

BASIL: It's a damn wonder she's not more banged up than she is.

SHOWERS: Well, the paint's kind a scratchy.

BASIL: No, the wife. I mean the wife.

SHOWERS: Yeah, she took quite a tumble.

BASIL: Says you helped out some.

SHOWERS: She's just a little shook is all, Basil.

BASIL: Still, you gave her a hand.

SHOWERS: Just helped her up.

BASIL: Well damn it! Can I thank you or not?

FERRIS: (*As* BASIL *and* SHOWERS *shake hands.*) For a good lookin fella he's all right, huh?

BUDDY: (*Turns to the men, and is now covered with grease.*) Would you look at that boy? He can't keep clean for nothin. He's got grease on his belly, his backbones, . . . he's got grease all over him.

BASIL: Feels good to the skin, huh?

BUDDY: Don't wipe the grease off him!

BASIL: Hold still, now! I want another look at you, boy.

BUDDY: How come?

BASIL: Cause you're so pretty.

BUDDY: (*Pleased, allowing him to look.*) He is?

FERRIS: Sure. Runs in the family.

BASIL: Course, your Dad's an exception.

BUDDY: Doodle bugs're pretty.

FERRIS: Yeah.

BUDDY: Jennie Mae's pretty, too.

SHOWERS: She sure is.

BASIL: (*Concerned*) Ferris, you ain't touched this boy, have you?

FERRIS: Kind a hopin it'll clear with the seasons.

BASIL: I don't blame you for hopin, but that ain't gonna cure him. Ferris, it's spread somethin awful! On his neck, in his scalp. Another week or two here it's gonna spread to his eyes. Now I told you to wash him!

FERRIS: I know, Basil.

BUDDY: Don't make him get wet.

BASIL: If you don't keep him clean it's gonna spread through his system.

BUDDY: You ain't gonna wash him.

BASIL: Well, Bud, it's the only cure for ringworm I know.

BUDDY: (*Running off.*) He ain't gonna go in no water!

FERRIS: Hey Bud . . . !

BASIL: You fellas're messin with these salts and this skin lotion and it ain't gonna cure a damn thing. You can't cure him a ringworm by puttin things on him. It's under the skin, don't you see?

SHOWERS: Now, hold on a minute. I can't see what you're talkin.

BASIL: I'm talkin the same damn thing I've told Ferris all summer. Warm water and lotions make the pores open up, and once the skin opens that ringworm'll head for high ground. But cold water draws the skin tight, don't you see? If the ringworm can't breathe, he don't bite . . . he don't bite, you don't itch. I'm not sayin it's easy the way the boy is, but if you'll just keep him clean he'll be fine.

FERRIS: (*Under* SHOWERS's *glare.*) Well, damn it, C.C., I can't take the boy's screamin.

SHOWERS: Why didn't you say somethin, Ferris?

FERRIS: You have to think how I feel when the boy's around water.

SHOWERS: You know how to help him and don't bother to tell me?

FERRIS: The boy gets near water and he's screamin and cryin—it just sets off my mind, don't you see?

SHOWERS: I been the whole summer here, Ferris!

FERRIS: You're not the boy's father, not family—you just work here is all!

SHOWERS: You just leave the boy go!

FERRIS: I'm tired of you tellin me what to do all the time!

SHOWERS: Well I'm tired a doin it all, Ferris!

FERRIS: Don't you understand? The boy's mother died in the water! My wife in the water. I was there.

SHOWERS: I don't care about your wife! I care about the boy!

FERRIS: I don't need you to push me!

SHOWERS: Well I'm gonna push you!

FERRIS: Then you can get to hell on down the damn road! We got along just fine before you, we can get on without you! You hear me?

SHOWERS: I hear you!

FERRIS: Well I'm sorry!

SHOWERS: (*Quietly*) So am I, Ferris.

FERRIS: (*Throws down a rag.*) Well damn it all! (*Pause. Then with control:*) I mean I'm sorry . . . I lose my damn temper too easy.

SHOWERS: I know the feelin . . .

FERRIS: Sometimes a man says things, he doesn't think what he's sayin.

SHOWERS: Sometimes a man's a little too pushy.

FERRIS: Yeah.

SHOWERS: Yeah. I guess I'm just pushy by nature. (*Pause.* SHOWERS, *lost in thought, is spinning one of the bike tires.*)

BASIL: Well. Uh, what do you say we give a push at this bike, fellas?

(SHOWERS *and* FERRIS *turn the bike upright.*)

FERRIS: I got her.

SHOWERS: There you go.

FERRIS: Listen, Basil, I thank you.

BASIL: I'm no doctor, Ferris, but I know what I know. And my advice is to try and relax. If I hollered like you boys I'd give myself the heart failure.

FERRIS: You got your balance now don't you?

BASIL: I'm fine. Just give me a little push is all.

SHOWERS: There you go, cowboy.

BASIL: Not too hard now, damn you!

FERRIS: Take her easy there, Basil.

SHOWERS: Be careful! (*They watch* BASIL *ride off stage. Pause. Then:*)

FERRIS: Well you got any idea how to go about this whole thing?

SHOWERS: Guess we got him in warm, we can get him in cold.

FERRIS: Can't tie the boy up.

SHOWERS: Nope.

FERRIS: And he's tough to hold down.

SHOWERS: Yep.

(JENNIE MAE *and* BUDDY *enter as the men exit.*)

JENNIE MAE: You got yourself all wrapped up in knots, Bud.

BUDDY: Well he was tryin to tie em.

JENNIE MAE: Since when did you start wantin shoes on your feet?

BUDDY: C.C. says he's supposed to keep his dogs in em.

JENNIE MAE: Why's that?

BUDDY: Cause his dogs a got ringworm. Plus he's got her all over the rest of him. Want a see?

JENNIE MAE: No. Now hold still a second. (JENNIE MAE *starts working at getting* BUDDY'S *shoe off and his pants legs rolled up.*)

BUDDY: Hurry up, Jennie Mae. S'gonna rain.

(SHOWERS *and* FERRIS *enter and go to the well. The preacher should draw the water from the well, the well light shining faintly.* BUDDY *doesn't notice them yet.*)

FERRIS: Strange sort a day, ain't it?

SHOWERS: Sky's changin, Ferris.

BUDDY: How come, Jennie Mae?

FERRIS: There's a wind risin fast.

BUDDY: How come you're rollin his pants up?

JENNIE MAE: Settle down, Bud.

BUDDY: Ain't you puttin his boots on?

JENNIE MAE: We'll get your shoes back on in a minute or two.

(SHOWERS *pours the well water into a large bucket.* BUDDY, *hearing it, turns and sees the men.*)

BUDDY: Hey! Hey . . . what you guys doin? What you got in that bucket?

SHOWERS: We're gonna try and fix you up, pal.

BUDDY: He says what's in a bucket, C.C.? Can't you hear? (*He realizes.*) Hey . . . hey, they's water in there. Dad?

SHOWERS: Come on, Bud.

(BUDDY *runs to his father as* SHOWERS *goes for him.*)

BUDDY: Dad!

FERRIS: Son, you're gonna be fine.

BUDDY: What you guys doin? Don't make him get wet.

SHOWERS: You're gonna have to sooner or later. (*They pull him toward the bucket. It's a real struggle.* JENNIE MAE *is waiting there with a rag.*)

BUDDY: C.C., he thunk you's his pal! Leave him go!

FERRIS: You're all right!

BUDDY: Leave go of him, Dad! He can't breathe in a water!

JENNIE MAE: Calm down!

BUDDY: Jennie Mae, make em stop! Ain't no air in a water! Leave him go! Leave him go! He can't breathe!

SHOWERS: It's not gonna hurt you! (*They nearly have his feet in the bucket.*)

BUDDY: (*Exploding*) His Mama's in a water! His Mama! His Mama! Leave him go! He can't breathe! (FERRIS *lets go and* BUDDY *breaks loose.*) Leave him go! (BUDDY *runs off.*)

SHOWERS: Buddy!

JENNIE MAE: Buddy, wait!

SHOWERS: Hey, Bud!

JENNIE MAE: (*Pause. Softly.*) He'll be back soon.

SHOWERS: Buddy—!

JENNIE MAE: (*To her father.*) There's a storm comin.

SHOWERS: Bud—!

JENNIE MAE: Daddy, did you hear me? There's a storm blowin in. He'll be home before long.

SHOWERS: (*Exiting*) He's in the woods, I guess.

(MELVIN *and* DEWEY *enter, watching the sky.*)

SHOWERS: Over those trees there.

JENNIE MAE: He'll be home. (*She exits.* FERRIS *exits after a moment.*)

MELVIN: I never saw clouds like that.

(SHOWERS *can be heard calling "Buddy" at regular intervals from off stage throughout the storm collage.*)

LUELLA: (*Entering with* GOLDIE) It's gonna rain soon.

NORMA: (*Entering with* DARLENE) It's fixing to rain awful hard, dear.

DEWEY: Would you look at that sky?

GOLDIE: You'll have to wait out the storm to get home.

MELVIN: Awful dark clouds.

DARLENE: I never saw the sky so full before.

LUELLA: It's been a good summer for rain.

GOLDIE: Nice summer.

NORMA: Are the windows closed?

BASIL: (*Enters and joins his farmhands.*) Are the tools in?

DARLENE: I think so.

MELVIN: Yeah, they're in.

GOLDIE: Gonna storm most the night I'm afraid.

NORMA: Would you listen to that wind?

LUELLA: It's the season for storms.

DARLENE: I can't sleep when it's stormin.

GOLDIE: (*Exiting with* LUELLA) Best get inside for the sky splits wide open.

NORMA: You'll be all right.

BASIL: I haven't seen the sky like this in years and years.

DARLENE: I never heard the wind so loud before.

DEWEY: Be lightnin and thunder.

MELVIN: Comin soon don't you think?

NORMA: (*Exiting with* DARLENE.) You'll be fine in the house.

BASIL: Won't be long now, boys. We best get inside.

(BUDDY *is heard calling "Mama" off stage as the men exit. Sound of thunder crashing and wind and rain breaking loose intermixed with the boy and the preacher calling.*)

BUDDY: (*Entering*) Mama—! Mama, the air's all turnin to water! All the air's turned to water! He can't find him no air! Mama—!

SHOWERS: (*Entering*) Buddy—?

BUDDY: Mama—?

SHOWERS: Buddy, it's all right!

BUDDY: He can't breathe!

SHOWERS: You're all right now, Buddy!

BUDDY: (*Moving away from* SHOWERS.) No, he can't find her! Can't find him no air!

SHOWERS: Buddy, listen to me!

BUDDY: Mama!

SHOWERS: Listen!

BUDDY: The air's all turnin to water!

(*As* SHOWERS *tries to make the boy understand they wrestle around the stage.* BUDDY *fights for all he's worth.*)

SHOWERS: Hold still and listen!

BUDDY: Leave him go!

SHOWERS: It's the rain! Not the water!

BUDDY: Leave go of him!

SHOWERS: No! You're gonna understand, Buddy! You're gonna figure this out if we have to stay here all night!

BUDDY: He can't breathe!

SHOWERS: You can breathe!

BUDDY: Leave him go! Leave him go! He can't find him no air!

SHOWERS: For a guy who can't breathe you're pretty strong! Now hold still! Hold still and listen!

BUDDY: He can't find her!

SHOWERS: You're not underwater—

BUDDY: Mama—!

SHOWERS: You're not in the water!

BUDDY: Mama!

SHOWERS: Can't you understand? You can breathe!

BUDDY: He has to find her!

SHOWERS: (*Exploding*) What do I have to do to you damn it? You're not gonna find your Mama here, Buddy! She's dead, don't you see, Buddy! Gone!

BUDDY: It ain't his fault, C.C.! Leave him go!

SHOWERS: No!

BUDDY: Leave go of him!

SHOWERS: No!

BUDDY: It ain's his fault how the water took his Mama!

SHOWERS: No! It's not your fault, Buddy! It's nobody's fault!

BUDDY: It ain't!

SHOWERS: No, it ain't!

BUDDY: It ain't Buddy's fault!

SHOWERS: It's not your fault, Buddy!

BUDDY: It ain't Buddy's fault! It ain't Buddy's fault! It ain't, it ain't, it ain't Buddy's fault ... (*He repeats himself, crying.*)

SHOWERS: (*After a pause. Softly.*) It's nobody's fault.

BUDDY: (*Softly*) It ain't?

SHOWERS: No.

BUDDY: God took her.

SHOWERS: That's not your fault, Buddy.

BUDDY: God's mad!

SHOWERS: He's not mad!

BUDDY: He's makin it rain!

SHOWERS: Now, Buddy—

BUDDY: God's mad at him, C.C.!

SHOWERS: It rains cause it's water!

BUDDY: (*Accusing*) It storms!

SHOWERS: Cause it's water! It rains so the plants can grow! It rains so the birds have somethin to drink! It rains because it's water, Buddy! That's what water does!

BUDDY: It does?

SHOWERS: Yeah, that's all it does. Now breathe.

BUDDY: No.

SHOWERS: Breathe!

BUDDY: He ain't gonna.

SHOWERS: You been breathin all along, pal! You might just as well face the fact and get her over with.

BUDDY: He ain't gonna breathe! You can't make him!

SHOWERS: You're breathin right now.

BUDDY: No, he ain't.

SHOWERS: Yeah, you are.

BUDDY: Nope!

SHOWERS: Are you ready?

BUDDY: What you gonna do to him, C.C.?

SHOWERS: We're gonna breathe.

BUDDY: But he can't breathe! (SHOWERS *takes a huge breath and holds it in. Pause.*) Hey, C.C.! It's rainin! He can't breathe in a rain! (BUDDY *becomes concerned for* SHOWERS *well-being.*) Hey, C.C.? You okay? (*He shakes him.*) You all right? Hey, C.C.? (BUDDY *takes a huge breath and holds it.* SHOWERS *immediately exhales.*)

SHOWERS: Now we're gettin somewhere. Feels pretty good, don't it, Bud? Hey, Bud? Buddy, listen. You're best to let out the old and take in some new, pal! (BUDDY *exhales, gasping for air.*) Now what'd you just do?

BUDDY: He breathed. Can't you see him?

SHOWERS: Now let's try her once more. You ready? One, two, three— breathe! (*They take a huge breath together, then another and another and so on—almost like the sound of a train starting up, until they're both breathing along at full tilt.*) You're doin pretty good, pal!

BUDDY: He is?

SHOWERS: Doin fine. Now the wonderful thing about breathin is you can't help but do it all the time, Bud.

BUDDY: He can't?

SHOWERS: Even when you're sleepin you're pretty busy breathin.

BUDDY: When he's sleepin?

SHOWERS: All the time, Bud. Even in the rain.

BUDDY: No siree, C.C.

SHOWERS: Buddy.

BUDDY: What?

SHOWERS: It's rainin.

BUDDY: It's rainin?

SHOWERS: It's lettin up some but it's still rainin.

BUDDY: (*Sudden*) He can't breathe!

SHOWERS: You can breathe, you are breathin, and you're gonna keep breathin!

BUDDY: In a rain? He's gonna breathe in a rain?

SHOWERS: If there's one thing you are, Bud, it's an A-Number-One breather. Word a honor.

BUDDY: (*Taking it to be a pact.*) Word a honor, C.C.? (*They rub palms together.*)

SHOWERS: Word a honor.

BUDDY: Hey, C.C., you know what? He ain't itchin so bad.

SHOWERS: You know why don't you?

BUDDY: Cause he's breathin!

JENNIE MAE: (*Calling from offstage.*) Buddy—?

SHOWERS: I got a sneakin suspicion it's not just cause you're breathin, but because you been breathin while rollin around in all this rain.

JENNIE MAE: (*Closer*) Buddy—?

BUDDY: Over here, Jennie Mae! Him and C.C.'re breathin!

JENNIE MAE: Oh, Bud, I been lookin for you half the night, little brother!

BUDDY: (*As she hugs him.*) He can breathe in a water, Jennie Mae. How bout you?

JENNIE MAE: (*To* SHOWERS) Are you sure he's all right?

SHOWERS: Looks fine to me.

JENNIE MAE: (*Crossing to* SHOWERS) Like to worry me to death, you two.

SHOWERS: Oh, Jennie Mae.

BUDDY: You guys gonna sweet-talk awhile? You want him to maybe go itch somewheres else?

JENNIE MAE: Buddy Layman.

BUDDY: He's itchin like nuts! His arm pitters, his backbones . . . (*Slight pause, amazed.*) Cept his dogs ain't itchin.

SHOWERS: That's cause your dogs're in a puddle a water, my friend.

(BUDDY *squats down and splashes some of the "puddle" in his arm pits.*)

JENNIE MAE: Buddy, what're you doin?

BUDDY: Puttin some a this puddle in his pitters. Feels good.

SHOWERS: Listen, you best find your dad and tell him we'll be down to the water.

JENNIE MAE: Right now?

SHOWERS: Go on. We'll be fine.

JENNIE MAE: Well can't you wait for us, C.C.? It won't take me long.

SHOWERS: Go on now. And stop lookin so worried.

JENNIE MAE: You two be careful. (*She exits.*)

BUDDY: He is.

SHOWERS: Come on, pal.

BUDDY: Where we goin?

SHOWERS: (*Walkin past the boy.*) We're gonna try and make you better.

BUDDY: Hey, C.C.—ain't you gonna carry him?

SHOWERS: Aw, Bud, my back's awful wore out.

(NORMA *enters with* DARLENE *and* DEWEY *in tow as* BUDDY *and* SHOWERS *exit. The young folks are slightly spiffed up.*)

NORMA: I am worn through and through with your stories, Darlene. I know you two been off dancin all night. I got eyes. I can see what you're up to.

DEWEY: But, Miz Henshaw—

NORMA: Not a word out a you, Dewey! You got no room to talk after taking my little girl where you been.

DARLENE: But it was beautiful, Aunt Norma. There was decorations and posters and those little toilet paper flower things.

DEWEY: And a band that played songs like they're right off the radio.

DARLENE: It weren't nothin sinful at'all.

NORMA: Dancin is sinful as sinful could be! I thought I could trust you, Darlene.

DARLENE: I'm sorry, Aunt Norma.

NORMA: You kids're gonna be sorry when you talk to the preacher.

DEWEY: But, Miz Henshaw—

JENNIE MAE: (*Calling from offstage.*) Miz Henshaw—

NORMA: Come on.

JENNIE MAE: (*Entering*) Miz Henshaw! Have you guys seen my Dad?

NORMA: We're marching straight out the garage to have a talk with the preacher.

DEWEY: Well Mr. Showers is down to the river.

NORMA: The river?

JENNIE MAE: If you see my Dad tell him Buddy's with C.C. and they're both to the water. (JENNIE MAE *runs off.*)

NORMA: Well bless me sweet Jesus. You find that man, Dewey. You find Ferris Layman if it takes you all mornin and you tell his boy's found the Lord. You hear me?

DEWEY: I'll fetch him.

NORMA: Well go on! Get a move on! (DEWEY *runs off.*) And as for you, Darlene—sneakin out of the house and carousin all night—I never been so ashamed in my life.

DARLENE: I didn't mean to make trouble.

NORMA: I want you to make a B-line for home and get out a that dress. I can't be bringin you to a baptizin in somethin you look like you were born in and been growin into ever since. (*They exit as* BUDDY *and* SHOWERS *enter.* SHOWERS *has the boy on his back. The river light comes up full force.*)

SHOWERS: Aw, Bud, you're gettin awful heavy.

BUDDY: You think he's a fatso?

SHOWERS: I think you're just growin.

BUDDY: Like a weed?

SHOWERS: (*Setting the boy down.*) To say the least.

BUDDY: (*Seeing the river.*) Hey, C.C.—you ain't gonna stick him in that river water?

SHOWERS: You still itchin?

BUDDY: Well he ain't so sure no more . . .

SHOWERS: Now just look at it a second. Come on, Bud. It's not gonna hurt you. You see, the river is more or less like the rain.

BUDDY: Kind a gives him the willies all over, C.C.

SHOWERS: No, now just try and touch it. (SHOWERS *dips his hand into the river and brings up a cupped hand full of water. He pours a little into* BUD-DY's *hand.*) Put a little in your hand. That's a boy.

BUDDY: S'like the rain?

SHOWERS: It's just water. (*He tosses the rest of his handful up in the air.*) You see how it falls?

BUDDY: (*Tossing his handful.*) Like the rain.

SHOWERS: Only there's a little more of it.

BUDDY: Yeah . . .

SHOWERS: Now what do you say we get that shirt of yours off?

BUDDY: Well he ain't so hot with his buttons.

SHOWERS: Stop scratchin a second and I'll help you.

BUDDY: You want him to get neked, C.C.?

SHOWERS: I'd imagine your shirt's close enough. The river's awful pretty this mornin, ain't it?

BUDDY: What color's that? S'that green, C.C.?

SHOWERS: There's all kinds of colors in the water here, pal. See the trees up above. See the leaves changin colors?

BUDDY: How come?

SHOWERS: Cause that's what leaves do in the fall.

BUDDY: You gettin neked?

SHOWERS: Just pullin my boots off.

BUDDY: Your dogs itch?

SHOWERS: Bud, a little water'll do me good, I imagine.

BUDDY: You sure that's like rain?

SHOWERS: Just about. (*He dips his feet in.*) Woooeeee! S'little colder'n I expected . . .

BUDDY: You okay?

SHOWERS: You stay right where you are and watch how I'm wadin. You want a splash it around on you a little. Get yourself used to it some. (*Freezing*) Feels pretty good, Bud. Real nice . . .

BUDDY: He's like to maybe go find him some breakfast, C.C.

SHOWERS: No. Now just get your feet in for starters. That's all I'm askin. If it's too cold we'll hold off awhile.

BUDDY: Just his dogs is all?

SHOWERS: Just your dogs for starters.

BUDDY: (*Tentatively lets* SHOWERS *dip his feet in.*) Wooooeeee, C.C.! S'freezin!

SHOWERS: Move em around some. (SHOWERS *has* BUDDY *standing in the shallow of the river now.*)

BUDDY: S'awful cold!

SHOWERS: S'awful nice.

BUDDY: Boy oh boy oh boy oh boy oh boy oh boy . . .

SHOWERS: (*Slight overlap.*) Keep movin. That's a boy. There you go.

BUDDY: How you doin?

SHOWERS: I'm doin fine, pal. Feelin dandy.

BUDDY: You gonna wash him all off?

SHOWERS: You warmin up some?

BUDDY: Well he's tryin.

SHOWERS: All right. (SHOWERS *lifts a handful of water and puts it over the boy's head.*)

BUDDY: Go easy, C.C.! Easy!

SHOWERS: (*Using less water, just a little.*) S'that better?

BUDDY: Hey, C.C.?

SHOWERS: Yeah?

BUDDY: He's a wonder.

SHOWERS: You are, huh? Well what are you a wonder about, Bud?

BUDDY: You think his Mama's okay?

SHOWERS: I figure your Mama's in heaven. (BUDDY *slips just a touch.*) Whoa now! You stick right here close by me.

BUDDY: He is.

SHOWERS: You want to feel your way along the bottom, you see.

BUDDY: Yeah . . . you been to Heaven?

SHOWERS: Well, Bud, to tell you the truth I been a little too busy bein here to be much a any place but here.

BUDDY: Well where's heaven at?

SHOWERS: Let me think for a second.

BUDDY: S'in the sky?

SHOWERS: Not exactly . . .

BUDDY: You still thinkin?

SHOWERS: I'm tryin. I guess you could say that Heaven's where you are when you ain't here no more.

BUDDY: When you ain't here no more ...

SHOWERS: Like your Mama.

BUDDY: She's gone.

SHOWERS: Well that's Heaven.

(NORMA, DARLENE, GOLDIE, *and* LUELLA *begin to sing* Shall We Gather At The River *off stage. They sound as if they're way in the distance and moving very gradually closer.*)

BUDDY: Hey, C.C. Listen. You hear it?

SHOWERS: What's that?

BUDDY: The river. S'talkin.

SHOWERS: The water, you mean? The waves?

BUDDY: S'talkin, C.C.!

SHOWERS: Well what's it sayin to you, Bud?

BUDDY: Well ... he don't know.

SHOWERS: Who doesn't know?

BUDDY: He don't.

SHOWERS: (*Pressing*) Who don't?

BUDDY: Him! Him, C.C.! Can't you hear?

SHOWERS: Yeah, I hear him. You're a pretty good guy, Bud. You know that?

(*The Women are still off, but very close.*)

WOMEN:
"Shall we gather at the river,
Where bright angel feet have trod;
With its crystal tide forever,
That flows by the throne of God?
Yes, we'll gather at the river,
The beautiful, the beautiful river.
Gather with the saints at the river,
That flows by the throne of God—" (*Etc.*)

(BUDDY *and* SHOWERS *totally overlap the singing.*)

BUDDY: Hey. Hey, C.C.—how come they's singin?

SHOWERS: It's all right. (*He calls to the women though they're still off stage.*) Hey, ladies? Ladies, we're trying to wash here, you understand?

BUDDY: He likes it in a water.

SHOWERS: (*To himself*) What're they doin? (*He calls.*) Hey, ladies? We'd like to be alone here, you see?

(*The women enter up high. They're singing very loud. The song should continue at high volume behind all the dialogue.*)

NORMA: I brought em, Pastor Showers! We're all here to witness!

SHOWERS: We'd like to be alone here.

NORMA: We're here for the baptizin, Pastor!

SHOWERS: This isn't a baptizin!

NORMA: Praise God, the Lord's with him! (*She goes back to singing full force.*)

SHOWERS: I'm just washing the boy. Don't you see?

(*The women sing even louder.* NORMA *acts as a song leader of sorts. As* SHOWERS *loses his temper he lets go of the boy's arm.* BUDDY, *enjoying himself immensely and thinking he can breathe in water, moves away from* SHOWERS *and the women.* SHOWERS *has his back to the boy as he rages at the women.*)

SHOWERS: (*Continued*) Would you stop singin and listen? This is nothing to do with the Church or the spirit! I'm done with the Church! Would you listen? Stop singin and listen!

BUDDY: He can breathe in a water!

SHOWERS: I'm not gonna baptize him, damn it! Don't make me a preacher!

BUDDY: He's breathin! (BUDDY *steps into the deepest area of the river and is suddenly underwater. At the same moment a sound of something representing underwater silence is heard—very loud, a sort of wail. Wind run at half speed and mixed with a little water sound works pretty well. All action immediately takes on the water's perspective and shifts to extreme or film-like slow motion. The preacher is yelling at the women. No one notices* BUDDY *underwater. When the boy rises the action suddenly shifts into normal stage speed and sound. The sound effects shifts off momentarily.*) C.C.!

SHOWERS: (*Overlapping*) Would you listen to me!

(BUDDY's *immediately back underwater and the sound effect and slow motion resume.* JENNIE MAE *enters in slow motion, looking over the water, and sees* BUDDY *as he rises for the second time.*)

BUDDY: Mama—!

JENNIE MAE: Buddy—!

*(The boy is immediately back under water, and the sound effect is im-
mediately up again. SHOWERS turns as JENNIE MAE screams and sees the
boy is missing. He goes underwater and searches the river bottom for the
boy. BUDDY, as if fighting the current, is slipping several yards cross stage
and fighting to pull himself back. SHOWERS searches the river bottom on
his belly, pulling himself along the raked stage, feeling along before him
with his hands. When he needs air he pulls himself back towards the
women, and bursts from the water.)*

NORMA: Thy Kingdom come! Thy will be done!

JENNIE MAE: *(Overlapping)* My brother! My brother!

*(As SHOWERS goes under again the sound comes back up as before. GOLDIE
is holding JENNIE MAE back from the water. NORMA is praying as if it will
somehow save the boy. As the preacher rises again:)*

NORMA: Forgive us our trespasses as we forgive!

GOLDIE: *(Overlapping)* It's all right!

JENNIE MAE: *(Overlapping)* My brother!

*(SHOWERS goes under water immediately and the sound comes back on.
He searches, nearly reaching the boy. He stays under as long as he can.
The boy dies as the preacher pulls himself toward shore. As he rises:)*

NORMA: And the glory forever and ever! *(Slight pause.)* Amen.

*(There is only the sound of the gently flowing water and SHOWERS cough-
ing, gasping for air. He pulls himself part way onto the river bank and
turns, looking over the water.)*

SHOWERS: Oh, my God. Oh my God my God my God . . .

*(The dulcimer begins to play "Amazing Grace" slowly, one string, one
note at a time—solemn and grieving in its music. The women and the
preacher hold their tableau.)*

Second Elegy

*(The river fades as two pin spots rise on either side of the stage, BASIL and
DEWEY entering. Except for the possibility of a morning sky behind them,
theirs are the only lights on stage. They speak directly to the audience, as
in the beginning. The dulcimer grows strong and full behind them.)*

BASIL: And like a slate wiped clean or a fever washed away where there
was fire to the sky now there's nothin. Where there was clouds there's
just blue and the sun.

DEWEY: His only son gone and it's me who brings the word when I find
Ferris Layman that mornin. I'd run to the river and I seen the boy there
and I run like the wind for his father! I says, "Ferris . . . I'm sorry." And

he don't move and don't speak. I says, "Your son, he's passed on beyond us."

BASIL: Buddy Layman's dead, don't you see? When he said it would rain we laid our fields in rows and we knew it would be a good season.

DEWEY: And now we harvest the fields and we turn the ground over.

BASIL: Turn the earth to the Earth like a child to his mother. And we think a the boy and we call it a blessin. We turn to each other and we call it a blessin.

(*The lights fade to black as the dulcimer strikes a final chord.*)

A Note On The Boy

Buddy can be played as either fourteen or seventeen years old, depending on the actor. If he's played as seventeen then several line changes are in order. His sister should call him "big brother" instead of "little brother"—or she should simply call him "Buddy" when "big brother" seems inappropriate. In the Cafe scene in the first act (*page 153*) the lines should read so that Goldie says, "He's only a boy, Ferris!" and Ferris responds, "The boy's seventeen! When I was his age I cussed all the time!", etc. Finally, in Ferris's monologue in the first act (*page 162*) he would say, "I wasn't married a year and she give me a son. I was just gettin used to a wife." His next line would then read, "then the girl came along."

Buddy's central trait is his innocence, his vulnerability. He shouldn't have too much of a speech impediment, though his speech should be hesitant when he's discovering something or confused or frightened. His gestures, his walk, and his whole physical attitude should reflect both an emotional and intellectual frustration, or more simply, sometimes a coordination problem. Clinically speaking, he isn't modeled on any specific emotional or physical disorder.

Costume Plot

BUDDY LAYMAN
> Overalls—very dirty
> Blue plaid flannel shirt—very dirty
> Black lace-up ankle boots—very dirty
> (must muddy body including hair—nightly)

JENNIE MAE
> Pale blue old cotton floral 20's style dress
> Slip
> Blue checked half-apron
> Brown leather tie shoes
> Off-white cotton socks
> Cut-off long johns under dress

FERRIS
> Pale blue striped shirt w/grease stains
> Suspenders
> Leather belt
> Baggy jeans
> Cap
> Cotton socks
> Brown leather ankle high boots
> Pocket watch
> Blue patterned handkerchief

C.C. SHOWERS
> Pale blue shirt w/pattern
> Brown striped tie
> Matching suit coat & vest-brown
> Brown suit trousers (not matching vest and coat)
> Black ankle-high lace-up boots
> Brown felt fedora
> Off-white man's handkerchief
> (*Everything should look very old*)

NORMA
> Rusty brown and cream floral 20's style cotton dress
> Black tie "sensible shoes"
> Gold-stiped faded work smock
> No stockings
> Gold pin on collar

DARLENE
> Pale yellow cotton 20's style dress
> Pink hand-knit cardigan

    Brown flat shoes
    Barette in hair

GOLDIE
    Blue and off-white striped cotton 20's style dress, w/white collar
    Pin at neck
    Cotton stockings
    Off-white laced "sensible" shoes
    Bib apron

BASIL
    Steel-rimmed glasses
    Jacket length jean work jacket-very faded
    Grey gabardine work trousers
    Black belt
    Blue and brown plaid flannel shirt
    Ankle-high black lace-up boots
    Old felt fedora
    Handkerchief
    White cotton socks

LUELLA
    Pink hat w/flowers
    Aqua-green cotton dress w/belt
    Gray laced "sensible" shoes
    Full rust apron
    Handbag
    Off-white sweater with embroidered flowers
    Wedding ring
    Cotton stockings

MELVIN
    Overalls
    Beige shirt
    Work boots

DEWEY
    Overalls
    Blue work shirt
    Work boots

*Important—All the clothes in *The Diviners* must look old and faded.

Joseph Pintauro

Snow Orchid

Joseph Pintauro lives in New York City and Sag Harbor, New York. Of his first full-length play, *Snow Orchid,* produced by The Circle Repertory Company, Frank Rich said, *"Pintauro reveals a talent for dramatising grand passions with almost operatic vigor. He unleashes a volcanic uproar of affection, obscenities and physical abuse worthy of* Raging Bull." Walter Kerr in his review of *Snow Orchid* singled him out as a writer of extraordinary energy and one to watch. Of his several one-act plays, Thomas Lask of *The New York Times* said: *"Pintauro has two considerable strengths: an ability to write pungent, idiomatic urban speech, and a willingness to let human passions overflow on the stage. His characters neither stifle their feelings nor express them with a stiff upper lip. In the full flood of their agony, they hammer at each other until their emotions are spent."*

The one-acts that make up *Cacciatore* were produced by the Actors Repertory Company at the Hudson Guild Theatre in New York City and at the Edinburgh Festival in Scotland. *Snow Orchid* was selected for the Eugene O'Neill Conference in 1980, where the role of FILUMENA was played by Rosemary Di Angelis. A series of one-act plays, produced at the Circle Rep Directors Lab, is scheduled for full production in the coming year.

Mr. Pintauro also writes fiction. His first novel, *Cold Hands* (Simon and Schuster, 1979), was widely reviewed and widely praised. In *The New York Times* review, Evan Hunter called it "a deceptively simple, hauntingly beautiful novel." Alan Cheuse, writing for *The Los Angeles Times,* described *Cold Hands* as a breakthrough novel. *Cold Hands,* singled out by *The New York Times Book Review* as one of the best novels of the year, has recently been republished by the Plume Division of NAL. Pintauro's most recent novel, *State of Grace* (Times Books, 1983), is now a Bantam trade paperback.

Mr. Pintauro has taught playwriting at Southampton College, fiction writing at Sarah Lawrence and filmmaking at Marymount and The School of Visual Arts, N.Y.C.

Author's Note: *Snow Orchid* is for my sister Mildred.

For information regarding stock and amateur rights, including all other rights, contact: Gilbert Parker, William Morris Agency, 1350 Avenue of the Americas, New York, NY 10019.

Snow Orchid previewed at The Circle Repertory Company on March 3, 1982 (Press Opening: March 11) under the direction of Tony Giordano with the following cast:

BLAISE .... Ben Siegler
SEBBIE .... Robert Lupone
FILUMENA .... Olympia Dukakis
ROCCO .... Peter Boyle

Characters

ROCCO LAZARRA is fifty-six. Born in Brooklyn, he is Italo-American, of Neopolitan extraction.

FILUMENA BATTAGLIA LAZARRA is thirty-eight. Born in Sicily and raised there, she came to America as ROCCO'S bride when she was only sixteen.

SEBB (SEBBIE, SEBASTIANO), their oldest son, is twenty-one.

BLAISE (Pronounced Blaze), their youngest, is sixteen.

The Set

The Lazarra house is a mythical vestige of Americana, a grey skeleton of a once elegant, one-family Victorian home in a run-down section of Brooklyn near the river across from Manhattan. The play turns on a wheel of scenes that take place mostly between two actors at a time. The scenes work best when the set is fluid enough to allow the actors to come forward, providing the audience with intimate access to them.

References to "stairs" and actors' exits to them, as well as to their rooms, may simply be choreographed to indicate the action. Still, all action should be put forward as realistically as possible. Good productions have taken place in the most minimalistic of settings, but props, in every case, should be fully employed when called for.

The orchids should be primitive varieties growing on tree bark or osmunda (a very lightweight, black, tropical wood-like mass to which greenhouse orchids attach themselves permanently and grow). Some plants might cling to masses of moss, but they should all hang, suspended from thin wires, primeval plants with visible, serpentine roots that live on air or even float in air.

The statue of Saint Anthony to which Filumena prays in her room must not be too large. If the statue must be fixed, then it should be dimly visible when not in play.

Technical Notes

The plants make sounds through microcomputers that feed through an amplifier and into speakers. These sounds may be a variety of beeps, interrelating in the manner of some works by minimalist composers such as Philip Glass. The sounds should be intelligent, tinkling, bleeping, fine, electronic. But the sound that occurs when Rocco touches his son's finger to the transmitting instrument is a deep, but friendly, organ-like note. Whenever hostility threatens the plants, the bleep-music should reflect this.

Act One

Scene One

(SEBB *and* BLAISE *tiptoe through front door.* SEBB *is carrying a large rectangular gift-wrapped box.*)

BLAISE: It's quiet.

SEBB: Where the hell am I gonna hide the box?

BLAISE: Hide it up in your room.

SEBB: She might bump into me on the stairs.

BLAISE: She's probably locked in her room talkin' to Saint Anthony. (*He calls softly, teasing* SEBB.) Ma?

SEBB: First your arms. Then your legs.

(FILUMENA *coughs offstage.*)

BLAISE: She's havin' a cigarette in the bathroom. We got a minute of peace before Vesuvius erupts.

SEBB: What you hafta waste a half an hour in Woolworth's for, huh, cauliflower-face?

BLAISE: Why'd you hafta go across the friggin' bridge into Manhattan for a lousy coat and dress? A new coat and dress ain't gonna get her to leave this house.

SEBB: I told you to read that magazine article. There's a place in Denver that cures people a'scared to leave their house.

BLAISE: So a coat and dress is gonna fly her there?

SEBB: I don't need you to help me with her.

BLAISE: What happened when her mother died in Italy and we hadda go get our passports? She turned into Niagara Falls on the subway . . .

SEBB: Blaise, I'm warnin' you . . .

BLAISE: She gets the sweats when she has to answer the freakin' doorbell.

SEBB: I'll take care of her.

BLAISE: You'd have to slip a dozen quaaludes in her macaroni to get her to New Jersey and he's talkin' about shippin' her to Colorado.

SEBB: They should put your mouth on top of every ambulance.

BLAISE: She looked like a vampire on the passport.

SEBB: She was in grief, you asshole.

BLAISE: She was in terror of the subways is what she was in. Did we get to Sicily? We didn't even get to Hoyt and Schermerhorn Street.

FILUMENA: (*Running downstairs*) You sonofabitches the two of you.

BLAISE: Here comes your hot lava.

FILUMENA: Where were you? You swore to me I wouldn't hafta be alone when that monster walks in.

SEBB: He kept me double parked for a half hour in fronta Woolworths.

BLAISE: Our father a monster.

FILUMENA: And what you hafta go to Woolworths for?

BLAISE: A welcome home sign.

FILUMENA: A welcome home sign for a man who tried to commit . . .

(*She grabs the bag out of* BLAISE'S *hand and rummages through it.*)

BLAISE: He's been gone a whole year for cryin' out loud.

FILUMENA: Party hats?

SEBB: Is that what I was wastin' gas for?

FILUMENA: He's not comin' home from the Army, you jerk. He's comin' home from the crazy house. I'm sittin' here afraid to take a bath in case he walks in on me, and this kid comes home with party hats?

BLAISE: So what if he sees your tits. He's your husband.

FILUMENA: (*Reaches to grab* BLAISE *to slap him.*) Catch that kid. I'm gonna torture him.

SEBB: Lookit you gettin' all dressed up for the monster.

FILUMENA: What're you crazy? I'm gettin' dressed for Saint Anthony.

SEBB: Saint Anthony?

FILUMENA: They're rollin' his statue in the streets.

SEBB: Saint Anthony ain't in December.

BLAISE: They're passin' out his bread for Advent. Five dollars a loaf.

SEBB: He's got a big dong, eh, Filumena?

BLAISE: Who? Saint Anthony?

SEBB: The ol' man, turkey. Like father like son . . .

BLAISE: I think we get it from her.

FILUMENA: Shut up, trouble-mouth. Wipe the fingerprints off the light switches before your father sees them and go upstairs and close my window.

BLAISE: Wait till he sees the oil bill. I'm tellin' him you keep your window open and turn the thermostat up so you could make believe you're back in Sicily.

FILUMENA: Do I spend your money?

BLAISE: You ain't gonna either.

SEBB: He got his first paycheck today.

FILUMENA: Oh yeah? You're gonna chip in here, big time. You're the one wanted to quit school ... (*To* SEBB) Come upstairs and help me get this dress on. I musta shrank the goddam thing. (*To* BLAISE) Go for olives, you. He likes olives ... and he hates the bread with the seeds. Get a loaf without the seeds. That Saint Anthony bread is full of seeds ... five dollars ... (*Exits*)

BLAISE: I hear your buddy Doogan is movin' to Texas tomorrow. I feel bad for you.

SEBB: C'mere ... I jus' wanna shake your hand.

BLAISE: I was just bein' sadistic.

SEBB: I ain't gonna do nothin—c'mere a minute ...

BLAISE: Ta ta ... (*Exits door.*)

Scene Two

(SEBB *makes his way up to Filumena's room as she is getting dressed and talking to her Saint Anthony statue.*)

FILUMENA: Some saint ... right now you hadda make them pass out the bread.

(*She bends to put on a black stocking. Her behind faces the doorway where* SEBB *is approaching silently.*)

FILUMENA: Who needs your bread? Who knows if they pick their noses those bakers or wipe their ass and not wash their hands? (*Then the other stocking.*) I shkeeve your bread. When I see you bakin' it with my own eyes, then I'll eat it.

SEBB: What gorgeous cheeks. (*He gooses her.*)

FILUMENA: Stop. You sonofabitch. (*She slaps him.*) Help me with this dress.

SEBB: Stop sweatin'. You'll stink.

FILUMENA: Where's my underarm ...

SEBB: Look at ya, primpin' and powderin' like King Kong was comin' to pick ya off the cliff.

FILUMENA: This powder ain't for your father.

SEBB: Then why you gettin' dressed? Huh? You goin' to go to the sidewalk this year? Huh, Filumena?

FILUMENA: Maybe I'll try to take the bread at the sidewalk. Why not?

SEBB: Good. I'll help ya down the stoop. Okay?

FILUMENA: Leave me alone.

(SEBB *waits for a response.*)

SEBB: Liar . . . You forget the days he used to give us black eyes?

FILUMENA: You're makin' me feel closed in.

SEBB: Would the Jews wear perfume for Hitler?

FILUMENA: Go look at Christ on the cross. You're supposed to forgive.

SEBB: Did you forget before Blaise was born . . . that shithole tenement over the Brooklyn Navy Yard where the three of us had ta sleep in one bed and he kicked us if we moved?

FILUMENA: Yeah, and you followed him around that tenement like a puppy. You cried when he went to work. All of a sudden he remembers the Brooklyn Navy Yard . . . He never said boo to you. When was the last time he talked to you?

SEBB: I just don't like seein' him around my house using my bathroom. Eatin' in my kitchen.

FILUMENA: The kitchen's under his name with the rest of the house. You say "hello" nice when he comes in and then you can forget him for the rest of your life. Now you work all day . . . and I'm the one who's got him. Twenty-four hours—Jesus!

MAN(O.S.): (*Far off*) Pane Sont Ondone.

FILUMENA: You hear? Saint Anthony's on Meeker Avenue. Tell the little bastard to throw the rigatoni in the boilin' water . . . if it's boilin'.

SEBB: (*Calling down*) Blaise . . .

BLAISE: (*Calling up*) The little bastard heard. Should I throw in salt, too?

FILUMENA: I salted it . . . I salted it. And did he turn on the gas under the gravy?

SEBB: Blaise?

BLAISE: I did.

FILUMENA: Low.

SEBB: Low, Blaise.

FILUMENA: Tell him to lower it. I know that kid.

BLAISE: I'm lowering it and I set the big table.

FILUMENA: (*Screams*) *Don't set the big table.* What's that little trouble-maker up to? He knows your father eats alone in the kitchen . . . Hey, the lipstick, throw it away, Sebbie, please . . .

SEBB: I paid three bucks for this lipstick.

FILUMENA: So give it to Doogan.

SEBB: I warned you not to make cracks.

FILUMENA: Take a joke, undertaker-face. You're scared your father'll find out, eh? Zip up the dress.

SEBB: Gorilla in a dress—(*With effort he yanks her dress down over her hips.*) Holy Christ . . .

FILUMENA: Oh! My tits are in my throat.

SEBB: Com'on . . . let's go down now and catch the bread. The people haven't seen you since we moved here.

FILUMENA: I don't wanna see no people. I'm catchin' the bread from the window. Lemme alone. Hide my cigarettes.

SEBB: I'll help you down the fuckin' *stoop.*

FILUMENA: Ravongool . . . Catholic high school. How sweet your mouth turned out with fuckin' this and fuckin' that. Bella sont, where's my money now? You, Saint Anthony . . . the breadmen, and Rocco all on the same fuckin' day. Hide these cigarettes.

SEBB: You don't have to hide nothin'.

FILUMENA: Put those cigarettes somewhere . . .

SEBB: If he ever hits you, you call me, you hear?

FILUMENA: Sure. So we can have a double murder. Brush my hair. (*She hands him the brush.*)

SEBB: How'm I gonna brush your hair if you don't sit?

FILUMENA: This dress is too tight to sit.

SEBB: (*Tries brushing*) Ma, you gotta sit.

FILUMENA: Okay, Ou Gesu Greest. (*She sits and the dress rips—rrriiiiipp.*) Che Gatz? Ou mange la madonna (*She consistently pronounces this "ma-dawn".*) ey tuttay sont.

SEBB: Holy Christ!

FILUMENA: I exploded the dress. Looka me. This saint wants me to stay trapped in this room with him forever.

SEBB: You wanna wear a new dress? Something terrific? Ma?

FILUMENA: (*She cries silently.*) It's no use. Sont Ondone, perche?

MALE VOICES (O.S.): (*Selling bread*) Pane Sont Ondone. Pane Sont Ondone.

FILUMENA: Brush! They're on the block. Brush!

(SEBB *brushes, roughly.*)

FILUMENA: Ouch!

SEBB: I'm sorry.

FILUMENA: No. I like it hard. Only you know how. It opens my sinuses. Mnnn.

SEBB: Ma, a grey hair.

FILUMENA: Pull it.

(SEBB *pulls the hair.*)

FILUMENA: Throw it away. What's the big bird that swims on top of the water in English again?

SEBB: A swan?

FILUMENA: Si. La cigna nera. That's what they used to call me in Sicily . . . the black swan, 'cause I wore my hair down to here. Sixteen years old. And your father? A thirty-two year old man with white pants. An American. He was so crazy for me he went to my mother: I die if you don't give her to me. Well, an Italian from America in white pants, Madonna . . . what connections he must have. Take her, my mother said. Who knew he was an electrician on vacation? Try to get him to fix a plug around here . . . and a Napoleedon on top of it.

SEBB: Ma, when are ya gonna let it be American time on that clock?

FILUMENA: Never. That's my mother's clock from Italy. I know the time from the electric clock, six o'clock, but it's midnight in Sicily right now. The stars are out. I hold the clock and I can smell lemons from my bed. I hear the bells on the goats . . .

SEBB: Ma, them goats died twenty years ago.

FILUMENA: (*She stares sadly out of her window.*) No. The goats are still alive, more than those skinny American trees outside that get hysterical soon as they smell the snow and tear all their hair out like crazy ladies. I hate the snow . . .

MAN'S VOICE (O.S.): (*Getting closer*) Pane Sont Ondone. Pane Sont Ondone.

FILUMENA: Ooop, Madonna, they stopped in front of the house. Where's my money? (*She jumps up and opens the window, waving her twenty-dollar bill, but looking up, she discovers, points to seagulls, and takes it as a lucky sign.*) Hey, seagulls. See?

MAN: Pane Sont Antone.

FILUMENA: (*Looking down*) Look. Up here, stupid.

MAN: No bread for the people who don't come to church Father Sullivan said.

FILUMENA: Tell him mind his business. There's a twenty-dollar bill. Throw me two loaves and get away from my door. We're expecting my husband.

SEBB: We'll go down and get your change, Ma... C'mon.

FILUMENA: Go 'way...

MAN: Next Sunday, Signora Lazarra, you people come to church.

FILUMENA: Is that supposed to be Saint Anthony on that wagon? He looks like you stole some stiff from the back door of Pizella's Funeral Parlor.

SEBB: Ma.

FILUMENA: You wanna see the real Saint Anthony? What you think them seagulls are makin' a circle over this house for? 'Cause he's right here in my bedroom. This is my church.

MAN: Catch your bread.

(FILUMENA *leans out, catches two loaves. Each loaf of bread has a purple Advent ribbon tied around it, and on the ribbon is pasted a paper reproduction of Anthony's face.*)

MAN: Hey, bend over for your change.

(*This brings* SEBB'S *head the window.*)

SEBB: She's my mother, money-hungry. Eat the change before I come down and shove it down your throat.

FILUMENA: Hey, you. You get inside.

(*Start fade out of* MEN *calling "Pane Sont Ondone" over following dialogue.*)

BLAISE: (*Running up stairs, enters UF.*) Ma... Ma... did you see Saint Anthony?

FILUMENA: Grab him.

(SEBB *teasingly grabs* BLAISE.)

BLAISE: What I do?

FILUMENA: Take down those decorations ... (*Slap*) ... and go to Scambatti's and get Provolone cheese for grating.

(ROCCO *enters quietly.*)

BLAISE: When're we gonna have an American dinner?

FILUMENA: Vongool America. Get Provolone.

BLAISE: Jungle woman.

(ROCCO *has entered quietly, unnoticed. He carries massive orchid plants attached to sphagnum moss and treebark; they are primeval-looking, but unseen as yet, wrapped in dark green tissue and then in transparent plastic to protect them from the cold.*)

FILUMENA: Grab that housedress ... hurry ... that clown grates Provolone on his macaroni.

SEBB: What clown? Cheeks. (*Gooses her.*)

FILUMENA: (*Screams*) Stop. The fat clown that sings in the opera.

SEBB: Pagliacci?

(FILUMENA *becomes confused and winds up with one sleeve of the dress on, but the torn dress is not fully removed. The boys move toward the stairs together, but* FILUMENA *holds back because she hasn't solved the dilemma of the two dresses.*)

FILUMENA: Get this ... arm out.

(Rocco *lifts the shades, letting in light. He proceeds to put on a cassette.*)

FILUMENA: (*Giggling to herself.*) Don't say Pagliacci to his face and make me laugh, you sonofabitch. Don't you do it.

BLAISE: Do you think they made him wear a straitjacket?

FILUMENA: Don't you try to made me laugh in fronta him or I'll kill ya.

SEBB: Cheeks.

(*Pinches her again; she jerks away, pretending she's annoyed, but she enjoys it.*)

FILUMENA: Stop! (*To* BLAISE) And you other sonofabitch, take down that welcome home.

MEN'S VOICES (O.S.): (*Far away now, turning to silence.*) Pane Sont Ondone. Pane Sont Ondone.

(*They freeze as beautiful music sounds throughout the house. It is spatial, angelic music, voices.* SEBB *slowly makes his way down the stairs.* BLAISE *and* FILUMENA *follow at a distance.*)

ROCCO: (*Startled*) Sebbie.

SEBB: Pa. Gee. You look good. (*Stares at the changes in* ROCCO, *sympathetically, then catches himself.*) How we sposta know who walked in here? What is that stuff playin'?

ROCCO: I thought it'd be a nice way ... I wanted to surprise you that I was home. Thanks for the sign. Where's ...

(FILUMENA *and* BLAISE *appear.*)

ROCCO: Filumena. Hey. Com esta?

FILUMENA: Rocco?

ROCCO: Yeah. She don't recognize me. Hey, I got thin, right?

FILUMENA: Didn't they feed you? You look like you just got out of a concentration camp.

ROCCO: You look like you just got hit with an airplane. (*No reaction*) So laugh at a joke. You go out while I was gone, Filumena?

BLAISE: She stuck her head out the window.

(FILUMENA *swings at* BLAISE.)

BLAISE: Lay off, beast.

ROCCO: Hey. Shut up. She'll go out when she feels like it. Right, Filumena? We'll get her out there. I learned a lot about that stuff. Whadya embarrassed to express yourself? ... Somebody kiss me or somethin'.

FILUMENA: (*To* BLAISE) Kiss your father.

BLAISE: Kiss him, Sebb. I gotta check the macaroni. (*Goes to the kitchen.*)

FILUMENA: And lower that music.

ROCCO: That's Brian Appelman. That new guy.

FILUMENA: (*She pretends to have heard of the composer.*) Oh, yeah.

ROCCO: You cut your hair, Filumena.

FILUMENA: Uh. Yeah.

ROCCO: I got a loaf of Saint Anthony bread ... and wine ... to go with the music. What're we eatin'?

BLAISE: Two minutes for the rigatoni.

ROCCO: Rigatoni? I'm so glad I'm home ... Jesus ...

(BLAISE *peeks into the blue drugstore bag* ROCCO *placed on the server.*)

BLAISE: Pa, these look like valiums.

ROCCO: Get outta that bag. We gotta learn to respect peoples' privacy.

FILUMENA: Then why'd you pull up the shades?

ROCCO: I'm gone a year and you greet me with why'd I open the shades? They pass valiums out like jelly beans where I come from.

BLAISE: You just got these around the corner. It says Lorimer Drugs.

ROCCO: What're you, a detective? Mind your business. Please. Hey. Welcome home, Rocco. This is it. Thank you for the sign.

FILUMENA: Thank you? Please? See what 'lectrizity does for your brain?

ROCCO: I didn't get no 'lectrizity. I got ... talkin' it out ... I'll teach you how to talk and how to hear. This is all new ...

FILUMENA: I'd rather have the 'lectrizity.

BLAISE: I set up your place in the kitchen, Pa, with a party hat.

ROCCO: No, I wanna eat out here with all of you. Please.

(FILUMENA *is attracted by Rocco's softness.*)

FILUMENA: That's up to you. I don't care.

BLAISE: A welcome home party.

SEBB: Count me out. I got an appointment.

ROCCO: Cancel it, Sebb.

SEBB: Who does he think he's ordering around?

FILUMENA: He'll stay for dinner. C'mon Sebbie ... for me.

ROCCO: Once, Sebbie, once. Like a real family.

SEBB: Listen to him. You're the one never wanted anybody to eat with you. Now you wanna play Daddy?

ROCCO: Daddy?

FILUMENA: Do it for me, I said.

BLAISE: Yeah, do it ... for someone else. (BLAISE *exits to kitchen.*)

SEBB: I'm twenty-one years old, you. He's somethin' in my past. I gotta screw around this table 'cause they gave him a guilty conscience in some nut house?

ROCCO: It ain't for me, poison-face, that I wanna eat with you. It's for your own good. Okay, you little sonofabitch, so don't bust my hump ten minutes after I walk in the door of my own fuckin' house ...

(ROCCO *stops short suddenly, hearing himself.*)

SEBB: What happened to "please" and "thank you?"

ROCCO: Look, I'm sorry. Okay? I'm scared. I'm nervous. I admit it ...

FILUMENA: We all sit down like he says for tonight ... just tonight ... 'cause tomorrow's a different story ...

SEBB: Absolutely not. I gotta go to a wake.

FILUMENA: Hey, prima dona. Swallow your pride. And Rocco . . . give us a chance to get used to the "please" and "thank-you's" 'cause you wasn't Jesus Christ last time we saw you.

ROCCO: Sebb, will you put my music back on? I wanna make a toast tonight. You'll see . . . Filumena. Honey, where's those pants of mine that you shrunk that time?

FILUMENA: In your drawer.

ROCCO: (*Bottoming out a little.*) These are the clothes I was wearin' when I went in . . . they're baggy . . . like anchors draggin' me backwards. Same house, same smell, same stairs . . . (*He disappears into his bedroom.*)

FILUMENA: Honey?

SEBB: A toast? (*He examines cassettes* ROCCO *brought home and puts one into play.*)

FILUMENA: Twenty-two years he's an iceberg. All of a sudden he walks in, he's a radiator that wants kisses.

BLAISE: Maybe he forgot who he is. Or maybe he got himself confused with some other guy . . . and Rocco went to that guy's house and that guy's the one we got.

FILUMENA: Smother this kid for me. Go for the olives, you little trouble-maker. Sebbie, you think he's got cancer?

SEBB: Who, Rocco? No such luck.

FILUMENA: What is that? Crazy-house music?

SEBB: It's Brian Appelman. (SEBB *knows of the music, and is both impressed and disturbed by* ROCCO's *discovery of it.*)

FILUMENA: What's he got there?

SEBB: This is the whole rain forest of Puerto Rico in here.

FILUMENA: Chi Brian Appelman . . . kee gotz?

BLAISE: This feels like a book in here.

SEBB: What the hell is this . . . ? (*Pulls up microcomputers and attached wires.*)

BLAISE: (*Reading*) "Audio butronic sensor? Patent number 045 R7 zero. Attach probes to plant and connect to amplifier" . . . Oh my God, this is like Frankenstein.

FILUMENA: The cheese.

BLAISE: Don't pinch, okay, or I'll punch you in the mouth.

FILUMENA: See?

SEBB: Move your ass, pimples, before I stick my fingers up your nose.

BLAISE: Poison face ... Rocco was pretty smart to come up with that. (*Exits*)

SEBB: Ma, don't be mad if I don't eat here tonight.

FILUMENA: Please.

SEBB: He makes me sick to my stomach. He had the right idea. He shoulda killed himself.

FILUMENA: Shut up. Maybe they taught him how to be good.

SEBB: I don't trust good men all of a sudden.

FILUMENA: So crucify me.

SEBB: Aggh, all that matters to you is that you get your rubdown tonight.

FILUMENA: Your filthy mouth drips. I don't ...

SEBB: Yeah you don't—I hope he chokes you in bed tonight. He's crazy as a ping pong ball.

FILUMENA: Sebbie, Sebbie, looka me. You, I love.

(BLAISE *reappears, panting from running. He stops silently in the doorway. He listens, overhearing them.*)

SEBB: I ain't eatin'.

FILUMENA: Not Blaise, not him ... only you I love. Who do you think I put up with everything for? You, you bastard. Eat with us. Don't leave me. Sebbie, come on.

BLAISE: (*Entering*) You forgot ... to give me ... the money.

FILUMENA: (*Startled*) Jesus. Madonna.

SEBB: Cash your paycheck, cheapskate. Scambatti'll cash it. (*He goes to alcove to turn off the music, but instead he turns it up.*)

BLAISE: Thanks, Filumena. (*He slams the door.*) Go get your cheese yourself.

FILUMENA: Ooof. I got three husbands ... and three loaves of Saint Anthony bread. Tonight the good luck's gonna hit this house like lightning.

(*MUSIC rises through the house.*)

(*In the course of the music playing,* SEBB, FILUMENA, *and* BLAISE *set the table.* ROCCO *appears, looking good in clothes that fit.*)

(*Music, soft at first, becomes crazy, paralleling the anxiety at table.*)

ROCCO: (*Pouring the wine*) Listen to this. I go into the liquor store. I want the most expensive wine, I says. The guy goes down in the cellar and comes up with this dusty bottle. A hundred thirty-five bucks.

FILUMENA: You paid what?

ROCCO: So I said, no, I don't even have that much on me. And I wound up with this . . .

BLAISE: How much?

ROCCO: Seven bucks, but I want you to know if I had the money, we'd have a king's wine. Uh . . . (*No one is impressed.*)

BLAISE: Put your party hats on, everybody. Be a sport, Pa. Put it on.

FILUMENA: Might as well all go crazy.

BLAISE: C'mon Sebb. (*He puts a hat on* SEBB.)

FILUMENA: See. We're nice people. We have parties.

BLAISE: Ma, you look gorgeous.

ROCCO: I want Sebb's glass.

BLAISE: (*Enjoying the music, while mocking it.*) Bee de beep bee de boop-bee de beep bee de doop. Be de dee de de de dede de de dee de de do. (*Or whatever suits the music.*)

ROCCO: All right now, this is important. You hear?

BLAISE: Don't I get no wine?

ROCCO: Here . . .

FILUMENA: Half. Sebbie, don't make me look at you . . . Ooop. (*She breaks into laughter.*)

ROCCO: Calm down. Now lemme toast . . .

(BLAISE *jumps up.*)

FILUMENA: Son of Pagliacci. Sit. And hands off the macaroni. Rocco, hurry up. Toasty . . . toast and jelly.

ROCCO: Okay.

SEBB: Spit it out, Hollywood.

ROCCO: What's this Hollywood?

FILUMENA: Hollywood?

SEBB: Hollywood came home skinny, with his hair combed over his ears. He forgot he's an electrician; he thinks he's Robert Redford.

ROCCO: Okay, Sebbie, I give up, go take a walk if you wanna.

SEBB: Now I don't wanna. (*Drinks his glass of wine.*) Gimme some more wine. (*Fills wine glass again.*)

ROCCO: First of all, I wasn't an electrician, Sebbie, okay? I was an electronics engineer.

SEBB: But they didn't pay you for that, did they? Ain't that what pissed you off so much?

FILUMENA: Blaise, turn off that goddamn music.

ROCCO: You ever see my paycheck, Sebb?

SEBB: Didn't have to see your paycheck, not with all those snowmobiles under our Christmas tree each year, and a Stingray to drive to Harvard with.

ROCCO: I give you fair warning, Sebbie, I'm a very different man than I was.

SEBB: If you're a different man, you should of gone to a different house, right, Rocco?

FILUMENA: (*To* SEBB) Son of a bitch.

ROCCO: I came back to this house to clean up my shit.

SEBB: Your *shit*. Is that us, Rocco? Well, you're gonna need a big shovel.

ROCCO: I got time.

SEBB: Oh, yeah? I heard your time was up.

FILUMENA: Close your mouth.

SEBB: I thought you got retired. Hey. Tell Blaise about the night of your retirement party.

FILUMENA: Enough, you.

SEBB: The kid's got a right to know.

ROCCO: You got any wedding plans, Sebbie?

BLAISE: Wedding plans? (*Giggles*)

FILUMENA: What's he talking about, wedding plans?

ROCCO: Guys his age already left home to start their own family, right?

FILUMENA: Mind your own business, Pagliacci, okay? We start eating right now or I turn the whole goddamn table over on top of all of you.

ROCCO: You heard the boss ... Lift your glasses.

FILUMENA: Lift your glasses. Sebbie, lift your goddamned glass, do me the favor. Now talk, Rocco, spit it out.

ROCCO: I wanna toast to my wife, I wanna promise her I'm gonna get her outta this house.

FILUMENA: Oh, yeah. Tomorrow. Don't worry.

ROCCO: And I wanna toast my sons. I want more than anything for my sons to die a natural death.

FILUMENA: (*Sipping, then coughing into her wine.*) Huh?

SEBB: What the fuck?

BLAISE: (*Has sipped, but not swallowed.*) Hmmmmmmmmmmnn?

FILUMENA: Spit out that wine. Spit it out.

ROCCO: No. You misunderstand. Sometimes a man is shy and he gets married anyway. He gets a family and insteada sayin', look, I'm scareda talk to ya, he just hits 'em. Ha. Like some ape. Man like that . . . thinks violent, like takin' his life . . . or wipin' out his whole family. Every one of ya. Clean you up or wipe you out. But . . .

BLAISE: Clean us up or wipe us out?

ROCCO: But I turned it on myself. Okay? Me, I took the dive, except . . . they stopped me . . . and showed me these statistics . . . that . . . that a man who commits . . . you know, suicide, his kids, they like follow his example. You should *see* these statistics. That's murderin' your sons, I said. No. I . . . gotta get home to save them boys . . . to . . . to . . . talk this over . . . because like there's a genetical tie-in.

(*They stare. FILUMENA breaks the ice.*)

FILUMENA: Okay, he's finished. Drink.

SEBB: Don't drink. You think your comin' home is saving my *life*? Rocco, I want you to know that nothing you can ever do can touch me, you hear? So go ahead and kill yourself, anytime you want.

ROCCO: You're wrong, Sebbie. Because I'm your father, it . . .

SEBB: I don't want no father. I don't need no father. And neither does he.

ROCCO: It's statistics. We gotta . . .

SEBB: We're Italian, okay? They're talkin' about other people. Don't you worry about us killin' ourselves. Now, Blaise, lift your glass. I wanna toast to the past, to the past of this family when there were no valiums to make our father such a good man.

FILUMENA: Shut up.

SEBB: Don't let him scare you, Ma. I know what he's tryin' here.

FILUMENA: Blaise, take the food inside.

ROCCO: No.

SEBB: You know what's makin' him so cool? These pills. (*He grabs the valiums.*) He's got a two-year supply of heaven here. No wonder he came home a saint.

(FILUMENA *grabs them from* SEBB.)

FILUMENA: Gimmie.

(ROCCO *grabs them from her and opens them.*)

ROCCO: Should I dump 'em?

BLAISE: Jeez.

FILUMENA: Please.

ROCCO: We'll make it a fair battle, okay Sebbie?

SEBB: Sure. Go ahead.

FILUMENA: Blaise, grab the medicine. Grab . . .

BLAISE: He dumped 'em!

FILUMENA: In my sauce!

BLAISE: He dumped 'em. The valiums in the rigatoni. Madawn, what sauce!

FILUMENA: This son of a bitch! I can't believe you did this. Tutto ruinate.

ROCCO: Gimme Sebbie's dish. (*He ladles it out.*) Here. Here Sebbie, get happy, eat my heaven.

FILUMENA: Leave him alone, you. He's got his own troubles, this kid.

ROCCO: That's okay.

FILUMENA: (*To* SEBB) You got people waitin', go. (*To* BLAISE) Get your hands outta there.

BLAISE: They didn't melt.

FILUMENA: Throw it all in the garbage.

SEBB: Thanks for the wine, Rocco. It was real civilized you eatin' in the dining room.

FILUMENA: Go upstairs, Sebbie.

(*She places herself between* ROCCO *and* SEBB; SEBB *goes to the stairs.*)

FILUMENA: And you (*To* ROCCO)—take care of those things (*The orchids*) you brought into this house.

ROCCO: I'll help you with these dishes. (*Lifts her dish.*)

FILUMENA: You really want to give me heart failure? Gimme my dish.

ROCCO: Go take care of your prince.

FILUMENA: Gimme my dish. (*They tug at the dish.*)

ROCCO: (*Winning the tug of war*) Go, goddamnit. Go to him.

(FILUMENA *slowly retreats to her room.* BLAISE *rushes toward the front door.*)

ROCCO: Hey, hold it, you. Go down the cellar and get me those speakers. The little ones. And I'll go get the wires.

BLAISE: But Pa, I gotta...

ROCCO: You gotta what?

BLAISE: Gotta... uh...

ROCCO: Go do me the favor. I wanna show you something you can tell your teachers about that'll make their hair stand on end.

BLAISE: What teachers?

ROCCO: At Brooklyn Tech.

BLAISE: Oh.

(BLAISE *goes toward the cellar.* ROCCO *clears dishes and goes into the kitchen.*)

Scene Three

(*In her bedroom,* FILUMENA *picks up her discarded lipstick lackadaisically. She contemplates using some, evaluating her sexiness in the mirrors, pulling her housedress tightly.* SEBB *enters as she does, startling her. He carries the large gift-wrapped box.*)

SEBB: Lipstick for Pagliacci after what he just did?

FILUMENA: Mind your business. You... you don't have to make the peace. You just make the trouble. When his last pill wears off and I'm alone with him in this bed, where are you gonna be?

SEBB: Still an' all, you put on lipstick for him.

FILUMENA: I got chap lips. Okay?

SEBB: He wants me to leave and start my family. Did you hear him?

FILUMENA: Don't you *dare*... you hear? Don't you dare leave me stuck in this trap with no protection from them two.

SEBB: Ma, we gotta get outta here and we can't get outta here till you learn to walk out that front door. Now will ya' open these? *Move*, for cryin' out loud.

FILUMENA: What is that?

SEBB: A gift. (*He tears the wrappers.*)

(FILUMENA *continues to open the box.*)

FILUMENA: Whose wake tonight?

SEBB: Mrs. Doogan.

FILUMENA: Vinnie Doogan? Your boyfriend?

SEBB: His grandmother . . . and don't let me ever hear you say that word in front of me again, or I swear . . .

FILUMENA: What word did I say now?

SEBB: You're all itchin' for him to find out.

FILUMENA: Boyfriend. A boy you hang out with.

SEBB: Shutup.

FILUMENA: Madonna! I don't know how I'm supposed to talk to you from one minute to the next. What's this? A black coat?

SEBB: With a fox collar. You know what a fox is?

FILUMENA: And a purple dress? What am I supposed to do with these? Die?

SEBB: You say you're ashamed to go in the streets 'cause you don't have good clothes . . .

FILUMENA: And I'm supposed to go to Scambatti's in funeral colors?

SEBB: Ma, I can't wait for you. This is it, Ma. You wanna leave with me?

FILUMENA: Shhh. Don't let him scare you. This is your house.

SEBB: You givin' me the deed? This is *his* house. This ain't my house, Ma. I'm splittin' . . . minavog . . .

FILUMENA: Don't you dare say that word.

SEBB: You ever hear of Colorado? There's a place where they cure people scared to leave their house.

FILUMENA: And where's Golarod . . . gooma si giam?

SEBB: Colorado. It's in the middle of this country.

FILUMENA: In the middle, not the edge . . . take back your coat; save your money. At least here I sit by my window and smell the ocean. Sometimes I smell Sicily . . . when there's a breeze.

SEBB: It's Pagliacci, isn't it? You make believe you hate him, but at night when this door is closed, you like his jabs . . .

FILUMENA: I keep peace is what I do . . . pigmouth. (*She slaps him.*) Wait.

Look at me. Swear on the Saint that you won't leave me here stuck alone with him.

SEBB: You got Blaise.

FILUMENA: Blaise is in his diapers, you sonofabitch. Swear.

SEBB: Ma, I'm sick of this house. It smells like Sicily, from the cellar to the roof.

FILUMENA: How do you know what Sicily smells like? All right . . . I'll wear your dress and the coat. Tomorrow's Sunday . . . I'll go to ten o'clock Mass if you take me.

SEBB: You swear it on the Saint.

FILUMENA: I swear that I'll really try. We're a good family, Sebbie.

SEBB: And no mention of Doogan. Please, Ma.

FILUMENA: He wouldn't believe it anyway. Swear you won't leave me.

SEBB: (*Hesitates, then slyly*) Hey, Saint Anthony, I promise I'll stay in this house with her forever, if she only comes with me to the ten o'clock Mass tomorrow.

FILUMENA: Remember when you were an altar boy? You used to look deep in my eyes and give me a Hollywood kiss, after you did my hair? Kiss me.

SEBB: Offah. (*He gives her a quick kiss and moves toward the door.*)

FILUMENA: Like a chicken he kisses.

SEBB: You don't need my kisses. Pagliacci's home. Here . . . (*Hands her a lipstick—forgivingly.*) Put some lipstick on. (*He exits.*)

FILUMENA: Offah.

(SEBB *runs into* BLAISE, *who is waiting for him at the front door. Both are standing at UC.*)

BLAISE: Sebb. He's gonna force me to go back to school, I know it. What am I gonna do?

SEBB: Sit on his face . . . wait . . . you really want to bring him into line? Make him tell you what happened in the Holland Tunnel.

BLAISE: I don't wanna know about that.

SEBB: I'll be in Pizella's. Lemme know what happens.

BLAISE: I ain't goin' into no funeral parlor.

SEBB: The dead don't bite. (*He exits.*)

BLAISE: Oh, yeah? I'll meet you in the candy store.

(ROCCO *comes up from the cellar with speaker wires. Enters UR.*)

ROCCO: Blaise, take these wires . . .

BLAISE: What do I do?

ROCCO: Attach them all to the amplifier.

BLAISE: I . . . I got a job. Workin' with Sebb. I'm a mechanic for Alphonse.

ROCCO: The Texaco Station? You quit Brooklyn Tech? My own doctor was tellin' me . . . he couldn't get his son in there.

BLAISE: I didn't know you knew where I went to school . . .

ROCCO: Then I went and got all proud and come home and find you a grease monkey.

BLAISE: How come you never hit me? Oh, I got a slap here and there, but you never made me black and blue like you did her and Sebb. He said you once broke every dish in the house, one at a time, like Frisbies. Psssh. Psssh.

ROCCO: Knock it off.

BLAISE: You threw him against the wall like he was a football when he was a kid, he told me.

ROCCO: Please . . .

BLAISE: How come you never was interested in me enough to throw me against the wall?

ROCCO: Blaise . . .

BLAISE: I got left out of everything.

ROCCO: Talk about going back to school.

BLAISE: Talk about the Holland Tunnel.

ROCCO: Okay, wise guy.

BLAISE: You never knew the difference between Brooklyn Tech and a reform school. The tunnel, Rocco. C'mon. What you do in the tunnel that night?

ROCCO: It's none of your business.

BLAISE: So it's none of your business if I work or go to school or whatever the hell I do . . .

ROCCO: Who let you know about the tunnel?

BLAISE: Everybody in the neighborhood says something else about the tunnel. I wanna know the truth.

(ROCCO *turns away in shame. Tears come.*)

BLAISE: Pa, you okay? Shit. You don't hafta tell me anything . . . you want a valium? Look, I got three of 'em. I'll get you some water.

ROCCO: Come back. Jus' stay here.

BLAISE: Forget the tunnel. I'm too young to know.

ROCCO: You're not too young. You . . . you changed a lot, Blaise. You got some girlfriend?

BLAISE: A couple.

ROCCO: You're not gonna be able to keep that thing in your pants much longer.

BLAISE: That was last year.

ROCCO: Here.

(ROCCO *hands* BLAISE *the wrapped book and attaches a microcomputer to one of the orchid plants. A red blinker starts, then soft bleeps sound.*)

BLAISE: Who put that on?

ROCCO: You'll see.

(BLAISE *unwraps the book.*)

BLAISE: *Vegetative Molecular Response?*

ROCCO: By Doctor Arthur Studebaker. He gave me these. They're species orchids. Out of the wild.

BLAISE: (*Reading inscription*) To my brother Blaise? Each of us is a bud that will bloom in its time? Well sure.

ROCCO: He was my friend up there. I helped him wire these plants. See? I attach this microcomputer. (*A small red light comes on.*) It blinks 'cause the plant is alive.

BLAISE: (*Suspiciously*) Yeah . . .

ROCCO: Now . . . I switch on this speaker to pick up the signal. (*He does and it causes tinkling bleeps.*) The plant is making those noises.

BLAISE: How do you know the plant's doin' that?

ROCCO: (*He touches the speaker to the chair.*) See? No light. Now give me your finger.

(ROCO *touches it to* BLAISE'S *finger. The light comes on and various deep sounds come out of one speaker.*)

BLAISE: Wow!

ROCCO: You gotta be alive. That was your sound.

BLAISE: It's awful.

ROCCO: Well, you're not a plant. Next month part of that book's gonna be in the *Scientific American.*

BLAISE: I know the magazine.

ROCCO: I met a lotta nice people at that place.

BLAISE: Did you?

(ROCCO *uncovers more of the orchids.*)

BLAISE: My God ... (*All plants have identification tags.*) Phael ... phaelen-opsis? And brazzalaelia?

ROCCO: Now attach these ...

BLAISE: Here?

ROCCO: Don't pinch them ... Yeah.

(*A tinkling comes from another of the speakers, and another small red light goes on.*)

BLAISE: Who did that?

ROCCO: Each plant gets his own speaker. Cut the volume. That's good. That's normal.

(*A tiny red light—½ inch to ¾ inch—accompanies each plant and goes on as* ROCCO *pulls out other microcomputers and attaches them to plants. The bleeps become more and more complex as more plants come into play. Each plant has a distinctive music.*)

BLAISE: Holy geez! Y'mean like these plants are expressing themselves? Like emotions?

ROCCO: Well, they don't know yet. Show that book to your biology teacher.

BLAISE: Funny, Pop. Ain't they goin' a little crazy?

ROCCO: They're scared (*To the plants*) Okay. Shhh ... you're safe. Lower the volume.

(BLAISE *lowers the volume.*)

ROCCO: Now open that latch.

(BLAISE *puts a chair up on the windowseat, climbs onto it, and opens the latch.* ROCCO *then turns out the light and squeezes onto the chair with* BLAISE. *Both squeeze their upper bodies through the roof opening of the alcove. (In Victorian times it was called the Fern Room.) They look up to the sky. Their heads and shoulders are outdoors through the roof. The sounds from the speakers become calmer. The red lights shine in the room below them like stars in a dark sky. But they are looking up, searching for stars in the night sky.*)

Rocco: Jesus, look at those stars.

Blaise: Oh, my God . . .

Rocco: There's a breeze from the river. You feel it?

Blaise: Yeah. I smell it, too.

Rocco: Big Dipper.

Blaise: Where's the Big Dipper?

Rocco: (*Pointing*) You kidding? It's right there. See the bright one?

Blaise: There?

(Blaise *points.* Rocco *places his hand over* Blaise's *pointing hand.*)

Rocco: Now follow your finger. (*He guides* Blaise's *hand.*)

Blaise: Oh. I got it. It's upside down. Big mother. Yeah. Pa, why'd Studebaker . . . say in the book . . . "To my brother Blaise"?

Rocco: I was his father sometimes. They usta conduct these hugging sessions . . .

Blaise: Huggin'?

Rocco: Primal huggin'.

Blaise: Sounds disgusting. So that must be north.

Rocco: Say "Welcome home, Dad."

Blaise: Oh, my God. I call you Pop.

Rocco: Just once. Like the American kids.

Blaise: Dad? Like that? Welcome home, Dad?

Rocco: Thanks.

Blaise: Just don't put me through it too many more times, huh?

Rocco: (*He stares, as if secure for the first time, to remember.*) I had a psychotic episode, Blaise . . . is what they call it . . .

Blaise: Forget it, it's okay.

Rocco: Blaise, you know how I usta hate to talk to anybody? Around here, anywhere? It was the same where I worked, except for one guy . . . this little Kenny Farrell. He usta bring me a peach every day. I don't know where the sonofagun got'em, even in the winter, him and his peaches were the only things ever made me talk a lot. So they give me this retirement party at the Canal Street factory . . .

Blaise: It's okay, Pa.

Rocco: Pink champagne and Lorna Doone cookies . . . and this plaque for your coffin that said thirty years . . . and Kenny . . . I think it was when he starts comin' toward me with this bag ... He's got a whole bag of peaches, I tell myself. Well, at first I'm really kiddin', ya know ... I grab the bag and I start throwin' peaches around the room ... They looked shocked at me. I'm embarrassed. I turn red, so I make believe I go to my locker. All I can think of is ... I don't wanna go back in there and I don't wanna come home here to get old, where nobody talks to me. And all of a sudden, when they ain't lookin', I take a quart of milk out of the refrigerator, I go to the medicine cabinet, and I swallow everything in there with the milk, and I go jump off the loadin' platform into the streets and ... I'm throwin' peaches at the buses and trucks. I'm punchin' taxi cabs and I go into the tunnel, two lanes, and I tell myself Jesus, Mary, and Joseph, help me close my eyes ... Close 'em, Rocco, you poor goddamn sonofabitch ... sonofabitch ... an' I'm waitin' ...

BLAISE: Shut up, Pa.

ROCCO: Not one of those goddamn trucks hit me ... not even a motorcycle ... just cops grabbin' me, puttin' me in handcuffs.

BLAISE: (*Shouts*) Shut up.

ROCCO: I tried to kill myself, Blaise. No more. Now you know. Just look up. Up.

(*They look up.*)

ROCCO: ... millions of worlds. You know somethin', Blaise, we could clean up the glass in here. And take off these curtains, and you know what we got here? Guess what we got here.

BLAISE: A greenhouse?

ROCCO: Yeah, a greenhouse. (*Pause.*) How would you get back into Tech? Say you wanted to ...

BLAISE: Too late to get back into Tech, Pop.

ROCCO: Did you try?

(BLAISE *nods yes.*)

BLAISE: I got kicked out finally. Wanna see proof? (*He jumps down.*)

(ROCCO *turns up the lights.*)

ROCCO: I believe you. (*Steps down and removes the chair.*) Hand me that plant. (*Reads tag.*) This one goes upstairs.

BLAISE: I'm sorry, Pop.

ROCCO: You'll be okay.

BLAISE: Pa, you gotta meet this girl of mine—Mercedes.

ROCCO: Just don't knock anybody up.

BLAISE: Pa, this son of yours 'sgot brains. Trust me.

(*Handshake*)

ROCCO: I trust ya. C'mon, beat it now, and let these orchids breathe.

(Rocco *turns down the lights again. The orchids are hanging, beautiful, in the soft light of night, including the budded brazzalaelia.* Rocco *gathers two small plants that need sun by their metal hangers and starts upstairs.*)

ROCCO: Thanks, Studebaker.

Scene Four

(ROCCO *enters* FILUMENA'S *bedroom. They ignore one another shyly as they prepare for bed.* ROCCO *is lifting the shades and hanging the plants on the shade rollers of* FILUMENA'S *south window.*)

FILUMENA: What are those?

ROCCO: Orchid plants that need the sun. This is a south window. (*He opens the drawer.*)

FILUMENA: Get the creepy things outta here, Rocco. I keep the shades down in the day so I can see my candles.

ROCCO: Just for a couple of days till we figure out . . . what's these here cigarettes?

FILUMENA: Who put cigarettes in my drawer.?

ROCCO: Maybe Saint Anthony.

FILUMENA: Okay, sarcastic.

ROCCO: Maybe your doll Marie Antoinette smokes when you ain't lookin'. Hey, Marie, these your Winstons?

FILUMENA: Sebbie playin' tricks on me . . . or Blaise.

ROCCO: C'mon, Filumena, I been smellin' the smoke in the bathroom fifteen years now. (*Finding it funny, laughs.*)

FILUMENA: Ask your son.

ROCCO: Go ahead—*smoke*!

FILUMENA: You think the little one don't smoke? You should smell the pot.

ROCCO: Smoke if you like, Filumena. I want you to be free here; I want you to smoke.

FILUMENA: It ain't me, I told you.

ROCCO: Lipstick?

FILUMENA: Gimmie that. Sebbie got it for my chap lips.

ROCCO: C'mon. Wear lipstick . . . it'd be good.

FILUMENA: Smoke. Wear lipstick. They did a good job on you in the nut house.

(Rocco *laughs, teasingly, seductively.*)

FILUMENA: Stop laughin', clown . . .

ROCCO: Clown, huh? You miss me, Filumena? Eh?

FILUMENA: Next thing you'll tell me you're glad I cut my hair.

ROCCO: Never. You'll always by my cigna nera . . .

FILUMENA: Oh, you remember that . . .

ROCCO: That's the only way I could remember things these past months, the way they used to be a long time ago.

FILUMENA: Help me turn down the bed.

ROCCO: C'mere.

FILUMENA: What for? Do your side.

(Rocco *opens the door.*)

FILUMENA: Close that door.

ROCCO: It's musty in here.

FILUMENA: *I don't want no draft* . . . I gotta thing in my neck.

ROCCO: A thing? Where? (*He touches her neck.*)

FILUMENA: No. Ow . . . Ugh . . .

ROCCO: Right there?

FILUMENA: Oh, my God! He touched right on the spot.

(Rocco *rubs.*)

FILUMENA: Agggh.

ROCCO: Tomorrow I'll help you wash your hair . . . when the kids are gone.

FILUMENA: Leave go my hair. Get the Vicks over there if you're gonna rub.

(Rocco *gets the Vicks. She takes off her dress.*)

FILUMENA: You should put some up your nose now that the heat's back on.

ROCCO: I can't with the Vicks.

FILUMENA: It opens your head up. Ou, the pain is travelin'.

ROCCO: It's travelin' where?

FILUMENA: Down my back . . .

(ROCCO *rubs.*)

Yeah . . .

(*Then suddenly, as if Rocco's rubbing has pushed the pain through her chest.*)

FILUMENA: I think its goin' to the front now.

ROCCO: Here? (*Her breasts*)

FILUMENA: Ou, yeah. You need more Vicks.

ROCCO: But the menthol . . . it'll burn your nipples . . .

FILUMENA: I don't care. I . . . you wanna rub or not? Whatsamatta?

(ROCCO *kisses her.*)

FILUMENA: What are you doing?

ROCCO: Kiss me, please, Filumena.

FILUMENA: What are you talking about? We don't kiss.

ROCCO: I can't do this . . . no more with the Vicks.

FILUMENA: Where's my dress?

ROCCO: You get a cramp, I rub. How many times have we gone through this ritual of the cramp, then close the door . . . "so my son won't see that I let my husband touch"? . . . We go from a cramp to biff, bam, boom with nothin' in between.

FILUMENA: Take a walk, Rocco.

ROCCO: We're done. You roll over and snore. I lay awake tryin' to figure out how we did all that without one single kiss. Kiss me, Filumena . . . why not a little kiss?

FILUMENA: Don't feel like it. (*She's busy getting dressed again.*)

ROCCO: I wanna show you how much like dogs we are.

FILUMENA: Well, dogs don't kiss.

ROCCO: That's what I mean . . . we're like dogs, Filumena. The young people, they don't do it like this anymore.

FILUMENA: Get out. I gotta say my prayers. (*She takes out books and a prayer book tied with a rubber band. This pack contains her glasses. She puts on her glasses and reads.*)

(*OVERLAP DIALOGUE*)

FILUMENA

ROCCO

Sant' Antonio Caro, padre dei poveri a degli afflitti, io povero peccatore, chiedo il tuo aiuto e il tuo consiglio e gengo all cura e protezione tua. Abbi pieta' di me, per la mano del signore che mi ha toccato e la divina guistizia che mi ha colpito per i miei peccati. Oh amato protectore, guarda la miserabile condizione mia e l'amaro tormento del mio cuore. Intercedi presso il mio amato redentore, affinche questo calice amaro possa passare da me sia fatta ancora la sua volonta al tuo povero servitore. Amen.

I'm sorry, Filumena...what're you hoardin'? You're gonna explode if you don't give it to somebody. Kiss somebody. Give it away for crissakes, before they put us in the ground. Filumena, I...I have a confession to make to you. Filumena, I never loved you. I never loved you. I found out I shouldn't'a married you. I thought I would learn, but I never learned. That's what the big mistake was. But now I wanna try to love you. I wanna take care of you. We can learn...I wanna turn this joke of me and you into somethin' human...

FILUMENA: This joke of me and you? Rocco...please...don't say you didn't love me in the beginning because that, that would really do it for me.

ROCCO: Who cares how we started out...look what we turned into...make love like dogs...rubdowns with Vicks...children born with no kisses.

FILUMENA: Who started with no kisses? Me? You're the one jus' now tellin' me you never loved me.

ROCCO: I admit it. I admit it. I started it off that way.

FILUMENA: Twenty-two years went by. The fireman comes to the fire twenty-two years too late...now you want kisses? Take these plants outta my house...he never loved me...good. Good. Now I know the secret of my misery in this house. (*She throws the plants at the door.*)

ROCCO: You sonofabitch.

FILUMENA: You forgot the days you used to put your face in my pillow and...

ROCCO: Huh?

FILUMENA: Open her legs, one, two, three, up inside me, ready or not. That's how my kids were born.

ROCCO: I'm not that man anymore...

FILUMENA: No. Now you're the man who kills himself, then comes home and says he never loved me, and then demands a kiss for it? Who do you think rules over this house? You? (*She points to Saint Anthony.*) Him. Saint Anthony. He gets my lips. He's the one took care of this family while you were eatin' and fartin' alone in the kitchen and puttin' your money in the bank . . . him, the Saint.

ROCCO: The Saint don't feel, the Saint don't bleed. This is chalk. (Rocco *slaps the statue to the floor.*)

FILUMENA: You crazy sonofabitch. You broke it!! Don't hit me. Don't you touch me. He'll punish you. The seagulls make a ring around this house.

ROCCO: 'Cause there's a garbage dump down by the river, three blocks, but you've never walked far enough to see it. Instead, you turned this bedroom into a mausoleum. So keep your shades down so no light comes in and keep your door closed so your wax fog doesn't creep down the stairs. But me? I ain't sleepin' in this room with you, Filumena. No, not without a kiss . . . no . . . (*He grabs his pillow and a blanket. He closes the door and descends to the alcove.*)

(FILUMENA *kisses the head of the broken statue as she picks it up; then she weeps.*)

ROCCO: (*Speaks to his plants in the dark—the bleeps are agitated, frequent. The red lights are glowing.*) Easy . . . don't be scared. Shhh. Shhh . . . you're safe. I won't let nothin' happen to you. It's not their fault. Sshh . . . shhsshhsshh.

(ROCCO *curls up to sleep among the orchids. The music, excited by his presence, calms gradually to a few infrequent bleeps.*)

(SEBB *and* BLAISE *enter through front doors.*)

SEBB: That Pizella. He paints their face like a birthday cake.

BLAISE: Don't talk about it.

SEBB: I swear I saw her eyelash move in the casket.

BLAISE: Sebbie, I won't sleep tonight.

(SEBB and BLAISE *move into the house.* SEBB, *seeing his father sleeping downstairs, runs up to check on Filumena.*)

BLAISE: Pa, you sleeping down here?

ROCCO: I'm gonna keep an eye on the orchids their first night.

BLAISE: I'll take the boxes down the cellar.

ROCCO: No, I'll do it. Go to sleep. (Rocco *exits to cellar with the box.*)

BLAISE: Goodnight.

SEBB: (*Knocking at Filumena's door.*) Ma? Ma?

FILUMENA: (*From behind the door.*) Go away. I'm okay.

(SEBB *goes to his room and lights a joint.* BLAISE *follows immediately.*)

SEBB: Shut that door, Blaise. Somethin' happened around here. I smell danger.

BLAISE: Between him and her? Gimmie. (*Joint*)

SEBB: Two tokes.

BLAISE: Cheapskate.

SEBB: Chip in for some of this shit now that you're workin'. What's this *Playboy* doin' in here . . . ?

BLAISE: There's an ad in there for that new diesel.

SEBB: You're full of shit.

BLAISE: You know what Caputo tol' me? You and Doogan are fuckin' one another.

SEBB: Oh, yeah? That's interestin'.

(BLAISE *throws dart at the Saint Sebastian dartboard.*)

SEBB: Leave go them darts.

BLAISE: And Doogan's pissed 'cause you ain't goin' with him to Texas.

SEBB: Caputo's a real special investigator, isn't he?

BLAISE: Can I ask you a personal question?

SEBB: No.

BLAISE: Sebbie . . . What ya think of when you jerk off?

SEBB: Get lost . . .

BLAISE: It reveals the deep, deep truth about ya.

SEBB: Just don't wipe your fingers on my face cloth.

BLAISE: I don't use a face cloth.

SEBB: Out.

BLAISE: I'm just tryin' to talk to ya. (*He opens the door.*)

SEBB: Did you bring up the Holland Tunnel to the old man?

BLAISE: Oh, yeah . . . He made me feel sorry for him.

SEBB: Feel sorry for your ol' lady. She'll turn to penicillin soon if we don't get her out in the sunlight.

BLAISE: Would you be mad at me, Sebbie, if I quit Alphonse?

SEBB: Maybe I should quit Alphonse too. Do you love your mother?

BLAISE: I don't really hate her.

SEBB: You just wish she had bleached blonde hair and wore high heels.

BLAISE: I got over that. Now I jus' wish she'd go to the corner to buy a quart of milk.

SEBB: Look... if we don't continue to work and save up, we'll never get her to that place in Denver...

BLAISE: You should talk to the ol' man about it. He knows a lot about that stuff now.

SEBB: I can't stomach his preachin'.

BLAISE: Don't tell me it don't suck, what he's been through. Funny, they got married, two people like that. You know, I betcha now he makes it up to her.

SEBB: How you gonna make it up to somebody after you blow their brains out? Huh? How's he gonna give her back twenty-five years? This is the postmortem, man, what d'ya think this is?

BLAISE: I feel like a hundred years old... (*Yawns*) Tired. Tomorrow's Sunday and I'm gonna do everything in my power not to wake up at seven o'clock. (*He opens Sebb's door, exits, goes to his room, and closes his door behind him.*)

(*A beat.* FILUMENA *emerges and can be seen on the stairway, carrying the bottom half of her coat box in both arms. The box contains the broken parts of her Saint Anthony statue. She lays the box down at the front door. Then she turns into the living room toward the alcove. She moves to the kitchen and returns with a bottle of ammonia. The* bleeps *begin as* FILUMENA *pours ammonia on each and every orchid plant.*)

FILUMENA: Here, drink... drink. Have a nice drink. Drink some more. Drink it all. I had poison poured in my heart too...

(*The* bleeps *are at peak rapid frequency now. The red lights are growing weak—coming on and off.*)

SEBB: Somethin's goin' on down there. Blaise?

FILUMENA: What's that noise... huh?

(BLAISE *runs out, meeting* SEBB *on the landing.*)

SEBB: What's makin' those bleeps?

BLAISE: The orchids.

(*They run down.*)

SEBB	BLAISE
Ma ... Where's Rocco? What's she pourin' on ... ?	What've you got there, Ma? Huh? What's that smell? Jesus!

FILUMENA: That's my business.

SEBB: It's ammonia. Take it off her.

BLAISE: Christ! Ammonia? Gimme.

SEBB: Crazy sonofabitch ... you want a hatchet in your head?

FILUMENA: I'm crazy?

ROCCO: (*Coming up from the cellar.*) That you up there, Blaise?

BLAISE: Uh, yeah, Pa.

SEBB: What in the ... Ma ... are you crazy?

BLAISE: She poured ammonia on his orchids.

FILUMENA: I'm crazy. Right.

SEBB: Ma, I can leave. You gotta stay here.

FILUMENA: Oh, now you can leave? Ohhh ... (*Sing song, sarcastic, paranoid.*) Did you see the broken statue on the floor there ... throw him in the garbage, you. (*To* BLAISE)

BLAISE: Christ. Saint Anthony.

ROCCO: (*Entering*) What she do? What happened?

SEBB: You ... brainless gorilla ... stupid Sicilian.

FILUMENA: What? What am I?

ROCCO: She what? Jesus! No.

FILUMENA: These should enjoy my house and I should be spit on? Let them put us both in a straitjacket ... I'm dangerous too. Okay?

ROCCO: Water, Blaise.

SEBB: You really want him to kill you? That's what you really want! Don't expect me to come between you. Have your bloodbath without me. You deserve one another. I pronounce you man and wife.

(FILUMENA *turns up the stairs, staring intently at* SEBB, *then slowly disappears, as she delivers her admonition to him.*)

FILUMENA: Now you got your excuse, eh, Sebbie? I know what you're up to, even with no brains. I know what's cookin' in that mind of yours. Go, Judas ... Now you got your excuse. And while you're at it ... tell your father about how you don't like girls. Tell your father about Doogan, your boyfriend. Go. Put on a dress for your father. Put on a dress, Judas.

CURTAIN
End of Act One

Act Two

(The time is early the next morning, Sunday, approximately 10 a.m.)

Scene One

(BLAISE *enters the house boisterously from the outside, through the front doors. He carries a container of coffee and the five-budded orchid with its wires still attached.*)

BLAISE: Pa, did you put these orchids outside on top of the garbage pail?

ROCCO: Oh, Blaise, please...

BLAISE: ...with the snow fallin' on them half the night?

ROCCO: They're dead.

BLAISE: Hold it... the book, the book... (BLAISE *pulls out Studebaker's book.*) Neglect... Neglect... Here. Neglect. (*Reading*) "Hobbyists often inquire why some species bloom under conditions of neglect, while others do not bloom when fed, misted, and fanned..."

ROCCO: Blaise, that's different.

BLAISE: "Orchid plants have been known to live over one hundred years..."

ROCCO: Not if somebody...

BLAISE: (*Still reading*) "Sensing they cannot recover, an orchid will sometimes set seed in order to regenerate itself."

ROCCO: Blaise... neglect is not ammonia. Ammonia is death. You know what ammonia does?

BLAISE: I'm reattaching 'em.

ROCCO: I don't want them in my sight, okay? And what's this?

BLAISE: I got you coffee from Scambatti's.

ROCCO: Oh. I can't. I got heartburn.

BLAISE: What is heartburn? I keep hearin' people sayin' heartburn, heartburn...

ROCCO: Gas. And a pain here.

BLAISE: Gas. That's how else they describe it. God, look at this poor orchid. You go sixteen years bored passin' the same garbage... leftovers, empty milk containers, coffee grinds... an' it all changes in one

day. There's Saint Anthony all broke up next to the valiums and the
rigatoni . . . and on the garbage pail cover, like funeral flowers, are these
murdered orchid plants that it's snowing on top of. Now that can give
you goosebumps. (*He belches.*) Gas and a pain here?

Rocco: Yeah.

BLAISE: I got heartburn.

Rocco: Blaise . . . will ya . . . help me to figure somethin' out?

BLAISE: Sure.

Rocco: I wanna know how come your mother can . . . can . . . come up
with this information about Sebb.

BLAISE: What information? Oh. Okay. Pa, she ain't stupid. She knows
everything that goes on.

Rocco: Oh? She knows then . . . ? How though . . . ? How does she
know?

BLAISE: Maybe Sebb told her himself.

Rocco: And how do you know?

BLAISE: Louis Caputo spilled it to me.

Rocco: Louis Caputo? Spilled what?

BLAISE: What? What we're talking about.

Rocco: What're we talkin' about?

BLAISE: Nothin' . . . I don't know.

Rocco: Someone tells you your brother's queer and you believe it? You
don't punch him in the mouth?

BLAISE: Caputo's a liar. What ya want from me?

Rocco: Sebbie can't be that way. He's a car mechanic, not a hair-
dresser.

BLAISE: He does *her* hair. Pa, whatya want from me? I don't know what
I'm talkin' about here . . .

Rocco: He must be puttin' us all on. To spite us.

BLAISE: Don't get me in trouble, Pa . . .

Rocco: Why don't you bring that coffee up to your mother?

BLAISE: Pa, it wasn't my intention to come in here and disrupt anything.

Rocco: Don't worry . . . Does she know he's packin'?

BLAISE: Why? Who?

Rocco: Your mother.

BLAISE: Who's packin'?

ROCCO: Your brother. He dragged a suitcase outta the cellar and he's up there banging drawers.

BLAISE: Christ. Sebbie!! (*He runs up the stairs and knocks several times on Sebb's door.*) Sebbie, open. Sebbie, it's Blaise, Sebbie. Sebbie, open this door or I warn ya...

(SEBB *opens the door.*)

Scene Two

BLAISE: What in the fuck do you think you're doin'?

SEBB: It's called leavin' home.

BLAISE: And who'd you consult about doin' this?

SEBB: Blaise, take a walk.

BLAISE: You're leavin', now... that you lit the fuse and they're all set to blow up?

SEBB: Fuck him. Fuck her. Doogan's gonna pick me up in ten minutes.

BLAISE: You gonna Texas?

SEBB: All the way.

BLAISE: What kinda guy don't hang around for his grandmother's funeral?

SEBB: That's Doogan.

BLAISE: I think I'm gonna have a heart attack or else I'm jus' gonna vomit. You're gonna leave me here with them two on the brink of bloodshed?

SEBB: Maybe this'll put them over the brink.

BLAISE: You're sticking me here with the problem.

SEBB: I paid my dues. I came outta her first. (BLAISE *is stealing a joint from Sebb's little box.*) I'm the sonofabitch they named Sebastian. I caught all the arrows.

BLAISE: (*Lighting the joint.*) Here.

SEBB: No.

BLAISE: Relax a minute. You're all hopped up.

(SEBB *succumbs and takes the joint, but continues packing.*)

BLAISE: He's an outpatient, you know.

SEBB: So what?

BLAISE: So you read in the fuckin' newspapers "Man Kills Self and Family"? Sebbie, maybe there's really a screw loose deep in him.

SEBB: Of course there's a fuckin' screw loose deep in him.

BLAISE: Sebb, you're makin' me sick to my stomach and it's the kinda thing I'm not gonna get over ... You ... you can't go to Texas on me. She's gonna die here ... Jesus, I can't even imagine what she's gonna do when she finds this out ...

SEBB: Wanna tie?

BLAISE: I'll take your Cardinal Hayes jacket.

SEBB: It's yours.

(BLAISE *is kidding, but* SEBB *takes off the jacket and flings it to him.*)

BLAISE: Naaa ...

SEBB: I don't think Cardinal Hayes is gonna appreciate his name splattered all over the gay bars of Texas.

BLAISE: Maybe he'd love it. Aw, come on, Sebb, you two go to Texas, getta sun tan, act like a couple cowboys down there, you come home and we go back to Alphonse's ... I'll go in tomorrow, okay? 'N tell 'em you hadda ...

SEBB: You better wake up, Blaise. You don't know what happens' to people like me. Don't expect to ever see me in this house again. This is it, kid brother.

SEBB: But it's startin' to snow.

SEBB: So don't hold me up.

BLAISE: Last night you wanted us to drag the ol' lady to Colorado.

SEBB: Today I say let her blow up like a big tumor till she explodes. I can't help her ...

BLAISE: Hey, calm down a minute and look at me here ... I'm your brother. *I'm your brother.*

SEBB: Not now, Blaise.

BLAISE: And when? Fifty years from now? You're walkin' outta here after talkin' to me about it for five minutes ...

SEBB: I'm not married to you.

BLAISE: Oh, yeah? Remember that old movie we saw on TV with James Mason and whatsername ... the blonde chick who was the piano player?

SEBB: Ann Todd. Get outta my way.

BLAISE: Remember how she played lousy till he started hittin' her hands with a stick and all of a sudden be-doom be-doom doom doom, bllllllllllllleeeeeeeeeeeeeeeee dum-dum ... (*Rachmaninoff's Fifth*)

SEBB: Okay, so ...

BLAISE: She fell in love with him.

SEBB: You're in love with James Mason?

BLAISE: He's dead. It's ... you—I don't know how to get along here without you.

SEBB: You'll get the knack of it.

BLAISE: Jesus, Sebbie, I was jus' startin' to talk to you ...

SEBB: You and me are two totally different stories ...

BLAISE: Shit! I know girls so hot for you they have to wash out their panties after you pass them on the street. Sebbie, it's heaven in there. Who's to stop you from diggin' chicks? I'll put an end to him with one punch.

(BLAISE *surprises* SEBB *with the amount of power he puts into punching his own hand.*)

SEBB: Get outta my way, you little creep.

BLAISE: (*Screams*)Who's to stop you?

SEBB: Me. I'm to stop me.

BLAISE: Only you? Then tell me, why are you doin' this to yourself?

SEBB: Blaise, you're givin' me a headache.

BLAISE: Hold it. Hold it ... somebody's rippin' *me* off here. Okay? *Me*. Was I gonna be your best man?

SEBB: Best man? What has that got to do?

BLAISE: I get cheated outta bein' your best man 'cause you say you're gay. You know that? I get cheated outta bein' godfather, bein' an uncle for your kids. Instead, I get them. And what happens if he hurts her?

SEBB: Him? With his snively dunce hat in his hands, shakin' an' ...

BLAISE: Or she kills him? ... or what happens when they die on me? Huh? I gotta put on some bomber's jacket and go drag you outta some goddamn weird bar?

SEBB: You little sonofabitch. You'll never find *me* in one of those bars, okay? Now get out ... and here ... (SEBB *flings Playboy into* BLAISE'S *face.*) Take your *Playboys*. You won't have to sneak them in here any more.

BLAISE: Jus' like the ol' man in the old days. You're gonna be him all over again. You motherfucker...

SEBB: I nearly killed somebody for that word.

BLAISE: Cocksucker.

SEBB: You...

(SEBB *slaps* BLAISE, *but* BLAISE *overcomes* SEBB *and pins him to the floor.*)

BLAISE: C'mon. Surprise, huh? The kid grew up. Now say "uncle."

SEBB: Get off me.

BLAISE: "Uncle"... "*Uncle.*"

SEBB: (*After a pause.*) Uncle.

BLAISE: Again.

SEBB: "Uncle." Uncle. Okay? Blaise? (BLAISE *softens, and cries.*) Whatsamatta?

BLAISE: I don't wanna be your uncle... Oh, God, Sebbie! I hate them...

SEBB: No, ya don't.

BLAISE: I'll hate it here alone with them. Please don't leave me here. I wouldn't do it to you. I could never do it to you.

SEBB: Yes, you would, kid brother... you would hafta. You would just hafta. Hey... You woulda been my best man.

BLAISE: Huh?

SEBB: You woulda been my best man.

ROCCO: (*Knocks on outside of door.*) Sebbie?

BLAISE: Come in, Pa.

ROCCO: (*Opens the door.*) Oh, Blaise.

BLAISE: 'Scuse me. This coffee's cold. How d'ya make it with the percolator? Never mind, I'll figure it out. (*He exits down to the kitchen.*)

SEBB: Pa, just do me a favor and don't lay any of your shit on me, okay?

ROCCO: I won't say anything.

SEBB: You gonna stand there and watch me?

(*No response.*)

SEBB: Pa, lemme pack.

ROCCO: Pack. (*Pause*) Where ya goin'?

SEBB: Fort Worth.

ROCCO: Fort Worth?

SEBB: That's right. Texas. My friend Doogan's uncle's got a big garage down there.

ROCCO: You got some girlfriend to take with you?

(This shocks SEBB a little.)

SEBB: Pa ... you didn't get married till you were way past thirty. What're you up to, Rocco?

ROCCO: You a homo?

SEBB: Go ask the black swan. *(Pause)* I'm queer ... that's right, Rocco.

ROCCO: What exactly is the meaning?

SEBB: Pa, I'm queer. I'm a fairy. Gabeesh? I ain't gonna marry no Alice in Wonderland. It's just you were the last to find out around here!

ROCCO: Mary Ann Benedetto ...

SEBB: Who is she?

ROCCO: Didn't you and her ...

SEBB: Pa, five years ago I took her to my prom.

ROCCO: It's curable.

SEBB: Pa ...

ROCCO: Jesus, it makes me laugh. I mean, in the hospital they used to round up the men and make us hug each other. Nurturing. Ever hear that word?

SEBB: Out.

ROCCO: What I say?

SEBB: You think you got somethin' I need you can give me? An ol' man with his hair and teeth fallin' out?

ROCCO: Hey, come on.

SEBB: Half-alive corpses don't bounce their sons on their knees, you shitball.

ROCCO: I'm only tryin' ...

SEBB: I'm hip to what you're tryin'. You want to put lipstick on the corpse and dance with it, but it's dead between you and me ... there's no life, no love between you and me.

ROCCO: Listen to me as a bump on a log or a goddamn radio ...

SEBB: Spit it out.

ROCCO: I was puttin' aside money, I dunno . . . in case somebody would need it, and now that you're goin' I think it's only fair . . . I got three thousand here.

SEBB: The King of Too Late. Pa, I'm almost twenty-two now and this is the first thing you ever done for me.

ROCCO: No. First thing was my stayin' alive for you.

SEBB: What nerve you got . . . far as I'm concerned, you shoulda gotten your way in the Holland Tunnel.

ROCCO: Sebbie . . .

SEBB: We'd get that money in your will.

ROCCO: Don't do this.

SEBB: Keepin' yourself alive. Who gives a shit? I've got hair under my arms over ten years now. I'm leavin'. You're in a time warp. Your life was. There's no more gonna be. Keep your fuckin' money.

ROCCO: Have it your way. (*He puts the money back in his pocket.*)

SEBB: Wait. Gimme the money. I got a good use for it.

ROCCO: What . . .

SEBB: All mine now? No strings?

ROCCO: No strings.

(SEBB *starts tearing up the money.*)

ROCCO: Sebb . . . Sebb . . . Gimme that. Don't rip it up. Gimme, you little bastard.

SEBB: It's mine, and this is what I choose to do with it, just like you did what you wanted when it was yours, and we lived in one room . . .

ROCCO: I lived in one room half my life. I was a father when I was eleven 'cause my father *died*. We had to take baths in the kitchen. I hadda see my mother . . . ashamed . . . covering her genital hair. I was a father at eleven years old, cleanin' the toilets in the sweat shop my mother worked in, for a dollar and a half a week.

SEBB: You're the same kind of father to me that yours was to you, so don't worry about me.

ROCCO: Nowhere near . . .

SEBB: I woulda liked to have turned down goin' to college, okay? I went to a good high school. I got marks in high school.

ROCCO: There's no comparison. Thousands of kids put themselves through college.

Sebb: That's not my point. You had that rotten money all the while. I saw those bank books in your black iron box...

Rocco: Sebbie, when I was a kid at night, I'd close my eyes and dream of bein' an aviator...

Sebb: (*Scoops out the bottom of an empty drawer, picks up pictures, and flings them at* Rocco.) Instead, here's what you turned out to be. Pictures of us on the fire escape... with our monkey faces. Those were the days when you were sockin' us if we moved in bed, and that gorilla in there used to hang on to me like she was drownin'... oh, my God, get out.

Rocco: Sebbie, please.

Sebb: You can't pay, don't you understand? I don't want you to think you're paid up. Ever. Money is the least you owe this family.

Rocco: You only remember what you wanna. You know how many times, when you were little, I was dyin' to bend down and hug you? But... I...

Sebb: But what? You were ashamed? Eh, squeaky?

Rocco: Maybe ashamed is the word...

Sebb: 'Shamed in front of who? Your wife? Ashamed of me, a little boy? Did I do somethin'? Was I ugly?

Rocco: You were an angel.

Sebb: Aw.

Rocco: She was like a tiger with you. She gave me the message from the beginnin' she wasn't gonna be too happy if I got too close to you.

Sebb: So she wouldn'ta been too happy.

Rocco: Well...

Sebb: You were scared of her?

Rocco: Who was scared?

Sebb: Pa, you shouldn't marry someone you're gonna be scared of. You shoulda taken the route I'm takin'... gabeesh? Not fuck up the world with fucked-up kids. I'll bet you're more queer than I am. Somethin' tells me.

Rocco: No, Sebbie...

Sebb: Okay then, lemme take my shower.

(Sebb *holds out his hand to shake and* Rocco *takes it.*)

Rocco: (*Leaves the money on* Sebb's *table.*) You take the money.

Sebb: (*Screams*) Oh, no. (*Flings the money.*) No payment.

(Rocco *picks up the money, as* SEBB *undresses for his shower.*)

SEBB: Pa . . . I'm behind schedule . . .

ROCCO: You remember when your mother was in the hospital havin' Blaise?

SEBB: Pa, I had my limit.

ROCCO: Bear with me. I took you to Mount Carmel Feast with that big ferris wheel? You remember that ferris wheel?

SEBB: No, Pa.

ROCCO: Sure you do. Blaise was just born . . . and . . . okay . . . I won you this. (*He reaches for the Pinocchio puppet sitting on top of the bookcase.*) Tell me you don't remember where you got this Pinocchio.

SEBB: Pa, I swear to God, I don't.

ROCCO: You don't remember ridin' the ferris wheel with me? Scared, inside my jacket jus' like a little mouse? Remember what you asked me?

SEBB: Pa . . .

ROCCO: Go along with me.

SEBB: What'd I ask?

ROCCO: You went, "Pa, what happens if we fall offa this thing?" and I said what?"

SEBB: What you say?

ROCCO: I said, "Sebbie, if we fall, I'll jus' turn over on my back so's you land on my soft tummy."

SEBB: That was nice . . .

ROCCO: You remember?

SEBB: Sorry, Pa . . .

ROCCO: I was wearin' that plaid mackinaw . . . What am I gonna tell ya? I didn't come in here only to drop this money, Sebbie.

SEBB: (*He is totally stripped now.*) What else did you come in for? Don't stand there like chocolate pudding . . . you wanna hug me and tell me you love me? Like those people in your hospital? Nurturing . . . you know?

ROCCO: Cover yourself.

SEBB: Why, whatsamatta? I'm gonna take a shower.

ROCCO: Don't make a fool of me, Sebb.

SEBB: Is that your excuse to cop out on me now?

Rocco: What am I copping out of? I don't follow you.

Sebb: The love. What're you ashamed of? We're men, for crissakes. (*He wraps a towel around his waist.*) I'm sincere . . . you send me a letter expressing your feelings if you're so ashamed here.

Rocco: You're being sarcastic.

Sebb: See? When your chance finally comes, you muff it.

Rocco: What am I muffing?

Sebb: I want proof. I have a right to it.

Rocco: I don't understand. What proof?

Sebb: Proof that you cared about me, like you said.

Rocco: I feel it in here. How does a person prove such a thing?

Sebb: You go down on your knees and swear it to God.

Rocco: You're makin' a joke of it.

Sebb: I'm *sincere*, you dope. You kneel.

Rocco: Don't make a fool outta me now . . .

Sebb: I swear on Christ on his cross. I won't.

Rocco: (*Kneels*) What you want me to say?

Sebb: Swear to me you always . . . you know?

Rocco: Cared about you?

Sebb: Exactly. I wanna take that away with me.

Rocco: What do I say?

Sebb: Just say I love you . . .

Rocco: I love you.

(Sebb *removes his towel.*)

Sebb: You wanna suck it? Go ahead . . .

Rocco: Fuckin' pig . . . you fuckin' pig . . . tou . . . tou . . . tou . . . (*He sprays spit into his son's face.*)

(Sebb *smiles into the spray. He enjoys it. He wipes some off his face and looks at his hand.*)

Sebb: Thanks for givin' me somethin' to remember you by . . .

Rocco: (*Swings at* Sebb.) I'll split your head open.

Sebb: Horray. We got the ol' Rocco back. He splits. He hits. He spits like the old days . . . Hit me, motherfucker . . . (Rocco *swings again and connects.*) Good. Now here's somethin' to remember your son by. (Sebb *grabs* Rocco *by his throat.*)

ROCCO: No. Sebb...

SEBB: I hate you, you silly motherfucker. You don't deserve to have me for a son. You didn't pay for it. You didn't pay for it. You didn't pay for it.

ROCCO: Sonny... no.

SEBB: You didn't pay... (*He is nearly choking Rocco.*)

(ROCCO *senses he should yield.*)

ROCCO: You're hurtin' me.

SEBB: You didn't pay. You didn't pay.

ROCCO: I'm sorry, Sebbie.

SEBB: You didn't pay. (*He weeps.*)

(ROCCO *composes himself a little as* SEBB *grabs for support, disoriented.*)

ROCCO: I know.

SEBB: I'll always hate you. Nothin', nothin' could ever change it.

ROCCO: I know. It's okay. Put your robe on.

SEBB: Pa, I feel dizzy. Sick.

ROCCO: Huh?

SEBB: I think I'm gonna...

ROCCO: What kinda sick? Sit. Sit. (ROCCO *guides him into a small, armless chair.*)

SEBB: Weak... I feel faint...

ROCCO: Put your head down. Put it down.

SEBB: No. (*He leans back in the chair—throws back his head, facing the ceiling, eyes closed.*)

ROCCO: You're sweatin'. Lemme wipe your forehead. Here.

(ROCCO *stands behind him and sweeps his hand over* SEBB'S *brow, back over his hair several times.*)

SEBB: Okay... okay. Leave me alone, Pa, and I'll be...

ROCCO: You sure?

(*Ignoring him,* ROCCO *continues wiping* SEBB'S *brow caressingly several more times.* SEBB *breathes deeply.* ROCCO *bends, kisses his head, embraces him.* SEBB *struggles, allowing a small part of it.*)

SEBB: Yeah. I'm all right now.

(*Pause*)

ROCCO: Can I leave the money?

Sebb: No. Jus' lemme alone. Please . . .

Rocco: Splash your face with some water.

Sebb: Okay.

(Rocco *exits*. Sebb *lifts the limp puppet as lights fade*.)

Scene Three

(Blaise *is coming upstairs with the coffee. He passes* Rocco *on the stairs*.)

Blaise: He gonna leave?

Rocco: Bring him that coffee.

Blaise: Thanks for bringin' home all this good luck. (*He goes to* Sebb's *door, knocks once, twice*.) Sebb? Sebb? (*Receiving no answer, he goes to* Filumena's *door and knocks*.) Ma? I got some coffee here.

Filumena: (*Her hair is down. She opens the door, pulls him inside, and slams it behind him*.) Get in.

Blaise: Ma . . . whattya doin'?

Filumena: I don't know. I don't know. But I gotta do somethin'. Count this.

Blaise: Where you get all this money?

Filumena: Did you take our passports outta my drawer?

Blaise: I never touched the passports.

Filumena: Saint Anthony. Blaise. You stay here with your father, if . . . if . . . I go 'way with Sebbie. Where in the manage a di madonna are the friggin' passports? (*Searches frantically for the passports*.)

Blaise: Ma, looka me. Doogan's comin'. Sebbie's goin' with Doogan to Texas. You know where Texas is?

Filumena: Yeah. In bluff land. Take a hundred. Go to Pizella's. Tell him to have a black car here in five minutes to take me to church . . . me and Sebbie . . . but tell him we're really goin' to the airport.

Blaise: The airport? Ma, have you been takin' them diet pills again?

Filumena: I'll slap your face till it bleeds. Go get the car.

Blaise: Sebbie's goin' to Texas I told ya.

Filumena: He swore on Saint Anthony he'd take me to church today. Okay? He won't go to no Texas when he sees me dressed for church. I know my son. Then we get in the car and I tell the driver: to the airport.

Don't you dare tell your father. Let him wait ten years for me to come back from church.

BLAISE: Ma, number one, you're the one who's bluffin' 'cause you ain't gonna make it even to the sidewalk and you know it.

FILUMENA: Don't worry... I'll make it.

BLAISE: Number two... Sebbie'll never go to Sicily in a million years.

FILUMENA: You know how many times he begged me to run away with him? Now he gets his wish. Where's my mother's gold ring?

BLAISE: Would you act like this if I was leavin' home?

FILUMENA: Hey. I'm gonna be trapped here with a nervous old man and you, you little jerk. He likes you.

BLAISE: Trapped with me and a nervous old man? But if Sebbie stays, you're not trapped, eh? You take the cake.

FILUMENA: You with your girlfriends. You'll be gone in a couple years and then where am I? Stuck in this country.

BLAISE: This is your country. You're married.

FILUMENA: I spit on the country. I hate it.

BLAISE: The why'd you come here?

FILUMENA: Another traitor. Help me.

BLAISE: You're the traitor with your... Italian mouth... with your stink and your sweats an'... an'... your Sicilian face. This country don't want you. Look in the mirror. That's the traitor. The Sicilian jungle woman. Don't expect me to brush that hair when he's gone.

FILUMENA: Gesu Maria aiuta...

BLAISE: Ma... I'm sorry I said that, but...

FILUMENA: Shhh. Jus' make believe you're my friend then.

BLAISE: Ma... Jesus! I'm your *son*. You would leave me here and go away with Sebbie? Why am I always second? I wanna come first for once.

FILUMENA: Okay. Sebbie was my favorite. It's jus' the way it was. In my mind... (*She stares a moment.*)

BLAISE: No. I don't want to hear this. (*Holding his ears.*) I ain't... (*Grabbing her face.*) Look at me. *I* wanna be your favorite... Say something.

FILUMENA: I... can't lie.

BLAISE: Say something...

FILUMENA: I slept with my face to the wall 'cause your father wouldn't talk to me in Italian. Hadda learn *English*. I wanted my mother's house so bad. Every night I prayed to the saints, Christ, His mother, anything: get me outta here. My answer was I got pregnant. I wasn't alone in America anymore. I had Sicily inside me. I named him Sebastiano after my father. But you, you're not like us. You're American. Look at your face.

BLAISE: Nooooo . . . Sebbie won't go with you.

FILUMENA: I'm the boss of Sebbie, not Doogan.

BLAISE: Why don't you take a walk before you fly over the ocean? We'll take a walk tomorrow.

FILUMENA: Don't baby me.

BLAISE: Funny that you could go all the way to Sicily but you're scared to go to Scambatti's. Your stockin's are fallin'. (*Laughs*)

FILUMENA: You think I'm a faker? What you think I been prayin' to that saint for all these years? (*She cries.*)

BLAISE: So don't cry. You want me to help ya?

FILUMENA: Sure I'm scared. I open the front door, and I can't put my foot down, not even one step.

BLAISE: You jus' drop the foot down.

FILUMENA: I get dizzy. I feel like I'm dyin'. I look at the house across the street. I see the cars and kids yellin', and I feel my bones melting.

BLAISE: Ma, you can trip on a rug.

FILUMENA: You don't wanna see what he's doin'. He got rid of Sebbie, and next you. Mark my words.

BLAISE: Not me.

FILUMENA: He'll send you to college. He'll pay for it. Then he'll close in on me. Get Pizella. Don't let that sonofabitch sneak outta here without me. Don't trick me, please . . .

(DOOGAN'S *car engine is heard pulling up.*)

FILUMENA: What's that noise?

SEBB(O.S.): Blaise?

BLAISE: Doogan's here with the car.

SEBB: (*From behind his door.*) Tell him I'll be right down.

FILUMENA: Go, you get Pizella first. Go fast and I'll love you. I swear.

(*She closes her door as* BLAISE *leaves.*)

(SEBB *opens his door and comes out with a suitcase and a duffle bag.*)

SEBB: Ma? Ma?

(FILUMENA *stands pressed against her door.* SEBB *pushes, gently. She walks into the room, leaving the door free to open.* SEBB *enters cautiously, shocked by her appearance.*)

FILUMENA: Ohhh . . . the undertaker face.

SEBB: Ma . . . what're ya dressed for?

FILUMENA: Ten o'clock Mass. You're takin' me to church, right? The lipstick okay?

SEBB: Huh?

FILUMENA: Here. Help me with my hair. (SEBB *accepts the hairbrush.*) C'mon, don't make such a puss. This dress is not long enough. (*She sits with her back to him.*) You think we'll look okay walkin' down the aisle together?

SEBB: Ma, I came to say good-bye.

FILUMENA: You not takin' me?

SEBB: I'm leavin', Ma.

FILUMENA: Who's gonna take me?

SEBB: Ma . . . I . . . uh . . . hafta . . .

FILUMENA: Okay. Don't tell me. Weakling.

SEBB: Don't call me that, Ma.

FILUMENA: Yes, you are. You let Rocco win. But he won't win with me. I'm goin' to Sicily.

SEBB: Right this minute?

FILUMENA: Laugh at me, you sonofabitch, and I'll stick this nail file in your face.

SEBB: Put that down.

FILUMENA: You think I can't go to Sicily?

SEBB: Sure you can.

FILUMENA: You think I can stick this in my throat?

SEBB: Gimme the nail file.

FILUMENA: And that's the way I can throw myself out the front door when the time comes. This house is a worse coffin than the plane. So go. Be proud that you tricked me.

SEBB: How'd I trick you?

FILUMENA: You swore on Sont Ondone you wouldn't leave me if I went to church today. (*Suddenly, for sympathy*) Looka me gettin' ready.

SEBB: Ma. I'm sorry.

FILUMENA: Sebbie...you...you're Sicilian. The lemons grow this big...the sun is always shining. I got money...

SEBB: Ma, I can't live in Sicily.

FILUMENA: I'm ready...look, Sebbie, I really am.

SEBB: Ma, lemme...lemme finish your hair. Sit. Go ahead. That feel good? What you cryin' for?

(*He brushes her hair, gently, affectionately.*)

(FILUMENA *melts under his tenderness and cries, realizing her defeat.*)

FILUMENA: You're gonna leave.

SEBB: I gotta...Ma.

FILUMENA: There's young people in Sicily...

SEBB: No. Ma.

FILUMENA: And what about gogathatz...goom a si chiam...where they'll cure me?

SEBB: Colorado? Ma, there's snow there. You hate the snow. Someday, I swear...

FILUMENA: No someday, please, please. You're makin' me scared.

SEBB: Ssshhhhhh.

FILUMENA: I'll die...I know. (*She clings to him, hard.*)

(SEBB *tries to pull out of her grip.*)

SEBB: Ma, lemme go now. Doogan's gonna get mad.

FILUMENA: Sebbie—

SEBB: Ma...leggo, Ma. Jesus! (*He pushes her off to break her grip.*)

(FILUMENA *responds by pushing* SEBB *toward the door.*)

FILUMENA: And when they bury me, don't you dare come across the ocean. I want none of youse. I got my passport.

SEBB: Huh? What're you tryin' to prove with the passports?

FILUMENA: Go. You think God is gonna bless you for trickin' me?

SEBB: I don't need God's blessing.

FILUMENA: He don't *need* it.

SEBB: Yours I want.

FILUMENA: Where's the nail file ... here ... take it in your cheek. (*She jabs* SEBB *in the cheek with the nail file.*)

SEBB: Ow! You crazy ... God ...

FILUMENA: You satisfied, Judas?

SEBB: You poor crazy woman.

FILUMENA: Now you can remember your mother when you look in the mirror. That's the kind of mother she was.

(SEBB *goes to the bathroom and* FILUMENA *slams the door behind him, but Sebb's bag is still in there.*)

(*O.S.: Doogan is beeping horn.*)

(SEBB *comes out of the bathroom with a small white towel wrapped in his fist. He's applying pressure to the cut on his cheek. He opens the door quietly.* FILUMENA *is still sitting, crying.* SEBB *picks up his bag, then pauses.*)

SEBB: Ma. Minavog.

FILUMENA: Go.

SEBB: You okay?

FILUMENA: (*Nods yes*) I'm okay ...

SEBB: I ain't a weakling, Ma.

FILUMENA: I know you ain't. Go.

(SEBB *kisses the top of her head then goes downstairs with his suitcase and bag.*)

ROCCO: What happened to your face?

SEBB: Shavin' ...

ROCCO: You got snow tires?

SEBB: No ... It'll be okay.

ROCCO: Don't let anybody ... ya know ... don't let anybody ...

SEBB: Just take care of her. (*Exits.*)

(ROCCO *meets* FILUMENA *on stairs, carrying her mother's clock.*)

ROCCO: Filumena ... What're ya dressed for? Huh? Where are you going with your mother's clock? (*Laughs at her.*)

FILUMENA: Where's Blaise?

ROCCO: I dunno.

FILUMENA: If you were dead that kid never would have left.

ROCCO: Don't you think it's good he left?

FILUMENA: No. The good man. He knows what's good for everybody.

ROCCO: He was old enough to leave home, Filumena. He wanted to go.

FILUMENA: Sure, to get fucked up the ass. And who made him that way?

ROCCO: Don't lay that on me . . . You . . . You Cigna Nera, you and your hair brush. You ate your own eggs, Black Swan. You got a full stomach? *You.*

FILUMENA: Whattya mean I ate my own eggs? Did you ever think it was 'cause I was starvin'?

ROCCO: That was the old days.

FILUMENA: And what is the new days? Today and yesterday?

ROCCO: Okay . . . I understand what you mean, Filumena, but now I wanna take care of you. I wanna love you . . . but you keep tryin' to hurt me, Filumena.

FILUMENA: Hurt? Who started with the hands twenty-five years ago? Who shoved cotton down my throat?

ROCCO: Cotton? What cotton . . . ?

FILUMENA: Speak *English*, Italian girl. You remember? Eat your love now . . . love now after your hand hit me, hit your kids. (*She's beginning to tremble.*)

ROCCO: Shshhhhh . . .

FILUMENA: Now he says love when his hair's white as snow. Love now that we're old . . . (*She disintegrates into Rocco's arms.*) Sebbie! . . . Sebbie!—

ROCCO: Shh . . . sh . . . shhhhh . . . Filumena. Please . . . please . . . please.

(*There is a moment of tenderness which* BLAISE *interrupts.*)

BLAISE: (*Panting*) Ma, Pizella's here.

ROCCO: Pizella? What for Pizzella?

BLAISE: Uh . . . Pa . . . the car . . . she wanted the car.

FILUMENA: I'm goin' home, Rocco.

ROCCO: Home? This is your home.

FILUMENA: No. Sicily.

ROCCO: Sicily? Sicily? Filumena, Sicily is different now. They're all dead over there . . .

FILUMENA: I don't care. Blaise'll take me to the airport. Passports, money . . . and Pizella.

ROCCO: A kiss good-bye, Filumena.

FILUMENA: You sonofabitch. What're you tryin' to torture me? How can I kiss you ever? Ever?

ROCCO: What's the big deal?

FILUMENA: I would disgust you. You never loved me. Remember?

ROCCO: I never loved anybody . . . but what the hell?

FILUMENA: Rocco. It's finished.

ROCCO: (*Grabbing* BLAISE) Look at this kid's nose.

BLAISE: Pa, lemme go.

ROCCO: This is your father's nose to a tee.

FILUMENA: Huh? My father was dead before you met me; how do you know what his nose looks like?

ROCCO: You usta say you had your father's nose.

FILUMENA: Me?

ROCCO: And this kid's got your nose, so . . .

FILUMENA: So?

ROCCO: You gonna leave this nose in America?

FILUMENA: Pagliacci.

ROCCO: Yeah. If you stay, I'll make you laugh, Filumena.

FILUMENA: Clown.

ROCCO: Yeah. Or make believe I'm your Marie Antoinette . . . stick me on your bed upstairs and put a hat on me.

FILUMENA: You . . .

ROCCO: Or make me your saint upstairs. Light candles to me. I'm Saint Anthony, ask me a favor. Go ahead. Ask me a favor.

FILUMENA: Rocco . . . There's a young girl dead in this house somewhere. Some day you may find the body. Do her the favor. Minavog.

ROCCO: Okay, go, I give up. Honest to Christ, let it all fall down. I can't live with hate either.

BLAISE: Wait, Pa . . . we're blowin' each other to the four fuckin' winds here. (*Turns to* FILUMENA.) Ma . . .

(FILUMENA *ignores him.*)

FILUMENA: (*Puts down her mother's clock and slowly, deliberately puts on her gloves, trying to mask her fear.*) The planes take off in snow like this?

BLAISE: Sure.

FILUMENA: And they sell tickets at the airport?

BLAISE: Uh-huh.

FILUMENA: What a wind passed through this house ...

(*Bells softly start far off.*)

FILUMENA: What's that? Are those bells? (*She knows perfectly well that they are bells for the ten o'clock Mass.*)

BLAISE: (*Realizing his opportunity.*) Yeah. For the ten o'clock Mass.

FILUMENA: If we let Pizella's car stop at the church, is there time?

BLAISE: (*Catching on*) Uh ... sure.

FILUMENA: Yep. All right. I'll try to light a candle for Sebbie ... maybe. We got time, yeah?

BLAISE: I said yeah.

FILUMENA: (*Trembling*) But if the priest talks, we get up.

BLAISE: Sure.

FILUMENA: Good. Then maybe we go to the airport or maybe we come back here. If. *If* I feel like it. (*Points a finger up, gesturing for Rocco.*) *If.*

ROCCO: I'll have some coffee waitin' ... *if* ...

FILUMENA: Well, don't count on it. 'Cause if I *do* come back, it don't mean I stay.

ROCCO: Whatever you want.

FILUMENA: (*Calls up the stairs as though there is someone she's leaving behind.*) Filumena? Hey ... Filumena Battaglia ...

BLAISE: Huh?

FILUMENA: I'll never forget you. Mai. Mai. Sola una persona always loved you from the beginning, and that was *me*, Pauvarella. (*Turns in the door frame to take her first step.*) Look at this one without a scarf. Put up your collar.

BLAISE: (*Descends backwards, facing his mother, while* FILUMENA *holds his shoulder as though it were a railing.*) Slide that foot ... off ... off ... Pa ...

(ROCCO *comes to help.*)

BLAISE: Let it go, off.

FILUMENA: Oh, where? Ou.

BLAISE: Down here. You should be wearin' your galoshes, Ma.

FILUMENA: I don't have any galoshes. Ou, it's slippery. Dio . . .

BLAISE: I gottcha. Now step again.

(*Jumps up and grabs* FILUMENA'S *arm;* ROCCO *has her other arm.*)

FILUMENA: Wait. My feet are getting wet. Lemme go back.

ROCCO: No. The snow is dry. Step . . . I gottcha. Blaise, you got her tight?

BLAISE: Yeah, I got her. You got her, Pa?

FILUMENA: Hold me tight, Rocco. If God gets me there, I'll light a candle with thirty dollars on the altar. If God gets me there . . .

BLAISE: God'll get us there. Now, step.

FILUMENA: (*Slides an inch*) Ou, ooop. Fifty dollars I'll leave, fifty dollars and a candle, right on the altar.

BLAISE: Good.

ROCCO: She's doin' wonderful.

FILUMENA: Ou, it's cold . . . blessed Mother . . . please get us there.

BLAISE: Step at a time, Ma.

(*The three step down one more step, then another.*)

FILUMENA: (*Voice fades.*) It's cold . . .

ROCCO: Easy . . .

FILUMENA: Step at a time, a step . . . Sant Ondone . . . Sant Ondone . . . oh . . . oh . . .

(*Snow falling can be seen through the open doors, but they have disappeared down the snowy steps to the sidewalk, as LIGHTS FADE in the empty house. We see one electronic light in the orchid area, glowing.*)

CURTAIN
End of play

Jules Feiffer

Knock Knock

JULES FEIFFER's first work for the theatre, *The Explainers*, was a musical review based on his cartoons, staged in 1963 at Chicago's Second City. *Little Murders*, his first full-length play, closed after one week on Broadway in 1967, but came into its own two years later in Alan Arkin's production at Circle in the Square. His next two plays were political: *God Bless* in 1968, and *The White House Murder Case* in 1969. Mr. Feiffer has published eleven collections of cartoons; a childhood memoir, *The Great Comic Book Heroes*, a book of drawings of the Chicago conspiracy trial, *Pictures at a Prosecution;* and a novel, *Harry, the Rat with Women*. He has also written the scripts for two films, *Little Murders* and *Carnal Knowledge*. He recently published yet another novel, *Ackroyd*.

Knock Knock is dedicated to Sherlee Lantz.

For information regarding stock and amateur rights, including all other rights, contact: The Lantz Office, Inc., 114 East 55 Street, New York, NY 10022.

Knock Knock was first presented in New York City by the Circle Repertory Company (Jerry Arrow, Executive Director) on January 14, 1976 (Press Opening: January 18). The play was directed by Marshall W. Mason, with the following cast:

COHN	Daniel Seltzer
ABE	Neil Flanagan
WISEMAN	Judd Hirsch
JOAN	Nancy Snyder

Joan's Voices, the Bailiff's voice, and other apparitions were played by Judd Hirsch.

The setting was by John Lee Beatty, costumes by Jennifer von Mayrhauser, lighting by Dennis Parichy, and sound by Charles London and George Hansen. Dan Hild was the Production Stage Manager.

Latter, producers Terry Allen Kramer and Harry Rigby moved the play to Broadway, where it opened at the Biltmore Theatre on February 24, 1976.

The time is the present. A small log house in the woods. It is unpainted, cramped, containing the worldly goods of two lifetimes, COHN's and ABE's. Books and periodicals litter every surface, including the floor, which is covered with an old Persian rug. Two out-of-use TVs, circa 1950. An aged radio-phonograph console; next to it on the floor a stack of classical LP's. A large oak table that serves as a dining table and ABE's desk. A typewriter, holding a blank sheet of paper at ABE's end of the table; next to it a ream of blank paper. The kitchen is separated from the living-dining room by a tattered screen, covered with magazine cutouts of famous faces: Einstein, Tolstoy, Beethoven, Toscanini, F.D.R., Gandhi, Joe Louis, Babe Ruth, Katharine Cornell . . . The kitchen is well equipped: a huge iron range, shelves of spices, canned goods, other supplies. A shelf of cookbooks. Two burlap-curtained doorways lead to the bedrooms. A tiny windowed door leads outside. The view through two dark windows is of vegetation: crawling vines, blackened leaves. Pictures bury the walls: simply framed, very small, mostly family photographs and postcard-size reproductions of Impressionist paintings. Near the fireplace: a large steamer trunk. Somewhere close to the kitchen: an open ironing board; on it a graying bundle of shirts, living there for days. On a side table: COHN's violin; near it, a music stand. In addition to the two dining-room chairs there is an old rocker: COHN's, and a huge, beat-up, overstuffed armchair: ABE's.

Act One

(AT RISE: COHN, overweight and fifty, is at the stove, reading from a cookbook and mixing ingredients into a pot. He is humming a Mozart aria. He hums, cooks, tastes. Across the room, ABE, underweight and fifty, lies in his chair staring into space. He lights a cigar and meditates.)

ABE: It's getting better.

COHN: *(Tastes)* Who says?

ABE: I say.

COHN: *(Mixes)* With what evidence?

ABE: My eyes are my evidence.

COHN: *(Turns to ABE and raises two fingers.)* How many fingers?

ABE: Five.

COHN: Some eyes. *(Goes back to his cooking.)*

ABE: All right, two.

COHN: *(Slams down the pot and turns to ABE)* So if you can see two, why do you say five?

ABE: I prefer five.

COHN: That's not a reason.

ABE: Why does there always have to be a reason?

COHN: Abe, I've known you for twenty-five years and for you there's never a reason.

ABE: And you? You're better off?

COHN: I don't invent.

ABE: I beg your pardon. Neither do I.

COHN: What kind of fool am I living with? You just made up five.

ABE: I didn't make it up.

COHN: Not a minute ago.

ABE: No.

COHN: I was holding up two *(Holds up two fingers.)* and you said I was holding up five! *(Holds up five fingers.)*

ABE: You *are* holding up five.

(COHN *quickly puts down his hand.*)

COHN: What's the use?

ABE: Cohn, I'll tell you something—you're rigid. I'm flexible.

COHN: Mindless.

ABE: You only believe in what's in front of your nose. That's not mindless?

COHN: I don't make things up.

ABE: (*Points to curtained doorway.*) What's that?

COHN: Don't bother me. (ABE *continues to point.*) It's my bedroom! (*Goes back to his cooking.*) Pest!

ABE: I don't see any bedroom.

COHN: You know it's my bedroom!

ABE: I beg your pardon. All I see is a curtain. (COHN *goes and pulls back the curtain.*) Ah hah! A bedroom! (ABE *rises, crosses to the doorway, and pulls the curtain back into place.*) A curtain. (*Pulls the curtain back and forth.*) A bedroom. A curtain. A bedroom. A curtain. A bedroom. Is it still a bedroom when you don't see it?

COHN: It's always a bedroom!

ABE: So for you it's always a bedroom and for me it's always five fingers. (COHN *slams the plate down on the table, pours stew into it, and begins to eat.* ABE *joins him at the table, studies the blank sheet in his typewriter, punches one key, and nods seriously at the results.*) I'm right, so I don't get any stew?

COHN: You want stew? Here! (*Hands him pot.*)

ABE: (*Looks into pot.*) It's empty.

COHN: (*Points to empty pot.*) What's that?

ABE: A pot.

COHN: You saw me cook stew in it? (ABE *nods.*) You saw me pour stew out of it? (ABE *nods.*) So eat your stew. (ABE, *unhappily, watches* COHN *eat.* COHN *wipes his mouth and points to the empty space in front of* ABE.) Eat! That's steak. That's potatoes. That's salad. That's beer. Hearty appetite!

ABE: That's vicious.

COHN: (*Smiles, self-satisfied.*) Abe, you can pull the wool over your eyes but you can't pull it over mine. I know you every step of the way. I know you inside and out.

ABE: I'm hungry.

COHN: So make something.

ABE: You know I don't cook. I burn everything.

COHN: Don't.

ABE: My mind wanders. (COHN *gets up, crosses to stock shelf, takes down a box of spaghetti, sets a plate in front of* ABE, *and pours the uncooked spaghetti into the plate.*) It's not cooked.

COHN: I say it's cooked. Two fingers. Five fingers. Eat your spaghetti. (ABE *looks disconsolately at the plate, picks the spaghetti sticks up in his hand, and begins to eat them.* COHN *watches for a moment, then relents. He takes the plate away from* ABE *and pours the spaghetti into a pot of water on the stove.*) When will you learn?

ABE: To be like you? I beg your pardon, is that such a blessing?

COHN: Don't get personal.

ABE: I don't like being made a fool of.

COHN: You asked for it.

ABE: I know I'm right. (COHN *groans.*) You can win the argument but it doesn't mean you're right. Inside I know who's right.

COHN: You think so?

ABE: I know so. With my ex-wife, I also lost all arguments. But you told me I was right.

COHN: With her you *were* right.

ABE: So if I lost with her and was right, you have to admit that when I lose with you I also could be right. It's consistent.

COHN: Abe, I'm going to tell you a little story. A parable. After I finish, you tell me what it means to you. O.K.?

ABE: Before I eat?

COHN: Here. (*Cuts him a slice of cheese.* ABE *wolfs it down.*) Once there was this beautiful, innocent, young maid, golden locks, of eighteen, who lived in a dark forest in the country with her very proud, strict parents, and it was her habit to sit by a pond day in and day out, and moon and mope about the moment when love would first enter her life. One day this lovely young thing is daydreaming by the pond when a frog hops out of the water and into her lap. The beautiful maid recoils. "Don't be frightened," croaks the ugly little frog. "I am not what I appear to be. I am in truth a handsome young prince cast under a spell by a wicked witch and this spell can only be broken when some fair maid takes me into her bed and spends the night by my side." So the girl calms down and decides why not? So she brought the frog home and she took it to bed with her and the next morning she woke up—and lying next to her was this tall, handsome, naked young prince. And that's the way she explained it to her parents when they walked in on the two of them. What's the moral of the story?

ABE: The moral is, you're a very cynical man.

COHN: You want dinner? Then discuss it intelligently.

ABE: (*Leaves the table and returns to his own chair.*) The moral is, you take a classic fable with charm and beauty, that deals with dreams and imagination, and you change it into men's-room humor. That's the moral. What you reveal of yourself. (*Leaves his chair, crosses to the typewriter, punches a key, and sits back down again.*)

COHN: You would believe the girl's story?

ABE: I beg your pardon, I wouldn't be her prosecutor. I leave that to you.

COHN: Supposing you're the girl's father?

ABE: I would face the problem with compassion.

COHN: First admitting it's a problem!

ABE: A man in bed with my daughter? At first—until the situations's cleared up, I have to admit it's a problem.

COHN: Then she tells you the story of the frog.

ABE: Which clears up everything.

COHN: You believe about the frog?

ABE: What's important is, she believes about the frog. We didn't bring her up to lie.

COHN: You'd rather have her crazy than lie.

ABE: Why is that crazy?

COHN: Or hallucinating.

ABE: Because her mind can conjure with change—with ugliness turning into beauty—you call that hallucinating? And what *you* see—only beauty turning into ugliness—you call that reality? I beg you pardon, Cohn, you're living in a stacked deck. You give me a choice, I prefer frogs into princes over princes into frogs.

COHN: Even if it's not so.

ABE: How do we know? All I'm saying is, we don't know.

COHN: Do we know that you're Abe and I'm Cohn?

ABE: In this life.

COHN: In this life. But in another life, maybe I was Abe and you were Cohn?

ABE: It's possible. Anything's possible.

COHN: —or that I was Mozart and you were Thomas Jefferson?

ABE: It's unlikely. But it's possible.

COHN: —or that I was Moses and you were Christ?

ABE: It's possible.

COHN: Abe, I'm going to give you a chance to listen to what you just said: It's possible you were Christ.

ABE: I didn't say probable. I said possible.

COHN: And it's possible that if I rub this lamp a genie will come out?

ABE: All I'm saying is, we don't know, do we?

(COHN *rubs the lamp.*)

COHN: Now we know.

ABE: I beg your pardon, we know about one lamp. We don't know about all lamps. Also, we don't know that a genie *didn't* come out. We don't know that there isn't a genie in this room this very moment. And that he isn't saying, "Master, I am the genie of the lamp and I have three wishes to grant you and anything you wish will come true." Maybe he's there and maybe we've been taught how not to see genies in our time. Or hear them. Or take advantage when they offer us three wishes. That's all I'm saying. That it could be us, not him.

COHN: Who?

ABE: The genie.

COHN: Abe, if I had three wishes, you know what would be my first wish? That instead of you to talk to, to drive me crazy for another twenty years, I had somebody with a brain I could talk to! That's what I wish!

(A sudden explosion engulfs ABE. Light and music effect. The smoke clears, and sitting in his place is a bearded WISEMAN in robes. He holds a clipboard and a pen.)

WISEMAN: Name?!

COHN: (*Shaken*) Cohn.

WISEMAN: (*Checks the clipboard.*) That's right—Cohn. Occupation?!

COHN: Musician.

WISEMAN: (*Smiles*) Musician. Where are you a musician, Cohn?

COHN: At the present I am unemployed.

WISEMAN: (*Smiles*) At the present you are unemployed, is that right, Cohn?

COHN: Yes.

WISEMAN: At the present—let me see if I have this straight—you are an unemployed musician.

COHN: That's right.

WISEMAN: Unemployed. But still a musician.

COHN: Yes.

WISEMAN: What are you first, Cohn? A musician or an unemployed?

COHN: I don't understand the question.

WISEMAN: You wanted someone intelligent to talk to?

COHN: Yes.

WISEMAN: Meaning that he will be on your level. That's what you mean by intelligent, isn't it Cohn? (*Waits*) Well? Isn't it?

COHN: I guess it is.

WISEMAN: By that we are to assume that you consider yourself intelligent. Or do I go too far, Cohn?

COHN: No.

WISEMAN: No what?

COHN: What you said.

WISEMAN: That I go too far?

COHN: (*Inaudible*) No.

WISEMAN: I can't hear you.

COHN: The other—what else you said first.

WISEMAN: That you consider yourself—don't let me put words in your mouth—intelligent. Though unemployed, out of work, a ward of the state, you consider yourself intelligent. And that you want as a companion—am I right in this?—someone of equal intelligence. I am not putting words in your mouth?

COHN: No. Equal intelligence. That's it.

WISEMAN: You want another unemployed musician?

COHN: Look—what's happened to Abe?

WISEMAN: Who?

COHN: Abe—my friend.

WISEMAN: You want Abe?

COHN: I want to know where he went.

WISEMAN: You miss this Abe? Is he another unemployed musician?

COHN: A stockbroker. Mutual funds. Retired.

WISEMAN: A wealthy retired stockbroker.

COHN: Yes.

WISEMAN: Supporting you?

COHN: He was sitting in that chair.

WISEMAN: In my chair?

COHN: It's Abe's chair.

WISEMAN: It's Wiseman's chair.

COHN: Who?

WISEMAN: Myself. Helmut Wiseman. It is my chair. You see? I am sitting in it. See how I sit in it, relax in it, lean back in it? So whose chair would you say this is? Does it look as if I've ever been out of this chair? Conversely, does it not look as if I have always been in this chair? How tall is this Abe?

COHN: Five foot eight.

WISEMAN: He is too short for this chair. You either have the wrong man or the wrong chair. Or the wrong height. If you had another height you might have the right man. But it would still be the wrong chair. No, I'm sorry, I can't help you. This is my chair. I, Wiseman. Mine. I know—you must have the wrong house! Try next door.

COHN: This is my house.

WISEMAN: (*He refers to his clipboard.*) Whose?

COHN: (*Quickly*) Abe's. Abe and I live here.

WISEMAN: In this house?

COHN: Yes!

WISEMAN: Or a house very much like this?

COHN: It's *this* house!

WISEMAN: It can't be this house because it's not the right chair.

COHN: It *is* the right chair!

WISEMAN: Then why isn't Abe sitting here? You see, Cohn, your argument collapses of its own weight. I'm sorry, I would like to spend more time with you, but there are others waiting. Will you send in the next applicant please?

COHN: What?

WISEMAN: (*Points to door.*) On your way out, will you send in the next applicant? (*A knock on the door.*) You see, they are getting impatient.

COHN: This is *my* house!

WISEMAN: You house? Well, I like that! Now you see here, Mr. Wiseman—

COHN: You're *Wiseman!*

WISEMAN: (*Indignant*) Oh! And I suppose I'm Cohn!

COHN: *I'm* Cohn!

WISEMAN: Now *you're* Cohn. It's your chair, your house, and your Cohn. Then who am I, may I ask?

COHN: I don't know who you are! You barge in here—

WISEMAN: Barge in? Did you see me barge in?

WISEMAN: In a manner of speaking.

WISEMAN: No, I'm sorry, Mr. Wiseman, or whatever you call yourself, I don't at all care for your manner of speaking. Your manner of speaking is offensive to me. Now if you had a nicer manner of speaking, something like: (*Sweet-voiced*) "Hello. How are you? I like you. Will you be my friend?" Well, that would be another manner entirely. But the way things stand now, the position is already filled. (*Knock on door.*) And tell the others to come back tomorrow. I'm going to bed. (WISEMAN *rises and disappears behind the curtained doorway leading into* COHN's *bedroom.*)—A terrible day. I want to leave a call for seven. (COHN *crosses to the doorway.*) If you don't have seven in stock, make it nine.

(*Another knock.* COHN *turns to the door.*)

COHN: Who—who's there?

JOAN: Joan.

COHN: Joan who?

JOAN: (*Sings*) Joan know why there's no sun up in the sky, stormy weather.

(COHN *growls and grabs the poker from the fireplace.*)

COHN: Enough's enough! (*To* JOAN) Did you hear? Enough is enough!

WISEMAN: Will you kids quiet it down in there!

COHN: (*Whirls toward bedroom.*) Wiseman!! (*Advances on bedroom with poker.*) I warn you I'm armed!! (*He disappears behind the curtain. Sounds of a fight. Curtain moves violently. After a moment* WISEMAN *skips out, opens the refrigerator, takes out a carrot, and skips back. Throughout* WISEMAN's *exit and return the sound of the fight and the bustling of the* *curtain continue. A moment later,* COHN *crawls out of the bedroom, his clothes in tatters. He throws open the trunk in the corner and pulls out a shotgun. He crawls back inside the bedroom with the shotgun. A loud blast.* COHN *staggers out, dragging the dead* WISEMAN. *Knock on the door.* COHN *freezes, holding* WISEMAN.*) Who's there?

JOAN: Joan.

COHN: Joan who?

JOAN: Joan ask me no questions and I'll tell you no lies.

(COHN *drags* WISEMAN *over to the trunk and with great difficulty manages to squeeze him into it. But not all of him. He pushes down on the head and the legs pop out. He sticks the legs back in and the head and shoulders slide up. This goes on for a while until finally all of* WISEMAN *is in the trunk and* COHN *slams shut the lid, at which point the side collapses and* WISEMAN'S *legs pop out.* COHN *stares sullenly at* WISEMAN'S *exposed legs. Another knock.*)

COHN: (*Wearily*) Joan who?

JOAN: (*Sings*) Joan sit under the apple tree with anyone else but me.

COHN: I thought so.

(*He folds back the edge of the rug, slides the trunk next to it, then unfolds the rug over* WISEMAN'S *legs. He skulks back into the bedroom and comes out with the shotgun. He crosses to the door and listens. During the above we hear the following outside the door.*)

JOAN: He won't let me in.

FIRST VOICE: He has to!

SECOND VOICE: Did you tell him who you are?

JOAN: No.

FIRST VOICE: Tell him.

JOAN: I can't.

SECOND VOICE: Why not?

JOAN: It sounds like name-dropping.

FIRST VOICE: Maybe he hasn't heard of you.

JOAN: He must have heard of me.

SECOND VOICE: How do you know if you don't tell him.

(*Pause.*)

JOAN: Knock. Knock.

COHN: (*Reloads shotgun.*) Who's there?

JOAN: Joan.

COHN: (*Getting ready.*) Joan who?

JOAN: Joan of Arc. (COHN *whips open the door and blasts away. A loud clang.* COHN *recoils in horror, drops the gun, and backs off. In walks a vision of loveliness wearing a suit of armor. The breastplate has a big black dent in it.* JOAN *glares at* COHN, *crosses herself, and starts talking to her body.*) Are you all right?

FIRST VOICE: I'm all right—a little shaky.

SECOND VOICE: I'm upset but I'm all right.

COHN: (*Gasping*) Who are you?

FIRST VOICE: That's some greeting.

SECOND VOICE: You got any more surprises like that?

COHN: Who are they?

JOAN: (*Taps the dent in her armor.*) My Voices.

(COHN *retreats to the curtained doorway, turns quickly, and throws the shotgun into the bedroom, then turns back to* JOAN.)

COHN: I'm not a violent man—

(*A loud blast from the bedroom.* COHN *ducks his head behind the curtain and out again.*)

FIRST VOICE: He's a pacifist.

SECOND VOICE: I'd like to pacifist *him* right in the mouth.

COHN: No harm done. Has this been a day! Look—(*Slowly regaining confidence through the sound of his own voice.*) Certain things we know. I'll make myself clear. We know that maturity is the weaning out of synthetics in one's life, so that where in one's childhood, one's life was a will-o'-the'wisp, fantasy-laden, hodgepodge, over the years it develops into a spare, clear-eyed, precise, concise, essentially organic whole. Ask questions. I'm not a pedant.

JOAN: You think life is a hole. Life is holy, not a hole.

COHN: An organic whole. (*Indicates with motion of his hand.*)

JOAN: Small wonder you go around shooting people. You don't know what's important.

COHN: I don't shoot people.

FIRST VOICE: You want to know where the hole is?

SECOND VOICE: In your head!

COHN: Look—(*A long exasperated pause.*) Who are they?

JOAN: My Voices? (COHN *nods.*) They're my Voices.

COHN: (*Restraining himself.*) What have you got inside there? A tape recorder?

JOAN: (*Crosses herself.*) You pitiful man. (*Places a hand on his shoulder.*) We must be on our way. Are these rags all you own?

COHN: I don't leave here.

JOAN: But you must come with me—

COHN: No!

JOAN: To see the Emperor!

COHN: Emperor— (*Quickly back-pedals, and bangs into the trunk. WISEMAN's legs kick up in the air under the rug.*) I'll make a contribution— (*Reaches into his pocket.*)

JOAN: I want you!

COHN: I live here. I stay here. Take the trunk! It's a gift!

JOAN: My mission is to bring you, among others, before the Emperor. It is your duty to follow me.

COHN: (*Retreats behind curtain.*) You're barking up the wrong tree. I never leave here. Ask anyone. They never see me leave here. They don't know me. Ask anyone if they know me. They'll say, "Who?"

JOAN: You must do as I say!

COHN: I have to go with you to see the Emperor. What Emperor? What for? To tell him the sky is falling?

JOAN: The sky is not falling.

COHN: (*Sarcastic*) Thank God!

JOAN: It is missing.

COHN: (*Comes out from behind curtain with change of clothes.*) What's missing?

JOAN: The sky is missing! We must find the Emperor to give him the wonderful news that the sky is missing and that mankind's path to heaven is at last unblocked and unimpeded, and that God calls on His Highness, the Emperor, to build a thousand spaceships and put on them two of every kind and blast off for heaven. Before the holocaust.

COHN: (*Sits her down.*) O.K. (*Pause*) Let's take this a little bit at a time. First of all, there's an emperor, right? (JOAN *nods.*) And he lives—where *does* he live? (JOAN *points.*) He lives that way. (JOAN *nods.*) And you are heading a delegation of citizens to petition the Emperor to build a spaceship—

JOAN: A thousand spaceships!

COHN: To take us to, you said heaven, am I right? (JOAN *nods*.) Because the sky which has always been up there is not up there any more. (JOAN *nods*.) In fact, it is missing. And we are to bring this piece of news to the Emperor, this man you call the Emperor. And he is to put two of every kind on the spaceships—and thus save us from the holocaust. (JOAN *nods*.) And everybody else dies. We're saved. Everybody else dies. Is that a mission or is that a mission!

JOAN: Don't be dense; it has nothing to do with dying. It's more or less like moving. Some people live in the city and some people live in the suburbs and some people live in the country and some people live in heaven.

COHN: You don't have to die to go to heaven any more?

JOAN: Not since the sky is missing. You simply *move* there. But first, of course, you have to know it's there. For example, if your entire life were spent in the city, would you know about cows and trees? No! Well, it's no different with heaven. True, we may know about it in a *religious* sense, but certainly not as a place to migrate.

COHN: (*With infinite patience.*) But isn't it cruel—maybe cruel is too strong a word—isn't it thoughtless to abandon everyone else to the holocaust?

JOAN: (*Brightly*) I'm glad you asked me that question. I, too, thought it was cruel, but my Voices tell me that people will never know it's a holocaust. They'll adapt themselves. Many may even find happiness. (*Goes to door.*) Are you ready?

COHN: Young lady, sit down, I have some shocking news to break to you. (*He sits* JOAN *back down in a chair.*) There is no Emperor.

JOAN: You might as well say there is no God.

COHN: There is no God.

JOAN: You might as well say there is no me and there is no you.

COHN: There is a me; that's all I concede.

JOAN: But there is no me?

COHN: For your information, you are not Joan of Arc.

JOAN: And my Voices?

COHN: There are no Voices.

FIRST VOICE: There are too!

COHN: There are not!

SECOND VOICE: Are too! Are too!

COHN: Are not! Are not!

FIRST AND SECOND VOICES: Are! Are! Are!

COHN: Not! Not! Not!

JOAN: Then whom are you arguing with?

COHN: (*Calms down.*) It's not an argument, just a discussion. I wish you'd tell me how you do that.

JOAN: Have you ever believed in anything?

COHN: I believe in me. After that there's room for doubt.

JOAN: But it's so lonely!

COHN: That's my problem.

JOAN: How can you bear it?

COHN: If you're strong, you can bear what's true. If you're weak, you make up fairy tales.

JOAN: You think I make up fairy tales?

COHN: I'm not singling you out. Abe, my best friend. Him also. *He'd* go with you to see the Emperor. Not that he'd believe. He wouldn't believe. But just in case. With Abe it's always just in case. He's built an ethic out of "maybe," "who's to know," "just in case." (*In a rage.*) He has no convictions! *No convictions!* I much prefer someone crazy like you who thinks she's Joan of Arc. That at least is a position. So that's another reason. I have to stay in the house to take care of Abe; I can't go with you to see the Emperor.

JOAN: We'll take him with us!

COHN: He's not here.

JOAN: Where is he?

COHN: That's the question. Vanished! Vanished to annoy me. You watch. I'll pay him back good. We had an argument—I won't bore you with the details—but it got around—who knows how?—to wishes. Two grown men, an argument over wishes. Abe said it's possible I had three, I said baloney. Abe said I couldn't know unless I wished, so I wished Abe would stop bothering me and vanish, and to make a long story short, in order to aggravate me, he did.

JOAN: Wish him back.

COHN: If life were only so simple.

JOAN: The first wish worked.

COHN: A trick.

JOAN: Are you afraid?

COHN: (*Smiles*) Afraid? Of what? Of wishes? Of voices? The only thing I'm afraid of is insanity. And that's a losing battle.

JOAN: I believe in your wishes!

COHN: That's reassuring.

JOAN: I do!

COHN: (*Shakes his head sadly.*) What do you know? Nothing. No background. I'll make a bet, no education. What do you have for credentials? Nothing!

FIRST AND SECOND VOICES: Us!

COHN: Less than nothing!

JOAN: I was once very much like you.

COHN: (*Enraged*) No one was ever like me! (*Calms himself.*) Don't be presumptuous.

JOAN: I was sad all the time.

COHN: I'm not sad.

JOAN: In despair.

COHN: This isn't despair.

JOAN: What do you call it?

COHN: Realism.

JOAN: Then why is it so much like despair?

COHN: I didn't say they're not connected. But they're not the same. With despair you feel there's no hope so you might as well die; with realism you feel there's no hope but you get a kick out of it.

JOAN: I wanted to die!

COHN: See? We're oceans apart.

JOAN: I lived in a sea of despair—

COHN: Not the same!

JOAN: —with my wicked stepmother and her two wicked daughters.

COHN: Wait. You're confused. That's Cinderella.

JOAN: Exactly.

COHN: You're Joan of Arc.

JOAN: Oh, I don't mean *now*.

COHN: You used to be Cinderella?

JOAN: Of course!

COHN: But now you're Joan of Arc? (JOAN *nods, patiently.*) Well, you're certainly working your way up in the world. Of course, instead of marrying Prince Charming, you get burned at the stake, but you do make sainthood, while all Cinderella gets is to live happily ever after. And in one case Shaw writes about you and in the other case Walt Disney. All in all, I'd say you made a wise choice.

JOAN: Choice? What choice? After the ball, I thought the Prince loved me and I dreamed—well, no matter what I dreamed—he came looking for me, door to door, with a glass slipper. Like a salesman! . . . Can you imagine my shame? That he, my true love, would only know me by trying a shoe on my foot! I walked barefoot on rocks, soaked my feet in brine, anything to fail such a test. But it was never to be made. One door away from ours the Prince was suddenly called to war and I was left with a broken heart and a size nine foot. So I became a nun. A very poor nun. Night after night, visions of Our Lord came to me bearing a glass slipper. So I fled the nunnery and traveled the land as a migrant fruit picker. I married and begat five Portuguese children. My husband was a sot and beat me. When my children grew of age, they beat me. So I threw myself off a bridge, into the river. I landed on my feet and, to my considerable surprise, saw that I was standing on the water. I walked on the water for miles trying to decipher the meaning of my fate. Half mad with the complexities of it all, I tried again to drown myself, this time by standing on my head and ducking it under the water. But the farther under I ducked, the more the water level receded, until finally, the river ran dry. I knew that it was a sign! I fell to my knees and prayed God for His forgiveness and that I should prove myself worthy of being His servant. And on the fortieth day my Voices came and told me who I was and what I must do. And now, praise God, I am Joan and I am here!

COHN: (*Stares at her. After a long silence.*) I really miss Abe.

JOAN: You don't believe my story.

COHN: You can walk on water, bring back Abe.

JOAN: Voices? May I?

FIRST VOICE: He shoots us and then he wants favors.

SECOND VOICE: He's got two more wishes. Why come to us?

JOAN: You *can* wish him back.

COHN: Oy.

JOAN: You can.

JOAN: Try.

COHN: I tried once. Look what happened!

JOAN: It came true.

COHN: It didn't come true. Certain things happened—I can't go into details—you don't know everything—

JOAN: You refuse to wish.

COHN: Let's drop the subject.

JOAN: You don't want it to come true.

COHN: I said—

JOAN: You don't want your friend back.

COHN: I want quiet! I want peace and quiet!

JOAN: But not your friend.

COHN: Him too! But first, quiet!

JOAN: Then wish!

COHN: You're a child!

JOAN: Wish!

COHN: Games!

JOAN: Wish!

COHN: Nag! Shrew! I wish! All right? I wish!

JOAN: What?

COHN: I wish Abe was back! (*Light and music effect.*) You satisfied? So where is he? You see him? Where is he? (JOAN *looks around.*) You're so smart. (*She looks in the bedroom.*) Miss Know-it-all.

(*He turns his back on her in contempt. She comes out of the bedroom, opens the lid of the trunk, and looks in.*)

JOAN: It came true!

(COHN *whirls, looks on in horror.*)

COHN: Close it! What are you doing in there? Mind your own business!

JOAN: Come! Look!

COHN: Who do you think you are!

JOAN: Dear God! He's dead! (*Crosses herself.* COHN *retreats.*) Your friend is dead.

COHN: He's not dead.

JOAN: He is dead.

COHN: *He's* dead. But Abe's not dead.

JOAN: But this is Abe.

COHN: He's not Abe. Abe is alive.

JOAN: You poor man. Your mind had cracked in grief. This is Abe.

COHN: Abe is shorter.

JOAN: This man is short.

COHN: Abe doesn't have a beard.

JOAN: This man is clean-shaven.

COHN: Abe is gray.

JOAN: In life this man was gray.

COHN: (*Crosses over the trunk, fed up.*) For once and for all—(*Looks in trunk.*) Abe! (*Falls into the trunk in a dead faint, headfirst. JOAN rushes to trunk, pulls COHN out by his shoulders, and tries to lift him off his knees.*) Go away. Leave me alone.

(*He rises shakily, staggers on the run behind his curtained doorway. After the briefest of pauses, JOAN follows.*)

JOAN: I know what's on your mind.

COHN: Go. The Emperor's waiting. *Give it back*!

(COHN's *shotgun comes flying out through the curtain, lands on floor beyond trunk.*)

JOAN: What if *I* brought him back to life?

COHN: Lady—

JOAN: Would you then go with me to see the Emperor?

COHN: Oy!

JOAN: If I brought Abe back to life?

COHN: If you brought Abe back to life, I'd believe you were Jesus Christ himself. Don't hit me!

JOAN: Don't blaspheme!

COHN: Don't nag!

JOAN: Would you believe?

COHN: Would I believe? I'd believe! I'd believe!

(ABE's *legs twitch.*)

JOAN: That I am Joan?

COHN: All right!

JOAN: And you will follow me?

COHN: All right!

JOAN: Praise the Lord!

(ABE's *legs twitch again. His head appears out of the trunk. He climbs out, looks at his typewriter, punches a key, and crosses to the refrigerator.*)

ABE: Cohn! What's to eat? (COHN *appears in the doorway. He cannot believe his eyes. He starts to collapse.* JOAN *catches him and helps him to a chair.* ABE *turns around and sees them. He shuts the refrigerator door and stares coldly at* JOAN.) Company?

COHN: You're dead.

ABE: (*Coldly*) I didn't know you were having a party.

COHN: You're walking—you're talking—(*He rises, starts to* ABE.)

ABE: I hope I'm not getting in the way. I know nobody invited me. I just live here.

COHN: (*Goes to* ABE *and embraces him.*) He lives, he breathes—(*Holds* ABE *away from him and stares at him happily.*) He smells!

ABE: You're drunk.

COHN: (*To* JOAN) Has there ever been such a friend, to rise from the dead in a rotten mood? I love this man! (*Hugs* ABE. ABE *breaks free.*)

ABE: I beg your pardon. That person?

COHN: That's Joan! Joan, here's Abe!

ABE: I beg your pardon. An old friend?

COHN: How old is old? Ten minutes? A half hour? It feels like half a lifetime. It was *your* lifetime, that I'll tell you!

ABE: Riddles. You invited her?

COHN: Not two minutes ago you were dead.

ABE: You wish.

COHN: I wished you back. They sent you back dead.

ABE: Intrigue is going on here. This is my house. I beg your pardon, miss. It's not personal. The house is in my name. But can I ever invite guests? Who was my last guest? Fifteen years ago. I'll show you the guest book. Look—here's the guest book. Blank, see? Hundreds of pages—wait, here's the guest—no, it reminds me—not even a real guest—a Jehovah's Witness. Came in out of the blue. We had coffee, a pleasant chat about religion. Cohn, here, throws a fit. Facts are facts, Cohn. It's nothing personal, miss. Cohn and I don't entertain. He agreed and I agreed. When we entertain we differ. It ends up in a fight. So we agreed to live and let live and not entertain. I didn't make up the rule. Now he breaks it. Is this a way to run a household? Anarchy? I beg your pardon, Cohn, I thought we'd agreed—anarchy is for outside.

COHN: (*To* JOAN) Is that a mouth? I love that mouth! (*Beaming at him.*) Abe, not five minutes ago you know what you were?

ABE: What?

COHN: You weren't! That's what you were. You were *not*! You were dead! You were dead! You were dead! (*Smile slowly fades.*) You weren't dead. (*Turns to* JOAN.) He wasn't dead.

JOAN: He was dead.

COHN: How could he be alive if he was dead?

JOAN: You saw him!

COHN: For half a second.

JOAN: He was cold.

COHN: Who felt him?

JOAN: I did!

COHN: I thought you were a saint. Now you're a doctor?

JOAN: You're reneging on your promise.

COHN: Don't be foolish; he only fainted.

ABE: I didn't faint.

COHN: You fainted.

ABE: Never!

COHN: In the trunk.

ABE: In what trunk?

COHN: That trunk!

ABE: I never fainted in a trunk in my life.

COHN: Not five minutes ago!

ABE: Five minutes ago I was sitting in my chair like always.

COHN: Then how come you didn't see her come in? (ABE *is stopped.*) Because you fainted!

ABE: Because you sneaked her in here before! When I wasn't looking!

COHN: *What* before?

ABE: Who knows, with a man as corrupt as you?! It could have been *years*! Who is she? Why is she wearing that armor?!

COHN: You're all excited. Calm down.

ABE: I don't like betrayal. I beg your pardon.

COHN: There's no betrayal.

ABE: Consorting with the outside.

COHN: No—

ABE: Spreading false rumors.

COHN: Abe, listen—calm now—what's the very last thing you remember?

ABE: Your betrayal.

COHN: (*Reasonably*) Abe, *I* fainted and *I* remember.

ABE: I never fainted in my life! I beg your pardon, but I have never vomited, I have never fainted, and I have never gotten drunk. Certain things I do not do. I have never done. So you and your chippie, don't try to pull a fast one.

COHN: (*Stares hard at him.*) You were dead. (*To* JOAN) It's the only explanation. He was dead.

ABE: I didn't faint so I must be dead. That's logic.

COHN: Not now, before.

ABE: How could I be dead before and alive now? That's consistency.

COHN: Wait a minute! Stop the presses! Is this my old friend Abe talking? The very Abe who believes in genies and three wishes and that I could be Mozart and him Jefferson?

ABE: There's no inconsistency.

ABE: It's perfectly plausible that I could die Abe and come back somebody else, but is it plausible that I should die Abe and come back Abe?

COHN: Is it plausible that you should die *Jefferson* and come back Abe?

ABE: —in the same house, with the same Cohn? A frog into a prince I could believe. Change! That's plausible! But sameness! Eternal sameness! No, I beg your pardon, I can't be convinced.

COHN: (*Exasperated*) I'm through wasting my breath.

(JOAN *crosses to* ABE. *He backs away. She takes his hand and stares into his eyes.*)

JOAN: I am Joan of Arc.

ABE: It's possible. You could be anybody. I won't fight over it.

COHN: He doesn't believe you.

ABE: It doesn't matter what I believe, it's what you believe.

COHN: She believes you were dead!

ABE: (*To* COHN) That's her privilege.

JOAN: You *were* dead.

ABE: (*To* JOAN) As far as you were concerned. You never saw me, I never saw you. In that sense I was dead.

JOAN: I brought you back to life.

ABE: In a physical way? Well, who knows? It's been a long time. But I do feel a certain arousal—

COHN: (*Groans and buries his head in his hands.*) It's not opinion! It's not an argument. It's a fact. A fact! A fact! She's Joan of Arc! She has Voices! She brought you back to life! (*To* JOAN) Strike him dead and bring him back again! (*To* ABE) And this time pay attention!

ABE: You ask me, is this Abe? I ask you, is this Cohn? You believe she's Joan of Arc?

COHN: No doubt about it.

ABE: And I was dead?

COHN: No question.

ABE: And she brought me back to life?

COHN: Believe me, it's a mixed blessing.

ABE: (*To* JOAN) Huh—must you be able to argue!

COHN: I believe in what's concrete—in what I see, until I see something different. That at least is consistent. (*To* JOAN) Are you ready?

JOAN: You'll come with me to see the Emperor?

ABE: Now comes an Emperor.

COHN: She and I have a mission!

JOAN: (*To* ABE) And you too.

ABE: Me? I'm dead.

JOAN: You won't come with us?

ABE: I beg your pardon. Two's company, three's a crowd.

COHN: Look, are we going to go or are we going to stay here and argue?

ABE: I don't want to keep you.

JOAN: (*Confused*) I'm not sure I should leave you.

COHN: Joan—any time you're ready.

ABE: Twenty years, Cohn, and now you go outside.

COHN: I'm not rigid!

ABE: You've changed!

COHN: Is that a crime?

ABE: (*Deeply disturbed*) It's—it's a miracle! (*To* JOAN) To change Cohn—to make him move an inch, not to mention he goes outside, is nothing less than a miracle. Who are you?

JOAN: I told you.

ABE: (*Stares at her for a long time.*) It's possible.

JOAN: Then you'll come?

ABE: Impossible.

JOAN: You have to come!

COHN: You can't stay here alone.

ABE: I'll manage.

COHN: Who'll cook for you?

ABE: I'll learn.

COHN: You won't learn.

ABE: Then I won't learn.

COHN: You'll starve.

ABE: It's possible. But unlikely.

COHN: (*To* JOAN) I don't have all day, you know.

JOAN: We must go. (*Opens front door.* COHN *goes out.*)

COHN: Hey, it's not so bad!

(JOAN *takes a long, sad look at* ABE.)

FIRST VOICE: Joan—

JOAN: (*Freezes*) Yes.

ABE: What's that?

SECOND VOICE: You can't leave.

ABE: Who said that?

JOAN: But my mission—

FIRST VOICE: Your mission is to take two of every kind.

ABE: (*Looks around.*) Who said that?

JOAN: I know.

FIRST VOICE: That includes schlepps.

ABE: (*Still looking.*) Who said that?

FIRST VOICE: You need one more.

(ABE *walks around looking for the* VOICES. JOAN *moves away from the door, back into the room.* COHN *appears in the doorway.*)

COHN: Well?

(*Nobody moves.*)

CURTAIN

Act Two

(*A month later. The house is no less cramped but much more orderly, like a military barracks. The screen has been moved from the kitchen to a corner near the bedrooms, where it partially hides a sloppily made Army cot, in which* Cohn *presently sleeps. Lying across the foot of the cot is a violin, several cookbooks, and the Bible.* Cohn *sits in his chair at the oak table. His head is bowed, his hands clasped, praying.* Abe *comes out of his bedroom, obviously ill at ease in* Cohn's *presence. He crosses to the typewriter, stares at the nearly blank sheet, and punches a key.* Cohn *looks up.* Abe, *refusing to meet his eyes, turns and disappears into his room.* Cohn *looks heavenward.*)

Cohn: God? Cohn again. How long? That's all I ask. The main thing is the waiting. How important in the scheme of things, one Abe more or less. The suffering I don't mind. In fact, so far it's minimal; to be frank, nonexistent; to tell you the truth, a pleasure. But if I had to, believe me, suffering! Sacrifice! You say the word, it's a commitment. For that girl— *and* you—it's you name it! (Joan *enters from* Cohn's *bedroom.* Cohn *jumps up in embarrassment.*) Speak of the devil!

Joan: How proud of you I am, Cohn.

Cohn: You're proud, I'm proud, we're both proud. You changed my life.

Joan: Not I. God.

Cohn: You first. You gave me proof. Tangibles.

Joan: Faith is the absence of proof.

Cohn: Still, it needs a beginning.

Joan: From within!

Cohn: You want something to eat? I have on a veal loaf. It'll be ready in no time. First start with this. (*Hands her a plate of antipasto.*)

Joan: I shouldn't, really. It's delicious.

Cohn: Eat. (*Watches her eat.*) You take small bites for a soldier.

Joan: I can't help but think of all those who go hungry.

Cohn: Soon that will end. (Joan *plows into her food.*) It *will* end soon, won't it?

Joan: (*Eating compulsively.*) What?

Cohn: Hunger. Famine.

Joan: When?

COHN: When?!

JOAN: (*In mid-bite*) Oh, heaven! You mean heaven! Of course! (*Resumes eating.*) I'm sorry, this is so delicious that I—(*Puts plate down.*)

COHN: No. Finish. Finish.

JOAN: (*Hesitates*) God's will be done. I am his servant.

(JOAN *resumes eating passionately. A warm exchange of stares.* ABE *enters, sees* COHN *and* JOAN *together, starts to back-pedal to his room.* JOAN *spots him and rises.*)

ABE: I beg your pardon. (*Crosses to stove as if crossing a mine field.*) I'll be out of your way in a minute. (*Pours himself a cup of coffee. With sudden resentment*) Far be it for me to make a pest of myself.

JOAN: (*Starts toward him.*) Abe—

ABE: (*Circles around her.*) Abe's my name. Invisibility's my game. (*Disappears behind his curtain.*)

JOAN: He won't let me talk to him.

COHN: (*Sullen*) That's his problem.

JOAN: *Our* problem!

(ABE, *his collar raised so as to make him invisible, slinks out again.*)

ABE: I'm not even here.

(ABE *crosses to the refrigerator and takes out a container of milk. On his way back* JOAN *plants herself in his path.* ABE *stops, turns, and starts back to the refrigerator. He opens it and sticks his head in as far as it will go, pretending to look for something.* JOAN *comes up behind him and stands there.* ABE *retreats even farther into the refrigerator, until more of him is in than out. Through it all* COHN *sits and glowers, jealous of the attention* ABE *is getting.*)

JOAN: May I say something, Abe? (*A long wait.*) I'd like to speak to you. (JOAN *does not move.* ABE *does not move. Finally he sneezes. Instinctively,* JOAN *puts a hand on his shoulder.*) Abe—

(ABE *reacts as if he's been shot. His head jerks up against the roof of the fridge with a resounding clunk. Stunned, his entire body, or what we see of it, sags. If we can see his head, it now lies on the first shelf.* JOAN *drags him out, closes the door, and half carries him to his chair.*)

ABE: I never felt better.

JOAN: Abe, why won't you speak to me? (ABE *doesn't answer.*) I've been here for weeks and we haven't exchanged a dozen words.

ABE: A dozen eggs?

JOAN: A dozen words.

ABE: What do you want to exchange a dozen words for ? Are they dirty? How do I know you even bought them here?

JOAN: You confuse me, Abe.

ABE: Confusme. That's a Chinese philosopher.

JOAN: That's Confucius.

ABE: Confucius is a color.

JOAN: That's fuchsia.

ABE: Fuchsia is what you say when there's a bad smell.

JOAN: That's phew.

ABE: Phew is a body of water in Norway.

JOAN: That's fjord.

ABE: Fjord is a car.

JOAN: That's Ford.

ABE: Ford is the number after three.

JOAN: That's four.

ABE: What's four?

JOAN: A number!

ABE: Absolutely right, I was so cold I was number. (*Rises.*) It's a pleasure finally talking to you.

(*He staggers on the run into his room.* JOAN *looks after him, then turns to* COHN *who all this while has been glaring sullenly at the scene. He turns away from her.* JOAN *crosses to him.*)

JOAN: Tell me what to do, Cohn.

COHN: (*Brusque*) Forget it.

JOAN: (*Squeezes his shoulder.*) God depends on you, Cohn.

COHN: God? (*He rises, very haughtily.*) Sometimes, very frankly, it's hard to take some of this stuff seriously.

(COHN *walks past her into the kitchen and busies himself at the stove.* JOAN *crosses to darkened window, looks out.*)

JOAN: (*Softly*) Voices? I see signs. I think it's going well. (*Looks around with some anxiety.*) Voices!?

FIRST VOICE: What now?

SECOND VOICE: Yes, Joan.

JOAN: I'm really very encouraged.

FIRST VOICE: She's encouraged.

SECOND VOICE: It doesn't take much.

JOAN: I have faith! They are almost ready.

SECOND VOICE: Joan—

FIRST VOICE: What are we going to do with her?

JOAN: I don't understand. Don't you think things are going well? Cohn is with me, that's one . . .

SECOND VOICE: I'll say he's one.

JOAN: And now that Abe is talking to me—

SECOND VOICE: Joan, come to your senses.

JOAN: Didn't you see it? *He is talking to me!*

SECOND VOICE: Talk to her.

FIRST VOICE: You talk to her.

SECOND VOICE: Who can talk to her? You talk to her.

FIRST VOICE: I don't want to talk to her. Frankly, I'm heartsick.

JOAN: What in the world is wrong with you today, Voices?

SECOND VOICE: Will you listen to the mouth on her?

FIRST VOICE: (*Warning*) Take it back, Joan!

JOAN: (*Fearful*) I'm unworthy! I take it back! (*Pause. Confused.*) What?

FIRST VOICE: She doesn't know.

SECOND VOICE: Hopeless.

JOAN: What? Am I displeasing you? I thought everything was wonderful. (*Grabs for her plate, eats compulsively.*)

SECOND VOICE: Stuffs herself like a pig.

FIRST VOICE: Any second now—crash!—armor all over the place.

JOAN: Why are you so angry with me? (*Hesitates in her eating. Reluctantly puts down plate.*) I am the servant of the Lord. I do his bidding.

FIRST VOICE: Will you look at her complexion? Breaking out.

SECOND VOICE: And why not? She hasn't been out of the house in a month.

FIRST VOICE: I think that you are losing your faith, Joan.

JOAN: Never!

SECOND VOICE: Not five minutes ago you forgot about heaven.

JOAN: Not for a second!

FIRST VOICE: Admit it! When you were eating.

JOAN: It slipped my mind for one second. Is that a mortal sin?

SECOND VOICE: Are you questioning us?

JOAN: I'm asking—

SECOND VOICE: Questioning!

JOAN: Not seriously—

SECOND VOICE: Losing faith.

JOAN: I have faith!

SECOND VOICE: Faith to do what?

JOAN: To believe!

SECOND VOICE: Believe in what?

JOAN: Believe in my Voices!

FIRST VOICE: We don't want you to say it if you don't mean it.

JOAN: With all my heart and soul! Before my Voices what was I? But with my Voices who am I? Do you think I can overlook such change? But it's so hard. Cohn, no matter what I say, he will agree. But to what end? No end. And Abe hates me. I know he hates me. Why should he hate me?

FIRST VOICE: Nobody said it would be easy.

SECOND VOICE: You must strengthen your faith. Strong faith sweeps all before it.

FIRST VOICE: Faith can move mountains, Joan.

JOAN: Voices! Let me go to a mountain!

SECOND VOICE: Joan, your trial is here.

JOAN: I beg of you, let me first move a mountain.

FIRST VOICE: Can you believe this?

JOAN: I promise, Voices, I shall make good on a mountain; then I shall return here.

FIRST VOICE: Hopeless!

SECOND VOICE: Admit it, we picked a real lemon this time.

(JOAN *whirls as a rock crashes through the window and lands at her feet.* COHN *and* ABE *come running. All stare down at the rock.* JOAN *stoops to pick it up.*)

COHN: Don't touch!

ABE: It's an animal!

COHN: It's a bomb!

ABE: It's not a bomb.

COHN: It's not an animal.

(JOAN *reaches for it.*)

ABE and COHN: Don't pick it up!

(JOAN *picks it up.*)

JOAN: It's a rock.

COHN: Get it away! Away! I hear ticking!

ABE: There's writing on it.

COHN: (*Scornfully to* ABE) Who writes on rocks?

ABE: (*Scornfully to* COHN) Who writes on bombs?

COHN: (*A wave of dismissal.*) Later!

JOAN: It's a message!

COHN: Don't read it!

ABE: Who writes on rocks? It says—

JOAN: (*Reading*) "You will meet new challenges, which can be turned into opportunities. Beware of January, February, and March."

COHN: (*Crosses to window. Shouts.*) Get away from here! This is no time for jokes!

(*A knock at the door. All jump.* JOAN *goes to the door. An aged, stooped* MESSENGER *in a cap.*)

MESSENGER: (WISEMAN) I have a rock for Joan of Arc.

JOAN: I'll take it.

MESSENGER: You Joan of Arc? (JOAN *nods.*) Sign here, please. (JOAN *signs his pad. He hands her the rock, then stares at her.*) You really Joan of Arc?

JOAN: I am.

MESSENGER: (*Begins to chuckle and shake his head.*) Joan of Arc.

(JOAN *gently closes the door on the chuckling* MESSENGER. *She reads the rock.*)

JOAN: "Beware of April, May, and June." (*With a loud squeal, the refrigerator door swings open.* JOAN, COHN, *and* ABE *look up. A rock falls out of the refrigerator.* JOAN *drops the second rock and crosses to the new rock. She kneels and reads it.*) "Also July, August, September, October, November, December."

ABE: That's it as far as I'm concerned.

(*He goes on the run into his bedroom.* COHN *crosses the door.*)

COHN: (*Whispers*) While it's still dark, let's make a break.

JOAN: Not without Abe.

COHN: (*Fed up*) Abe?! Who knows what's out there?

JOAN: And I believed you had faith.

COHN: (*Conspiratorial*) You want Abe? (*Takes drugs off stock shelf.*) A pinch of this in Abe's soup. In no time, out like a baby. I guarantee after twenty years inside, we get him outside. He won't leave our side.

JOAN: (*Disbelieving*) You want me to trick Abe?

COHN: Tactics. You never heard of tactics? All right, you don't like pharmacology, here's plan two: While he was inside hiding, he missed a second messenger. A Hollywood offer. Big money. A documentary. A movie pilgrimage to the Emperor. Trust me, if Abe falls for it, we can handle the others.

JOAN: (*Puzzled*) You want me to fool Abe?

COHN: Who wouldn't want to be in pictures? They'll fall for it, two of every kind. I guarantee: a cast of thousands.

JOAN: (*Shocked*) You want me to lie?

COHN: First and last we remember the mission. Later is time enough for the truth.

JOAN: From the beginning!

COHN: The beginning's too soon for unorganized truth. It needs preparation. You don't like movies? Here's plan three: We'll say we're the police, charges have been made but it's a free country. They'll have their day in court, they should come with us to appeal before the Emperor.

JOAN: Coh, what's come over you?

COHN: You give them a little fear, they get a move on. No dilly-dally. No explanations. The main thing is the mission.

JOAN: You actually want me to lie!

COHN: It's no bed of roses out there. In me, you're fortunate to find a man of imagination, but out there, you tell them you're Joan of Arc, I guarantee it's no laugh riot.

JOAN: They will believe me.

COHN: What? Two bricklayers? Two carpenters? Two truck drivers? Two taxi drivers? Two advertising-agency executives? Joan. Joan, what am I going to do with you? It's a whirlpool you're walking into. Not even you can walk on whirlpools. It takes fiddling. A story here. A little piece of business there. You maneuver. You manipulate. Push comes to shove, a wheel, a deal, we got ourselves an army. Trust me.

JOAN: I trust God.

COHN: No argument. No argument. He gives policy, I carry it out. Where's the contradiction?

JOAN: I trust my Voices.

COHN: Voices always have to be right. Beliee me, Joan I've worked this out.

JOAN: Believe you? I can scarcely believe my senses!

COHN: Voices talk, they don't listen. They're Voices. What do they know? Two of every kind. Abe and me? Never! Not in a million years! Even superficially—Glutton. Gourmet. If they could see they'd know.

JOAN: They do know.

COHN: I can make a mistake, you can make a mistake. Voices can't make mistakes? That's not in the realm of possibility?

JOAN: How can you have faith and still question?

COHN: I don't question.

JOAN: Cohn, has questioning ever given you satisfaction?

COHN: The opposite. I don't question.

JOAN: Has it ever made you happy?

COHN: Not once. I don't question.

JOAN: Do you believe I am Joan?

COHN: *Yes.*

JOAN: Do you believe in my mission?

COHN: Yes!

JOAN: Do you believe the sky is missing?

COHN: Yes! Yes! Yes!

JOAN: Praise the Lord!

COHN: Praise the Lord!

JOAN: (*Takes his hand.*) You are my right hand, Cohn.

COHN: (*Falls to his knees, clasps her hands.*) You want to know who's two of the same kind, not Abe and me, *you* and me! More than that is a complication. Do we need it? In my opinion: no. Travel fast, travel light. We go it alone! Trust me!

(He strides to the door and throws it open. A SOLDIER *in combat dress, wearing a gas mask and carrying an automatic rifle, stands in the doorway.* COHN, *still staring at* JOAN, *does not see him. He holds his hand out, beckoning her to the great outdoors. His hand brushes against the* SOLDIER's *gas mask. He turns, very slowly, to see what he's touching, sees, and slams shut the dor. A siren sounds. The room is flooded with searchlights.)*

POLICE VOICE: (WISEMAN) (*Miked*) Send out the girl! We only want the girl!

ABE: (*Crawling out of his room on his belly.*) I knew it!

POLICE VOICE: We don't want you. We only want the girl.

JOAN: I'll go!

COHN: (*Stops her.*) No!

ABE: (*Shouts*) You can have her! You can have her!

COHN: (*To* ABE) *You* go!

ABE: Ah hah! Didn't I know it?!

POLICE VOICE: We don't want Abe, we want the girl.

JOAN: Let me speak to them!

COHN: They're your enemies.

JOAN: I have no enemies.

COHN: (*Restraining* JOAN) No! *I'll* go!

POLICE VOICE: We don't want Cohn, we want the girl.

COHN: (*Shouts*) It's all or nothing! You want her, you got to kill us all!

ABE: All? What all?!

POLICE VOICE: We don't want to kill you all, we only want to kill the girl.

COHN: (*To* JOAN) See?

JOAN: They won't harm me. They are my army!

COHN: Are you crazy? You're Joan of Arc! They want to burn you at the stake!

POLICE VOICE: There'll be a hot time in the old town tonight!

JOAN: Voices!

POLICE VOICE: Yes?

JOAN: I want *my* Voices!

POLICE VOICE: The game's up, sister. Throw out your armor and come out with your hands up!

JOAN: He's drowning out my Voices!

POLICE VOICE: (*Croons*) I dream of Joanie
With the light blond hair,
Floating like a vapor
On the soft summer air.

(*As* POLICE VOICE *sings,* ABE *leaps into the trunk and pulls the lid down over him.* COHN *dashes for the bedroom and comes out with his shotgun.* JOAN, *at the door, tries to pull it open. It is locked. She fiddles with the bolt. By this time,* COHN *is at the window and fires a blast.*) Very nice! (*A white flag is poked through the shattered window.*) Don't shoot. I'm coming in to parley.

(*The door opens.* JOAN *leaps back. In walks* WISEMAN, *in robes as before, but with a silver star pinned to his chest. He crosses to the table, sits, puts on a green eyeshade, and begins shuffling a deck of cards.* COHN *backs off in horror.*)

WISEMAN: To make it interesting we play for the girl. (*Looks at them.*) Who plays?

(*Stares at* COHN, *who backs into the trunk.* ABE *lifts the lid and peers out at* WISEMAN. *He climbs out of the trunk as* COHN *climbs in and pulls shut the lid.* ABE *crosses to* WISEMAN *and sits.*)

ABE: We play for peace and quiet.

WISEMAN: I win, I get the girl; you win, you get peace and quiet. (*He deals the cards. They study their hands. As each discards, he calls out his card.*) Fifty-five.

ABE: Seventy-one.

WISEMAN: King.

ABE: Einstein.

WISEMAN: Queen.

ABE: Garbo.

WISEMAN: Jack.

ABE: Daniel's.

WISEMAN: One.

ABE: Meatball.

WISEMAN: Ashtray.

ABE: Match.

WISEMAN: Deuce.

ABE: Game.

WISEMAN: Loophole.

ABE: Manhole.

WISEMAN: Fix.

ABE: Parking ticket.

WISEMAN: Horse.

ABE: Fire engine.

WISEMAN: Love.

ABE: Stock market.

WISEMAN: Cadillac.

ABE: Morphine.

WISEMAN: Mortuary.

ABE: February.

WISEMAN: Wake.

ABE: Corn flakes.

WISEMAN: Banco!

ABE: Bunko!

WISEMAN: (*Fans out his cards.*) An inside straight!

ABE: (*Fans out his cards.*) An outside patio with a rose garden!

(WISEMAN *growls, kicks over his chair, and storms out.*)

JOAN: (*Crosses to* ABE.) You are a wonderful card player.

(ABE *doesn't look at her. He shuffles the cards.* JOAN *sits next to him.* ABE *continues to shuffle.*)

ABE: I'll give you the answer, you give me the question. Chicken teriyaki.

JOAN: I don't understand.

ABE: I'll give you the answer. You give me the question. It's a game.

JOAN: Oh.

ABE: Chicken teriyaki. (JOAN *looks at him nonplussed.*) You don't know? The question is: Who is the oldest living kamikaze pilot? Here's another: Nine-W. (JOAN *doesn't respond.*) Now you give me the question.

JOAN: I wasn't listening.

ABE: The answer is nine-W. What's the question?

JOAN: I don't know.

ABE: The question is: Do you spell your name with a "V," Herr Wagner? You ready for another?

(JOAN *reaches out to him.*)

JOAN: Abe—

(ABE *pulls away. A pause.*)

ABE: All right, here's another. The answer is: From birth, I was taught to believe: Where there's a will there's a way. But nobody wrote me into his will, so I had to make my own way. Still, I had hope. Someday I would find the right situation. In the meantime, I piled up money. For when I found the right situation. Also I married. A mistake, but bearable. It didn't take too much of either of our time. Whenever we exchanged understanding stares, I found out later it was a misunderstanding. So I wondered: Is this all? I couldn't accept yes for an answer, so I left my wife and I started looking. She sent Cohn to bring me back. Instead, he talked me into looking where he wanted to look instead of where I wanted. Finally, we split up. I went on looking. High and low, inside and out, until I got so depressed I couldn't hold my head up. So not being able to hold my head up, I saw straight in front of me for the first time. And looking right in my face was the answer. In life you don't look too high and you don't look too low, you look straight down the middle. The answer lies in the middle. In the middle there's always room for hope and not too much room for disappointment. So the lesson of life is to settle. So I came to the woods. To settle. I found this house, I knocked on the door and Cohn opened it. He had settled the year before me. It's not terrific. But also it's not painful. I don't hurt anybody. It's an across-the-board settlement. I don't love it, I don't hate it. That's the answer, what's the question?

JOAN: The question is: If you want to believe in something, can't you come up with anything better than that?

(*They continue to stare at each other.*)

ABE: I beg your pardon. (*Rises, looks at typewriter, punches a key, looks at paper, pulls it out, and crumples it.*) I'll put it this way. I'll start. How far I get is another question.

JOAN: (*Slowly realizing*) You'll go? You'll come?

ABE: (*Smiles*) I'll accompany.

(*Backs off into his doorway, where he lingers for a moment, then disappears.*)

JOAN: You'll accompany! You'll accompany! Cohn! (*Looks for him.*) Abe will accompany! (COHN *lifts the lid of the trunk an inch or two and peers out.*) Abe will accompany! He'll accompany!

ABE: (*Pokes his head out from behind his curtain.*) Miss? Joan? Could you possibly—

(JOAN *charges through* ABE's *curtain.* COHN *stands up in the trunk and looks after her.*)

COHN: He'll change his mind! I know him!

JOAN: (*Pokes her head out from behind curtain.*) He's beginning to pack! (*Ducks back in.*)

COHN: It's a lie! He's lying!

JOAN: (*Pokes her head out.*) He's packing! He's actually packing! (*Ducks back in.*)

COHN: I've been through this before!

JOAN: (*Pokes her head out.*) Do you know where he put his muffler? He won't go outside without his muffler! (*Back in.*)

COHN: He's backing down!

JOAN: (*Head out.*) He found his muffler! (*Back in.*)

COHN: It's the wrong muffler!

JOAN: (*Head out.*) He's packed! (*Back in.*)

COHN: He's not to be trusted!

JOAN: (*Head out.*) He's putting on his galoshes! (*Back in.*)

COHN: We can't wait! He'll slow us down!

JOAN: (*Head out.*) He's coming!

COHN: We'll never get there!

JOAN: (*Throws open curtain and introduces* ABE.) He's *here!*

(ABE *emerges past* JOAN, *bandaged in winter clothes, lugging a huge suitcase.*)

ABE: What a sensational day for a trip!

JOAN: Onward to the Emperor!

FIRST VOICE: Onward to thc Emperor!

SECOND VOICE: Onward to the Emperor!

(ABE *and* JOAN *move to the door.* JOAN *throws open the door.* COHN *disappears into the trunk and slams shut the lid.* ABE *and* JOAN *stand waiting.*)

COHN: (*Raises the lid one-half inch.*) You know what you can do with those buttinsky, wiseacre Voices of yours? I *wish* you never heard of them! You know what I *wish*—I *wish* you never heard of Joan of Arc! (*Slams shut the lid. Light and music effect.*)

JOAN: (*Puts on bandanna cap, grabs broom, starts sweeping. Turns to* ABE.) Abe, what are you all bundled up for? (*Starts unwrapping him.*) You're not going out in this weather. After dark? In the night air? Without your dinner? Cohn, can you imagine? Honestly! You two!

(*She continues to unbundle the stunned* ABE. COHN *stands up in the trunk and looks on.*)

CURTAIN

Act Three

(*Five months later. The house is as cramped as before and far more dis-organized. Everything looks as if it's been moved and for no particular purpose. Altogether the impression is of impending chaos.* JOAN's *tarnished armor hangs in sections on several hooks of a clothes tree. It is dinnertime. Two pots on the stove give off lots of steam. The dining-room table is littered with dirty dishes.* ABE's *typewriter and stacks of paper are nowhere in sight.* ABE *comes out from behind his curtained doorway wearing a bathrobe, carrying a half-empty glass of milk. He brushes past* JOAN's *armor.*)

ABE: In the way. As usual.

(*He stops, scowls at the armor, then tentatively touches it. He takes the headpiece off its hook, is about to try it on when* JOAN *rises out of the steam from behind the kitchen counter. She wears an old-fashioned, long flowered dress and a frilly apron. Her complexion is pale and waxen.*)

JOAN: (*Excited*) Almost ready!

(*She lifts the cover off a pot, burns her hand on the handle, and lets go with a loud scream. The cover flies across the room through* COHN's *curtained doorway.* COHN *rushes out, holding pot cover. He is a nervous, contrite, less abrasive* COHN.)

COHN: Joan—

JOAN: (*Whirls on him.*) Stay put!

COHN: (*Freezes*) But—

JOAN: If it didn't belong there I wouldn't have thrown it there! (*Turns back to stove.*) One more minute!

COHN: (*Not daring to move.*) It smells delicious!

ABE: (*Crosses to table and sits.*) It was one more minute fifteen minutes ago.

JOAN: Cooking one thing at a time is no problem, it's cooking combinations.

ABE: If excuses were only edible.

COHN: (*To* ABE, *placating*) She's trying.

ABE: If reasons were raisins I wouldn't go hungry.

JOAN: (*Whirls on* ABE.) What did you say?

ABE: Me? Not a word.

JOAN: (*Turns back to stove.*) The trick is to get the roast and the beans and the cauliflower and the potatoes all done at the same— I think it's ready.

(*Opens the oven door. Thick black smoke spurts out, darking* JOAN's *face and sending her into a fit of coughing. She grabs a dish towel and covers her face. Staggering around, she backs into the stove and knocks the pots off.*)

COHN: (*Alarmed*) Careful!

(JOAN *manages to escape the downpour of boiling water and vegetables. In her jumping about she sends the spice shelf flying. In her attempt to regain her balance, she flails out and grabs hold of the bottom shelf of the dish cabinet. The shelf gives way and all the dishes descend on her.* JOAN *disappears from view under a pile of debris.* COHN *leans forward tensely,* ABE *leans back, contemptuous.*)

ABE: Typical.

(COHN *starts toward the kitchen.*)

JOAN: (*Out of sight.*) Everyone stay out of here. (COHN *keeps coming. He gets to the kitchen.* JOAN *screams.*) Stay out! I had a little accident. No one's hurt. (*Snarls to* COHN.) Everything's under control.

COHN: (*Advances a step.*) Let me—

JOAN: (*Screams.*) I don't need help! (*Rises from the floor, her hair in disarray, her blouse ripped, but with a blackened roast pig on a platter, an apple in its mouth. She marches proudly to the dining table and slams down the platter.*) No vegetables tonight. (*Glares at* COHN.) All right?

COHN: (*Feigned cheerfulness*) Fine.

JOAN: (*Glares at* ABE) All right?

ABE: I had vegetables yesterday.

(COHN *starts carving the pig.* JOAN *goes back to the kitchen and begins sweeping up the wreckage. It makes a terrific clatter.*)

COHN: Don't you want to eat, Joan?

JOAN: (*Snaps*) Later.

COHN: Don't you at least want to sit with us?

JOAN: (*Snaps*) Later.

(COHN *sighs and starts eating.*)

ABE: A terrific companion. If she wasn't so handy around the kitchen, I'd suggest we get rid of her.

COHN: (*Low*) She hasn't been well.

ABE: (*Picks up a charred slice of pig.*) Look at that. By what stretch of the imagination could this possibly be called food?

COHN: It's not so bad.

ABE: This is a pig not even a pig would eat.

COHN: A little charity!

ABE: You want charity? Ask the Emperor!

JOAN: (*Recoils suddenly, as if in reaction to* ABE's *harsh reminder.*) Ouch!

COHN: (*Jumps up.*) What happened?

JOAN: Nothing.

COHN: (*In fear*) You cut yourself!

JOAN: It's all right.

ABE: (*To* COHN) Stop making a fool of yourself. Sit down.

COHN: Let me look!

JOAN: Stay put. It's only a cut finger.

COHN: Oh my God!

JOAN: (*Comes out of the kitchen, one finger aloft.*) Oh, stop it, Cohn. Nobody dies of a cut finger.

(*She faints dead away.* COHN *runs to her, scoops her up in his arms, and carries her to the couch. He empties the couch of its litter and lays* JOAN *down.*)

COHN: Abe, quick! Bandages! Gauze! Iodine! Brandy! (ABE *leans back in his chair, streches his arms, and yawns.*) Heartless!

ABE: She's faking.

COHN: Heartless! Heartless!

ABE: I know a faker when I see it. You talk heaven to her, she burns a pig; talk mission, she cuts a finger; talk going outside, she falls asleep. Free room and board. In exchange for what? Minnie the Moocher. In my life among bad deals I include this with the worst.

COHN: She's dying!

ABE: She fainted. I died. And believe you me, I didn't get all this attention. (COHN *rushes off for medical equipment.* ABE *strolls over to* JOAN) All right. Have it your way for now. I'm patient. Nobody outwaits Abe. I only get fooled once. A stranger cries "Heaven!" You take a look. It's only polite, what could it hurt? If it turns out heaven, so much the better. If not, what's to lose? One more disappointment. In my life that's hardly an event. I worked on Wall Street thirty years, but for hope I was ready to take a plunge. So what do I get for my investment? People jump out the window for less.

(COHN *rushes back in.* ABE *walks back to the table.*)

COHN: (*On his knees beside* JOAN.) The bleeding stopped. Look how white she is, Abe.

ABE: (*Indicates door.*) She's free to get all the air she wants. With my blessing.

COHN: You're upset, that's why you're talking that way.

ABE: Me? Do I look upset? (*He doesn't.*)

COHN: (*Eager to make up.*) I apologize for calling you heartless. It was a moment of excitement.

ABE: Who listened?

COHN: (*Confidential*) Listen, while she's out, you want me to make you a little something?

ABE: I'm not hungry.

COHN: An omelet? You love my omelets.

ABE: I'm full. On pig.

COHN: You name it, I'll cook it.

ABE: Don't trouble yourself.

COHN: Trouble? It would be a pleasure.

ABE: Thank you, but food no longer interests me.

COHN: She's breathing more regular. (JOAN wakes.) Stay still.

JOAN: (*Sullen*) That's easy enough for you to say.

COHN: What's so important you can't rest a minute?

JOAN: The kitchen.

COHN: I can't clean it up?

JOAN: I don't want you in my kitchen.

COHN: I won't go near it.

JOAN: Stop humoring me.

COHN: I'm only trying to be friends.

JOAN: I have no friends.

COHN: I'm not a friend?

JOAN: You say it but you don't mean it.

COHN: I mean it with my heart.

ABE: Abe's not my friend.

COHN: Abe is crazy about you.

JOAN: He hates me. And you're his friend, so you must hate me.

COHN: Abe loves you, I love you. You're a little sick so you feel bad.

JOAN: He makes me feel useless. He's the one who's useless. If I ever get my health back, I'm going to tell him that. He's right. I am useless. I mess up everything. I don't blame him for not liking me. Sometimes I hate you.

COHN: (*Hurt*) Don't worry about it.

JOAN: I bore you.

COHN: You don't!

JOAN: I bore me, so I must bore you.

COHN: The other way around.

ABE: You mean I bore Abe too?

COHN: I mean I bore you.

JOAN: You do bore me.

COHN: (*Fearful*) You want to leave!

JOAN: You want me to leave.

COHN: You're bored and you want to leave.

JOAN: I don't want to leave.

COHN: Why shouldn't you?

JOAN: I'll go if you want me to.

COHN: Never!

JOAN: Where would I go?

COHN: (*Upset*) That's all that's keeping you. If you knew where to go, you'd be out of here like a shot.

JOAN: (*Angry*) I don't want to leave.

COHN: You're saying it to make me feel good.

JOAN: What could possibly be out there that I'd want?

COHN: (*Guilty*) Nothing is out there! But if there was—

JOAN: But there isn't!

COHN: But you'd go!

JOAN: I don't care what there is—I wouldn't go.

COHN: I just want you to be happy.

JOAN: (*Helpless; pause.*) Well, I'm mostly happy.

COHN: (*Anxious*) But you're sick.

JOAN: I'm much better.

COHN: You're weak. You take on too much. You should do less.

JOAN: If I did less I'd die.

COHN: (*Insistent*) But you're happy. (JOAN *nods.*) Well, that's all I care about. If I could believe that, then I'd sleep easy.

JOAN: (*Frightened*) Aren't you sleeping well?

COHN: I worry.

JOAN: I will never go.

COHN: So I won't worry.

(COHN *lays his head in her lap and starts humming a Mozart aria.* JOAN *moves* COHN's *head off her lap and stands. She takes two steps and falls into a dead faint.* COHN, *on the couch, continues humming and does not notice.* ABE *comes out of the kitchen, where he's been sneaking a cold meal out of the refrigerator. He stops and looks down at* JOAN.)

ABE: (*To* JOAN) You should be an actress on the stage. (*Stares down at her while gnawing away at a chicken leg. Suddenly he bends down to take a closer look. He feels her pulse.*) She's dying.

COHN: She's happy. (*Resumes humming.*)

ABE: (*Listens to her heart.*) She's dead. (*Rises. To* COHN) You really did it this time.

(COHN *jumps up and runs to the fallen* JOAN. ABE *walks off.*)

COHN: Water! Smelling salts! Pepper! Garlic! Brandy! (*Shakes* JOAN's *lifeless body.*) I wanted her to take it easy. But no, she has to have her own way! (*Shakes her more violently.*) She won't listen! (*Strokes her face.*) Pale like a ghost. (*Flutters a hand back and forth across her face.*) She's not well enough to go out. Wake up, Joan! (*Slaps her lightly.*) Abe, where's the water? (*Looks up at* ABE, *who has not moved.*) What is this? Sadism?! *Cooperate!*

ABE: It's over. You did it.

COHN: (*Shakes* JOAN, *slaps her face repeatedly, with increasing alarm.*) Wake up! (*Shakes her.*) I get no cooperation! (*Lifts her angrily and throws her on the couch.*)

ABE: Very nice.

COHN: (*Desperate*) Not one ounce of cooperation from anyone around here. It's her who's sick, not me, but does she help? Fat chance! No help! Never helps! Just faints. Faints! Faints! Faints! You could clock it on the hour. As if she has anything really wrong with her; don't tell me! Hysterical reaction. Getting even. Childish! Childish! What did I do? What was my crime! Why all this torture? If I'm a criminal, get it over, put me on trial!

(*Door flies open.* WISEMAN *enters in his robes, wearing a judge's wig and carrying law books.*)

BAILIFF's VOICE: Oyez! Oyez! The Second Hessian of the Fourth Circuit Court of the Fifth at Aqueduct is now inoperative. Judge Helmut Wiseman presiding.

WISEMAN: (*Uprights the trunk and bangs a gavel on it.*) This court is now in session. Who represents the accursed—uh—accused?

ABE: I do, your honor.

WISEMAN: Who represents the prosecution?

ABE: I do, your honor.

COHN: So that's what you're up to! I knew it all the time! I wasn't born yesterday!

ABE: Your honor, the defendant alleges he wasn't boring yesterday

WISEMAN: Is he aware he's under oath?

COHN: I'm not under oath. I'm not under anything!

ABE: If your honor pleases, I have an expert witness who will testify that the defendant was boring yesterday.

WISEMAN: Let me admonish the defendant of the danger of committing perjury.

ABE: Your honor, I have additional expert testimony which will prove that the defendant has been boring for twenty years; that, in fact, the defendant has a history of being boring to a point of tears, death, and distraction.

WISEMAN: (*Picks up imaginary phone.*) Hello. Tears, Death, and Distraction. I'm sorry. Mr. Tears is dead, Mr. Death is distracted, and Mr. Distraction's in traction. I'll put you on to our Mr. Cohn. *Cohn!*

ABE: Take the stand!

WISEMAN: Do you swear to tell the truth, the whole truth, the half-truth, for better or worse, for whom the bell tolls, for me and my gal, in sickness, in health, in darkness, in light, in Newark, in Irvington, indecision, innuendo, so help you God?

COHN: Not on your life!

WISEMAN: Oh yeah?! Well, a knot on *your* life! (*Swings at* COHN's *head with the gavel.* COHN *ducks.* WISEMAN *falls off balance, over the trunk.*) Order! Did you hear me call for order?!

ABE: Fried eggs over light, with bacon.

WISEMAN: Toast?

ABE: (*Raises a glass.*) To Joan of Arc.

WISEMAN: (*Stands, raises his gavel.*) To Joan of Arc.

COHN: Ah ha! I gave you enough rope, you hung yourselves. I know your game! I admit nothing.

ABE: You admit you are Cohn?

COHN: I admit I tried. Can more be asked of any man?

ABE: And you were acquainted with this Joan of Arc?

COHN: She wasn't Joan of Arc!

ABE: I object, your honor. Giving adverse testimony about a deceased person who is in no position to defend herself.

COHN: She fainted. She's not dead. Who knows if she even fainted? (*Glares at them.*) Three of the same kind! I'm the one person here who can be trusted. *You* object? *I* object!

WISEMAN: Objection sustained.

ABE: I object!

WISEMAN: Objection sustained.

ABE: Where does that leave us?

WISEMAN: I object! Objection overruled! Are there any further questions to be asked of this witness?

ABE: Cohn, do you recognize this object? (*Holds up* JOAN's *suit of armor.*)

COHN: It's a dress.

ABE: A dress. And do you recognize this object? (*Holds up* JOAN's *sword.*)

COHN: It's a broom.

ABE: A dress and a broom. Mr. Cohn—(*Raises five fingers.*) Please identify what I am now holding up.

COHN: You want to know what you're holding up?

ABE: What am I holding up?

COHN: You're holding up these proceedings. (*Turns to* WISEMAN.) Ha! (WISEMAN *bangs his gavel.*) You're all against me.

ABE: The judge is against you?

COHN: He's no judge. I know him from the old country.

ABE: I'm against you?

COHN: Tell me something I don't know.

ABE: The deceased was against you?

COHN: The worst of the lot. Look at her. I trusted her. The rest of you I knew better. You especially.

ABE: Me especially.

COHN: You especially.

ABE: Who pays for this house?

COHN: Every argument he brings it up. Move, I won't stop you.

ABE: It's my house!

COHN: I found it!

ABE: You rented. I bought!

COHN: So money makes everything all right? Is that the story? Plutocrat. Didn't I always know it? Plutocrat!

ABE: Nobody made you live with me.

COHN: I felt sorry for you. That's my weakness. Softness of heart. I took you in. I felt sorry for her, I took her in. So tell me, where's the gratitude? Him twenty years, her six months, I'm still waiting. I won't hold my breath. I'm guilty all right, guilty of being an innocent set loose in a world full of thieves. Cutthroats. Ingrates. That's my crime. Never again.

WISEMAN: The defendant has pleaded guilty of being innocent. I sentence him to hang by the neck until dead. (*To* COHN) You want to appeal the sentence?

COHN: Drop dead.

WISEMAN: Appeal granted. Say thank you.

COHN: You could first cut my tongue out.

WISEMAN: Motion granted. (*Whips out scissors.*) Witness, do you have anything to say before I pass sentence?

COHN: No.

WISEMAN: Do you have anything to say before I pass out?

COHN: No.

WISEMAN: (*Rings a bell.*) Recess! (*Tips back in chair and falls to the floor, asleep.*)

COHN: (*Quietly, after a long pause.*) I hope you're satisfied.

ABE: I didn't start it.

COHN: We were made fools of.

ABE: Not me.

COHN: You too.

ABE: You first!

COHN: You were of no help whatsoever!

ABE: Help *you?* You've got a mind like a closed fist. Who can argue with it? You believed that she heard voices!

COHN: I didn't!

ABE: You told me so yourself!

COHN: A metaphor!

ABE: You believed she had a mission.

COHN: No.

ABE: Yes.

COHN: Never!

ABE: Always!

COHN: Sometimes. Never always. Not even when I said it.

ABE: So why did you say it? (COHN shrugs.) To get back at me, that's why!

COHN: *You?*

ABE: So she'd like you better!

COHN: She *did* like me better.

ABE: Because you knew her first. Do you deny you told me she was Joan of Arc?

COHN: (*Evasive*) I don't remember. (ABE *turns away in disgust.*) A charming conceit. Did it do harm? (*Improvising desperately*) She was cute. I liked her. She was nice—in my opinion—who knows? I wanted to please her. Pleasing a pretty girl. Is that so out of the question? I did it as a favor. A little game. A flirtation. Who understands women? I thought, in time, with patience, with understanding, the power of logic, I could talk her out of it.

ABE: You *wished* her out of it.

COHN: I didn't wish! (*A confession*) So I wished. You never wished?

ABE: You killed her!

COHN: Liar!!

ABE: You!

COHN: Killed her? Killed her? What are you saying? What a thing to say. I loved her! I believed in her! Killed her? Before her, I'd kill myself! (*Rushes over to* JOAN *and picks her up in his arms.*) The one person in this world who gave me anything! You gave me joy, I gave you doubt! You gave me hope, I gave you despondency! You gave me a second chance! And what did I do with it? What I did with my whole life! (*Overwhelming guilt*) I killed! I'm a killer! I should be killed. Locked up till I learn my lesson! (*Flash of insight*) I can't learn! I never learned! Never! Never! Never! (*Staggers over to* ABE.) Don't deny it, Abe, you're a saint! A saint! How could you put up with it? (*Embraces* ABE.) A man's best friend! (*Whips out a pistol.*) Kill me! Shoot me! (ABE *shoots—and misses. He blows a big hole in the back wall. Sunlight pours in.* COHN *and* ABE *squint in the sudden light.* JOAN *is bathed in light. She sits up slowly, rubbing her eyes.* COHN *does not see her. To* ABE) Idiot! Numskull! Can't you do anything right? (*Grabs pistol from* ABE *and turns it on himself.*)

JOAN: Cohn!

(JOAN *cry causes* COHN'S *hand to jerk at the moment of fire. A great hole is blown in the side wall. Sunlight pours in.* COHN *whirls on* JOAN, *drops the gun, and falls to his knees beside her. He covers his face with his hands and weeps.* JOAN *strokes his head.*)

COHN: A miracle! An angel from heaven!

JOAN: No, it's only me.

COHN: Say you forgive me.

JOAN: For what?

COHN: (*Angry*) Never mind for what! Say it! (*In self-reproach*) I did it again! (*Starts banging his head.*) Dog! Vermin! Pestilence!

JOAN: (*Gently*) Cohn—(COHN *looks up.* JOAN *rises from couch, shakily.*) I must leave you.

COHN: What are you saying?

JOAN: Farewell.

COHN: You're too sick to go out. It's freezing out there. Snow. Rain. Sit. Rest.

JOAN: Farewell, Abe.

ABE: More tricks?

COHN: Don't go! I deserve it, but don't!

JOAN: Abe, can you ever forgive me?

ABE: What's to forgive?

JOAN: You hate me.

ABE: Who hates? I'm objective.

JOAN: You're angry with me.

ABE: Anger is a waste. I'm objective.

JOAN: You're disappointed in me.

ABE: Disappointment is subjective. I'm objective.

JOAN: Abe, I'm sorry. I must go. Something is calling me.

COHN: Nothing! What? Something?

JOAN: —something inside—

COHN: Calling you?

JOAN: Inside. Something.

COHN: Voices?

JOAN: No. Yes! Voices! Oh, Cohn, how did you know?

COHN: I have to hear!

JOAN: How can you hear what's inside me?

COHN: Don't cut me out, Joan! I'm a dying man.

JOAN: I'm a dying woman.

COHN: Don't compete. (*Puts his head against her belly.*) Let me hear! Tell them it's me! Cohn! *Voices!* Name it! Cohn does it! No more kidding around.

JOAN: (*Tries to break away.*) I must go.

COHN: (*Holds her.*) It's not fair!

(*They struggle.*)

COHN: (*Begins to stagger.*) You must let me—

COHN: Voices! (JOAN *topples over.* COHN *catches her in his arms.*) What is this? (*To* ABE) What's the matter with her?

ABE: You did it again.

COHN: Joan. Don't joke, Joan. (*Drags her into the light.*) You want to go? Is that it? Is that all you want? You're free. Free as a bird. Go. Go, Joan. Go. (*Drags her to hole in the wall.*) You're free. Did I say no? Wake up, Joan. Go. Go! Go! (*To* ABE) She won't go.

ABE: She's dead.

COHN: She won't go. See! I'm holding her loose. What can I do? It's her decision. Look how loose I'm holding her.

(JOAN *rises out of* COHN's *arms and floats high above his head.*)

JOAN: Farewell!

COHN: You'll hurt yourself!

JOAN: I am off.

COHN: Without me?!

JOAN: I'm off to heaven. Happiness is waiting. Fields of green, sunlight—

COHN: You can't get there that way! You need a rocket ship! You told me yourself!

JOAN: Not if you're dead.

COHN: You're not dead.

JOAN: I am dead.

COHN: No! I deny it!

ABE: Stop arguing! Can't you see she's dead?

COHN: If she's dead, why is she up there?

ABE: If she's alive, *how* did she get up there? Bow your head. A little respect.

COHN: (*Cannot bow his head.*) How can I not see her for the last time?

JOAN: I am going far but I have come far. I have been several people, seen terrible things, had my heart broken and then spliced, have been shot at—

COHN: No!

JOAN: —have escaped, have been trapped, have escaped, have found God and lost him, found hope, lost it, grown weak, grown ill, passed out, recovered, walked on water, performed miracles, died, and floated up to the ceiling. And out of these myriad experiences I have learned all that I know and this is the sum of it: I have learned that however prosperous you should get out of the house, however satisfied you should be dissatisfied, however disillusioned you need hope, however hopeless you need patience, however impatient you need dignity, however dignified you need to relax, however relaxed you need rage, however enraged you need love, however loved you need a sense of proportion, however dispassionate you need passion, however possessive you need friends, however many friends you need privacy, however private you need to eat, however well fed you need books, however well read you need trials, however tried you need truth, and with truth goes trust and with trust goes certainty and with certainty goes calm and with calm goes cool and with cool goes collected but not so cool and collected you can't be hot and bothered. And if you're hot you need affection and if you're affectionate you want perfection, but however imperfect you needn't complain all the time. However lost you need to be found, however found you need to change, however changed you need simplicity, however simple not *too* simple or oversimple, however righteous not self-righteous; however conscious not self-conscious or self-hating or self-seeking; but you should be self-sufficient, but not alienated, not despairing, not sneering, not cynical, not clinical, not dead unless you are dead, and even then make the most of it. As I hope to do now. But first: My Last Will and Testament.

COHN: No!

JOAN: You must hear me.

COHN: It's not true!

ABE: (*To* COHN) Now at the end a little respect.

JOAN: To Abe I bequeath my armor in the hope of inspiring strong resolve and the courage to find a conviction. To Cohn I bequeath my Voices because he needs all the help he can get.

FIRST VOICE: I won't go!

SECOND VOICE: I object!

(COHN, *in amazement, looks down at his stomach.*)

WISEMAN: (*Leaps up from his napping place and bangs gavel.*) Objection overruled. Case dismissed. (*Scoops up* JOAN'S *armor and runs for the hole in the back wall.*)

ABE: (*Starts after him.*) That's my armor!

WISEMAN: Miarma? That's in Florida! (*He leaps out of the hole.* ABE *leaps after him. Both disappear from view. Sounds of a terrific struggle.*)

COHN: (*Stumbles*) Who's pushing me?

FIRST VOICE: Him.

SECOND VOICE: It's you I'm pushing, not Cohn.

COHN: (*Stumbles*) Well, quit pushing.

FIRST VOICE: Well, you tell him to quit pushing.

(COHN *stumbles backward.*)

COHN: Cut it out!

SECOND VOICE: You heard him.

FIRST VOICE: He meant you!

SECOND VOICE: You started it.

COHN: You didn't behave this way with Joan!

FIRST VOICE: We're influenced by our environment.

ABE: (*Rises into view, dressed in* JOAN'S *armor, her sword raised in victory.*) Onward! (*Sword high, he stalks out of sight.*)

COHN: (*Runs to hole in wall.*) Abe! It's pouring! You'll catch your death of cold! Viral pneumonia! A stroke! (*Suddenly stumbles toward hole.*)

SECOND VOICE: Quit shoving!

(COHN *struggling to stay erect, loses the struggle and tumbles backward through the hole, disappearing from view.*)

FIRST VOICE: Now you did it!

SECOND VOICE: Who did it?

FIRST VOICE: I didn't

SECOND VOICE: No. You're the innocent one around here.

(COHN *rises into view, blinking in the strong sunlight.*)

COHN: It's not as bad as it looks. (*Holds out a hand.*) It's only a drizzle.

FIRST VOICE: It's getting better.

SECOND VOICE: By whose evidence?

FIRST VOICE: The evidence of my senses.

SECOND VOICE: Your senses should have their head examined.

COHN: Shut up. Follow me.

(COHN *walks off. Lights fade on* JOAN, *in space, apparently heaven-bound.*)

CURTAIN

Julie Bovasso

Down By the River
Where Waterlilies
Are Disfigured Every Day

JULIE BOVASSO has won five Obie Awards, three of them for her writing, directing, and acting of the ANTA Theatre production of *Gloria and Esperanza*. Other plays include *Schubert's Last Serenade, the Nothing Kid, Standard Safety, The Moondreamers, Monday On the Way to Mercury Island,* and *Angelo's Wedding*. A recipient of a Guggenheim Fellowship for playwriting and two Rockefeller Foundation playwriting grants, Ms. Bovasso won her first Obie Award in 1955 for her establishment of the Tempo Theatre where she produced, directed, and acted in the American premieres of Jean Genet's *The Maids*, Eugene Ionesco's *Amedee* and *The Lesson*, Jean Cocteau's *The Typewriter*, and Michel deGhelderode's *Escurial*. She won the Drama Desk and Outer Critics' Circle awards for her performance in the American premiere of Genet's *The Screens*. She has also appeared extensively in major roles in regional theaters, including The American Shakespeare Festival at Stratford and Cincinnati's Playhouse in the Park. She is known to film audiences for her appearances in Sidney Lumet's *The Verdict* and *Daniel,* as well as Lumet's televised production of *The Iceman Cometh*. Other movies include Paul Mazursky's *Willie and Phil,* Brian de Palma's *Wise Guys,* and with John Travolta in *Saturday Night Fever* and *Staying Alive*. She has served on the faculties of Sarah Lawrence College, The New School for Social Research, and Brooklyn College Graduate School. She is a native New Yorker and lives and works in New York City.

For information regarding stock and amateur production rights, including all other rights, contact: Helen Harvey Associates, 410 West 24 Street, New York, NY 10011.

Waterlilies was first produced at the Trinity Square Repertory Theater, Providence, Rhode Island, under the direction of Adrian Hall, in 1972–73. Its second production previewed on March 12, 1975 (Press Opening: March 16) at the Circle Repertory Theater, under the direction of Marshall Oglesby, with the following cast:

PHOEBE	BOBO LEWIS
CLEMENT	NEIL FLANAGAN
COUNT JOSEF	RYLAND MERKEY
CONSTANTINE	LINDA HUNT
HERSCHEL	RUTH HERMINE
COUNT JUNIOR	CHARLES T. HARPER
SISSY	VERNA HOBSON
MISSY	SARALLAN
QUEEN NELL	CATHRYN DAMON
PRINCE PERCY	HARRY BROWNE
KING ARNIE	BRIAN CALLOWAY
COUNTESS ELIZABETH	CATHRYN DAMON
BARRY ZAP	BAXTER HARRIS
SMITHERS	CHARLES T. HARPER
GENERAL BUCKLEY	BAXTER HARRIS
ADMIRAL DUNCAN	BRIAN CALLOWAY

Characters

PHOEBE SNOW—An eccentric old woman
CLEMENT—An elegant gentleman of indeterminate age
COUNT JOSEF—The Prime Minister
CONSTANTINE—His Aide, a very small man
COUNT JUNIOR—Josef's idiot son
HERSCHEL—Another Aide, also very small
MISSY—A cleaning woman
SISSY—A cleaning woman
QUEEN NEIL—The Cockney queen
KING ARNY—The Cockney king
PRINCE PERCY—The Cockney prince
SMITHERS—A paratrooper

The Joint Chiefs of Staff
GENERAL WILLIAMSON
ADMIRAL DUNCAN
GENERAL BUCKLEY
ADMIRAL MITCHELL
GENERAL HUNT

The play should be performed with a cast of 12 actors, with doubling. In the original production at Trinity Square, the play was performed as written, with an all-male cast. This is not necessary, but if this concept is used, the only role that should not be played by a man is COUNTESS ELIZABETH, who was written into the play during the second production.

Act One

Scene One

(The sun parlor. White wicker furniture; a four-paneled screen; a Cheval mirror; a large window facing out.)

(At curtain: Distant noise of children's voices in sing-song chorus, chanting. Loud explosions followed by huge flares of light, crowds cheering and the crackle of a tremendous fire. War hoots, horns, drums.)

(PHOEBE SNOW is seated in a rocking chair in front of the window, looking out through a pair of pearl-handled opera glasses. She is very aged and wrinkled, but her face is made up to approximate a once dolllike prettiness. She wears an elegant, voluminous gown of fine grey silk with a ruffled, high-necked white lace bodice. On her head she wears a grey silk bonnet trimmed with forget-me-nots. Attached to the bonnet are long, silky, lavender curls which fall softly around her shoulders.)

(CLEMENT is in front of the mirror, practicing ballet steps. He wears a black leotard and appears quite pleased with his image.)

(There is a loud explosion followed by a great flare of light and crackling of fire.)

PHOEBE: Fifteen! They got the old oak at the south end. They'll get them all soon. In a very short while all the trees will be gone. Look at it. Nothing but charred stumps and flaming branches and leaves. Those rotten little punks are ruining the neighborhood.

(More shouts and cheering from without.)

PHOEBE: I've been watching children play in that park for thirty years but I've never seen anything like this. And when they finish burning the trees they'll turn to the houses. *(She takes a bit of snuff.)* Well, we're safe here at the north end for awhile, anyway. Nothing but basketball courts and cement at this end. But yesterday—yesterday I saw them pouring hot tar in the sandbox. And early this morning—broken glass all over the dog run. *(There is another explosion followed by a flare of light and crackling fire.)* Sixteen! The willow! They got the willow, those black-hearted little bastards! The weeping willow is in flames!

(CLEMENT crosses to a phonograph and puts on a practice record.)

© 1972 by Julie Bovasso

PHOEBE: Maybe it will never end. Maybe it will just go on until everything is in ashes. The authorities have fled. The king and queen are in hiding. Nothing but children, thousands of children, all of them with molotov cocktails and flame throwers in one hand and Ph.D's and Masters degrees in the other. Doctors of destruction, that's what they are. Masters of annihilation.

CLEMENT: Don't be ridiculous. None of those children is more than fifteen years of age. The Ph.D's and the Masters have fled with the authorities.

PHOEBE: *(Indignantly)* Are you speaking to me?

CLEMENT: Well, old dear, I thought you were speaking to me.

PHOEBE: I haven't spoken to you in fifteen years, why should I suddenly start speaking to you now?

(He crosses to the phonograph and turns it off.)

CLEMENT: How long are you going to sulk? You're not going to live forever, you know, and you wouldn't want to die that way, would you? Sulking? That would be a terrible way to die. She died sulking. *(He is wiping himself with a towel in front of the mirror, admiringly, with sensuous, caressing gestures.)*

PHOEBE: Vain.

CLEMENT: What?

PHOEBE: *(Loudly now)* Vain, vain.

CLEMENT: You're jealous, that's all—because you can't look into the mirror yourself without seeing all the ghosts and corpses of everything that was.

PHOEBE: If you have half my memories when you're my age—

CLEMENT: Here. Would you like to say hello to one of your dead shadows? Converse with one of your bloodless shades?

(He holds a hand mirror to her face. She pushes it away. He laughs.)

PHOEBE: But you'll never live to be my age.

CLEMENT: Why do you say that? Why shouldn't I live to be your age?

PHOEBE: *(Evenly)* Do you want to?

(He stiffens, turns abruptly and goes behind the screen. She shouts.)

PHOEBE: No, I shouldn't think you'd want to. Not with a life built on vanity. He wants to be a young, beautiful corpse, but he's afraid to die. He wants to live to be my age without growing old. You can't have it all ways, my dear. If you want to carry on you've got to give something up. If you want to go on to next year you've got to give something up from last year.

CLEMENT: *(Comes out from behind the screen, dressing to go out.)* What are you screaming about, you old hag? Drink your martini and shut up.

PHOEBE: I haven't got a martini.

CLEMENT: Then I'll got you one.

PHOEBE: There's nothing to look forward to anyway except death. Nothing's going to change that. *(Shouting again)* But if you want to continue the journey across the river you've got to jettison the things of this life. You've got to learn how to die a little bit every day if you want your death to be something more than just a darkness and an end. *(Pause)* I don't want that martini unless you have one with me.

CLEMENT: Ahhh, coming out of your stubborn sulk, are you?

PHOEBE: No, I just don't like to drink alone.

CLEMENT: Cheers. *(He returns to the mirror.)*

PHOEBE: Out again.

CLEMENT: Yes, out again.

PHOEBE: Where to this time?

CLEMENT: Here, there, and everywhere.

PHOEBE: *(Singing, in a soft, cracked voice.)*
Over the hill and through the dale
To grandma's house we go,
Riding the Lackawanna trail,
Riding with Phoebe Snow.

(She takes another sip of the drink and sings with more energy now, in a jazzy old beat.)

The Lackawanna Trail, the Lackawanna Trail
Will take you where you wanna go.
The Lackawanna Trail, the Lackawanna Trail
Goes the Route of Phoebe Snow . . .

CLEMENT: *(Laughing)* What's that?

PHOEBE: *(Grandly)* My theme song.

CLEMENT: Oh, yes. Your theme song, of course! *(He laughs again.)*

PHOEBE: "Of course! Of course!" What do you mean, of course? I haven't sung that song since I was eighteen, you couldn't possibly know it.

CLEMENT: Oh? Weren't you about eighteen when we met?

PHOEBE: Yes, that's right, tease me about my age. Torment me about my age. You've been doing it for thirty years. Why stop now?

CLEMENT: Thirty years? Now see here, we haven't been together for thirty years. More like twenty.

PHOEBE: Thirty! *You* were twenty.

CLEMENT: If I were twenty thirty years ago, old dear, I'd be fifty.

PHOEBE: And if you were thirty twenty years ago you'd still be fifty, so it amounts to the same thing. You're fifty.

(She cackles. There is a long silence. CLEMENT is absorbed with his image, smiling at himself, examining his teeth, opening his eyes and examining them, fussing with his hair.)

PHOEBE: Oh, beautiful, beautiful. You're just beautiful.

(He glances at her, annoyed. She cackles with delight and takes another sip of her drink.)

PHOEBE: Bad imvestment.

CLEMENT: What did you say? I didn't hear you.

PHOEBE: I didn't intend for you to hear me. I'm talking to myself. *(Brief pause, then, shouting.)* Bad investment.

CLEMENT: Was I supposed to hear that or not?

PHOEBE: Hear it or not you'd be the wiser to heed it.

CLEMENT: What is that, a riddle? Have you taken to talking in riddles now? What's a bad investment? What should I heed in order to be the wiser for?

PHOEBE: *(Slyly)* I was speaking of the past. Ellsworth.

CLEMENT: *(Not sure he has heard correctly.)* Ellsworth? Did you call me Ellsworth?

PHOEBE: It's your name, isn't it?

CLEMENT: *(Turning away)* Devil take you, dotty old sop.

PHOEBE: Ahh, that's right. Ellsworth isn't your name at all, is it? Ellsworth was *his* name. *(Slight pause)* I wonder where he is.

CLEMENT: Give me that martini! You've had quite enough!

He reaches for the glass, but she tosses the remainder of the drink down in one throw, then hands him the glass.)

PHOEBE: Here you are, Chippie.

(He takes the glass. She cackles with pleasure at his annoyance.)

PHEOBE: Chippie—that *is* your name, isn't it? That *is* what you like to be called, isn't it?

CLEMENT: Go to hell. *(He returns to the mirror.)*

PHOEBE: Chippie! Ridiculous name for a man of fifty-five, I must say.

CLEMENT: Oh, it's fifty-five now, is it? Why not sixty-five or seventy? You'd like that, wouldn't you, if I were a dottering old thing like yourself. You've been doing that ever since I've known you—trying to make me closer to your own age, robbing me of my youth, trying to make an old man of me. For thirty years now . . .

PHOEBE: Thirty! Ha!

CLEMENT: *(Returning to the mirror.)* Why do I even bother to talk to you at all. Just get dressed and go out. Horrible old witch. How in the name of God I ever got mixed up with you—

PHOEBE: Then why don't you leave? Why do you stay?

CLEMENT: I should have left. Years ago.

PHOEBE: And done what? Played with yourself in a room full of cats for the rest of your life, the way I found you? Terrified of your manhood?

CLEMENT: That's not true! I'd had affairs before I met you!

PHOEBE: Affairs! With what? Your cats?

CLEMENT: Pamela!

PHOEBE: Oh, Pamela! Yes. Pamela. For three months at the age of seventeen you scratched around on a bed with Pamela. I taught you everything. It is I who should have left you.

CLEMENT: Well, it's too late now, isn't it? Hardly likely that you'll find somebody to take care of you now, isn't it? Somebody to put up with your peevishness, cater to your whims. It isn't likely you'll find that now, is it? At this late date.

PHOEBE: At this late date! That's what you said when I was forty! You preyed like a maggot on my woman's fear that forty is the end of everything. Your youthful arrogance at the age of thirty made me feel old and desperate at the age of forty!

CLEMENT: Are you saying now that I was thirty when you were forty? *(He laughs in disbelief.)* You really are too much! If that were so you'd be fifty now, when in actual fact you are seventy!

PHOEBE: Which in actual fact would make you sixty!

CLEMENT: We are not ten years apart, Madame! We are thirty years apart!

PHOEBE: If we are thirty years apart, my friend, you had a nine-inch pecker at the age of ten!

(He goes angrily behind the screen. She mutters and cackles.)

PHOEBE: It isn't quite nine inches, anyway.

(There is another loud explosion and the noise outside increases in volume.)

PHOEBE: What's going on out there? What are they up to now? (*She opens the shutters and looks out through her opera glasses.*)

PHOEBE: Good heavens! Look at it! They're pouring into the square in droves. Thousands of them. Come here! Look! The children are sweeping into the square from all over . . . !

(CLEMENT enters from behind the screen, polishing shoes.)

CLEMENT: What are they doing?

PHOEBE: Garbage . . . !

CLEMENT: What?

PHOEBE: They're carrying garbage to the center of the square. *(He moves to the window for a moment, then back to his shoes.)* What are they going to do with all that garbage, leave it there? The little rotters! We'll be overrun by every rat in the city.

CLEMENT: We're too high up. Rats don't climb this high.

PHOEBE: (*Agitatedly*) But I'll have to look at them. I'll have to look at the rats if they come. What's that? What's going on over there? Clement, I can't see, it's too far away. Something is going on over there. Come take the glasses and look.

CLEMENT: Where?

PHOEBE: There, at the east entrance. It looks like a procession of some kind. What is it? What is it? Let me see. Let me see.

CLEMENT: Just a moment, you gave me the glasses, didn't you?

PHOEBE: Tell me what's happening! Tell me!

CLEMENT: More children, that's all . . . marching in unison . . . dressed in funny rags . . .

PHOEBE: What are they dong? Where are they going?

CLEMENT: Be still a moment, will you? They're carrying torches—moving toward the center of the square—moving toward the mountain.

PHOEBE: The mountain? What mountain?

CLEMENT: The garbage mountain. Just a moment! They're beginning to encircle it now.

(*Chanting is heard without.*)

CLEMENT: They're probably going to burn it.

PHOEBE: Good god!

CLEMENT: I must say—the children nowadays seems to have much more fun than we did. Their games are far more imaginative than ours were.

(*He hands her the glasses and returns to his activities.*)

PHOEBE: Clement, I don't think you ought to go out tonight. It's an ominous night.

CLEMENT: Nonsense.

PHOEBE: Please. Break your appointment. It's dangerous out there.

CLEMENT: I can't break my appointment. I don't want to break my appointment.

PHOEBE: But look at it. You can't just carry on as usual in these unusual times.

CLEMENT: There's nothing unusual about the times. History is simply repeating itself and we happen to be sitting in a grandstand seat. Relax and enjoy it. If the children want to heap garbage in the center of the square, let them. If they want to burn it, let them. What's it got to do with me? I'll simply walk 'round the park instead of through it. (*He continues with his preparations.*)

PHOEBE: Are you bringing friends home with you tonight?

CLEMENT: Perhaps.

PHOEBE: May I request that you not tell them that I am your mother.

CLEMENT: Then what shall I tell them? How shall I explain your presence?

PHOEBE: (*Shouting*) I am not your mother. I resent your telling your friends that I am your mother, when in actual fact we have been lovers for thirty years and are still lovers!

CLEMENT: We are not still lovers.

PHOEBE: Then what was all that business last night?

CLEMENT: What business?

PHOEBE: All that business! All that business!

CLEMENT: You were dreaming.

PHOEBE: I was not dreaming!

CLEMENT: Then it must have been the dog!

PHOEBE: It was not the dog! The dog doesn't do such things! Besides the dog is dead! Or don't you remember having murdered him?!

CLEMENT: I did not murder your dog.

PHOEBE: You murdered the dog. You deliberately dropped that watermelon on his head!

CLEMENT: It leaped out of my hands.

PHOEBE: A watermelon doesn't leap! You murdered the dog!

CLEMENT: All right! Have it your way! I murdered the dog! There never was a dog to begin with, goddammit! It's all in your head!

PHOEBE: All in my head, you say? The dog . . .

CLEMENT: Yes, the dog . . . and everything else.

PHOEBE: And what about the murder weapon? Was that in my head, too? Did that begin with me?

CLEMENT: No, that began with me, I admit—

PHOEBE: There, you see! Premeditated murder! Murder, murder, murder!

CLEMENT: But you're the one who dreamed up the idea that it killed him!

PHOEBE: But you're the one who did it!

CLEMENT: In your mind! Not in mine!

PHOEBE: But you were thinking about doing it! Admit you were thinking about it!

CLEMENT: Inconsequential!

PHOEBE: Guilty, guilty, guilty!

CLEMENT: It started with you!

PHOEBE: Hang him! Hang the murderer!

CLEMENT: You can't hang someone for thinking about something—

PHOEBE: You planned the whole thing—!

CLEMENT: —you can only hang them fr committing an act—! And you, Madame, are the one who shall hang because it was you, Madame, who took my thought and turned it into an act! It was you, Madame, who made the whole thing a *fait accompli*!

PHOEBE: Not true! What motive would I have—?

CLEMENT: Blackmail!

PHOEBE: Not true!

CLEMENT: You framed me, Madame—!

PHOEBE: False!

CLEMENT: You had the murder weapon in your possession, is that not right? You took the murder weapon, is that not right? Answer me! Is that not right? And you did what you would with it! Is that not right? And what you did with it was *kill him*! Is that not right, Madame! Is that not right!

PHOEBE: No, no, it was an accident!

CLEMENT: Very likely—!

PHOEBE: I swear it was an accident—!

CLEMENT: Very likely, indeed. (*He turns to the window.*)

PHOEBE: Oh, God. God forgive me. Forgive me, dear God. I'm guilty. I confess. I did it. I killed him.

CLEMENT: (*At the window, solemnly.*) Yes. But I was an accomplice.

(*Another explosion, followed by shouts and cheers from the children.*)

PHOEBE: No, no, Clement. You're cleared. You're clean. It was my thought.

CLEMENT: What difference does it make? You thought, my thought—

PHOEBE: God will forgive you. His death began with me—

CLEMENT: And whether or not he ever was he got murdered all the same (*He remains looking out of the window, his face illumined by the reflection of flames from without.*)—by you or by me, what difference? If you had not killed him, I probably would have done it. And if I had not dreamed it up, you probably would have dreamed that I had. It's all one, isn't it? We live in the same house, sleep in the same bed, look out of the same window, eat from the same table—when people are so very much the same, when everything about their lives is so very much the same, it's bound to produce the same thoughts, the same dreams, the same nightmares. (*He remains fixed at the window, staring out reflectively.*)

PHOEBE: You have such a keen mind, Clement. It's a pity that you didn't do more with your life. You'd have made an excellent lawyer, for instance. Or a politician. Why, with your good looks you might even have become a president, or a king, or a high and powerful potentate.

CLEMENT: Potentate, indeed.

PHOEBE: Or perhaps you should have been a priest. There is something pious lurking around under all that vanity. Yes, you might have been a politician or a priest. Or a high potentate or a holy prophet.

CLEMENT: Why not all four? Yesterday's priest is today's politician and today's high potentate is tomorrow's holy prophet.

PHOEBE: Yes, quite right. You might have been all four. Like *him*.

(CLEMENT *turns to her.*)

CLEMENT: What do you mean, like *him?* He was none of those things.

PHOEBE: He was *all* of those things.

(CLEMENT *turns away. She eyes him for a moment, then:*)

PHOEBE: You haven't seen him by any chance, have you?

CLEMENT: Stop talking nonsense.

PHOEBE: You've seen him! I know you've seen him!

CLEMENT: Stop talking as if he were living down the street!

PHOEBE: (*After a moment, enigmatically.*) Maybe closer than that.

CLEMENT: (*Slightly alarmed.*) What do you mean?

PHOEBE: I have a feeling that he's close by, that he's coming back. To find out the truth.

(*Another explosion from without, followed by a loud roar of children's voices.* CLEMENT *glances at his wristwatch.*)

CLEMENT: I'd best get a move on or I'll be late for my appointment. (*He turns away from the window, takes a silk shirt from a hanger, puts it on.*)

PHOEBE: My God . . . ! They got the bush! The old bush at the west end of the square. It's in flames. The bush is in flames . . . !

(CLEMENT *is drawn again to the window as the lights and sounds of the revolution cross-fade and come up on:*)

Scene Two

(*The Ministry. The office of* COUNT JOSEF, *the Prime Minister. The set is a combination Gothic and Art Deco: mirrored walls, glass columns, dark velvet drapes; a long flight of stone steps leading to a stained glass Gothic window, high up and extending across the upstage area, a cathedral effect.*)

Half-way up the stone steps, an Art Deco door leading to the chamber. At the top of the stone steps and to the left of the Gothic window, another door with steel bars leads to the tower. Stage level area has a large Art Deco desk an chair, a row of High-Tech equipment, three video screens, panel control boards.)

(AT CURTAIN: Count Josef, dressed in formal morning coat, striped trousers, grey suede spats over black patent leather pumps, is at work on a large figure sculpture. He wears a canvas apron over his clothing, and a silk top hat on his head.)

(Constantine, a small man under four feet tall, dressed in black tights, doublet and cape, slips into the room from between the part in the velvet drapes.)

Count Josef: Where have you been, Constantine? I've been looking for you.

Constantine: Visiting with the Archbishop, Your Excellency.

Count Josef: Again? You seem to be spending a lot of time these days with the Archbishop.

Constantine: His condition is getting worse, you Excellency. He's lonely, lying there all day, and he seems to enjoy my company.

Count Josef: I appreciate your concern for the old man and your solicitude does you honor, but your place is here with me. There's a lot of work to be done.

Constantine: Yes, Your Excellency.

Count Josef: Where is my son?

Constantine: In his chamber, Your Excellency.

Count Josef: Alone?

Constantine: No, my cousin Herschel is with him.

Count Josef: What's he doing? Is he occupied?

Constantine: No, Your Excellency. He simply sits and stares out the window.

Count Josef: I've told you that he was to be kept occupied.

Constantine: But nothing holds his attention, Your Excellency. He stares out of the window with the tears streaming down his face, muttering those same words over and over. Then he will suddenly begin to gnash his teeth and start that awful humming sound, or leap from his chair and begin to flail about the room, slashing the air with his good arm and beating his withered leg.

Count Josef: All right! That's quite enough! You can spare me the details. I have been living with my son for eighteen years and I am fully aware of the manifestations of his illness.

CONSTANTINE: I'm sorry, Your Excellency.

COUNT JOSEF: What's going on out there?

CONSTANTINE: The Members of the Press are beginning to arrive. Will you be ready for the conference in a few minutes, or shall I have them wait?

COUNT JOSEF: Let them wait. (*There is a silence as he continues to work on the statue. Then:*) Well, how do you like it?

(CONSTANTINE *does not reply.*)

COUNT JOSEF: Don't you think the resemblance is extraordinary?

CONSTANTINE: How would I know, Your Excellency? I have never met the man.

COUNT JOSEF: Neither have I. but I imagine him to look like this.

CONSTANTINE: A god, Excellency?

COUNT JOSEF: I wouldn't have an adversary who was anything less. It would be unheard of.

(CONSTANTINE *snickers.*)

COUNT JOSEF: What are you snickering at?

CONSTANTINE: Forgive me, Excellency, but the irony of it—that even you should worship him, along with all the children.

COUNT JOSEF: And should I despise him, then, because he is a renegade?

CONSTANTINE: I would think so, Your Excellency. He's a dangerous revolutionary.

COUNT JOSEF: And instead I am building an idol to him. That's impossible for you to understand, isn't it?

CONSTANTINE: Yes, Your Excellency.

COUNT JOSEF: Constantine, you have a narrow mind. You don't understand the finer subtleties of life. The minute complexities. The dichotomy of existence confuses you, embitters you, turns you sour. Whereas I—*J'accepte!* With a knowing and wistful smile. (*He smiles very knowingly and not at all wistfully at* CONSTANTINE.) Bellica pax, vulnus dulce, suave malum. It is no wonder that you are no further along in your career than a mere Aide. Why, at your age I was already in the Senate, such as it was.

CONSTANTINE: Begging your pardon, Count Josef, but I did not have the benefit of your family's wealth, your family's name, your family's heritage.

COUNT JOSEF: You sound like one of those revolutionary children. Why don't you go out and join them? What are you doing here, shining the boots of a conservative old ogre like myself?

CONSTANTINE: Not all people from my station are revolutionaries, You Excellency. Some are loyal to the Crown.

COUNT JOSEF: Yes, especially those of you on government payroll. Get out of my sight, you vassel. I can't stand to look at you.

(CONSTANTINE *withdraws to a corner.*)

COUNT JOSEF: How he—Pango! He is something else. The Great God Pango! He has organized those wild children and he leads them, even though he is not one of them. He is of my class. He comes from a good family, he was educated abroad. He is a man of sensibilities.

CONSTANTINE: Pardon me, Your Excellency, but how do you know that? Nobody knows anything about Pango.

COUNT JOSEF: I imagine him to be that. He is like me. A man who has experienced life's ironies, one who knows that certain inevitables cannot be changed. (*Addressing the statue.*) And yet you have dedicated yourself to achieving the impossible, whereas I have dedicated myself to achieving only that which I know to be most possible. But that is why I am a prime minister and you a revolutionary.

(*He crosses from the statue, puts out his hand.* CONSTANTINE *places a wet towel in it.*)

COUNT JOSEF: But we are brothers, he and I. My life would be very dull without him, Constantine.

CONSTANTINE: What if he wins?

COUNT JOSEF: What? Wins? (*He laughs.*) How can he win? With an army of children? He's not a fool. He knows he will lose. He knows that I have six hundred years experience putting down skirmishes of this kind. However, he is making an impression.

CONSTANTINE: (*A note of sarcasm*) Yes. Don't underestimate . . .

COUNT JOSEF: I never underestimate, you idiot!

CONSTANTINE: I merely wished to point out that he has mobilized over ninety percent of the children in the country. His objective is to overthrow you, Your Excellency, and our government.

COUNT JOSEF: Beautiful! Beautiful! And for having such lofty ambitions I shall have to arch his nose a bit more. (*He molds the statue's nose.*)

(CONSTANTINE *turns away, snickering to himself.*)

COUNT JOSEF: What are you snickering at now? You're imagining the confrontation between him and me . . . my disappointment when I finally meet Pango face to face and discover that he is a middle-aged, balding intellectual with a sunken chest and a bulbous nose. That's what you're imagining, isn't it? Hoping for, in fact, eh. Constantine? Oh, I can read your thoughts. I know how your mind works. It is a mind twisted by failure, festering in its own bitterness and disillusionment; a mind uable to grasp the Idea; a mind which clings to reality because it does not have the imagination to transcend it. Yes, Pango may very well be a balding, middle-aged intellectual. Don't you think I am prepared for that, too, you fool? If and when he finally holds the sword to my throat and makes the final thrust which sends me into oblivion—Don't you think I am prepared to die at the hands of a horse's ass, you horse's ass!?

(*A bell rings.* CONSTANTINE *hurries out through the draperies.* COUNT JOSEF *turns to the statue and caressing it:*)

COUNT JOSEF: But if you are to be my executioner, Pango, I prefer to imagine that you are beautiful, noble, dedicated and in full possession of your faculties. The only unbearable irony is the thought of dying at the hands of a fool or a madman.

(COUNT JUNIOR *has entered and stands in the doorway. He is a gentle-faced, sad young man with a withered left leg which he must drag along in order to walk. His left arm is crooked and the fingers of his left hand gnarled. His face bears the expression of consummate innocence, along with the unmistakable look of idiocy.*)

COUNT JOSEF: Ah, Junior, my boy. Don't stand there in the doorway. Come in.

(*He extends his arm and the boy drags himself toward his father.* COUNT JOSEF *puts his arm around the boy's shoulders.*)

COUNT JOSEF: I understand you had a visit from Herschel today. Did you and he have a good time?

COUNT JUNIOR: Hunnnnh . . . hunnnh . . .

COUNT JOSEF: That's good. I like Herschel, too. He's very sweet, very kind. I much prefer him to his cousin Constantine. You must be careful of Constantine. He's very treacherous.

COUNT JUNIOR: (*Wandering aimlessly away.*) Hunnnh . . . hunnnnh . . .

(CONSTANTINE *enters.*)

COUNT JOSEF: Constantine, get a chair for Count James, will you?

CONSTANTINE: Excuse me, Your Excellency, but the members of the press . . .

COUNT JOSEF: (*Interrupting*) How do you like my statue, Junior?

(COUNT JUNIOR'S *attention is turned to the statue. He drags himself across the stage.*)

COUNT JOSEF: Hunnnh . . . Hunnnh . . . (*He reaches out to touch the statue, his hand caressing the left leg and arm.*)

COUNT JOSEF: He looks a bit like you, don't you think?

(COUNT JUNIOR *looks up at* COUNT JOSEF, *then smiles.*)

COUNT JOSEF: Ah, that pleases you. I'm glad. I like to see you smile.

(CONSTANTINE *has placed a chair beside* JUNIOR, *but he does not sit.*)

COUNT JOSEF: Why don't you sit down?

COUNT JUNIOR: (*Shaking his head and wandering away.*) Hunnnnh . . . hunnnh . . .

COUNT JOSEF: Suit yourself.

CONSTANTINE: Excuse me, Your Excellency, but the Members of the Press are becoming impatient. Are you ready to see them now?

COUNT JOSEF: There will be no press conference, Constantine.

CONSTANTINE: But they're all gathered, Your Excellency . . .

(COUNT JUNIOR *has wandered back and seats himself at* COUNT JOSEF'S *feet.*)

COUNT JOSEF: I shall simply make a brief statement on the issue. Anything more elaborate than that would blow the government's cool. Am I right, Junior?

COUNT JUNIOR: (*Smiling and swaying*) Hunnnnh . . . Hunnnnh . . .

COUNT JOSEF: There, you see? Count Junior agrees. Hand me the microphone.

CONSTANTINE: You're not even going to appear before them, Your Excellency?

COUNT JOSEF: No. We shall keep it all shrouded in mystery for awhile. If a mystery is allowed to go on long enough it very often solves itself. Remember that, Junior.

COUNT JUNIOR: Hummmmmh . . .

COUNT JOSEF: When we are prepared to move, we shall move—dynamically. And they will know about it, you can be sure. (*He takes the mic-*

rophone and turns to the audience.) Good evening, Ladies and Gentlemen of the Press. This is Count Josef speaking . . .

(*There is an explosion in the distance, followed by shouts of children.*)

COUNT JOSEF: In the matter of the recent rumor of a royal flake-out: If His Majesty the King is losing His Royal Mind, you can be sure, Ladies and Gentlemen, that it is in the interest of the people. (*He switches off the microphone nd hands it to* CONSTANTINE) End of statement.

(*Another explosion is heard.* COUNT JUNIOR *perks up his head like an animal alerted and then begins to drag himself over to the window, where the sky is red with flares of light.*)

COUNT JUNIOR: (*Becoming agitated*) Hunnnnggg . . . Hunnnnnggg . . .

COUNT JOSEF: Now I want to send a message to the Chairman of the Joint Chiefs of Staff.

(CONSTANTINE *readies himself at the table in front of an odd-looking, somewhat makeshift machine with buttons, keys, antenna.*)

COUNT JUNIOR: (*Scraping at his withered arm and leg, gnashing his teeth.*) Hunnnnnh . . . Hunnnhhh . . .

COUNT JOSEF: Dear Walter: This is Count Josef. Please advise all members of the staff that there will be an emergency meeting in my office at nine o'clock this evening to discuss plans for immediate action in regard to our plan of action . . .

(*There is another loud explosion.*)

COUNT JUNIOR: Cast upon thee . . . Hunnnnhhh . . .

COUNT JOSEF: The hiding place of the king and queen will be revealed to you at that time, and you may then proceed to put into operation the plan of action planned by us . . .

COUNT JUNIOR: (*Beating upon himself.*) Hunnnnnnh . . . cast upon . . .

COUNT JOSEF: . . . planned by us in the operational plan entitled "Operation, Action Plan." Signed, Count Josef. End of Message.

COUNT JUNIOR: Cast upon thee . . .

COUNT JOSEF: Have you got that?

CONSTANTINE: Yes, sir.

COUNT JUNIOR: I am a worm . . . hunnnnh . . .

COUNT JOSEF: Send it off as quickly as possible. And ring for your cousin Herschel to come and take Count Junior back to his room.

COUNT JUNIOR: Cast upon thee . . .

COUNT JOSEF: (*Gently*) What is it, Junior? What's wrong?

(COUNT JUNIOR *stops beating himself and stares at* COUNT JOSEF. *Then he turns his head distractedly away.*)

COUNT JUNIOR: I was cast upon thee . . . (*He turns back and looks at* COUNT JOSEF.)

COUNT JOSEF: Why don't you sit down?

(*He places his hands on the boy's shoulders and tries to get him seated. But* COUNT JUNIOR *remains rigid and fixed.*)

COUNT JOSEF: . . . from the womb. Hunnnnh.

COUNT JOSEF: Come on, now . . .

COUNT JUNIOR: Thou art my God from my mother's belly.

(*There is a pause.* COUNT JOSEF *stares into the eyes of his idiot son, then:*)

COUNT JOSEF: Come on, now. Come on. Sit down like a good fellow.

(COUNT JUNIOR *allows himself to be seated and he slumps now, his energy spent.*)

CONSTANTINE: What are those words he keeps uttering, Count Josef?

COUNT JOSEF: He doesn't know what he's saying. he repeats them by rote. His mother used to read to him from Scriptures and he remembers words, phrases, sometimes whole sentences. Perhaps he's merely recalling the sound of her voice. But he doesn't understand what he's saying.

COUNT JOSEF: But I am a worm and no man . . .

COUNT JOSEF: Did you ring for Herschel?

CONSTANTINE: Yes, Your Excellency.

COUNT JOSEF: A reproach of men . . . hunnnnnh . . .

CONSTANTINE: (*Craftily*) I have heard people say that his mother, The Countess Elizabeth, was a holy woman.

COUNT JOSEF: (*Tersely*) She was very devout.

COUNT JUNIOR: Despised by the people. Hunnnnnnh. Despised . . . hunnnh . . .

CONSTANTINE: . . . and that your son, too, is holy.

COUNT JOSEF: My son is close to God by reason of his affliction.

CONSTANTINE: In that case, I too, should be close to Him by reason of mine. (*He snickers.*) What a ptiy the Countess could not have been given a Christian burial. The Archbishop told me that he was powerless under the circumstances.

COUNT JOSEF: Dried up ... hunnnnggg. Dried up ... Thou hast brought me into the dust of death.

(HERSCHEL *enters. He is a small man, about the same size as his cousin.*)

COUNT JOSEF: Herschel. Will you take Count Junior back to his room, please?

HERSCHEL: Yes, Excellency.

(*Extending his hand to* COUNT JUNIOR, *who takes it.*)

HERSCHEL: Come along ... come along, mon petit Compte de Penombre.

COUNT JUNIOR: (*Softly, to* HERSCHEL) My strength ... is dried up. Hunnnngg.

HERSCHEL: (*Leading him to the door.*) Yess, yes, mon petit. I understand, little shadow. Come along. Herschel will play with you.

COUNT JOSEF: Herschel. When you've taken him to his room, please come down to my private chamber. I wish to speak with you.

HERSCHEL: Yes, Your Excellency.

(*He exits with* COUNT JUNIOR.)

COUNT JOSEF: Now another message, Constantine, if you please. This one is to the Queen ... to be delivered by hand.

CONSTANTINE: Delivered by hand? By whom, Your Excellency?

COUNT JOSEF: By you, Constantine.

(CONSTANTINE'S *eyes widen.*)

COUNT JOSEF: Yes, I must take you into my confidence and reveal to you the hiding place of the Royal Family. You will be the only person other than myself to have this information. I trust that I can trust you. Can I trust you?

CONSTANTINE: Oh, yes, yes, Count Josef. Implicitly. I am honored ...

COUNT JOSEF: Here is the message. It is to be delivered before Midnight. 'From Count Josef to Her Majesty, the Queen ... (*He stops suddenly, sways slightly, and grips the edge of the desk.*)

CONSTANTINE: Are you all right, Your Excellency?

COUNT JOSEF: Yes, yes, I'm all right. Where was I?

CONSTANTINE: "From Count Josef to Her Majesty ... "

COUNT JOSEF: Yes, yes ... (*With some difficulty*) "Your Majesty ... " (*He pauses. Then, distractedly:*) "The Comedy ... is over ... " (CONSTANTINE *looks up, puzzled.*) No, no, that's not it. Strike that out. (*He pauses again,*

then still somewhat distractedly:) "The Comedy...is not yet...
over..."(*Pause*) No, strike that..." (*His hand goes to his forehead and
he closes his eyes.*)

CONSTANTINE: Does His Excellency *know* what he wants to say?

(COUNT JOSEF *turns on him abruptly.*)

CONSTANTINE: I beg your pardon, Excellency.

(COUNT JOSEF *makes an effort to recover himself, straightens up and, in full
command of the situation:*)

COUNT JOSEF: "From Count Josef to Her Majesty, the Queen: Dear Nell.
Sit tight." End of message. (*He crosses to the stone steps.*) I shall be in my
chamber.

CONSTANTINE: But Your Excellency, where shall I deliver the message?

COUNT JOSEF: What?

CONSTANTINE: The hiding place, Your Excellency. You haven't told me the
hiding place.

COUNT JOSEF: Oh. Yes. The hiding place... (*He stops as if he'd suddenly
heard something, then turns his attention back to* CONSTANTINE.) The hiding place of the king and queen is as follows: (CONSTANTINE *writes frantically.*) Five thousand four hundred and twenty four paces of a size ten
shoe, north, in a direct line from the center of the square. (*Pause*) Have
you got that?

CONSTANTINE: Yes, Your Excellency.

COUNT JOSEF: Good. Now Swallow it and repeat it from memory.

(CONSTANTINE *eats the paper and gulps it down.* COUNT JOSEF *is still
deeply preoccupied.*)

CONSTANTINE: (*Repeating from memory.*) "The hiding place of the king
and queen is as follows: Five thousand four hundred and twenty-four
paces of a size ten shoe, south..."

COUNT JOSEF: North! North! You idiot!

CONSTANTINE: North. Yes, north... "in a direct line from the center of the
square."

COUNT JOSEF: Good.

(*He starts out.* CONSTANTINE *stops him.*)

CONSTANTINE: But Your Excellency... I only wear a size three shoe.

COUNT JOSEF: Dammit. Complications. (*He removes his own shoes.*)
Here. Take these. They're a size ten. But be sure to return them. They
were my grandfather's opera pumps. (*He crosses to the door.*) I shall be

in my chamber. Call me when the Joint Chiefs of Staff arrive for the meeting.

(*He exits.* CONSTANTINE *hugs the big shoes to his chest.*)

CONSTANTINE: Fool! To reveal the hiding place of the king and queen to me, of all people. Even you, Count Josef, are capable of making the one fatal error which will cost you everything. Yes . . . the Archbishop will be most pleased to have this information which you have so kindly put into my mouth.

(*He suddenly begins to retch and, clutching his stomach, rushes behind the desk as the lights fade and come up on:*)

Scene Three

(*The sunparlor.* CLEMENT *is still at the window looking out through the opera glasses.* PHOEBE *sits, eating chocolates.*)

CLEMENT: Good God, every bit of garbage in the world must be in that heap.

PHOEBE: I wonder if my old wicker tea tray is in there.

CLEMENT: Don't be ridiculous. How could it be? You threw that thing away ten years ago.

PHOEBE: Well, it might be there. One never knows what happens to the junk one discards. A lot of it is resurrected and given new life.

CLEMENT: (*A note of sarcasm*) Yes, I daresay.

PHOEBE: I beg your pardon?

CLEMENT: (*Riveted to the activities outside.*) What in the name of heaven are they doing? Looks like some kind of war dance.

PHOEBE: Are you suggesting, sir, that you resurrected me?

CLEMENT: They're putting their torches to the edges of it—

PHOEBE: That I was ready for the junk heap when we met?

CLEMENT: By Christ, they really are going to send it all up! (*Turns to her, preoccupied.*) What? Oh . . . Well, you did still have a very nice figger for your age.

PHOEBE: (*Banging her cane.*) For my age! Yes! For my age! That's what you've been saying for thirty years. "Not bad, for your age." (*Shouting at the world at large.*) At forty I had breasts as firm and as high as a girl of twenty . . .

CLEMENT: (*Without taking his attention from the outside.*) Phoebe, be still a moment and look.

PHOEBE: (*Barrelling on*) And still you said "Nice for your age."

CLEMENT: The smoke is beginning to rise . . .

PHOEBE: At forty I was a queen in the full bloom of my life, but you made me feel as if it was the end of everything!

CLEMENT: All the garbage in the world is about to burn before our eyes.

PHOEBE: When in fact it was the beginning!

CLEMENT: It's an historic moment!

PHOEBE: (*Wailing*) Oh, if only I had known then what I know now and not been so afraid!

CLEMENT: There it goes!

PHOEBE: But you bore into me like a worm with your youth . . .

CLEMENT: It's going up.

PHOEBE: Flaunting it because you had nothing else.

CLEMENT: It's in flames!

PHOEBE: I have thrown away the best years of my life!

CLEMENT: Look at it burn!

PHOEBE: Oh, my God! . . .

CLEMENT: A mountain of flaming shit! . . .

PHOEBE: There is nothing more beautiful than a beautiful woman at forty.

CLEMENT: A universe of worthless trash!

PHOEBE: But it takes a man to know it! Not a boy! A man! Not a faggot! . . .

CLEMENT: Putrifaction is in flames!

PHOEBE: All my life I have had nothing but boys and faggots, faggots and boys!

CLEMENT: The universal sewer is illuminated at last!

PHOEBE: (*With both arms raised, standing center.*) I MUST FIND MY-SELF A MAN BEFORE I DIE!

(*There is a silence. He turns.*)

CLEMENT: Sit down before you fall.

PHOEBE: If I sit down before I fall I'll wind up in the same place any-way . . . Down! What difference does it make? Down on the floor or down in the chair? Down is down!

(CLEMENT *puts the opera glasses on the table and moves away from the window.* PHOEBE *falls to the floor.*)

CLEMENT: There! You see!

PHOEBE: Leave me alone! Leave me alone! Don't touch me! I'm down!

CLEMENT: (*After a moment he crosses to her.*) Come on, now.

PHOEBE: Get away, get away! Let me crawl. Let me slither with the serpent in hell!

CLEMENT: Phoebe, you're being silly.

PHOEBE: No, no. Leave me alone. I shall find my own way back, thank you very much.

CLEMENT: Very well. (*He puts on his white gloves.*) I really must be going now. I'm very late. (*He puts on his stiff-brimmed hat and picks up his cane.*) Is there anything I can get you before I leave?

PHOEBE: The pot. I need the pot.

CLEMENT: (*Angrily flinging his cane aside.*) Damn!

PHOEBE: Well, you asked me, didn't you?

(*He crosses to the cupboard and removes a chamber pot.*)

CLEMENT: Where do you want it? On the chair?

PHOEBE: No, no, right here. Quickly. I won't make it to the chair. Quickly. Quickly.

(*He places the pot on the floor, center stage, and helps her while she arranges her voluminous skirt around the pot and sits, regally. He paces around impatiently. There is a pause. She sits, staring straight out.*)

PHOEBE: Could I have some music please?

(*Exasperated, he goes to the phonograph and places a record on the machine: a rather lyrical selection, possibly a Viennese waltz or* Les Sylphides.)

(CLEMENT *paces about impatiently, glancing at his watch.*)

CLEMENT: Are you finished yet?

PHOEBE: (*With great gentility*) I haven't even begun.

(CLEMENT *flings himself into the chair as the lights fade.*)

(*The music from the phonograph cross-fades with a recorded voice:*)

RECORDED VOICE: This is a memo to Count Josef from General Walter Hunt, Chairman, Joint Chiefs of Staff . . .

(*The lights fade up on:*)

Scene Four

(Count Josef's *Office.*)

(Constantine *appears and moves quickly to the intercom.*)

Recorded Voice: Your message acknowledged. All members of the staff will be at your office within the hour to discuss plans for immediate action in regard to our plan of action as planned by us in the operational plan entitled "Operation, Action Plan." Please be further advised that it will be necessary for us to wear disguises in view of the danger of apprehension by the children. End of Message. Signed, General Walter Hunt, Chairman, Joint Chiefs of Staff.

Constantine: (*Snickering*) Disguises. Those lily-livered bastards. And do they think for a moment that the Archbishop is not aware of their plans for a military coup d'etat? They may have Count Josef fooled, but not His Holy Reverence, the Archbishop of Capistrano.

(*Enter* Herschel, *cautiously. He wears a long black cape, a hat pulled down over his eyes, and a muffler that conceals most of his face. He looks around cautiously and, hugging the wall, sneaks towards the door.*)

Constantine: Where are you going? (*He darts forward, blocking* Herschel's *exit.*)

Herschel: (*Terrified*) For a walk.

Constantine: At this hour of the night?

Herschel: Yes.

Constantine: What did Count Josef want to see you about? Come on, come on, speak up you little gnome or I'll cut out your heart and stuff it in your mouth. (*He twists the scarf around Herschel's neck and squeezes it tightly.*) Remember, my little country cousin, you are here only out of my good graces. My good graces, you little chicken farmer! And if you don't tell me everything that goes on between you and Count Josef and his idiot son I'll turn you in to the Archbishop as a heretic and nobody will be able to save you, including Count Josef. Now tell me! Where are you going? He's sending you on a secret mission, isn't he? Speak up! Where are you going?

Herschel: To the music store, the music store, that's all. I swear. Count Junior's flute has disappeared and I must get to the music store and buy him another before they close.

(Constantine *releases* Herschel.)

Constantine: (*Laughing*) The idiot's flute has disappeared? I wonder what can have happened to it?

(*He laughs again as* HERSCHEL *exits.*)

(*Enter* MISSY *and* SISSY *with mops and pails.* CONSTANTINE *straightens up authoritatively and moves to* COUNT JOSEF's *desk, where he sits, with an air of importance.*)

CONSTANTINE: Don't let me disturb you, ladies. Just carry on.

SISSY: Yassah, we is carryin' on.

MISSY: (*Surly*) We is carryin' on fo' sho'. Don' know how we is carryin' on, but we is carryin' on.

SISSY: (*Whispering fearfully*) Mind yo' manners, Missy.

MISSY: Ah ain' mindin' nuthin'.

SISSY: Missy, please! Yo! is addressin' a important official government millionaire.

MISSY: Ah is addressin' shit.

CONSTANTINE: (*Sharply*) What was that?

SISSY: Nothin', nothin'. She din't say nothin', boss.

MISSY: Shee-it, boss.

SISSY: Missy, hush up yo' mouf an' do yo' work 'fore you gets us bofe in trouble.

MISSY: We cain't be no wuss off dan we is, de way ah sees it, so might jes' as well speak mag min'.

CONSTANTINE: (*Rising abruptly*) What's the matter, my good woman? Why are you so hostile?

MISSY: (*Hostile*) Why am ah so wut?

CONSTANTINE: Aren't you satisfied?

MISSY: Satisfied wid wut?

CONSTANTINE: With your lot.

SISSY: Wid our wut?

MISSY: Wid our lot. Dat means is we satisfied wid wut we got.

SISSY: (*Quickly*) Oh, yassah, boss. Ah is satisfied wid mah lot.

MISSY: Wut yo' got, woman, dat yo' is satisfied wid?

SISSY: Ah got a lot.

MISSY: You got shit.

SISSY: Why no, Missy. Ah got nine chillun, foh husbands and three fryin' pans.

MISSY: Thas shit!

CONSTANTINE: (*To* SISSY) Your friend sounds like a revolutionary, Madam.

SISSY: Oh, nossuh. She jest a pickinniny lak mah sef.

MISSY: Ah ain' no pickinniny, yo' pickininny.

CONSTANTINE: (*To* MISSY) That's all right, my good woman. I understand your hostility.

MISSY: Take yo' han' off'n mag shoulder, white boy!

SISSY: Oh, Mercy, Missy...

CONSTANTINE: But you see, my good woman, it is necessary in this life to rise above our circumstances.

MISSY: Mista, Ah ain' got no circumstances, an' if'n Ah had Ah'd sell 'em. But wut Ah got? Ah got plen'y o' nothin', thas wut Ah got.

SISSY: Thet ain' true, Missy. You got twelve chillun, seven husban's an' foh fryin' pans.

MISSY: Set yo' mouf' wid yo' fryin' pans. We is talkin' about wut goes inta da fryin' pans. An' at de moment dis government official millionaire is givin' us hawg shit to put in ours.

(CONSTANTINE *moves angrily away.*)

SISSY: Oooo Lawd, Missy, you gonna git us locked up fo' sho'.

MISSY: He can't lock us up. He ain't such a big number. He ain' de boss aroun' dis government. He jes' anudder piece o' hawg shit wid a little pineapple glaze.

(CONSTANTINE *picks up the microphone and speaks into it with great self importance.*)

CONSTANTINE: A message to His Holy Reverence, the Archbishop of Capistrano. (*He clears his throat and glances at the two women, who are now silent.*) I am in possession of the valuable information concerning the whereabouts of their majesties, the king and queen.

SISSY: Oooooo, Missy, wut'd Ah tell you?

CONSTANTINE: More details to follow. End of message. (*He rises importantly.*) If I weren't so busy with matters of State, ladies, you would both find yourselves under arrest for insulting a government official. (*To* MISSY, *who is stuffing papers into a wastebasket.*) What are you doing? Weren't you given strict orders not to throw out any papers from this office? Now get to work. (*He exits through the drapes.*)

(*She dumps the papers from the basket onto the floor.* SISSY *is in the corner with her mop and pail.*)

SISSY: Was dis here? All over de floor. Ah mus' say, dese high government official millionaires is a bunch o' pigs. (*She picks up a slip of paper gingerly between two fingers.*) Do we needs to save it, accordin' to de strict orders?

MISSY: No lessen it got writin' on it.

SISSY: Yas, it got writin' on it. Looks like writin'. (*Reading slowly*) De hidin' place o' de king and queen is as follas: Yas, it got writin' on it.

MISSY: Give dat here.

SISSY: Wut?

MISSY: Give dat here, ah said! (*She snatches the paper from* SISSY)

SISSY: Wut you doin', Missy? Wut you want wid dat smelly piece o' vomit paper?

MISSY: Vomit paper mah ass. Do you knows what dis is, Sissy? Dis here is a piece of vallable info'mation. Dis here is de hidin' place o' de king an' queen.

SISSY: So wut?

MISSY: Don' you read de newspapers, you dumb shee-it? Don' you know dat de newspapers is jes' dyin' t'know where de king an' queen is at? Dey is always talkin' about where's de king? Where's de queen? Where's dey hidin' out?

SISSY: Ohhh. So now we kin tell 'em, is dat it?

MISSY: Fo' a price, we kin tell 'em.

SISSY: You mean de newspapers wud buy dat smelly piece o' vomit paper?

MISSY: Bet yo' ass dey wud. We is gonna git at least five dollas fo' dis piece of vallable info'mation, seein' as de newspapers is so interested in de whereabouts o' de peoples in question.

SISSY: Five dollas? Dey wud pay five dollas fo' dat?

MISSY: Sure as shit dey wud! Don' you realize wut we got here, Sisy? Dis piece o' vomit paper come right outa da belly o' de horses mouf. Come on, Sister. Pick up yo' bucket an' les go.

(*They exit. As the lights fade to dim we hear the strains of* Loch Lommond *and the singing of birds.*)

(KING ARNOLD *enters, dancing across the stage with a bucket of birdseed, his crown askew and a sappy little smile on his face. He glides across the stage flinging the birdseed into the air and disappears as the lights come up on:*)

Scene Five

(The roof of a tenement. A wind is blowing. Sounds of the revolution below. Flames from the fire are reflected all around.)

*(*QUEEN NELL, *a tall, energetic blonde, dressed in an elaborate white gown and white royal cape trimmed in white fox, stands looking over the roof tops through a white jeweled telescope.)*

*(*PRINCE PERCY *is seated on the ledge of the roof cleaning a rifle. He is a chunky little ruffian with curly red hair and a snub nose.)*

PRINCE PERCY: See anything?

QUEEN NELL: No' a thing. Where's my h'army, Percy?

PRINCE PERCY: Gone, Mum.

QUEEN NELL: An' the Palace Guard? H'are they gone, too?

PRINCE PERCY: All gone. E'every last one of 'em.

QUEEN NELL: Gore Blimey. H'all that h'activity down there makes me very nervous. H'it ain't safe. Somebody might 'ave seen H'all the palace furniture comin' into this lousy tenement . . .

PRINCE PERCY: Relax, Mum. H'if Pango and 'is children 'ave any suspicion that we're h'in the vicinity, H'I'm quite sure they'd think we're over there at the North h'end in one of those classy neo-Greek Revival 'igh rises, and not 'ere at the South h'end in this rotten place.

QUEEN NELL: H'it is a rotten place, hain't it, Perce? An' my white furniture does look awful in 'ere, don' it?

PRINCE PERCY: Yes, Mum, but our 'eads would look even worse h'on top o' the flagpole.

QUEEN NELL: Gore, you're h'right. An' that's just where our 'eads'll be h'if Pango finds us. We're sittin' ducks, that's wot we h'are.

PRINCE PERCY: Calm down, Mum. Count Josef will 'ave the h'entire h'affair h'under control h'in a very short time. Pango an' 'is guerrilla children will be squelched, we will return to the palace, an' the king's condition will be 'ushed h'up an forgotten.

QUEEN NELL: Where's 'e at, h'anyways?

PRINCE PERCY: 'Ho?

QUEEN NELL: The king, your father!

PRINCE PERCY: 'E's in the parlour h'eatin' h'away at 'is pie, wher'd'j'a think 'e was?

QUEEN NELL: An' them? Where h'are they h'at?

PRINCE PERCY: 'Ho?

QUEEN NELL: (*Shouting*) The four an' twenty, that's 'ho!

PRINCE PERCY: Oh. Them. Why, they're h'right in there with 'im.

QUEEN NELL: Wot! 'E's got them bloomin' blackbirds in my white parlour droppin' bird shit h'all over my white satin divan h'an' my white fur rug?!

PRINCE PERCY: Eh, Mum, watch you language, eh?

QUEEN NELL: H'I'll bake 'im h'in a pie, that's wot H'I'll do. (*Suddenly*) Wot's 'at? Shhh. Somebuddy is be'ind that door.

PRINCE PERCY: (*Alert*) Stand back. (*Holding his rifle ready, he steps between* NELL *and the roof door.*) (*Shouting at the door.*) I'll blast h'anybody 'ho comes through that door, h'in the name of the Prophet Figs!

QUEEN NELL: (*Trying to avert the rifle.*) Percy, don' be crazy! H'it might be the king, your father!

PRINCE PERCY: I'll blast 'im anyway!

(*He fires a great blast.* HERSCHEL *walks through the door, unharmed, the shot having gone over his head.*)

PRINCE PERCY: Oh, h'it's you.

HERSCHEL: Your Majesty.

QUEEN NELL: 'Ark, wot news?

HERSCHEL: No news.

QUEEN NELL: No news? (*She turns to* PERCY *who is standing with the gun aimed directly at her, playfully. She screams.*) Ooooaawwh!

PRINCE PERCY: Sorry, old girl, h'I didn't realize h'I 'ad it aimed directly at you.

QUEEN NELL: Put h'it h'away, do'ya 'ear? Just put h'it h'away!

HERSCHEL: Your Majesty, Count Josef sent me to tell you to get off the roof. You can be seen by the enemy.

QUEEN NELL: Jesus Gawd! Percy, get h'off that ledge 'afore you gets your 'ead blown off.

(PERCY *ignores her.*)

HERSCHEL: He also told me to tell you to turn off the kitchen light on the second floor.

QUEEN NELL: Kitchen light. Second floor.

HERSCHEL: And to please tell King Arny to stop throwing birdseed out of the window on the people below.

QUEEN NELL: Gawd in 'eaven! H'is that wot 'e's h'up to? 'E'll get h'us all captured yet with 'is bloody lunacy. (*She starts toward the door.*) Thank you, 'Erschel, an' may Gawd 'ave mercy on your soul. (*She exits.*)

HERSCHEL: Thank you, Your Maj . . . (*He stops*) May God have mercy on my soul?

PRINCE PERCY: My mother simply means that 'E didn't show much mercy h'on your body, h'and therfore 'E may 'ave some mercy on your soul. (*He laughs at his own mean joke.*) Sit down, 'Erschel. I want to talk to you.

(*He smiles as he caresses his rifle, which is aimed casually at* HERSCHEL, *who remains standing, petrified.*)

PRINCE PERCY: Sit down, h'I said!

(*Slowly* HERSCHEL *sits.*)

PRINCE PERCY: Well, now, 'Erschel, 'ow are things h'at the Ministry?

HERSCHEL: The same, Your Highness.

PRINCE PERCY: (*Snapping*) The same? What does that mean, the same?

(HERSCHEL *is trembling and cannot speak.*)

PRINCE PERCY: Answer me when h'I speak to you!

HERSCHEL: The same, Your Highness.

PRINCE PERCY: (*Smiles suddenly and lowers the rifle.*) The same. And your cousin Constantine? 'Ow is 'e? Still h'as treacherous h'as ever?

HERSCHEL: Yes, Your Highness.

PRINCE PERCY: What h'about my cousin Count Junior? Still beating 'imself for 'is father's sins?

(HERSCHEL *is silent.* PERCY *sneers.*)

PRINCE PERCY: Never min', you needn't h'answer. (*Then, mocking*) Your loyalty h'an' discretion does you h'onor. But tell me, 'Erschel—tell me h'about the h'Archbishop. H'is 'e still planning to murder the Royal Family? (*Grabbing him suddenly by the throat.*) Or is Count Josef planning to do that? H'is that the plot? Eh? H'is it?

HERSCHEL: I don't know. I swear I don't know. Why do you pick on me?

PRINCE PERCY: Because you're h'a dwarf, h'an' dwarfs h'are supposed to know h'everything. (*He shoves* HERSCHEL *roughly aside.*) No matter. H'I'm not concerned with plots. H'I am much to h'interested h'in the moment. (*He smiles suddenly and playfully aims the rifle into the air.*)

The h'only future h'is in the moment. (*He swings the rifle suddenly around and aims it directly at* HERSCHEL, *then swings it away again.*) The final moment . . . when the future h'is death.

(HERSCHEL *has begun to inch towards the door.* PERCY *turns suddenly.*)

PRINCE PERCY: Where 'a you goin'?

(HERSCHEL *freezes in fear, nervously eyeing the rifle, which is aimed at him.*)

PRINCE PERCY: This may be your final moment.

(*With one swift gesture,* PERCY *raises the gun and fires just over* HERSCHEL's *head.* HERSCHEL *nearly collapses with fright.*)

PRINCE PERCY: H'I've just given you a glimpse of your future. Now thank me h'and get out!

(*He laughs.* HERSCHEL *rushes to the door, stumbling and tripping as the lights fade and come up on:*)

Scene Six

(*The sunparlor.* PHOEBE *is still seated center, on the pot.* CLEMENT *is slumped in a chair, waiting. The music heard at the end of Act One, Scene Three is still playing on the phonograph.*)

PHOEBE: Yes, I'm sure my wicker tea tray is in that burning garbage heap out there. I'm sure somebody resurrected it ten years ago and gave it new life.

(CLEMENT *rises impatiently.*)

PHOEBE: Did you know that I served tea to Admiral Peter Swanson of the Norwegian navy on that tray?

CLEMENT: Yes, yes, you told me about it. Look, Phoebe, can't you hurry it up a bit? You've been sitting on that pot for an eternity.

PHOEBE: You can't rush these things. Physis, naturai, naturalis . . .

CLEMENT: Whatever that means. Look, will it help for me to turn on the water faucet?

PHOEBE: No, I'm not doing that one.

CLEMENT: But you did the other one this morning.

PHOEBE: Well, it's possible to do it twice in one day, isn't it?

(*He flings himself wildly into the chair again.*)

PHOEBE: Are you sure I told you about Admiral Swanson and the tea tray?

CLEMENT: Yes, I'm sure.

PHOEBE: How he picked it up . . .

CLEMENT: . . . and smashed it against the wall in a fit of rage—look! I really can't wait any longer. I am quite late as it is.

PHOEBE: Well, go then! Go! Who's stopping you?!

(*He gets up and collects his things.*)

PHOEBE: Just like you to leave me alone in my old age sitting on a shit pot with the world coming to an end.

(*Resigned, he sits down again, his face tight with exasperation.*)

PHOEBE: Are you quite sure, Clement, that I told you how Admiral Swanson hurled the wicker tea tray against the wall and then turned on me in a rage and struck me hard across the mouth with his open palm?

CLEMENT: Yes, quite sure. And-you-uttered-a-little-cry-and-fell-backwards-into-the-Queen-Anne-chair.

PHOEBE: And he stood there with his face all red and his hand over his eyes muttering—what? What was Admiral Swanson muttering? Come on, come on, what did he mutter?

CLEMENT: Oh-God-forgive-me-what-have-I-done.

PHOEBE: And then he threw himself upon his knees—

CLEMENT: A-very-uncomfortable-position-for-Admiral-Swanson-who-bowed-to-no-one-except-God . . .

PHOEBE: Right!

CLEMENT: And-he-begged-our-forgiveness. Are you finished yet?

PHOEBE: Then he pleaded with me to pardon his abominable behavior and assured me that he'd never struck a woman before and would never . . .

CLEMENT: . . . ever . . .

PHOEBE and CLEMENT: . . . do-it-again.

PHOEBE: There! I'm finished!

CLEMENT: At last! (*He goes quickly to the cupboard and takes a roll of tissue from the shelf.*)

PHOEBE: No, no, I don't need any, thank you.

CLEMENT: What?

PHOEBE: There was nothing. It was all in my head.

(He flings the roll of tissue across the room. PHOEBE *rises now with a bit more energy and returns to the chair at the window.)*

PHOEBE: But it felt wonderful. Almost as good as the real thing.

CLEMENT: Now that you have finished your little game, *may I please leave?*

PHOEBE: Game? What game? Put the pot back. (*She picks up the opera glasses and resumes her watching*) Now! What are they up to out there?

CLEMENT: What game! These little games you play to keep me from ever getting out of this house!

PHOEBE: Oh, my! Look at all that garbage burning.

CLEMENT: Every night it's the same thing. If it isn't one thing it's another.

PHOEBE: Oh, look. They're hoisting something up to the top of the heap.

CLEMENT: You've been doing it every night for twenty years . . .

PHOEBE: Good heavens! It looks like figures . . .

CLEMENT: . . . and every night for twenty years I've been missing my appointments!

PHOEBE: People. They're hoisting people to the top of the garbage pyre, Clement.

CLEMENT: I have missed everything for twenty years because of your little tricks . . .

PHOEBE: Oh, no—effigies—

CLEMENT: . . . your little traps, your games, your ruses!

PHOEBE: The children are burning effigies. Looks like the king, the queen and the prime minister.

CLEMENT: I have missed my life because of you!

PHOEBE: I don't know what you're talking about. You're free to go. You've always been free to go. Ever since *he* left . . .

CLEMENT: What? He? Are we going to bring him into it again?

PHOEBE: You drove him away! He was the only real man I've ever known and you drove him away!

CLEMENT: It was you who drove him away!

PHOEBE: You stood between us. That's why he left.

CLEMENT: He left because he hated you. I was the one he cared about, not you.

PHOEBE: You're the one he hated. He loved me. And now he's gone. Gone forever. Forever and forever and forever.

CLEMENT: And he's never coming back. Never; never, never. So you'd better get used to it.

(*The telephone rings.*)

PHOEBE: (*Suddenly fearful*) Who's that?

CLEMENT: (*Apprehensively*) I don't know. I'm not expecting any calls. Are you?

PHOEBE: No.

(*The telephone rings again.*)

PHOEBE: Maybe it's him. (*She starts for the telephone.*)

CLEMENT: (*Grabbing her arm.*) Don't be a fool! It can't be him. Why would he call after so many years?

PHOEBE: He might.

CLEMENT: He wouldn't.

PHOEBE: That's what you always say!

(*She breaks away. He grabs her again as the telephone rings again.*)

PHOEBE: That phone has been ringing every day for thirty years and every day for thirty years you've been saying it can't be him, he wouldn't call after so many years. Then it rings once more and stops.

CLEMENT: Well, it can't be him. He wouldn't call after so many years.

(*The telephone rings once more and stops. She lunges for it and grabs the receiver.*)

CLEMENT: What do you think you're doing?

PHOEBE: Hello. hello. Hello. Jim? Jim?

(*He tries to wrest the receiver from her. There is a scuffle.*)

CLEMENT: Give that to me. It can't be him.

PHOEBE: Jim? Ellsworth, are you there? (*The scuffle ends.*) There was nobody there. He'd already hung up. It might have been him. I'll never know if it was.

CLEMENT: Of course it wasn't him.

PHOEBE: I'll never know. I'll never know.

CLEMENT: No, you won't. So it's best that you forget about it. I'm going. I'll be back around midnight. Are you all right?

PHOEBE: Yes, yes, I'm all right.

(*He crosses to the door.*)

CLEMENT: Well . . . goodbye.

(*She glances at him and turns away.*)

CLEMENT: Goodbye.

(*She turns back and stares at him.*)

CLEMENT: What's the matter? What are you staring at?

(*She continues to stare at him in silence.*)

CLEMENT: Is something wrong?

(*She then turns disdainfully away.*)

CLEMENT: Well, what's the matter? Obviously something is wrong. What is it? Is it the way I look? Is there something wrong with the way I look?

(*She glances at him again with great disdain.*)

CLEMENT: Well, what is it? What's wrong with the way I look?

PHOEBE: Everything.

CLEMENT: Everything? What do you mean, everything?

PHOEBE: (*Shrugging*) Well, you asked me and I'm telling you.

CLEMENT: But what, specifically? My tie? My trousers? What?

PHOEBE: Everything, everything. It's all put together wrong. It's wrong, wrong, wrong!! You look ridiculous.

(*He has rushed to the mirror and is examining himself anxiously.*)

PHOEBE: If you go out like that you'll be laughed off the street.

CLEMENT: But I don't see . . .

PHOEBE: You don't see! That's the trouble! You don't see yourself as others see you!

CLEMENT: But what is it? Do you mean the tie doesn't go with the suit? Is that it? Or perhaps the shirt doesn't go with the tie . . . ?

PHOEBE: Nothing goes with anything and everything is all wrong! Wrong, wrong, . . .

CLEMENT: All right! You've said that! It's wrong. Now what shall I do to make it right?!

PHOEBE: (*Shrugs*) Why ask me? What do I know?

CLEMENT: (*Angrily and impatiently begins to strip his clothing off.*) You know! You know! You know exactly what's wrong but you're just not telling! (*Wildly flinging his clothes about.*) I'm already half-an-hour late as it is . . .

PHOEBE: Well, it isn't my fault that you don't know how to dress.

CLEMENT: And I shall probably miss it altogether . . . again!

PHOEBE: You never did know how to dress.

CLEMENT: Again and again and again and again! Every night for thirty years I have missed getting out of here. You couldn't have said something earlier, could you?

PHOEBE: You didn't ask.

CLEMENT: For thirty years I have not spoken to nor set eyes on another human being and probably never shall for another thirty years. And I haven't had any exercise since the day the elevator broke down and I had to walk up fifteen flights from the laundry room.

PHOEBE: And then you forgot the laundry.

CLEMENT: You'll never forgive me for that, will you?

PHOEBE: And you never went back to get it!

CLEMENT: If you think I was going to trot down fifteen flights and up again just to collect a bag of your old bloomers . . .

PHOEBE: (*Angrily banging her cane.*) But the elevator's been fixed for fifteen years and the laundry is still down there!

CLEMENT: Let it rot! (*He has stripped down to his shorts and undershirt.*) Now! What shall I wear? Time is running out!

PHOEBE: (*After a pause*) The green suit.

CLEMENT: (*His face falls.*) The green suit?

PHOEBE: Yes. The green suit.

CLEMENT: You mean . . . the green *velvet* suit?

PHOEBE: What other green suit do we have?

CLEMENT: But . . . that would be ridiculous.

PHOEBE: No, it would not. It would be the height of chic.

CLEMENT: But I don't think it will even fit me anymore.

PHOEBE: Nonsense. Your figger hasn't changed since you were eighteen.

CLEMENT: (*Flattered, but still uncertain.*) Well . . .

PHOEBE: The green velvet suit is the epitome of elegance. If you wear it you will be superb.

CLEMENT: (*Pleased*) Will I really?

PHOEBE: Yes. When I see you in the green velvet suit it makes me want to sing.

CLEMENT: (*Very pleased*) Does it?

PHOEBE: Yes. You are exquisite in the green velvet suit. And I am quite sure that if you wear it tonight your appointment will burst into song at sight of you and fall instantly in love.

CLEMENT: (*Extremely pleased*) Will he really?

PHOEBE: (*Catching him out*) He?

CLEMENT: I mean she.

PHOEBE: (*Trapping him*) You said he.

CLEMENT: I meant she.

(*Pause*)

PHOEBE: (*To herself*) He. He.

CLEMENT: So you really think . . .

PHOEBE: You're going to meet *him*, aren't you?!

CLEMENT: What? No. I mean . . . don't be ridiculous . . .

PHOEBE: It's *him* you're going to see, isn't it?!

CLEMENT: Whatever gave you that idea? Why would I be seeing him after thirty years? I don't even know where he is.

(*There is a pause. She laughs smugly.*)

CLEMENT: So you really think the green velvet suit would be . . .

PHOEBE: Yes.

CLEMENT: You're sure?

PHOEBE: I am very sure.

CLEMENT: Well . . . I must admit . . . I am . . . not so sure.

PHOEBE: But sure is as sure does.

CLEMENT: That's true, isn't it? Yes, of course. You're right. Sure is as sure does. You're right. I'll do it. (*He disappears behind the screen.*) I hope the trousers fit.

PHOEBE: If they don't we'll think of something. (*She rises now and looks slowly around the room.*)

CLEMENT: Yes, but what? I don't have a pair of trousers that would match.

(PHOEBE *begins to move slowly around the room collecting his clothing. The noise ouside increases and the stage again becomes flooded with flaring light.*)

PHOEBE: Where are you going to meet him?

CLEMENT: Under the clock tower at the south end of the park.

(PHOEBE *laughs quietly to herself.*)

CLEMENT: This jacket seems to fit all right . . . (*He breaks off abruptly and slowly raises his head so that he appears over the top of the screen. His face is extremely somber.*) What are you doing?

PHOEBE: Just collecting your things. If you bring your friend home tonight to meet mother, you wouldn't want her to think I kept a messy house now, would you?

(*She stops and looks directly at him for a moment, then resumes her activities.*)

PHOEBE: Why don't you come out and show mother how you look?

(*He pauses, then appears from behind the screen dressed in the top half of an elegant 17th Century green velvet suit. The trousers and ruff are slung over his arm.*)

PHOEBE: Splendid. Magificent.

(*Pause. He remains quite still.*)

PHOEBE: Why don't you look at yourself in the mirror?

(*He obeys.*)

PHOEBE: Now put the trousers on and you'll be all set to go.

(*Slowly she moves towards the screen. He turns abruptly just as she disappears behind it. There is an apprehension about him that reflects an awareness that she is up to something. He turns his attention to the mirror again and begins to put on the trousers.*)

CLEMENT: I'm not sure . . . they'll fit.

(*The lights dim and cross-fade from the sunparlor and come up on:*)

Scene Seven

(*The Queen's white parlour, which is situated just below the roof. Bird music.*)

(*As the lights come up, KING ARNY is seen in the room flinging birdseed into the air and out of the window. QUEEN NELL is heard shouting, off.*)

QUEEN NELL: (*Off*) Arnold! Arnold!

KING ARNY: Oh, Gawd. 'Ere she comes.

QUEEN NELL: (*Off*) Where h'are you, h'Arnold?

KING ARNY: We're goin' to get 'ell again. Go on, shoo, shoo. Get h'out. Quick, 'afore she wrings your li'ule necks. Go on, shoo, shoo.

(QUEEN NELL *enters, in a rage.*)

QUEEN NELL: 'Ow many times 'ave h'I told you not to bring those bloomin' li'ule bastards inta my white parlor?

KING ARNY: Please, Nell, you're frightenin' the poor li'ule fings.

QUEEN NELL: H'I'll choke the livin' daylights out o'em.

KING ARNY: Nell, please, don' kill 'em. Leave the li'ule creat'iors h'alone, Nell. They's on'y poor li'ule fings wot din't mean no 'arm.

QUEEN NELL: Look h'at this room! Bird droppin's h'all over the place!

KING ARNY: H'I'll wipe h'it up, Nell. H'I swear H'I'll wipe h'it all up.

QUEEN NELL: An' the bloody fings 'ave h'already begun to mult-i-ply! There was on'y four an' twenty when they first come outa that pie, h'an' now look! They's six h'an' thirty, seven h'an' forty—Gawd on'y knows 'ow many of these bummy birds'll be followin' h'us h'aroun' for the h'rest of h'eternity!

KING ARNY: You're just h'upset, Nell, that's h'all. You're h'upset because we've lost the mortgage h'on the kingdom, so to speak. But you mustn't takt h'it out on my frien's, Nell. These li'ule blackbirds is my frien's. H'an' besides, wot h'if they do leave their droppin's h'all over the place? We'll be out of h'it all soon, anyways, so let the blackbirds do wot they will an' leave the new regime to clean h'up the bird shit, that's wot I say.

QUEEN NELL: Oh, that's wot you say, h'is't? Ready to give h'it all h'up, just like that! Well 'ho gives h'a damn wot you 'ave to say, you batty old blister, with h'all your plugs gone 'aywire h'in your h'upper story you don' 'ave much to worry h'about, do ya? You've h'already lost your 'ead! But wot h'about Percy h'an' me? We's lucky h'if we gets h'away wif ours!

KING ARNY: Don' worry, Luv, we'll find h'a way. H'old Arny will find h'a way.

QUEEN NELL: The on'y way h'ld Arny h'ever found was 'is way from the stitchin' machine to the crapper h'an' back! You'll find h'a way!

KING ARNY: But maybe h'it's all for the best, Nell, 'ho knows? Sometimes h'I fink we was 'appier 'afor h'all this, back there h'in Soho 'afore we won that bloody Literary Digest Sweepstake wot made h'us king h'an' queen.

QUEEN NELL: Don't gimme that!

KING ARNY: H'an h'I don' fink this h'is h'a very good life for Percy, Nell. 'E's changed. 'E used t'be such h'a studious boy. First h'in 'is class, spoke like h'a gen'l'mun—but 'e's h'always with them guns now. Nell, h'aimin' 'em h'a you h'an' me h'ana' the 'hole world. Tormentin' fings wot h'is smaller than 'imself. H'I fink the power 'as gone to 'is 'ead, Nell, h'an' you knows 'ow dangerous poer c'n be h'if h'it goes to an 'ead wot h'aint't prepared for h'it.

QUEEN NELL: There ain't nothin' worng wif Percy. 'E's a spirited boy, thas h'all.

KING ARNY: But look ha wa' 'e done to your white cat, Nell.

QUEEN NELL: 'E h'ain't done nothin' to my white cat!

KING ARNY: 'E killed it, Nell! 'E killed 'at li'ule white cat h'as sure we're sittin' 'ere.

QUEEN NELL: 'E didn't kill no cat! That cat committed suicide, thas wot h'it did. Jumped h'right h'off the roof because h'it was h'as balmy h'as you!

KING ARNY: H' all right, h'all right, 'ave it your way. H'it committed suicide, then. But h'I still finks we was 'appiar 'afore h'all this.

QUEEN NELL: Don' gimme that smoke! Maybe you was 'appier back here h'in that crummy lousecage of a 'ome, whipstitchin' your life h'away for h'a mouldy twopennce that wouldn't pay for the dynamite hi'it needed ta blow h'it h up! Maybe you was 'appier, but H'I wasn't! H'I wasn't 'appier, d'ay 'ear? H'an that lottery ticket was the one good fing we h'ever 'ad h'on h'ice h'in h'our lives h'an you knows it!

KING ARNY: But wha' did h'it get h'us, Nell? You h'always worryin' h'about gettin' spots h'on your white furniture, h'us h'always h'at h'each h'other h'all the time, an' Percy—

QUEEN NELL: *(Shouting hysterically)*
H'I don' wanna 'ear no more h'about Percy! H'an' my white furniture stays white, d'ay 'ear? No more soot h'an' grime h' of the stinking past!

KING ARNY: Maybe h'it was Gawd wot sent h'us h'all these li'ule blackbirds, Nell. Maybe h'it's h'all too clean h'an' white h'in your 'ead now, so 'E sent h'us these li'ule black creatiors to remind h'us that we're just a couple of Soho Sheenies wot 'appened to win the Literary Digest h'election sweepstake.

QUEEN NELL: Gawd didn't send h'us no blackbirds! Them blackbirds was put h'in that pie for h'a reason, h'an' hoever the traitor h'is wot done h'it know'd h'exactly wot 'e was doin'. H'if h'it wasn't for them blackbirds we'd still be h'in charge h'aroun' 'ere. H'it was them blackbirds wot flaked you h'out h'an' you knows it!

KING ARNY: But wot was h'I ta-do? H'anybody would've flaked out, Nell. That was such h'a sight ta set 'afore h'a king.

QUEEN NELL: Yew gimme h'a pain. Sometimes h'I fink you put them in 'ere yourself because yew jus' don wan' the h'respon-si-bility.

KING ARNY: Well, h'I still fink we should've taken the cash h'instead o' the crown. Then we could'a gone h'an retired to Loch Lomond for the rest h'of h'our days, nice h'an' peaceful.

QUEEN NELL: Nice h'an' peaceful! Nice h'an' peaceful! Thas h'all you h'ever wanted was nice h'an' peaceful. H'an' the one time we gets somethin' h'in h'our lives which h'is h'important h'an' h'excitin', you go h'an' blow h'a gaffer h'on the 'hole fing!

KING ARNY: H'I've h'always dreamed h'of goin' ta Loch Lomond. H'ever sincle H'I was h'a li'ule kid. Some'ow there h'ain't nothin' on this h'earth which h'is more betiful to my mind than Loch Lomond.

QUEEN NELL: Oh, you gimme h'a pain wif your bloody Loch Lomond! H'if you wants ta go ta Loch Lomond, take your bloomin' blackbirds h'an' go! H'I'll take Percy h'an' 'ook myself h'up wif the h'International Set, thas wot h'I'll do.

KING ARNY: Wot h'International Set h'is that?

QUEEN NELL: Which d'ay fink? The h'International Set h'of dispossessed kings h'an' queens wot 'angs out h'in the gamblin' casinos h'all h'over the world.

KING ARNY: Gore blimey, H'i bet they got h'a bit o' birdshit drippin' offa them.

QUEEN NELL: Maybe h'I'll even 'ook myself h'up wif the king o' Spain, 'ho knows? H'after h'all—H'I'm a queen, h'an' h'I ain't done yet!

(A loud rifle shot. QUEEN NELL is struck before she knows it and goes flying across the room. KING ARNY rises, turns. Another shot rings out and he flies across the room and falls beside NELL.)

(After a moment, the strains of "Loch Lomond" are heard and PRINCE PERCY enters carrying his rifle in one hand and a cassette machine in the other. He glances calmly around, places the cassette on the table, and leaves as the lights fade.)

End of Act One

Act Two

Scene One

(COUNT JOSEF's *private chamber. Flute music is heard, off: a selection from Mozart.* COUNT JOSEF *is seated in an armchair. He wears a lounging jacket and is smoking a pipe.* HERSCHEL *is occupied at a side table pouring brandy into a glass which he places on a small silver tray with coffee. He then serves this to* COUNT JOSEF.)

COUNT JOSEF: Thank you, Herschel.

(HERSCHEL *clears plates from the small table.*)

When did he begin working on the Mozart?

HERSCHEL: Only a few weeks ago, Your Excellency.

(COUNT JOSEF *listens in silence to the music. There is a sudden loud explosion from without, followed by a great flare of red light and the sound of children cheering.*)

COUNT JOSEF: Close the window, Herschel.

(HERSCHEL *climbs on the window sill. The flute music stops suddenly, and from offstage we hear* COUNT JUNIOR's *voice, wailing loudly.*)

COUNT JUNIOR: (*Off*) Cast upon thee . . . hunnnnngg . . . Thou art my God from my mother's belly . . . hunnnnnhhhhg . . . huuuunnnng . . .

(COUNT JOSEF *rises impatiently.*)

COUNT JOSEF: Go to him, Herschel. Never mind the window.

(HERSCHEL *climbs down and exits quickly.* COUNT JOSEF *crosses to the window, closes it and stands looking out.*)

COUNT JUNIOR: (*Off*) I am a worm and no man . . . hummmnnnnng . . . (COUNT JOSEF *leaves the window and moves impatiently to the statue.*) Thou hast brought me into the dust of death . . . hunnnnnmmggg . . . (COUNT JOSEF *moves restlessly to the chair and sits. Another loud explosion, from without, flares of red light.*) Beloved only in the sight of my mother . . . hunnnggg . . . hunnngg . . .

(*There is a sudden silence.*)

COUNT JOSEF: Why those phrases? Why constantly those same phrases? (*He waits and listens. In a moment the flute music begins again.*) Yes, Elizabeth. You are taking your revenge through him. (*He sits for a moment, then rises and goes to the side table where he pours another brandy. He stands looking up at the door at the top of the flight of stone steps. After a moment he moves resolutely to the table, opens a drawer from which he removes a large ring of keys. He locks the entrance door to the room and turns out the light. The room is now in dim shadows with only the red flares from without illuminating the area. He now lights a taper and starts up the stone steps to the tower door. He pauses for a moment, then unlocks it and pushes it open and waits. Then:)* Elizabeth ... Elizabeth ...

(He waits another moment, then, leaving the door ajar, moves down the stone steps and sits in the chair, waiting.)

*(*Elizabeth *appears from the dark room above. She is dressed in white. Her long hair is grey at the temples, her eyes enormous in her sunken face—a beautiful face with the soft, yet penetrating look of the ascetic. Her eyes are not, however, without a glint of humor. After a moment, she speaks.)*

Countess Elizabeth: You called me, Josef?

(He remains seated with his back to her.)

Count Josef: *(Barely a whisper)*

Is that you, Elizabeth?

(She smiles to herself. He now rises and turns.)

Elizabeth.

(He moves towards the steps, but she stops his approach with a gesture.)

Countess Elizabeth: You mustn't touch me, Josef, or I shall crumble.

(He stops.)

Why did you call me, Josef? Why don't you let me rest, let me die in peace ... ?

Count Josef: If I had wanted you to die I would have let them kill you.

Countess Elizabeth: *(More than a slight touch of irony.)* Ah, yes, that's right. You rescued me from the dungeon in the dead of night—

Count Josef: *(Turning aside)* Please—

(Slight pause)

Countess Elizabeth: What do you want from me, Josef?

Count Josef: Your forgiveness.

Countess Elizabeth: After all these years—?

Count Josef: I have no peace—

Countess Elizabeth: My forgiveness?

Count Josef: I cannot rest.

Countess Elizabeth: Absolution.

Count Josef: Call it what you like—

COUNTESS ELIZABETH: Redemption.

COUNT JOSEF: I am tormented, Elizabeth.

COUNTESS ELIZABETH: By your guilt?

COUNT JOSEF: You were the keeper of my vision, the guardian of my soul.

COUNTESS ELIZABETH: And your conscience, yes. Those were my roles. But you betrayed me, Josep—short-changed me, as it were.

COUNT JOSEF: What do you want me to do, fall on my knees—

COUNTESS ELIZABETH: No, no spare me that.

COUNT JOSEF: Please, Elizabeth. I must shake off this yoke of blame for my unpardonable trangressions—

COUNTESS ELIZABETH: Then what you are saying is that you need me again.

COUNT JOSEF: Yes! Oh, my dearest, yes!

COUNTESS ELIZABETH: For your own peace of mind.

COUNT JOSEF: Yes! *(He simply does not understand.)*

COUNTESS ELIZABETH: For the sake of your sanity.

COUNT JOSEF: Yes!

(She laughs lightly, not unkindly. Then, sadly:)

COUNTESS ELIZABETH: Poor Josef. You still don't understand, do you? Still as dense as ever.

(He looks at her, bewildered.)

I am no longer your conscience, Josef. In the solitude of my imprisonment I learned that I am more than that. Much more. There is your conscience—*(She gestures at the statue.)* You have buried it in cement and stone, locked it away in a marble image, hidden it and forgotten it in the secret womb of a stone idol. *(Then, with heavy sarcasm.)* What ishe, another one of your trumped up martyrs?

COUNT JOSEF: *(Turning away, to hide his guilt.)* History, Elizabeth. I was caught in the web of history. But we must heal these wounds inflicted by fate.

COUNTESS ELIZABETH: Ah, history—so now you are a victim of history. I thought you were a maker of it.

COUNT JOSEF: I am a politician, Elizabeth . . . !

COUNTESS ELIZABETH: Then you are both victim and maker, in which case you are a victim of your own making.

COUNT JOSEF: *(Desperately)* Don't joke, Elizabeth, please . . . !

COUNTESS ELIZABETH: Why not? Is a dead woman not supposed to have a sence of humor? God knows the living haven't got much of one left. *(Slight pause)* Don't speak to me about vision and the soul—*(She turns to him)* Could your vision, as you call it, find no better place to come to rest than in the likes of that? *(She gestures at the statue again.)* And your soul—could it find no better place to fly than back to the pagan gods for comfort? Pango, indeed!

COUNT JOSEF: *Don't mock me! I am standing before you with my world falling apart—*

COUNTESS ELIZABETH: Your world! I don't give a damn about your world! I am no longer in the service of your world! When you betrayed me you forfeited everything—your vision, your soul, your conscience!

(He turns away.)

And you *became* a politician! One of the woodpeckers on the world tree of *history*! One of the worms who never die and who return eternally from the depths of hell to feast upon the future, having successfully mutilated the past!

COUNT JOSEF: Please . . .

COUNTESS ELIZABETH: You renounced me, Josef, to save yourself—locked me away, hid me and forgot me. But I am not made of stone, Josef, and the secrets of my womb will never be yours to have ever again. And I will never again give you sons in your own image to sacrifice to these mad gods of yours.

COUNT JOSEF: I didn't know you oculd be so cruel.

COUNTESS ELIZABETH: Bright. I am bright. In the darkness of my tomb I became very bright.

COUNT JOSEF: You will not forgive me . . . ?

COUNTESS ELIZABETH: Only dull women and Christian martyrs turn the other cheek, Josef. I am neither.

COUNT JOSEF: The people think of you as a martyr.

COUNTESS ELIZABETH: Well, that has nothing to do with me, does it? The people believe what you tell them. *(Then:)* Could I have a drink?

COUNT JOSEF: A drink?

COUNTESS ELIZABETH: Yes, a drink. If you're gong to invite a martyr back from the dead the least you might do is offer a drink.

COUNT JOSEF: Why yes, yes, of course.

(He crosses to the side table. There is a sudden explosion from without, followed by shouting, drums, war chants and hoots by the childen. Then, from offstage, COUNT JUNIOR.)

COUNT JUNIOR: *(Off)* I am a worm and no man—cast from my mother's belly—huunnnggg—hummmnnnggg—

COUNT JOSEF: Bourbon, wasn't it?

COUNTESS ELIZABETH: Vodka.

COUNT JOSEF: Oh, yes, vodka, of course.

(She moves to the window and stands looking out at the activities below.)

COUNTESS ELIZABETH: Does he exist?

COUNT JOSEF: What?

COUNTESS ELIZABETH: Pango.

COUNT JOSEF: Of course he exists.

COUNTESS ELIZABETH: Have you ever seen him?

COUNT JOSEF: Nobody has. *He hands her the drink.)*

COUNTESS ELIZABETH: Well, perhaps he's some sort of—spontaneous psychic phenomenon—a numinous fantasy, perhaps.

COUNT JOSEF: There you go with your wild talk—Psychic phenomenons, numinous fantasies. You always did read too much.

COUNTESS ELIZABETH: And drink too much.

COUNT JOSEF: *(Slightly offended)* I never objected to your drinking.

COUNTESS ELIZABETH: But you did object to my reading. *(She moves to the table and takes a cigarette from the silver case.)* Is he a saviour, then?

COUNT JOSEF: What?

COUNTESS ELIZABETH: Obviously those childen need a saviour. I thought perhaps you had drummed one up for them in order to avoid a *real* revolution.

COUNT JOSEF: *(Growing more uneasy.)* Don't be absurd.

(Slight pause.)

COUNTESS ELIZABETH: Be careful, Josef. Saviours are crucified. *(The flute music is heard again, off.)* Could I have a bit more vodka in this, please? And not so much ice.

(He takes the glass and moves to the side table. She sits in the armchair now and listens to the flute music.)

COUNTESS ELIZABETH: Is that James playing?

COUNT JOSEF: Yes.

COUNTESS ELIZABETH: I always did like Schumann.

COUNT JOSEF: Schumann? That isn't Schumann, it's Mozart. How on earth could you confuse Schumann—

(She laughs.)

COUNTESS ELIZABETH: Oh, is it? Well, what difference does it make. They're both a part of history.

COUNT JOSEF: No, my dear. They are a part of eternity.

COUNTESS ELIZABETH: You acknowledge the difference? You didn't, twenty years ago. If you hadn't been so busy making history twenty years ago, perhaps I'd still have my head—*(Pausing, then wistfully)*— and the will to leave.

COUNT JOSEF: Leave?

COUNTESS ELIZABETH: Go back to my rock in the middle of the rushing river, where you found me.

COUNT JOSEF: *(Handing her the drink.)* Where *you* found *me*. Shipwrecked, as it were—down by the river— *(He raises his glass.)*

COUNTESS ELIZABETH: *(Raising her glass.)* Yes. Down by the river—

COUNT JOSEF: My little mermaid—*(With sudden passion)* Elizabeth ...!

COUNTESS ELIZABETH: No, no, I told you not to touch me, Josef—

COUNT JOSEF: *(Falling to his knees.)* Please, Elizabeth. If you knew how much I long to take you in my arms and crush you passionately to my breast.

(She rises.)

COUNTESS ELIZABETH: I don't want to be crushed. Passionately or otherwise.The last time you crushed me passionately to your breast, you turned around the very next moment and just as dispassionately had my head removed. I have come to distrust passion on the basis of that event, Josef.

COUNT JOSEF: I did not have your head removed! I saved you from the dungeon!

COUNTESS ELIZABETH: Oh, yes, that's right. You resucued me from the dungeon in the dead of night—that's how it goes, doesn't it?—and brought me here to live with you in the shadows of your existence. *(Evenly)* Is there a difference?

COUNT JOSEF: Elizabeth, please! If it were possible for me to live it all again—

COUNTESS ELIZABETH: As impossible as it would be for me to melt that block of marble, Josef. *(She turns away.)* I'm tired. I'm going back ...

COUNT JOSEF: Wait, please! You have that power. Only you have that power.

COUNTESS ELIZABETH: I? A madwoman? Are you forgetting that I'm mad, and that I, Lady Madness—Countess of the Shadows—am officially dead?

COUNT JOSEF: You have the power to melt that stone, Elizabeth, to free my spirit, my will. Even my will has turned to stone, and like a stone it doesn't have the power to stop its own motion.

(She stops and turns. They look at each other for a moment, then he rushes to her.)

COUNT JOSEF: Elizabeth ... *(They embrace.)*

COUNT JOSEF: Show me the true face of my soul—

COUNTESS ELIZABETH: *(A profound sadness)* Ah, Josef, Josef. I have already done that for you, Josef, but you did not like what you saw. It emerged speaking only in Tongues.

(He releases her slowly. They look at each other for a long moment, then she turns and starts up the stone steps.)

COUNT JOSEF: I love him, Elizabeth. Believe me, I love him.

COUNTESS ELIZABETH: Yes, but do you listen to him?

(COUNT JUNIOR is heard, off.)

COUNT JUNIOR: *(Off)* Cast upon thee ... I was cast ... upon thee ... from my mother's womb ...

COUNT JOSEF: Elizabeth! Do you condemn me to this farce? This joke? When will it end? When will this comedy end!

COUNTESS ELIZABETH: When tragedy begins.

(She exits off into the tower, closing the door behind her. COUNT JOSEF leans against the wall, his face drawn, his eyes wide and staring. Flares of red light from the windows, distant sounds of the revolution increase in volume.)

COUNT JOSEF: Then let it begin! Oh, God! Let the tragedy begin!

(Pause. After a moment the buzzer rings. COUNT JOSEF turns, distracted. The buzzer rings again. He recovers himself with some difficulty, then turns on the light and unlocks the door. CONSTANTINE enters.)

CONSTANTINE: The Joint Chiefs of Staff are here, Your Excellency.

COUNT JOSEF: Ah, yes. Good.

CONSTANTINE: They are wearing disguises, Your Excellency—

COUNT JOSEF: *(Still distracted)* Disguises—?

CONSTANTINE: Saints, martyrs, crippled begars—

COUNT JOSEF: The Joint Chiefs of Staff?

CONSTANTINE: The children have taken to roaming the streets in armed battalions, hiding in buildings and on rooftops with rifles.

COUNT JOSEF: Yes, yes, of course. Show them into the Conference Room. I shall be there presently.

(CONSTANTINE exits.)

COUNT JOSEF: Saints, martyrs and crippled beggars—*(A touch of irony)* Yes, of course. General Hunt, the Prophet. *(He turns to the statue and addressed it somberly.)* Well, my friend. It seems that we have constellated a masquerade of monstrous proportions. The childen are bringing everything into focus. They call us what we are. They insist that we be what we are, even though we may be nothing more than a joke. *(Slight pause)* Perhaps I, too, should appear at this meeting in disguise. Yes, perhaps I should. I may not find the truth in it, but certainly there shall be comedy. And who knows? Comedy, too, may come in disguise and lead me to the truth of my tragedy.

(He exits. After the a moment PRINCE PERCY appears at the window. He opens it quietly and climbs into the room, looking around cautiously. He then darts quickly behind a drape as HERSCHEL enters and begins to straighten the room. PERCY then appears suddenly from behind the drape.)

HERSCHEL: Who's there?

PRINCE PERCY: It is I, Erschel.

HERSCHEL: Your Highness! *(He bows and reaches for PRINCE PERCY's hand.)*

PRINCE PERCY: Never mind h'all that. H'I came to visit with my cousin, Count Junior. Go h'aed and get 'im.

HERSCHEL: But your Highness . . .

PRINCE PERCY: *(Fiercely)* Get 'im!

(HERSCHEL backs off in horror and disappears. PRINCE PERCY looks around the room and sees the statue. He crosses to it with great curiosity.)

PRINCE PERCY: Hello? H'and 'ho are you? H'another h'one of my uncle's h'aberrations? *(He touches the statue. Then, with growing realization.)* Why yes. Yes, h'of course . . . ! *(He bursts out laughing.)* 'Ow stupid h'of we not the 'ave recognized you immediately. Why, h'it's perfect. H'it's divine. H'it's h'exactly wot you h'ought to look like.

(HERSCHEL enters with COUNT JUNIOR.)

COUNT JUNIOR: *(Happy to see* PRINCE PERCY.) Hunnnnggg ... hummm-mmmnnngg ...

PRINCE PERCY: 'Ello, cousin. 'Ow good to see you.

*(*COUNT JUNIOR *is affectionately trying to embrace* PRINCE PERCY.)

COUNT JOSEF: Hunnnng ... huuuummm ... have mercy upon me ... hunnnng ... for I am weak ... hunnnnngg ...

PRINCE PERCY: Yes, yes. That you h'are, cousein.

COUNT JUNIOR: Heal me, O Lord ... hunnnng ... for my bones are vexed ...

PRINCE PERCY: H'and mine eye, like yours, cousin, h'is consumed because h'of grief. H'and like yours, h'it waxeth h'old because h'of h'all mine h'enemies.

COUNT JUNIOR: Hunnnn ... hunnnnnggg ... sore vexed ...

*(*PRINCE PERCY *lifts* COUNT JUNIOR *with one arm and drags him along.)*

PRINCE PERCY: Come h'along now, cousin. Come h'on. We're going to take h'a li'ule trip. H'a li'ule journey. Just the two h'of us.

HERSCHEL: But your Highness, he isn't allowed to leave the premises. *(He blocks their exit.)*

PRINCE PERCY: H'out h'of my way, li'ule man ...

HERSCHEL: You cannot take him! *(He draws his little sword.)*

PRINCE PERCY: Ho! H'and wot 'ave we 'ere? H'a duel, h'is'it?

(He draws a dagger from his belt and with a light tap knocks HERSCHEL's *tiny weapon from his hand. He then kicks him roughly aside and exits with* COUNT JUNIOR, *who is emitting strange wailing sounds.)*

HERSCHEL: Count Josef! Count Josef! Sound the alarm! Count Josef!

*(*CONSTANTINE *enters hurridly.)*

CONSTANTINE: What's the matter with you? Stop your shouting! Count Junior has been kidnapped. We must sound the alarm ... !

*(*CONSTANTINE *grabs* HERSCHEL *around the neck in a deadlock.)*

CONSTANTINE: Kidnapped, you say? By whom, little cousin?

HERSCHEL: Let me go! Count Josef must be ...

CONSTANTINE: By whom?!

HERSCHEL: Prince Percy! Let me go!

*(*CONSTANTINE *releases him.* HERSCHEL *darts toward the door, but* CONSTANTINE *quickly blocks his exit.)*

CONSTANTINE: Where has he taken him?

HERSCHEL: I don't know. Let me pass. Count Josef must be informed.

(CONSTANTINE *draws his little sword.*)

CONSTANTINE: Count Josef shall not be informed. This news is for the Archbishop's ears and his alone.

(HERSCHEL *stops, stunned. He then stoops down slowly and picks up his own little sword. They duel.*)

CONSTANTINE: Ah, you fight well, cousin, for a little man. Arragghhh ... ! (*He runs* HERSCHEL *through.*)

HERSCHEL: (*Staggering and falling*) Not nearly so well as you, cousin ... for a littler one.

(*He dies. The lights fade and come up on:*)

Scene Two

(*The sunparlour. Sounds of explosions; flares of red light; children shouting and chanting.* CLEMENT *is still in front of the mirror, struggling to get into the green velvet trousers. The lights from without illuminate the room even more now, and the appearance of an inferno is more intense.*)

CLEMENT: I can't ... They don't seem to ... Oh, God! I know I shall be late. Damn these trousers. Damn this green velvet suit. Why did I listen to her in the first place? (*Struggling even more.*) Never! ... They'll never ... fit! (*The sound of airplanes is heard overhead.*) What's that? What now? (*He hobbles to the window.*) What ... ?

(*The sound of airplanes grows louder, many squadrons flying directly above.*)

PHOEBE: (*Calling from behind the screen.*)
Did you get the trousers on?

CLEMENT: Phoebe, look! Airplanes. Hundreds of airplanes flying overhead.

PHOEBE: Did you get the trousers on?

CLEMENT: What? No. They don't seem to ... Phoebe! What are those planes?

PHOEBE: It must be the 82nd Airborne.

CLEMENT: The 82nd ... ? What? (*He hobbles back to the window.*)

PHOEBE: They always send in the 82nd Airborne at times like this. Have you got the trousers on?

CLEMENT: (*Confused, his attention divided between the mirror and the window.*) 82nd Airborne. Yes. So it is. No. I can't get them on. They're too tight. I never should have ...

PHOEBE: The 82nd Airborne always arrives in the knick of time.

CLEMENT: Phoebe, they won't go on! What am I going to do?

PHOEBE: *(Shouting over the din.)* Won't go on, you say?

CLEMENT: *(Shouting back)* They won't even go over my knees.

PHOEBE: What are they doing?

CLEMENT: *(Desperately)* They're hanging around my knees.

PHOEBE: The 82nd Airborne.

CLEMENT: What . . . ? Airborne? Oh. *(He stumbles to the window.)* Damn it. I know I shall be late. *(Shouting)* They're jumping. *(Then, to himself.)* I shall probably miss him altogether. Oh, dear God, help me. Wait for me, Jim. Don't leave. I'm coming, I swear, tonight I'm coming.

PHOEBE: What?

CLEMENT: They're jumping. The 82nd Airborne are jumping. Phoebe, what am I going to do? I can't get these trousers on. I'm going to miss my appointment and it's all your fault. You knew they wouldn't fit.

PHOEBE: Jumping, you say? They're jumping?

CLEMENT: Yes, jumping. Hundreds of them. Thousands. Phoebe, please! You said you'd think of something if these trousers didn't fit! Well, they don't fit! Think of something!

PHOEBE: What did you say?

CLEMENT: Help me, Goddamn it, Phoebe! They won't go on!

PHOEBE: Well, try this!

(She hurls the voluminous silk gown over the screen, enwrapping him in it.)

CLEMENT: *(Stunned, holding the gown.)* So that's your game, is it?

(She appears from behind the screen.)

PHOEBE: Yes. That's my game. *(She is dressed in his clothing. In her hands she holds the bonnet, attached to which are the curls. Her own hair is very short and dark, cut in the style of a man's hair. In fact, she is a man.)* You'll need this as well. *(She hands him the bonnett and curls. He accepts it mechanically.)* Is there anything I can get you before I leave? *(She puts on the stiff-brimmed hat.)*

CLEMENT: Take off my clothes.

PHOEBE: *(Putting on the white gloves.)* Under the clock tower, you say?

CLEMENT: Give me back my clothes.

PHOEBE: Well, I shall be there. In your place.

CLEMENT: I'm warning you. Take off my clothes!

PHOEBE: I shall be there to meet him. *My Jim!*

CLEMENT: *(Wildly)* Your Jim!

PHOEBE: For thirty years now you've been planning these secret rendez-vous under the clock tower with him, haven't you?

CLEMENT: Take off my clothes!

PHOEBE: For thirty years you've been deceiving me . . .

CLEMENT: Take off my clothes or I swear I'll . . .

PHOEBE: Your clothes! Your clothes, indeed! Your clothes! These are my clothes! Mine! Stolen from me! Yes, Madame! Stolen! For thirty years you've kept me wrapped in a woman's skin, tied to you, bound to you, imprisoned under your voluminous skirts! Sucked up by your fat, hairy lips into that hungry belly . . .

CLEMENT: Imposter!

PHOEBE: . . . swimming around in the waters of your fetid womb, a mis-shapen hermaphrodite with an eternally embryonic heart which could not beat independently of you!

CLEMENT: Serpent!

PHOEBE: Captured by the arrows of the huntress! Laid low in the woodlands of love under Phoebe's light! Yes, Phoebe! Phoebe! *(He is pointing at* CLEMENT.*)*

CLEMENT: Janus!

PHOEBE: No more! I am free! Phoebus has risen from the dark waters!

CLEMENT: Conjurer!

PHOEBE: My sun is rising and will shine again! *(Pointing accusingly again.)* You have destroyed the trees, Madame! Not the children! You have destroyed the trees by shadowing the sun! This night . . . this inter-minable night . . . your night . . . must end!

*(*PHOEBE *raises the cane, prepared to strike.)*

CLEMENT: *(Shrieking)* Would you strike your mother?!

PHOEBE: As the sun would strike the moon if it o'ershadowed it!

(A heavy blow. CLEMENT *falls to the floor, unconscious.)*

PHOEBE: You're lucky I didn't finish you off for good, you old dragon. Taken away your power for good and all. (PHOEBE *begins to dress* CLE-MENT *in the voluminous gown.)* Eight twenty. I can still make it if I rush. He won't be gone. He'll wait. He'll be there. Wait for me, Jim. Please wait. I'll be there. This time I'll be there. You'll see. I'm finally out of her clutches now, Jim. You and I can be friends now. Get to know each other. The way we should have long ago when I was a child. Football...hunting...fishing...*(He has finished dressing* Clement *and staggers drunkenly to the window and shouts out.)* I'm coming, Jim. I'm coming. I've cut my way out of her burning belly, Jim. I've let the mother's blood run out of me, Jim. I can hold up my bleeding arm to yours and let your man's blood flow into me now, Jim. Hold out your arm! Hold out your arm, Father Jim! Tonight...I am...a man!

(There is a high-pitched supersonic sound which reaches a climax ending in a thunderous crashing of glass, followed by a heavy thud as:)

(The Paratrooper crashes through the ceiling. The lights fade and come up on:)

Scene Three

(A street; Missy *and* Sissy *are standing near a telephone booth.)*

Sissy: You sho' dat newspapa fella said he wud be here at nine, Missy?

Missy: Das wut he said. Stop flappin' aroun' like dat, you makin' me nervous.

Sissy: Wut if'n he don' come? Wut if'n he ain' comin'?

Missy: He comin'. You kin be sho' he comin'. When Ah tole him about dis here vallable piece o' info'mation he done near shee-it right over da phone.

Sissy: Did you tell him we wuz sellin', not givin'?

Missy: Bet yo' ass ah did. O' 'course ah din't discuss price wid him. Ah merely says "Bring a lot o' cash, white boy, ah don' discuss monies over de phone.

Sissy: Oooooooo-E. Wut we gonna do wid all dat monies?

Missy: We is goin' inta bizness, dats wut we is gonna do.

Sissy: Bizness! Ooooo, Missy!

Missy: Fo' our selfs!

Sissy: Amen.

Missy: Puhsonally, o'course, ah allus fancied de antiques bizness, mahself.

Sissy: Antiques bizness! Us? Mercy, Missy. We don' know nuffin' about antiques.

MISSY: Ain' nuffin' to know. Alls ya gotta do is get dere befo' do sanitation department, das all.

(*The phone rings in the booth.*)

MISSY: Shhh. Das him.

SISSY: Who?

MISSY: De newspapa fella, das who!

(*The phone rings again.*)

SISSY: Ain' you gonna answer it?

MISSY: You ain' got da brains you wuz born wif! Don' you remember he say let it ring six times and den answer?!

(*It rings again.*)

MISSY: How many is dat?

SISSY: Ah don' know. Ah wuzn't countin'.

(*It rings again.*)

MISSY: Ah betta answer.

SISSY: (*Hysterically*) But wut if'n it wuzn't six?!

MISSY: (*Stymied*) Ah dunno.

(*The phone rings again.*)

MISSY: Dat mus' be at least six.

SISSY: Ah don' think so. Ah thinks it wuz on'y fo'.

MISSY: Are you sho'?

(*It rings again.*)

MISSY: Sounds mo' like eight.

SISSY: Seven, maybe. But not eight.

MISSY: Seven?! Dat come after six!

(*They wait anxiously. It does not ring again.*)

SISSY: Ah don' think it gonna ring again.

(MISSY *rushes into the booth and picks up the receiver and, frantically:*)

MISSY: Hello. Hello. Hello dere, newspapa fella? Hello? Is you dere, Zap? Hello! (*She hangs the receiver up and comes out of the booth dejectedly.*) He's gone. We missed it. De one big chance in our lifes an' we misses it because o' de number six.

SISSY: (*In tears*) Das a bad number.

Missy: Well, Sissy, ah guesses we don' go inta de antiques biznuss after all. (*She throws the paper away.*)

Sissy: (*Bawling*) Ohhhh, Missy, life is jes' a sleigh ride full o' ups and downs.

(*The telephone rings.*)

Missy: Sweet Jesus! (*She rushes into the booth, then out again.*) Find dat piece o' paper, Sissy, quick! Ah'm sho' it's him.

(Sissy *rushes around looking for the paper.* Missy *picks up the telephone.*)

Missy: Hell? ... Yes, dis here is de party you is referin' to. . . . No, suh! We wuz here! You musta had de wrong number . . .

(Sissy *stands at the booth making wild gestures.*)

Missy: Jes' a minute dere, Mr. Zap. My partner here is tryin' to communicate somethin' to me. (*To* Sissy) You find it?

(Sissy *shakes her head frantically.*)

Missy: Never mind. (*Back into the receiver.*) Everythin' is fine, Mr. Zap. We is expectin' you in a short while, as the sayin' goes. (*She hangs up.*) Gimme a piece o' paper, quick!

Sissy: It flew away!

Missy: Any piece o' paper. Hurry up!

(Sissy *searches through her shopping bag and produces a piece of paper.*)

Missy: *Wut difference do it make? He don' know wut de piece o' paper look like. (She hands* Sissy *a pencil.*) Write it down jes' like it wuz.

Sissy: (*Screaming hysterically*) Ah cain't write! You know ah cain't write!

Missy: (*Snathching the paper and pencil.*) Den give it here.

Sissy: But you cain't write neither!

Missy: Dat don' matter. Ah remembers wut it said. (*Holding the pencil awkwardly, like someone holding one for the first time, she scrawls.*)

Sissy: Wut you doin', Missy? Wut all dem funny scratches and lines and scribblin' you is puttin' down dere? He gonna know dat ain' writin'. He a newspapa man.

Missy: Dis here is known as symbol writin'.

Sissy: Ah don' think we is gonna get away wid it, Missy. You tell him dis here is symbol writin' an' he gonna say "Symbol, shit!"

Missy: Den we tell him it's in code. Dey all understands de code.

SISSY: Wuts de difference between de symbol and de code?

MISSY: De code is for the dumb shits what don' understand de symbol, and de symbol is for the dumb shits what don' understand the code.

SISSY: Den ah think we oughta play it safe an' call it both.

MISSY: Amen! You still got a piece o' brain wukkin' in dat head, sister. We tell dat newspapa fella dat dis here piece o' vallable info'mation is written in de *Symbolic Code*. (*They both laugh.*) If'n he don' un'erstand one, he sure to un'erstan' de udder.

(BARRY ZAP *enters from Upstage. He wears a trenchcoat with collar pulled up, a fedora had drawn low over his eyes, and he moves furtively, like a character in a spy movie. Upon seeing the two women he assumes a deliberately casual manner and, careful not to make eye contact, moves down to the opposite end of the stage.* MISSY *glances at him, he turns quickly away. Then he glances at her, and she turns quickly away.*)

MISSY: Dat's him. Don' turn aroun'. Look de udder way.

SISSY: (*Whispering*) Why?

MISSY: Because dats de way dese things is done.

(BARRY ZAP *begins to whistle and moves around with his hands in his pockets, casually looking up in the air.*)

SISSY: Wuts goin' on now? Why don' you talk to him?

MISSY: Becase we is involved here in a very heavy undercover number. We gotta play it de way he deals it, an' he's dealin' it slow.

SISSY: Ooooooo-Eeeeee!

(BARRY *begins to dance, still with hands in pockets and eyes in the air.*)

SISSY: Wut's he doin' now?

MISSY: Looks like he wants to do a little waltzin' aroun' befo' we gets down to our negotiatin'.

SISSY: Oh, Lordy.

MISSY: Here ah go.

(*She begins to waltz and hum now, moving slowly in* ZAP's *direction. He starts to waltz toward her and they meet center, still avoiding eye contact.*)

BARRY ZAP: Are you . . . uh . . .

MISSY: Das right.

BARRY ZAP: You . . . uh . . . got the . . . uh . . . information?

MISSY: Bet yo' ass ah got it, mister.

BARRY ZAP: How much?

Missy: Five.

Barry Zap: (*He stops waltzing.*) Five? That's pretty steep, don't you think?

Missy: Das our price, white boy. Take it or leave it.

Barry Zap: Okay. Let's have the paper.

Missy: Uh-uh. Not 'til after you gives us de five dollas.

Barry Zap: Five doll . . . ? Uh . . . certainly. Of course. Five dollars. Five dollars coming up. (*Takes out his wallet eagerly.*) Five dollars coming right up. (*Flipping through his roll of bills.*) I . . . uh . . . don't think I have anything quite that . . . uh . . . Do you by chance have change of a C note?

Missy: A C note? (*Pause. She gets the picture.*) Give it here. (*He hands her the bill, which she puts in her bosom.*)

Barry Zap: Well, where's the change?

Missy: No change. Our price jes' went up.

Barry Zap: But that's . . . that's . . . you can't change the agreement right smack in the middle of the transaction.

Missy: WHO SEZ AH CAN'T! . . .

Barry Zap: But that's like changing the rules in the middle of the game.

Missy: We ain't changin' the rules, mister, we is learnin' dem.

Sissy: A-men!

Barry Zap: Alright. A C note. I'm . . . I'm glad to let you have it.

Missy: Oh, hear dat, Sissy? He is glad to let us have it. Dis white boy has really got aheart of gold. He is glad to let us have it. (*Turning on him.*) You is glad to let us have it because we's got it!

Sissy: A-men!

Barry Zap: All right, all right!

Missy: You is glad to let us have it because if you wuz in our place, white boy, you'd ask ten times wut we is askin'. So shet yoh mouf an' count yo' blessins, 'cause you is still ahead o' the game. Fo' de time bein', dat is.

Barry Zap: (*Mopping his brow nervously.*) All right, all right. You've made your point. Now where's the paper? Time is important. The whole revolution is at stake.

Missy: (*Cackling with laughter.*) Revolution. You hear dat, Sissy?

(Sissy *begins to cackle with laughter.*)

Missy: What revolution you talkin' about, white boy? De one in yo' head or de *real* one? You mean dat barn fire where doe's lily white chillun is roastin' their marshmellas? Dat what you mean?

(They both laugh hysterically.)

Missy: Das wut he mean, Sissy. He mean all dem little ghosties down dere wut is doin' de revolution number in de park—all dem little fade-out space freaks wut don't know shit from shinola. (*She stops laughing. Her tone changes.*) Here's de paper. Wipe yo' ass wid it.

(Barry *grabs the paper. He looks at it in confusion, turns it upside down, looks at* Missy *and* Sissy, *who are grim-faced.*)

Barry Zap: What's this?

Missy: Dat is wut is known as de SYMBOLIC CODE.

Barry   Zap: (*Growing   furious.*)   Symbolic . . . symbolic . . . Symbolic shit!

Sissy: (*Aside to* Missy) Wut'd ah tell ya?

Barry Zap: What is this? Come kind of a knockdown? Some kind of a high-grade hype? Now you listen to me, you pair of slum hustlers—don't try to nutroll me, understand? I'm not some wet-behind-the-ears-cup-reporter-from-some-donkey-town-in-the-hinterlands! I'm Barry Zap! Responsible to millions of readers, understand? And when I write a story I give it to the public the way it is, understand?

Missy: Ain' nobody tryin' to pigeon-pluck you, Mister. You got it jes' the way it is. Ain' Mah fault you don' un'er'stan' de symbolic code. Ain' Mah fault you learn nothin' in dem bullshit schools up dere in boola-boola land.

Barry Zap: What am I going to do with this! How am I going to tell the public what this is all about!

Missy: Das easy. You jes' do wut you been doin' fo' as long as you been doin' it—When you don' un'er'stan' somethin', you jes' make somethin' up. Ain' dat wut you newspapa fellas does alla time?

Sissy: A-men!

Missy: Jes' cain't admit dat dey don' know shit. (*They bothe cackle with laughter.*) You know de trouble wif you, Mister? You ain' humble in de presence o' de Lawd.

Sissy: A-men!

Missy: Dat dere piece o' papa in yo' han's is de han'writin' o' de Lawd. You wanna know wut it mean? Well, all you gotta do is take de time to axe Him. An' He tell ya. He tell ya. Jes' axe de Lawd. Get down on yo' knees an' axe de Lawd . . . !

SISSY: A-men, Sister!

(*They go into a wild Holy Roller number.*)

MISSY: You wan' de trufe? On yo' knees if'n you wan' de trufe. On yo' knees if'n you really wants to decipher dat code, dat Symmmmmmmmm-bolic Code! Dat hannnnnd-writin' o' de Lawd. De trufe is found on yo' knees brother . . .

SISSY: On yo' knees. Aaaa-men!

MISSY: You wan' de trufe? Den you gotta go down on yo' knees an' wait fo' it! (*She pushes* BARRY *to his knees.*) Yo' gotta wait on yo' knees an' aaaaaxe de Lawd!

SISSY: Axe de Lawd . . .

MISSY: De trufe don' come wid words alone. No, brother. It come in de Symmmmmmmm-bolic Code . . .

SISSY: Hallelu-ya!

MISSY: Axe de Lawd. Go on, boy. Axe de Lawd. Axe Him to traaaaanslate dat symmmmmmmbolic code. Axe Him. Hear me? Axe Him. Ohhhhhhhh, Lawd!

SISSY: Lawdy-Lawd . . . !

BARRY ZAP: (*Mezmerized, carried into the spirit of it.*) Ohhhh, Lord . . . decipher the code.

MISSY: Das right. (*She takes out a cigar and lights it.*)

BARRY ZAP: Tell me, Oh Lord . . . the truth of this message . . .

MISSY: Right on!

BARRY ZAP: Speak to me . . . Oh, Lord . . .

MISSY: Give it a little more juice, boy. (*Wild Holy Roller*) LET ME HEAR THY VOICE, O LAWD . . . !

SISSY: (*Singing out*) LAWDY!

BARRY ZAP: Let me hear Thy voice . . . !

(*They begin to move slowly off.*)

MISSY: Das right.

SISSY: A-men!

BARRY ZAP: Tell me the truth, Oh Lord. Let me hear Thy voice again . . .

MISSY: (*Exiting*) Das right, boy. You is doin' fine.

BARRY ZAP: ...as I heard it when I was a child. Dear Lord, give me a sign. Send me a vision. Decipher the code, Oh, Lord...!

(*The lights fade on* BARRY ZAP *on his knees and come up on:*)

Scene Five

(*The sun parlor. A huge parachute covers the entire area. As the lights fade up a figure is seen moving under the white silk, struggling to find a way out. In a moment* PHOEBE *appears, still dressed in* CLEMENT'S *clothing.**)

(*He lifts an end of the chute and* SMITHERS, *a young paratrooper, is revealed, lying unconscious on the floor. Beside him there is a large canvas mail sack.*)

CLEMENT: My God! Right through the skylight. (*He kneels down and lifts the boy's head.*) Hello, there. Hello there, young man.

(SMITHERS *groans.* CLEMENT *feels his arms and legs for damage.*)

CLEMENT: Nothing broken.

SMITHERS: (*Dazed*) Ohhhh... what...?

CLEMENT: Easy. Take it easy, young fellow. You'll be all right. Good fall, though, I must say. They really taught you how to land, didn't they?

SMITHERS: Where am I? (*He looks around, dazed.*) Who are you? (*He tries to rise, swaying unsteadily.*) What happened? Where am I? Is this Sing Nang Poi?

(CLEMENT *is confused.*)

CLEMENT: No, no, it isn't. Actually, it's only a rather overpriced apartment in one of dreadful Greek Revival high rises at the north end of St. Cloud.

SMITHERS: St. Cloud? Did you say St. Cloud?

CLEMENT: (*Tentatively*) Yes.

SMITHERS: Yes. yes. That's it. St. Cloud. It's beginning to come back now. St. Cloud. (*He pauses and looks at* CLEMENT *then turns away distractedly.*) We were flying around for what seemed an eternity, looking for Sing Nang Poi.

CLEMENT: Sing Nang Poi? Where is that?

SMITHERS: I don't know. We couldn't find it.

CLEMENT: Ahh.

---

*From this point on PHOEBE shall be called CLEMENT and CLEMENT shall be called PHOEBE.

SMITHERS: We had orders to bomb the shit out of it. But we couldn't find it. Months ... years ... up there in the sky, flying around looking for Sing Nang Poi. (*He pauses again, then wanders off distractedly. Suddenly his hand goes to his head as if he'd just remembered something.*) The navigator went mad! That's right! The navigator—he jumped out of the hatch! He jumped without his chute! Shouting all the way down— "There is no Sing Nang Poi ... !"

(*The clock strikes in the distance.*)

CLEMENT: (*In utter defeat*) Nine o'clock.

SMITHERS: He took it personally, I guess. Took it on himself that he couldn't find it.

CLEMENT: An hour too late.

SMITHERS: That's what the Sergeant said.

CLEMENT: Again.

SMITHERS: Poor devil took it all on himself and that's why he blew his mind and jumped. (*He pauses, remember. Then:*) Poor old Jim.

CLEMENT: Jim? Did you say Jim?

SMITHERS: The navigator.

CLEMENT: He jumped, you say?

SMITHERS: Yes.

CLEMENT: Without his chute?

SMITHERS: Do you hear flute music? I hear flute music. (*Sudden panic.*) Where am I? What ... what are my orders? (*Turning to* CLEMENT. *Slight pause.*) Too late? For what?

CLEMENT: For me.

SMITHERS: Don't say that. It's never too late.

CLEMENT: For you, perhaps. You're young, and you were confirmed before you died.

SMITHERS: Died ... ? Am I dead, then?

CLEMENT: (*Distracted*) What ... ? No, no. You're not dead. If you're dead then I'm dead. If you're dead then we are all dead.

(SMITHERS *turns his attention out the window again.*)

SMITHERS: I still think about Jim. When we got the order to peel off over St. Cloud, I thought I was Jim. And just now when I landed—I swear I thought I was Jim looking for Sing Nang Poi.

CLEMENT: Would you like a drink? You're very shaken.

SMITHERS: Yeh.

(*A stirring under the parachute.* PHOEBE *flails around, trying to get out.*)

PHOEBE: Clement? Where are you, Clement?

(SMITHERS *does not appear to hear. He remains far off into his own thoughts.*)

PHOEBE: What happened, Clement? Why is it so dark? (*She emerges from under the chute.*) Clement? Is that you? Where are my glasses? I can't see a thing.

(CLEMENT *hands her a pair of eyeglasses from his pocket.*)

PHOEBE: These are not my glasses. They're your glasses.

CLEMENT: What difference does it make? Put them on. (*He hands* SMITHERS *the drink.*)

PHOEBE: (*Putting on the eyeglasses.*) Ah, that's better. Where have I been? Asleep?

CLEMENT: Yes. You've been asleep.

PHOEBE: How long did I sleep? It feels like a long time.

CLEMENT: Yes, it was. A very long time.

(PHOEBE *sits in the rocker, adjusting her skirts.* CLEMENT *stands Center between her and* SMITHERS.)

SMITHERS: I was the only one who saw him jump. Everyone else was asleep.

PHOEBE: (*Turns, noticing* SMITHERS *for the first time.*) Who is that?

CLEMENT: His name is Smithers. He's a paratrooper.

(PHOEBE *eyes* CLEMENT *with suspicion.*)

PHOEBE: I hope you didn't tell him that I'm your mother.

CLEMENT: No. No, I didn't (*He remains preoccupied with* SMITHERS, *answering* PHOEBE *perfunctorily.*)

PHOEBE: What's been happening while I slept? Anything interesting?

CLEMENT: Not much. A few wars. Numerous revolutions. A tidal wave took five hundred thousand lives.

PHOEBE: Anything of local interst?

CLEMENT: The Empress of Greece used the public toilet at the Parthenon yesterday.

PHOEBE: (*Very interested*) Oh?

CLEMENT: You can read about it if you like. There was a headline.

(PHOEBE *picks up the newspaper.*)

SMITHERS: It happened just before we got the order to return home.

(CLEMENT *turns his full attention on* SMITHERS, *who remains staring out, remote and distant.*)

SMITHERS: I saw him rush for the hatch and force it open.

PHOEBE: Did you make your appointment all right?

CLEMENT: What . . . ? Oh, yes, yes, I did.

SMITHERS: I caught hold of his legs and grabbed the hook rail as he flung himself over—

PHOEBE: And did you have a nicc time?

CLEMENT: Oh, yes. Yes. Splendid.

SMITHERS: I tried to pull him back in, but the wind was too strong. I couldn't hold him.

PHOEBE: And how is Jim?

CLEMENT: Jim? Oh. Fine. The same.

SMITHERS: (*Turning and looking directly at* CLEMENT.) He committed suicide, didn't he.

(CLEMENT's *face has begun to express some premonitory fear.*)

CLEMENT: What . . . ?

PHOEBE: (*Focused on the newspaper.*) Oh, my—!

CLEMENT: Suicide . . . ?

PHOEBE: That is a nice picture of her, I must say.

(CLEMENT *turns to* PHOEBE, *completely disoriented.*)

SMITHERS: Do you suppose he left a mother?

PHOEBE: The Empress of Greece coming out of the public toilet at the Parthenon. Did you see it?

CLEMENT: Yes, yes—(*He is in a state of slow disintegration. He rubs his forehead and eyes and appears to have difficulty breathing.*)

SMITHERS: Do you know what I heard her say once?

CLEMENT: What . . . ? Who . . . ?

SMITHERS: She would gladly pour my blood onto the battlefield. (*He turns to* CLEMENT, *who is simply staring at him.*) She said it. How d'you think I got those scars all over my body? I got them from the forceps. They had to drag me out with forceps when I heard her say that. Why do you look so surprised? You know the scars I'm talking about. You've seen them. Touched them. Kissed them. Cold nights in the barracks house, eh, Jim? (*He winks at* CLEMENT, *who stands stiffly, in a state of near shock.*) You're not going to deny it now, are you? Your fingers doing a waltz on my back? Oh, man, you got a light touch, I must say. So light, in fact, that I didn't even know it was happening. (*He laughs softly, distantly*) Your head under the blanket, your lips pressed against the crescent moon on my ass. Left cheek, remember? That was your favorite scar—the crescent moon. And man, I sure thought you were gonna skin me alive when I came so fast without any warning. But I just couldn't help it, man. I just went sky high and blasted off like shit through a greased pipe. (*He laughs again, a fond memory.*) Oh, Wow! I sure thought you were gonna put your foot in my ass and kick me outta the crib and send me into the night like a naked snowman. (*He continues to laugh, quietly to himself. They stare at him in disbelief.*)

CLEMENT: (*Nervously reaching for the glass.*) Look here, Smithers—perhaps you oughtn't to drink that—

(SMITHERS *pulls the glass away and with open hostility.*)

SMITHERS: Why not! You afraid I got disconnected wires in my tank? You afraid I might put the blast on you and your hard-legged bitch dog and vomit lead death all over this birdcage?

CLEMENT: (*To calm him*) No, no, please . . . don't get excited . . .

PHOEBE: Clement, I don't like him. Where did you meet him?

SMITHERS: Pour my blood into the battle, will she? (*turning to* PHOEBE) Easy for you to talk about what you'll do with my blood, isn't it? Easy for you to talk . . . !

PHOEBE: Clement! Get him out of here!

SMITHERS: It isn't your blood you're giving away so generously, it's mine! And I'll be damned if you're gonna pledge it away before I'm even out of the womb—

CLEMENT: (Trying to restrain him.) Easy, easy, everything's all right. Calm yourself, my by. It's all right. I'm here. I'm here now.

SMITHERS: (*Whirling on* CLEMENT) You're here now? And where the fuck were you then, you watery-assed weakling! What did you ever do except say yes to her all your life and bring home the bacon so she could scramble us both in her frying pan—two eggs over light, that's what we are, Dad! Soft yellow centers, like father like son!

CLEMENT: Stop it! You're delirious!

SMITHERS: All circus water and cat beer but no spud! Right? Am I right, Dad? Am I right? (*He flings* CLEMENT *roughly against the wall.*) Oh, Christ in heaven! Am I the product of this impotent piss?! What am I doing here? Who sent me here? Jim! Jim! You were right Jim! You were right! *There is no Sing Nang Poi!*

(*Sounds of planes flying overhead in squadrons.* SMITHERS *is alert.*)

SMITHERS: Listen! Listen! (*He pulls a pair of earphones from his jacket.*) Demon One to Satan. Demon One to Satan. Do you hear me, Satan? This is Demon One. What are my instructions, Satan? My position is ten o'clock at seventy-two miles, tracking one, two, zero degrees. No bogey in sight. Do you hear me, Satan? This is Demon One. It doesn't look like I'm gonna make it, Satan. The ignition switch isn't working. I'm gonna have to leave it, Satan. I'm gonna have to blow the canopy!

(*The sounds increase in volume: squadrons of planes, dogfighting, dive bombing, crash diving, all overlapped.*)

SMITHERS: Oh, my God! They're burning! They're burning alive! I hear them screaming! Oh, God! Their flesh is in flames!

(*Silence. Pause.*)

PHOEBE: Clement—what's that sack?

CLEMENT: What . . . ?

PHOEBE: That sack. What is it? Where did it come from?

(*The lights fade slowly as they bend over the sack and come up on:*)

Scene Six

(COUNT JOSEF'S *chamber and, simultaneously, the Conference Room. In a corner of the chamber,* HERSCHEL'S *body is laid out on a funeral bier.* COUNT JOSEF *is standing in front of a mirror, back to the audience, dressed in military fatigues and boots.* CONSTANTINE *is handing him accessories: a gunbelt, a kerchief, etc.*)

(*In the Conference Room, four of the* JOINT CHIEFS OF STAFF *are present, dressed in authentic-looking garbs of martyrs, saints, beggars, and prophets. They wear long, grey beards and long, grey wigs.*)

(*The lights fad up on silence, only the distant crackling of fire. Flames continue to illuminate the stage. There is no movement at all, except between* CONSTANTINE *and* COUNT JOSEF. GENERAL WILLIAMSON, ADMIRAL DUNCAN *and* ADMIRAL MITCHELL *are seated aorund the conference table.* GENERAL BUCKLEY *is standing at the window, staring out.*)

GENERAL WILLIAMSON: What's keeping him? He's been locked in his chamber for an hour now.

ADMIRAL DUNCAN: (*Expressionlessly*) He's dressing.

ADMIRAL MITCHELL: (*As if in a daze*) What on earth for?

(CONSTANTINE *hands* COUNT JOSEF *a wig of wavy brown-gold hair, which he puts on.*)

GENERAL BUCKLEY: (*At the window.*) This silence. I don't understand this silence. What are they doing out there? What are they up to?

ADMIRAL DUNCAN: (*Suddenly rises, restlessly.*) I'm concerned about General Hunt. He should be here by now. I'm sure something's happened to him.

ADMIRAL MITCHELL: Sit down, Robert. There isn't much we can do at the moment.

GENERAL BUCKLEY: (*With more energy now*) I don't understand it. I simply don't understand it. How can it have happened? How?

(*Above,* COUNT JOSEF *now turns from the mirror. His face is disguised in a most uncanny transformation, artfully made up to resemble the beautiful youth in his statue.*)

COUNT JOSEF: Why aren't all the tapers lit?

(CONSTANTINE *quickly removes the one lit taper and lights the other three surrounding the bier, as* COUNT JOSEF *exits from the chamber and reappears on the steps of the Conference Room where he stands for a moment, looking down at the* CHIEFS OF STAFF, *who are seated with their backs to him, quite still. The only movement on stage now is that of* CONSTANTINE *who, upon finishing the lighting of the tapers, pauses for a moment to look into the face of* HERSCHEL. *An expression of genuine terror appears on his face as he backs away and rushes to the door. It is locked. He tugs at it, glancing back at the bier in terror. Unable to open the door, his fear mounting, he runs to the window. It, too, is locked. He begins to cry out, runs back to the door, and, finally, with a loud cry, sinks into a corner, huddled with his knees to his chest and his arms over his head, where he remains for the rest of time, whimpering in fear of the body of his cousin.*)

(*At the moment of* CONSTANTINE'S *final cry the* CHIEFS OF STAFF *turn and see* COUNT JOSEF. *They rise in alarm.*)

COUNT JOSEF: Good evening, gentlemen. It seems that my disguise outdoes you all. (*They glance from one to the other as* COUNT JOSEF *moves down the steps.*)

COUNT JOSEF: Sit down, gentlemen. Where is General Hunt?

GENERAL BUCKLEY: He hasn't arrived yet, Your Excellency—

GENERAL WILLIAMSON: We're very concerned—

COUNT JOSEF: Well, then, General Buckley, would you be good enough to make a preliminary report and bring me up to date as of this moment?

(*They glance at each other again, with the same apprehension.*)

GENERAL BUCKLEY: Yes. Yes, of course. Paragraph One, Section One of our plan was put into action an hour ago over the part at St. Cloud . . .

(*He clears his throat and continues with some difficulty.*) . . . at the height of the . . . revolutionary activities. (*He wipes his brow.*)

COUNT JOSEF: Yes. Go on.

(*Unable to continue,* GENERAL BUCKLEY *returns to the window.*)

GENERAL WILLIAMSON: Unfortunately our paratroopers were unable to surround the park as planned, Your Excellency and . . . (*He stops, unable to continue.*)

ADMIRAL DUNCAN: (*Quickly getting it out.*) The operation was a failure.

(*There is a silence.* COUNT JOSEF *looks from one to the other. They each avert their eyes.*)

COUNT JOSEF: What happened?

(*They glance at each other again, their apprehension now turned to dread. No one can bring himself to answer. Finally:*)

ADMIRAL MITCHELL: They fell into the fire.

(*Another silence.* COUNT JOSEF *face appears suddenly drawn of blood.*)

COUNT JOSEF: Into . . . the fire?

GENERAL WILLIAMSON: Yes, Your Excellency. Every last one. Down to a man.

(COUNT JOSEF *sways slightly, then steadies himself by gripping the edge of the table.*)

COUNT JOSEF: I see. (*He sinks slowly into the chair then, looking up at them, sharply:*) Can you explain how the troopers came to be dispatched directly over the burning garbage heap?

GENERAL BUCKLEY: We think it was the wind, Your Excellency.

COUNT JOSEF: (*With sudden fury*) What do you mean, the wind?! Since when does the wind determine the success or failure of a military venture?

ADMIRAL DUNCAN: The elements, Your Excellency . . .

COUNT JOSEF: Since when have we allowed the elements to dictate our destinies?

ADMIRAL MITCHELL: Nature, Your Excellency . . .

COUNT JOSEF: And since when have we alloed nature to interfere with war!

GENERAL BUCKLEY: I'm sorry, Your Excellency! But the wind—

COUNT JOSEF: The wind, the wind! The wind be damned! Are we to be defeated by the wind? The wind is a madman! The wind is an irrational fool! The wind flits and changes like mercury! (*Pause. he finally collects himself.)* I'm sorry, gentlemen. Of course, The wind. It is quite possible that the wind . . . it has been known to happen before.

(An awkward silence.)

GENERAL WILLIAMSON: *(Finally, venturing)* Why, yes. In nineteen forty two, or was it forty three—the 82nd over Italy . . .

COUNT JOSEF: *(Flaring up again.)* It has been known to happen before! Let it go at that! *(Pause)* When did this occur?

GENERAL BUCKLEY: Barely fifteen minutes ago.

GENERAL WILLIAMSON: We saw the whole thing on the radar screen. Nothing we could do . . .

ADMIRAL DUNCAN: It was horrible . . .

COUNT JOSEF: Was Air Command notified immediately?

GENERAL BUCKLEY: Of course! We tried to make radio contact, but we couldn't get through. We kept meeting with interference.

COUNT JOSEF: What interference?

(They hesitate and glance at each other again. COUNT JOSEF *slams his fist on the table.)*

COUNT JOSEF: What interference?!

GENERAL WILLIAMSON: Flute music, Your Excellency.

COUNT JOSEF: *(As though he had not heard correctly.)* Flute music?

GENERAL BUCKLEY: Yes, Your Excellency. Flute music.

(There is another pause. COUNT JOSEF *turns slowly away from them and sits staring off into the distance of his own thoughts as though they were no longer present.* THE CHIEFS OF STAFF *awkwardly attempt to continue the meeting among themselves.)*

GENERAL WILLIAMSON: I still think my thoery is correct, Robert. The enemy troops were probably all tuned in to a flute concert on their transistor radios at the same time . . .

ADMIRAL DUNCAN: I told you that's absurd.

ADMIRAL MITCHELL: *(Dazed)* Ridiculous.

GENERAL WILLIAMSON: How else can we explain it? It was impossible to intercept that many sound waves of the same frequency, occurring at the same time and in the same place.

GENERAL BUCKLEY: No, no . . .

ADMIRAL DUNCAN: Totally unscientific.

ADMIRAL MITCHELL: Poppycock.

Count Josef: (*In a strange voice*)The wind blows in a thousand different ways, gentlemen . . .

(*They turn to him.*)

Count Josef: . . . and the sound it makes is not unlike the sound of a flute.

(*They are bewildered.*)

Admiral Duncan: Why yes, yes . . . quite so. I've heard that said . . .

General Buckley: Yes. Who was is said that . . . ?

General Williamson: Lao Tzu . . .

(*All: 'Yes, yes,' 'That's right', 'Lao Tzu, of course', 'Art of War'.*)

Count Josef: (*Interrupting*) And may I remind you, gentlemen, that the wind does not shift and change at will, but at the instruction of the gods. (*He rises, somewhat unsteadily.*) Fate too has arrived in disguise. And it is Fate's disguise which outdoes us all. It seems that Pango and his children are on the side of the gods—and the mysterious flutist. This meeting is adjourned. (*He starts towards the steps.*)

General Williamson: But this is only one defeat, Your Excellency.

Count Josef: One defeat, but a prophetic one. The wind has whispered to us, General. It should stir our wisdom. We must therefore suspend all operations until . . . (*His eyes wander off, distractedly.*)

General Williamson: Until what, Your Excellency?

Count Josef: Until we learn to harness the wind. (*He moves slowly up the stairs and exits into his office, where he sits at his desk, the statue beside him.*)

(*Enter, General Hunt, staggering and clutching his side. Blood trickles from the corners of his mouth; his hands are covered with blood, as are his arms and legs.*)

General Hunt: I'm sorry . . . to be so late . . . gentlemen . . .

General Buckley: General Hunt!

(*They rush to him and support him to a chair.*)

General Hunt: . . . but I was overtaken . . . by revolutionary . . . reconnaissance officers . . .

Admiral Duncan: My God, he's bleeding all over . . .

General Hunt: (*Waving it aside.*)These children . . . are evidently in search . . . of prophets . . .

General Williamson: Knife wounds.

General Hunt: . . . and they took me . . . for the real thing

GENERAL BUCKLEY: Don't try to talk, Walter . . .

GENERAL HUNT: They . . . descended upon me . . . and proceeded to pull me off . . . in the direction . . . of St. Cloud . . . kissing my feet . . . touching the hem of my robe . . . salaaming to me . . .

GENERAL WILLIAMSON: There must be something we can do for him . . .

GENERAL HUNT: (*A final burst of energy*) And then, suddenly . . . one of them . . . raised his knife . . .

ADMIRAL DUNCAN: Oh, my God.

GENERAL HUNT: . . . and then all of them . . . (*Growing more weak.*) but I remember . . . my Machiavelli, gentlemen . . . (*Feebly he raises his hand, in which he holds a revolver.*) A wise prophet . . . always carries a weapon . . . beneath his hair shirt.

(*He slumps over and rolls off the chair, dead at their feet.* GENERAL BUCKLEY *kneels down and shakes his head.*)

GENERAL WILLIAMSON: We've got to tell Count Josef.

ADMIRAL DUNCAN: No, no, not now . . .

(ADMIRAL MITCHELL, who has remained seated at the conference table in a daze throughout, looks up:)

ADMIRAL MITCHELL: But, Robert . . . we haven't even told him about his son.

(*The lights fade on them and come up full on* COUNT JOSEF.)

COUNT JOSEF: (*Addressing the statue*) Well, my friend. I am not surprised. I've known it for some time; long before Mercury embarked upon the wind, I knew the wishes of the gods. My holy prophet visited my palatine in an unplayed scene and warned that any attempt to stop your advance would be like holding up my hand to stop a tidal wave from the oceans of heaven.

(*Slight pause*)

COUNT JOSEF: And yet the Airborne was dispatched. (*Pause. Then, with sudden anger.*) Yes! The Airborne was dispatched! Don't be a fool, man! Surely you are not as naive as your child followers! Surely you realize that I must play out my role, uphold the Law in spite of my inner voice. I am responsible to history! Not to God! The Airborne was dispatched and will be again and will again go to their certain destinies in dung and death and fire because I must continue in motion; just as anyone caught by the tail of history must continue in motion in spite of the inner voice which declares that the motions are fruitless; in spite of the inner vision which is capable of isolating the truth from that smokescreen set up by the body politic. (*Turning to the statue again.*) Yes. I am a politician. You are the saviour. Two half-truths tottering on the edge of the cosmos in the subterranean corners of a separated self. Politician, priest. Potentate, holy prophet. How shall we know them? By their words, my savior. By their words. For two thousand years I have shut away the truth under guard of law, separating it from the law of God. And in that very act of separation taken upon myself the entire weight of evil. Would you have me fall to my knees, fall back on my word and ask forgiveness? I? The Body Politic? For two thousand years the Palatine has murdered the Prophet, the Politician has murdered the Priest . . . ! Would you have me cut off at the wrist the hand which holds the leash on this mummery, this monkey-trick farce? No, my saviour! Praise defeat! I am who I am! (*Slight pause. He wavers.*) And yet . . . and yet . . . I . . . who would have been in my highest dreams . . . (*Sudden anguish*) Words! Words! You shall know us by our words! We speak in a dead language. Our words are buried in the shifting sands. You, my saviour, speak in tongues, and your words are written in stone. ((*He covers his eyes with his hand.*) Forgive me . . . Elizabeth. I could have saved you. But I feared you. My Lady Madness, and your son—our son—child of my spirit. Oh, God! (*He falls to his knees.*) What have I done? My vision . . . my soul . . . give it back!

VOICE IN THE DARKNESS: You may 'ave it back, h'Uncle . . .

(*The lights come up on* PRINCE PERCY *in a* PANGO *disguise identical to the one worn by* COUNT JOSEF. *In his arms he carries the body of* COUNT JUNIOR.)

VOICE: . . . for h'a price.

(*He places the dead body on the floor at* COUNT JOSEF's *feet as the lights fade and come up on:*)

Scene Seven

(*The sunparlor.* SMITHERS *is still seated on the floor, down left,* CLEMENT *is bending over the sack, examining the contents.*)

SMITHERS: We were flying high over the waters somewhere in the East. As I floated through the air my body cast a huge shadow on the sea, reflected in the sun.

PHOEBE: What is it?

CLEMENT: A mail sack. It must have come through the skylight.

SMITHERS: When I looked down I saw this enormous shape rise up from the water. It grabbed hold of my shadow and drew me down closer and closer until I felt myself become very small . . .

CLEMENT: These letters . . .

SMITHERS: Then I slipped into the waves and disappeared.

PHOEBE: (*Sensing something fearful.*) What about them?

(CLEMENT *looks at* SMITHERS, *then up at* PHOEBE. *He is trembling.*)

CLEMENT: They're all addressed to us.

SMITHERS: Again I saw my shadow beamed against the sky, reflected by the flames from the fire below. Again something rose up from out of the flames, grabbed hold of my shadow and drew me down closer and closer, until I felt myself become very small . . .

(PHOEBE *stands, holding a letter.*)

PHOEBE: Look Clement—an official announcement of some kind. Look at the seal. (*Slowly she opens it. Her voice is choked and trembling.*) Oh, it's . . . very fine . . . paper, Clement. (*She reads.*) Dear Madame . . . (*She begins to sway into a faint and falls into the rocking chair.* CLEMENT *takes the letter from her.*)

CLEMENT: (*His hand shaking, his voice tremulous.*) Dear Madame . . . It is with deep regret that we inform you that your son— (*He stops, drawing in his breath.*) James P. Snow, Navigator, First Class— (*Continuing, with great difficulty.*)—was lost in action over the Eastern Sea surrounding the island of . . . Sing Nang Poi . . . on September 4, this year of our Lord . . . (*He stops and turns to* SMITHERS.)

SMITHERS: Then I slipped into the flames and disappeared. When I woke up I was here.

CLEMENT: Who are you? Where did you get this sack? Answer me! Who are you?

SMITHERS: (*Snapping to attention and saluting.*) Snow, sir. First Lieutenant James P. Snow. Also known as The Demon Count of Squadron Ten. (*Suddenly alert*) Listen! (*The sound of planes overhead. He puts on the earphones.*) Roger. Demon. This is Demon Count. I hear you, Satan. Over. Demon to Satan. Can you hear me, Satan? What are my instructions, Satan? Demon has sighted the bogies. Do you hear me, Satan? I have sighted the bogies. What are my instructions?

(*A fusion of pilot-to-Ground Command voices, indiscernable and overlapped. Speaking over the din:*)

SMITHERS: Check. I read you, Satan. Destroy the bogies. Roger and out.

(*Sudden silence.* SMITHERS *rises slowly, lifting his revolver and aiming it at* PHOEBE *and* CLEMENT. *As they back away in terror the lights fade to very dim. Two shots are heard. The lights fade and come up on:*)

Scene Eight

(*The Office.* Count Josef *is kneeling over the body of his son.* Prince Percy *is at the window, staring out sullenly.*)

Count Josef: Why? Why did you do it?

(Prince Percy *remains standing with his hands in his pockets, kicking the floor with the toe of his shoe, very much like a naughty child who has been caught doing something wrong.*)

Prince Percy: H'I dunno—

(Count Josef *springs at him like a madman and grabs him by the throat.*)

Count Josef: WHY!

Prince Percy: (*Screaming*) H'I duunno! Don' kill me, please! H'I dunno!

(Count Josef *releases him and moves to the desk and sits.*)

Count Josef: He was an innocent.

Prince Percy: (*After a moment, a clumsy attempt to establish some rapport.*) H'I guess H'I'm Pango now, h'ain't I? (*He waits for a reply.* Count Josef *remains seated in silence, his back to* Percy) You should've seen those kids when h'I dragged my mother h'an' my father down the street h'an' into the square. H'O! They shouted h'an' cheered me like . . . (*He stops. An awkward silence.*) Really made me feel like some shucks, h'it did. H'an' when we 'oisted 'em bofe h'up h'on top o' that burnin' 'eap o' garbage h'an' dropped 'em down 'hinto the land o' the settin' sun—H'O! The kids h'all h'opened their bluggers h'an' began to shout h'an' cheer h'an' lifted me h'up h'on their shoulders, ballyhooin' my name! Pango! H'all 'ail Pango! The king is dead! Long Live Pango! Boy, h'it was somethin'. H'I never felt so slopped h'over h'in my life. (*Pause*) Then 'e began to play 'is flute.

(Count Josef *turns now and looks at the body of his son.* Percy *continues, as if eager to please him; to reassure.*)

Prince Percy: H'oh, h'it was beautiful, believe me. H'it was beautiful. Everything suddenly went quiet. H'all the kids 'ushed h'up h'an' listened to that flute, they did. H'an' then the wind began to blow, h'an' all the blokes come floatin' down from the sky. Silent they fell h'into the fire, with nothin' but the flute playin'. No' h'a sound. H'it was beautiful. H'a beautiful moment, know wot H'I mean? (*Pause. Softly now. A touch of guilt, remorse.*) H'I din't know wot ta do. H'I wanted ta cry, h'I think, h'it was so beautiful. But h'I din't know wot ta do. Really h'I din't. (*Pause.*) So h'I blasted 'im. (*Pause. Then, almost gently, again, to reassure.*) But h'I h'ain't gonna kill you, sir. This don' mean nothin's changed for you.

You c'n still go h'on bein' Prime Minister, h'or what'h'ever it is you was. (*He laughs now, childlike.*) The kids h'all say yor the pres-i-dent. They says you was last seen floatin' down the river h'on a rubber tube smokin' h'a corn cob pipe. (*The image delights him, but he restrains his laughter.*) Some h'of 'em says that you've h'already took yoo place h'among the disfigured waterlilies wot clusters h'about h'on the bands o' the Styg-i-an shores. Wot's that mean—Styg-i-an shores? H'is at like the Potomac or somethin'? H'or the River Thames? (*He waits for a reply. Then, an almost desperate, rather pitiful plea.*) Look, we c'n be frien's, can't we? H'I mean, you c'n work h'under me. H'an h'I c'n sort h'of be like your son. H'I mean, H'I c'n take 'is place. (*Attempting cheerfulness.*) 'Ows's 'at? Fair h'exchange? (*Desperately now*) 'E wan't too right in 'is 'ead, h'anyways. H'I mean, h'I'm smarter than 'e was. You c'n at least teach me somethin'. You c'n teach me h'a lot.

(COUNT JOSEF *rises now and starts towards the door without looking at him.* PERCY *calls desperately after him.*)

PRINCE PERCY: Where you goin'? Don' leave! Don' leave me 'ere h'alone! somebuddy's got'ta teach me ... !

(COUNT JOSEF *exits, closing the door behind him.* PERCY *pounds on the door, shouting.*)

PRINCE PERCY: SOMEBUDDY'S GOT'TA TEACH ME SOMETHIN' ... !

(*He sinks to the floor, his head cradled in his arms, dissolved in tears.* COUNTESS ELIZABETH *appears from the tower and stands at the top of the flight of stone steps.* PERCY, *sensing a presence, turns and looks up, stares at her as she now begins to descend the stone steps. The lights begin to fade as she reaches the bottom of the steps.*)

PRINCE PERCY: 'Ho are you?

COUNTESS ELIZABETH: Elizabeth. My name is Elizabeth.

(*She extends her hand.* PERCY *takes it and rises as the lights fade to black on:*)

The End

A (Brief) History of
The Circle Repertory Company

1985-86

Lanford Wilson   *Talley and Son*

Paul Osborn   *Tomorrow's Monday*

Nancy Donohue   *The Beach House*

Albert Camus   *Caligula*

Lanford Wilson   *The Mound Builders*

Anne Chislett   *Quiet in the Land*

1984-85

William Shakespeare   *Love's Labor's Lost*

James Paul Farrell   *Bing and Walker*

Patrick Meyers   *Dysan*

William Hoffman   *As Is*

Julie Bovasso   *Angelo's Wedding*

1983-84

Anton Chekhov   *The Sea Gull*

Conrad Bishop & Elizabeth Fuller   *Full Hookup*

Timothy Mason   *Levitation*

John Bishop   *The Harvesting*

John Patrick Shanley   *Danny and the Deep Blue Sea*

Lanford Wilson   *Balm in Gilead*

1982-83

Lanford Wilson   *Angels Fall*

Michael Cristofer   *Black Angel*

A.R. Gurney, Jr.   *What I Did Last Summer*

Corinne Jacker   *Domestic Issues*

The Young Playwrights' Festival

Sam Shepard   *Fool for Love*

1981-82

Jonathan Bolt   *Threads*

Confluence: Three One-Act Plays

    Lanford Wilson   *Thymus Vulgaris*

    John Bishop   *Confluence*

    Beth Henley   *Am I Blue*

Joseph Pintauro   *Snow Orchid*

William Shakespeare   *Richard II*

John Bishop   *The Great-Great Grandson of Jedediah Kohler*

Jules Feiffer   *A Think Piece*

1980-81

Jim Leonard, Jr.   *The Diviners*

William Shakespeare   *Twelfth Night*

Gerhard Hauptmann   *The Beaver Coat*

Romulus Linney   *Childe Byron*

Roy London   *In Connecticut*

Lanford Wilson   *A Tale Told*

1979-80

David Mamet   *Reunion 3 Plays*

William Shakespeare   *Hamlet*

Friedrich von Schiller   *Mary Stuart*

John Heuer   *Innocent Thoughts, Harmless Intentions*

Milan Stitt   *Back in the Race*

William Mastrosimone   *The Woolgatherer*

1978-79

Patrick Meyers   *Glorious Morning*

James Farrell   *In the Recovery Lounge*

Milan Stitt   *The Runner Stumbles*

John Bishop   *Winter Signs*

Lanford Wilson   *Talley's Folly*

David Mamet   *The Poet and the Rent*

1977-78

Patrick Meyers   *Feedlot*

Albert Innaurato   *Ulysses in Traction*

Frank Wedekind   *Lulu*

Lanford Wilson & John Bishop   *Two from the Late Show*

Lanford Wilson   *5th of July*

1976-77

David Storey   *The Farm*

Arthur White   *A Tribute to Lili Lamont*

Corinne Jacker   *My Life*

Albert Innaurato   *Gemini*

James Joyce   *Exiles*

Cole Porter & Norman Berman   *Unsung Cole*

1975-76

Berrilla Kerr   *The Elephant in the House*

Andrew Colmar   *Dancing for the Kaiser*

Jules Feiffer   *Knock Knock*

A.R. Gurney, Jr.   *Who Killed Richard Cory?*

John Heuer   *Cavern of the Jewels*

Lanford Wilson   *Serenading Louie*

Roy London   *Mrs. Murray's Farm*

1974-75

Tennessee Williams   *Battle of Angels*

Lanford Wilson   *The Mound Builders*

Julie Bovasso   *Down by the River Where the Waterlilies Are Disfigured Every Day*

Corinne Jacker   *Harry Outside*

A.E. Santaniello   *Not to Worry*

1973-74

Mark Medoff   *When You Comin' Back, Red Ryder?*

Richard Lortz   *Prodigal*

Roy London   *The Amazing Activity of Charlie Contrare and the Ninety-eighth Street Gang*

Edward J. Moore   *The Sea Horse*
e.e. cummings   *Him*
Aeschylus   *The Persians*

1972–73
Lanford Wilson   *Three New Plays by Lanford Wilson*
Claris Nelson   *A Road Where the Wolves Run*
Lanford Wilson   *The Hot l Baltimore*
Henrik Ibsen   *When We Dead Awaken*
Ron Wilcox   *The Tragedy of Thomas Andros*

1971–72
Anton Chekhov   *Three Sisters*
August Strindberg   *Ghost Sonata*
Berrilla Kerr   *The Elephant in the House*
Helen Duberstein   *Time Shadows*
Lanford Wilson   *Three New Plays by Lanford Wilson*

1970–71
Witold Gombrowicz   *Princess Ivovna*
Lanford Wilson   *Sextet (Yes)*
August Strindberg   *The Ghost Sonata*
Moliere   *The Doctor in Spite of Himself*

1969–70
David Starkweather   *A Practical Ritual to Exorcise Frustration After Five Days of Rain*
Anton Chekhov   *Three Sisters*